WHAT IS RELIGIOUS AUTHORITY?

Published by Princeton University Press
41 William Street, Princeton, New Jersey 08540
6 Oxford Street, Woodstock, Oxfordshire OX20 1TR

press.princeton.edu

ISBN 978-0-691-20430-7
ISBN (pbk.) 978-0-691-20431-4
ISBN (e-book) 978-0-691-20429-1

British Library Cataloging-in-Publication Data is available

Editorial: Fred Appel, Jenny Tan and James Collier
Production Editorial: Jenny Wolkowicki
Cover design: Pamela Schnitter
Production: Brigid Ackerman
Publicity: Kate Hensley and Kathryn Stevens
Copyeditor: Maia Vaswani

Cover art: Prince Selarasa paying respect to Sèh Nur Sayid
From the Serat Selarasa © The British Library Board (MSS Jav 28, f. 8r)

This book has been composed in Arno Pro

Printed on acid-free paper. ∞

Printed in the United States of America

10 9 8 7 6 5 4 3 2 1

For my parents

For it is He who has brought into being gardens—the cultivated ones and those growing wild—and the date-palm, and fields bearing multiform produce, and the olive tree, and the pomegranate: [all] resembling one another and yet so different!

—THE HOLY QURʾĀN, THE CATTLE (6:141)

Whoever institutes [*sanna*] a good *sunna* [*sunna ḥasana*] in Islam, he and all those who act upon it shall be rewarded until the day of resurrection.

—THE PROPHET MUḤAMMAD

CONTENTS

NOTE ON NAMES, DATES, TRANSLATION, AND TRANSLITERATION

ASIDE FROM historical and notable public figures, including Habib Luthfi and Habib Bagir, and those whose written works are cited, all names have been changed. The abbreviation b. refers to bin or ibn, meaning "son of" in Arab names. All dates are Common Era unless otherwise noted. All translations are mine, unless stated otherwise. The book uses a standardized transliteration of Arabic words, including for Indonesian words that are derived from the Arabic language (e.g., *ḥadīth* instead of *hadis*). I make exceptions for special nouns that appear too frequently in the book (e.g., *habib* instead of *ḥabīb*). Otherwise, transliteration follows the standard of the *Encyclopaedia of Islam* with full diacritics. To ease readability for non-Arabic speakers, plural forms of Arabic terms are given in the Arabic singular with the English plural -s added (e.g., *manṣab*s instead of *manāṣib, bid'a*s instead of *bida'*). Exceptions are made with words that are better known in English in their plural forms (thus *'ulamā'* instead of *'ālim*s). Indonesian and Javanese terms and proper names are written in their modern spellings. I have retained the older name when context decrees, such as when I speak of Batavia, and not Jakarta. Personal names follow the spelling employed by the people themselves. Thus, I used Habib Luthfi Bin Yahya and Habib Abdullah Bagir instead of Ḥabīb Luṭfī Bin Yaḥyā and Ḥabīb 'Abdallāh Bāqir, except when it pertains to historical individuals who wrote their names in Arabic.

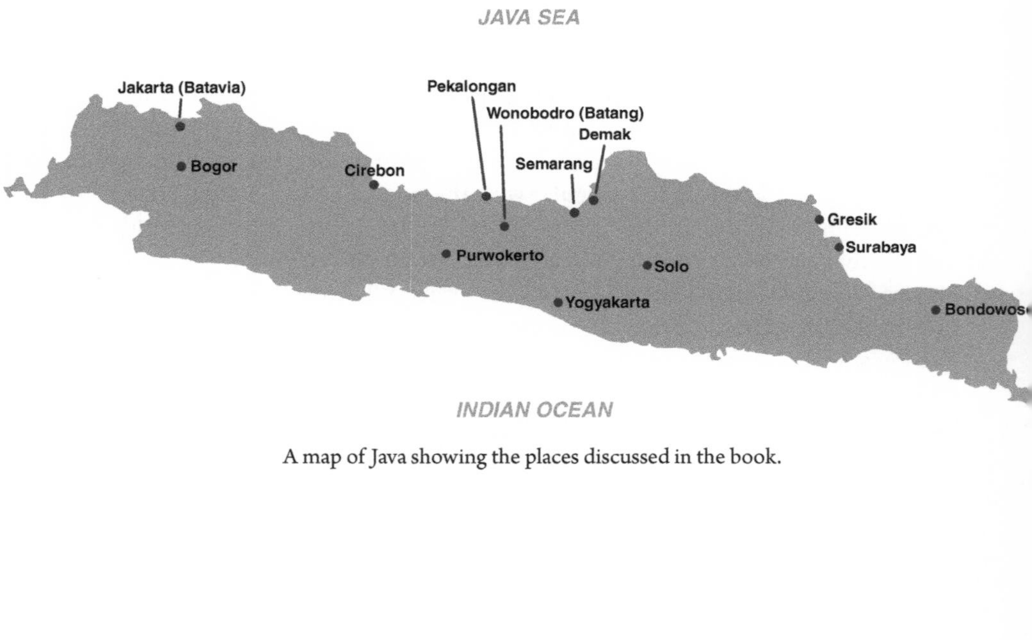

A map of Java showing the places discussed in the book.

INTRODUCTION

Cultivating Islam

PEKALONGAN, Central Java, 4 August 2012. It was just after 9:00 p.m. when a middle-aged Javanese man appeared at the house of Indonesia's most prominent Sufi master, Habib Muhammad Luthfi b. Ali Bin Yahya (b. 1947).[1] Dressed in a green checkered sarong and shabby cream long-sleeved shirt, the man looked as if he had traveled a great distance. Later I learned that his name was Suryo. As he entered the brightly lit reception chamber, Suryo saw the Sufi master seated solemnly in an armchair surrounded by his disciples, all of whom were sitting on the rug-covered floor. A disciple was reciting the chapter on ritual ablution from the *Fatḥ al-bārī*, a multivolume fifteenth-century commentary of the sayings and acts of the Prophet Muḥammad (*ḥadīth*).[2] Realizing that a class was in session, Suryo quickly took his seat among the disciples. Moments later, Habib Luthfi gave a signal to the reciter to stop. He then talked for thirty minutes, describing to his audience in Indonesian mixed with Javanese how the Prophet Muḥammad performed the ablution, while enacting it through bodily gestures. The disciples eagerly watched their master's reenactment of a Prophetic practice. Habib Luthfi told his disciples that he learned how to perform ablution in accordance with the Prophetic precedent not only from reading textual accounts but also from witnessing his teachers. "Textual descriptions of a Prophetic act may be perplexing," he explained, "which is why we need to supplement our textual reading with direct witnessing of the act being performed by someone connected to the Prophet." Most disciples were busy observing Habib Luthfi and taking notes. Suryo, however, did not seem to be interested. His eyes were fixated on the blue octagonal figures of the Afghan rug on which he was sitting.

Shortly after Habib Luthfi dismissed the class, Suryo stood up and approached the Sufi master. He told the *habib* that he had traveled from South Sumatra. Habib Luthfi smiled and thanked Suryo for making the long journey. Much to everyone's surprise, Suryo informed the *habib* that the Prophet Muḥammad had directly appointed him as the Mahdi—that is, the prophesied eschatological redeemer who will lead Muslims prior to the Day of Judgment and restore Prophetic teachings. He claimed that the Prophet had instructed him to meet Habib Luthfi and demand his allegiance:

> I am giving Habib twenty-four hours to consider. If you and your *jamāʿa* [followers, congregation] pledge your allegiance to me, then you will all attain salvation. But if you choose to ignore my warning, then you will all be destroyed together with all the evils of this world. Remember Habib, I speak on behalf of the Prophet Muḥammad.

The disciples burst into laughter and began to ridicule Suryo. Habib Luthfi told them to keep quiet and put his arm around Suryo. In an avuncular manner, the *habib* asked Suryo a series of questions unrelated to the latter's eschatological claims. "How is the family?" he asked. "Are they well?" . . . Are you in need of money? . . . What has disappointed you? . . . Is there anything I can help you with?" Realizing that Habib Luthfi was not taking his demand seriously, Suryo's face turned red in anger. He stood up and gave the *habib* a piece of paper with his cell phone number on it. In a stern voice, Suryo repeated his warning: "Habib, I am only giving you twenty-four hours to join the genuine people of the *sunna* and the *jamāʿa* [*ahlu sunnah wal jama'ah yang sejati*]." This time, Habib Luthfi chose to completely ignore him. He turned his face away from Suryo and lit a cigarette as the disciples resumed their giggles. Without saying anything, Suryo left the house. He was never seen again.

The brief encounter between Habib Luthfi and Suryo encapsulates the central concern of this book: Islamic religious authorities and their roles in cultivating communities of Muslims that revolve around Prophetic teachings, which can nevertheless vary widely from one another. Both Habib Luthfi and Suryo claim connections to the Prophet and deploy such claims to constitute a religious community. But, whereas Habib Luthfi has been able to seamlessly transmit Prophetic teachings to his disciples without much effort, Suryo was perceived as an eccentric and became an object of ridicule. While a study of "eccentric subjects" can indeed shed light on sites and mechanisms of exclusion, creativity, and struggle beyond dominant categories and discourses, this book is not about Suryo.[3] It is about Habib Luthfi and other Muslim saints and scholars who through arduous labor have succeeded in cultivating communities that can serve as sites for the transmission and social realization of Prophetic teachings.[4] Such actors articulate specific and oftentimes contending visions of the *sunna*—that is, the normative teachings and practices of the Prophet Muḥammad. Consisting of the words, actions, and habits of the Prophet, Muslims posit the *sunna* as the concrete elucidation of divine revelations enshrined in the Qurʾān, from dress codes and performance of worship to rules for war. While the Qurʾān does not contain most of the specific theological, legal, and ethical teachings that make up Islamic norms, it repeatedly commands Muslims to "obey God and His Prophet" (Q. 8:1) and pronounces Muḥammad as "a most goodly example" (Q. 33:21). In doing so, the Qurʾān posits the Prophet's life as "the lens through which the holy book is interpreted and understood."[5] Together with the Qurʾān, Muslims regard the *sunna* as a foundational source of Islamic theology, law, mysticism, and ethics.

The *sunna*, however, was never written down during the Prophet's life. Entextualization and compilation of reports that describe the *sunna*—known as *ḥadīths* (Ar. pl. *aḥādīth*)—occurred "over a period of decades and even centuries" after the Prophet's death and, as such, they "are not in themselves contemporary historical documentation of what Muḥammad said and did."[6] As a result, Muslims have never agreed on the specific content of the *sunna*, even when they all recognize its authority as one of the religion's foundational sources. Different actors claim to speak on behalf of the Prophet by revealing connections to the Prophetic past in the hope of borrowing the authority of the *sunna*. They reconstruct the Prophetic past using various means to delimit the *sunna* in response to distinct social challenges that they confronted in their own localities and historical moments. Consequently, the questions of what can be regarded as *sunna* and who can articulate it lie at the heart of the historical diversification of Islam. Attempts to address these questions have generated a high-stakes competition of unstable claims among Muslim scholars, saints, and leaders and the communities they cultivate. At the broadest level, this book presents a polyphonic story of how the *sunna* becomes rooted in and modulated by distinct sociocultural realities. It argues that the abiding issues of translation, mobilization, collaboration, competition, and conflict are the very dynamics that continue to give the *sunna*—and, hence, Islam—its particular content and force. At stake is the fundamental point that there is no one common, global Islamic community, or *umma*. Instead, there have always been, historically, many communities, each revolving around a different articulation of the *sunna*.

Owing to the intervention of Talal Asad, anthropologists have come to recognize Islam as a discursive tradition that includes and relates itself to the scriptures and to the changing forms of social practice.[7] In contrast to these works, this book does not begin by asking how Muslims draw on textual traditions to inform social practices. Instead, it departs from the notion of a vanished *foundational past*, as opposed to existing foundational texts.[8] Temporal estrangement from the Prophetic past necessitates the labor of connecting to, along with reconstructing and representing, that past as a model, or *sunna*, to others. Such labors involve authenticating transmitted reports and evaluating inherited practices. In the religion's formative period, they even include the work of delineating the boundary between Divine and Prophetic speech.[9] These labors are historically, geographically, and culturally situated. Concurrently, as an ideological and narrative product, time itself is constantly being made and remade, generating multiple constructions of time that add layers of complexity and diversity in how Muslims comprehend the Prophetic past from a particular present and think about their relationship to it.[10] The present on which these labors occur serves as the ground that modulates the past in the attempt to find *not* what is authentically Islamic, but rather what is essential to Islam for that very present and future. The concern with essence, as Asad reminds us, is not necessarily to be equated with a concern with authenticity, and what is essential in a religion, in turn, is not neutrally determinable because it is subject to agonistic and antagonistic arguments.[11] The reconstructions and representations of the Prophetic past by different actors may thus look dissimilar from one another. Such dynamics diversify and particularize the *sunna*. They generate a variety of Islamic texts, practices, and institutions that engender diverse forms of religious authority, from caliph and jurist to charismatic saint, holy warrior, and Sufi master, each claiming to connect Muslims to their foundational past.

To be taken as authoritative, a connection to the Prophetic past needs to be recognized by others. Authority, as Hannah Arendt explains, is a hierarchical relationship that connects a group of people with a past that they recognize to be foundational, thereby endowing those in authority with the capacity to transmit and transform that past into examples for the present.[12] Authority "rests neither on common reason nor on the power of the one who commands," but on the recognition of the hierarchy deemed by all parties involved to be right and legitimate.[13] Arendt's definition of authority is helpful to think with for the present purpose of comprehending Islamic religious authority, as it highlights three constitutive elements that make up authority. These are the notion of and connection to a temporal foundation, the capacity to transform that foundation into examples, and the ability to effect obedience without coercion. The authority of Islamic religious leaders, this book argues, is premised on the recognition of their connection to the Prophetic past and hinges on a hierarchical relationship that allows them to articulate Prophetic teachings for others without resorting to coercion. This, in turn, suggests that the formation of authority demands ongoing labors of (re)producing and maintaining such a relationship. A relationship is an achievement, an outcome of contingent and precarious labor, and not a given. The labor cannot stop if the relationship is to endure and develop into a durable community.

Pushing back against Weberian notions of "charisma" and "routinization" that have dominated studies of Islamic religious authority, this book uncovers the centrality and contingency of labor in the formation and maintenance of religious authority and community, including those authorities that have frequently been described as charismatic.[14] While the notion of charisma may perhaps be useful when considering the founding of a religious tradition, it is of limited utility when it is deployed to comprehend postfoundational religious authority. Instead, the approach I develop here seeks to destabilize religious authority by uncovering the networks and relationalities that simultaneously constitute and jeopardize authority, while highlighting the centrality of labor. My use of the term "labor" owes, once again, to Arendt, who defines it as a form of making that is different from "work." If work denotes the making of finished products or economic production, labor refers to the ongoing and recurring life-reproducing activities characteristic of farm or household that do not necessarily produce distinct or independent objects.[15] Arendt's notion of labor is particularly useful to think with when comprehending the formation and maintenance of religious authority and community because it "undermines any clear distinction between production and action" and "locates itself firmly in the sphere of the ordinary."[16] Concurrently, it allows us to think about outcomes that are internal to the labor itself, like mastery, virtuosity, and excellence in performing the labor.[17]

By focusing on the networks, relationalities, and labor that make up religious authority and community this book takes *politics* and *infrastructure* into serious consideration. Politics is central because the labor of cultivating community tends to take place in competitive social terrains where other Islamic communities have come to be formed by different religious leaders claiming alternative connections to the Prophetic past. Cultivating community also occurs in a landscape where "nonreligious" social formations, including states (whether precolonial, colonial, or postcolonial) and other structures of power, concurrently take shape, thereby generating not only complex overlaps and synergies but also conflicts and contestations. As a result, what are commonly considered "religious" and "secular" domains of life are, in reality, variously articulated. How these articulations are formed and regulated, and what happens when they are altered, are questions for anthropological and historical inquiries.[18] Equally important to the politics of religious authority is the question of infrastructure. Cultivating an Islamic community demands infrastructure that connects religious leaders to the foundational past and helps solidify their relationship with their followers, thereby affording them the ability to articulate that past as *sunna* for others. While infrastructures make transmission possible, they also work to "transform, translate, distort, and modify the meaning or elements they are supposed to carry."[19] This entails the need to think about how varying infrastructures shape divergent contours of relationship that link religious leaders to their followers and open up distinct articulatory possibilities.

In illustrating these general arguments, the book traces the movement and labor of Bā ʿAlawī saints and scholars from the Ḥaḍramawt valley of Yemen to Java, Indonesia, from the eighteenth century to the present day. Claiming descent from the Prophet Muḥammad, the Bā ʿAlawīs have for long migrated to

Southeast Asia from the Ḥaḍramawt. These mobile actors traversed complex cultural fields, and built channels for the transmission of Prophetic teachings and their social realization as *sunna*. They competed with one another as well as with other actors belonging to different Islamic lineages and intellectual genealogies. Following these vectors of transmission accentuates the ways in which these actors have been caught up in local issues of translation and mobilization in their attempt to articulate the *sunna* and cultivate community without ever having the capacity to guarantee success or realize their moral visions. To a large extent, however, the Bā ʿAlawīs have succeeded in maintaining eminence among local populations and becoming recognized as leading Islamic authorities, although there are also less successful cases, as will be shown in this book.[20] Thus at the most specific level, this book seeks to capture the ways through which Habib Luthfi, and other historical and contemporary Bā ʿAlawī saints and scholars like him, have been able to become recognized as religious authorities, as living connectors to the Prophetic past. By following these mobile actors, the book traces the movement of Islam between two regions that have been commonly posited to be "peripheral." It demonstrates how Islam does not simply radiate from the "central lands," but instead is perpetually formed in between heterogeneous cultures. In adopting a transregional perspective, the book shows close up how Arabic and Javanese elements and people articulate within the same religion. Such a cross-cultural aspect of world religion is seldom noted but is of fundamental importance in developing a more nuanced and grounded way of understanding the diversification of Islam, one that attends to the politics, infrastructure, and labor that engender different forms of religious authority.

The *Sunna* and the Community

"As Indonesian Muslims, we should know how to plant coconuts, and not date palms." Habib Luthfi uttered these words in front of thousands of disciples and followers who flocked to his congregational center to hear the Sufi master's monthly sermon. Upon hearing these words, the crowd began to cheer and clap with excitement. I remember asking myself why a simple statement about the cultivation of dates and coconuts electrified the audience. In fact, what is the relationship between Islam or being Muslim and the cultivation of dates or coconuts? To make sense of Habib Luthfi's statement and the outburst of enthusiasm that followed, we need to consider the resonances evoked by both date and coconut palms for contemporary Indonesians.

Date palms evoke exotic images of the Arabian physical landscape, perceived by many Indonesian Muslims to be the cradle of religious authenticity. Such images are mediated by, among others, the producers of popular culture who assemble visual imageries of barren desert dotted with oases and date palms for Islamic television programs. Television documentary series, like the highly rated *Jejak Rasul* (Footsteps of the prophets), trace the sacred history of Islam while reproducing imageries of Arabian desert as mythic chronotopes of religious authenticity, sincerity, and piety. Desert scenes, complete with images of camel caravans and date palms, are consistently reproduced as stage sets for Islamic musical performances. During the Islamic holy month of Ramaḍān, high-end malls in Indonesian urban centers feature seasonal displays of desert scenes with effigies of camels and date palms, while employees dressing up in Bedouin garb greet passersby with the Arabic greeting *ahlan wa sahlan* (figure I.1).

The image of coconut palms, on the other hand, conjures a panoramic picture of captivating congeries of tropical islands that make up the vast Indonesian Archipelago. Such imageries have been immortalized by, among others, the legendary nationalist composer Ismail Marzuki (d. 1958) in his "Rayuan Pulau Kelapa" (The allure of the coconut islands). Indonesian children are taught to sing the patriotic song in school, while every evening, television channels and radio stations play it as their closedown. The Indonesian boy scout movement, a requisite component of the public school system, uses the image of a germinating coconut seed as its emblem. The official explanation of the symbol notes that a coconut seed represents continuity, versatility, and rootedness in the land.

When heard alongside the contemporary salience of date and coconut palms, Habib Luthfi's statement sounds like a critique of those who attempt to transplant what they take to be a more authentic articulation of Islam from Arabia to Indonesia. From numerous conversations with the *habib*'s followers, I got the sense that many were appalled by some of their compatriots who prefer to speak like an Arab (without knowing the language), dress like an Arab, and idealize Islam in Arabia while criticizing local customs. As one of my interlocutors said, "if Habib Luthfi, who is an Arab and a descendant of the Prophet endorses *Islam Jawa* [Javanese Islam], then why would the Javanese Gatot change his name to Khaththat and start dressing up like an Arab?" The man was referring to Muhammad al-Khaththat—the chairman of the hard-line Islamic Nation Forum—whose real name, Gatot, is a common Javanese name derived from Gatotkacha, one of the protagonists of the Hindu epic Mahabharata. During my fieldwork, I have repeatedly heard similar jokes and criticism. Indeed, Habib Luthfi's popularity among Javanese Muslims stems from, among other things, his Javanese orientation and disposition, his ability to deliver sermons in refined Javanese, and his vast knowledge of Javanese history and mythology. For that reason Habib Luthfi is often characterized as *Arab tapi njawani* (a Javanized Arab).

FIGURE I.1 Ramaḍān displays at a Jakarta high-end mall. (Photo by the author)

Indonesian media have often portrayed Habib Luthfi as a proponent of *Pribumisasi Islam* (indigenization of Islam).[21] The term is often used to describe a number of different intellectual and cultural projects that aim to arrive at a functioning synthesis between what is taken to be a foreign religion and a local culture. *Pribumisasi Islam* emerged from various discussions, debates, and conferences held by several Indonesian Muslim scholars, thinkers, and activists.[22] It took shape as a response to multifarious, and often conflictual, processes and itineraries that are often lumped together under the term *Arabisasi* (Arabization). One of its leading proponents, the late Muslim scholar turned Indonesia's fourth president, Abdurrahman Wahid (d. 2009), defined *Pribumisasi Islam*:

> as neither Javanization [*Jawanisasi*] nor syncretization. *Pribumisasi Islam* is merely to take local necessities into account in formulating religious law, without having to alter the construct of the laws themselves. It is not an attempt to put aside [religious] norms for the sake of culture, but simply to ensure that those norms accommodate the necessities of culture by using the opportunity provided by variations in understanding the texts.[23]

Since its initial emergence in the 1980s, *Pribumisasi Islam* has morphed into different forms, the most recent of which is an essentialized notion of *Islam Nusantara* (Archipelagic Islam—i.e., of the Malay-Indonesian Archipelago) posited as antithetical to an analogously essentialized *Islam Arab* (Arab Islam) and presented—in the words of one Indonesian scholar—as "a promising response to religious intolerance and radicalism."[24] One cannot help but notice how the opposition between a positive and humane Archipelagic Islam and an intolerant and turbulent Arab Islam resonates with an old colonial juxtaposition of "good Muslim" and "bad Muslim."[25] This colonial framing resurfaced as a key diction in the rhetoric of the US-led War on Terror, and has now been adopted by the Muslims themselves.[26]

Ongoing debates on *Pribumisasi Islam* have generated essentialized terms like Arab Islam, Indonesian Islam, and Javanese Islam, all of which carry strong ideological force in contemporary Indonesia. As ideological products, these terms certainly deserve careful study.[27] One should refrain, however, from reproducing such terms as analytic categories to help us comprehend Islam as a sociological reality in contemporary Indonesia, or in any other place for that matter. The underlying problem with such terms or with the notion of indigenization lies in its assumption of the existence of, or possibility to demarcate, a universalized and acultural Islam that can integrate into different cultures. Wahid's aforementioned essay, to give one example, begins with this very assumption:

> Religion (Islam) and culture are independent, although they are often interrelated. . . . Religion (Islam) is based on revelation and has its own norms. Owing to its normativity, religion tends to be permanent. Culture, on the other hand, is man-made and for that reason subject to evolution and fluctuation in accordance to historical development. This difference, however, does not foreclose the possibility for religious life to manifest in cultural forms.[28]

Note how Wahid presupposes the existence of a universal and acultural Islam. Such an Islam is usually posited in a legalistic framework, thereby giving the impression that law itself is not a cultural process.[29] An assumption of the existence of an acultural Islam is also shared by proponents of Salafism and other more literalist readings of Islam, and has fueled their zeal for purifying the religion from what they see as its cultural accretions.[30] It is indeed interesting to note the resonance between such an assumption and what Wendy Brown has identified as liberalism's conceit regarding the universality of its basic principles, which are assumed to operate independently of politics and culture, rendering culture extrinsic to—or as something that can be "entered" and "exited"—and not constitutive of such principles.[31]

So what analytic tools, then, can one adopt to make sense of Islam as a sociological reality without perceiving it as independent of the politics, cultures, infrastructure, and labors that produce it? Historians have increasingly come to deploy terms like *hybridity*, *translation*, and *transculturation* to characterize the historical encounters between Muslims and other cultures or religious traditions.[32] For example, Devin DeWeese's work on the Islamization of the Golden Horde describes how elements of Islamic religious tradition often personified by saintly figures displaced the Inner Asian conception of the First Man/Communal Founder, allowing local groups to identify them as their communal ancestors. This initial recognition set in motion a gradual and seamless transformative process that was understood as both Islamic and native.[33] Zvi Ben-Dor Benite's and Kristian Petersen's works on Islam in late imperial China point to how Islamic knowledge was framed in Confucian paradigm, generating the production of Islamic literary works, known collectively as the *Han Kitab*, that envision a Chinese way of being Muslim and a Muslim way of being Chinese.[34] Rian Thum's historical ethnography of Uyghur Muslims suggests how locally composed hagiographical texts, saintly shrines, and pilgrimage practices historically defined what it meant to be Muslims for the Uyghurs. This religious infrastructure enabled mass participation, generating a shared imagination of Islam as a form of communal belonging that is historically deep (going back to the region's saintly past and, ultimately, the Prophetic past), locally embedded, and experiential.[35] Tony Stewart's work on the Islamization of Bengal illustrates how Muslims reimagined Islamic ideals in "a new literary environment" through modes of translation that look for local "terms of equivalences in order to approximate the ideas they wanted to express."[36] This, in turn, enabled them to share commensurate terms with Bengalis of different faiths. Finbarr Barry Flood's work on intercultural and interreligious contacts and transactions in medieval Afghanistan and North India illustrates how practices like architectural borrowing, gift exchange, and circulation of loot translate and simultaneously engender the creation of new cultural forms situated in between exclusively Hindu and Islamic cultural spheres.[37]

On the whole, these significant works demonstrate how culture and religion ought to be understood as composite products of historical interactions. A term like "syncretism," in turn, is no longer deemed useful considering that all "pure" cultures and religious traditions are outcomes of "intercultural and intracultural transactions."[38] In its own way, each of these works has highlighted the need for an analytic approach to Islam that can account for its contextually embedded (re)production. The challenge remains, however, in ensuring that such an approach does not succumb to, or end up reproducing, purportedly neutral dichotomies like global Islam versus local Islam, scriptural versus vernacular, central versus peripheral, or Arab versus Archipelagic. One should be careful of not positing the existence of a culturally purified or abstracted Islamic normativity that interacts with local cultures and religious traditions to produce more complex and culturally bound instantiations of Islam. The problem with notions of Islamization (or indigenization) is that they often assume local or regional Islam as the historical outcome of "Islam + *y*," where *y* points to the various local cultural and religious elements deemed to be different from Islam. But what is Islam in such a case? What are the Islamic ideals or elements of Islamic religious tradition or Islamic knowledge that are understood to have entered into creative transaction with local cultures or religious traditions? If one assumes the existence or a precultural, presynthetic, pretranslation, prehybrid, or pretransculturation Islam, who gets to decide what it is in the first place? To assume that local cultures were previously extrinsic to Islam, and only gradually came to complicate the religion through historical transactions is to miss the culturally situated labor that aligns and modulates the Prophetic past and the community, contingently determines the alignment between the two, and, as a result, produces an *instantiation* of Islam.[39] To illustrate this point further, I want to return to Habib Luthfi's agricultural metaphor and explore its analytic potentials. Instead of comprehending the symbolic salience of date and coconut palms among contemporary

Indonesians as I have done, I want to now take both plants and the labor of cultivation literally.

* * *

Date and coconut palms are members of the monophyletic Arecaceae (also known as Palmae) botanical family. Environmental changes brought about a long and slow process of adaptive radiation that diversified a common ancestor into around 200 subdivisions and 2,600 subspecies, exhibiting shared morphological and physiological traits. Among the most extensively cultivated plants, palms have been central to the formation of human sociality in different parts of the world. Towns, villages, and cities emerged around them. Palm cultivation demanded workers who came from different places, and engendered divisions of labor. The trunks and leaves of palms were crucial for creating infrastructure. The timber was a primary component for building the transportation technologies, whether Arabian dhows or Trobriand canoes, that have historically facilitated the expansion of human sociality. At the same time, parts and products of both date and coconut palms were used for ritual purposes.

So here we have a common ancestor whose actuality has long vanished and whose existence can be grasped only virtually and partially by cultivating its botanical descendants. Cultivation, however, involves understanding different climes and topography, as well as mastering various skills and technologies to improve growth, quality, and yield, and develop the plants' resistance to diseases, pests, and environmental stresses. Cultivation is a social formation. It is a project that gathers different actors, materials, and other entities onto a tract of land that needs to be systematically ordered and sown, and in itself is conditioned by climatic and topographical variables. In the process, these disparate elements become entangled with one another, forming an assemblage that revolves around a shared concern. Cultivating dates in a desert valley and planting coconuts in a sandy tropical beach are projects that lead to the emergence and growth of autochthonous but nevertheless monophyletic agricultural fields, although their constitutive elements—like the laborers, the seeds, and the tools—may come from different places. Equally important is the fact that the temporality of an agricultural field is not synchronic precisely because the elements that compose it did not all begin at the same time.

As a sociological reality, Islam is similar to dates and coconuts. Islam is the fruit of an ongoing project of cultivating a living entity. It seeks to cultivate particular characters and traits in living individuals that are deemed to be beneficial for their flourishing and strengthen their resistance to things that stunt their development.[40] Islam is the outcome of a situated project of constituting sociality, assembling collectivity, controlling and expanding its field, and delineating its boundaries. The Prophet Muḥammad cultivated a social field, in ways that were similar to but at the same time different from the dominant tribal sociality of his day, by relying on the conceptual and material infrastructure that was available to him.[41] When he died, others continued the labor that he had initiated or cultivated a new field elsewhere. As might be expected, they began to disagree about the proper way to cultivate this expanding social field. Allow me to present a caricatural representation of the historical disagreements during Islam's formative period (and do note their consistent gender):

MR. A. Let us introduce new cultivation techniques. As we travel and cultivate fields in different environments, we notice that some of the old techniques are no longer suitable for the changing topography. Nevertheless, these innovations are still in line with the Prophet's way. What is important is the act of cultivation, not its technical details!

MR. B. We in Medina have carefully maintained the field that the Prophet once cultivated. As inhabitants of the Prophet's city, we are most familiar to his way and we know every detail passed down by the locals. Other cultivators elsewhere should follow what we do. We should be the standard.

MR. C. No one knows the proper way to cultivate the field except for the Prophet's immediate family and descendants! We should recognize them as the genuine cultivators and follow their guidance.

MR. D. Look at us, we have painstakingly compiled oral reports detailing how the Prophet cultivated his field and gathered them into written anthologies. We even know how he walked and talked, the clothes he wore, and the various objects he possessed.

MR. E. Let us think carefully about this notion of cultivation. I think what is essential is not the act of cultivating the field. Look at those who claim to be cultivators only to sit on thrones and enjoy worldly power! What is important is how to cultivate ourselves. Only those who have cultivated themselves can cultivate others. Do you know that some of the cultivated ones can even learn directly from the Prophet through visionary experience?

MR. F. Enough! All this talk about the proper way to cultivate the field is not going to help us. I think from now on we should stick to the reports that Mr. D and his colleagues have compiled. You guys cannot just say that what you are doing is consistent with what the Prophet did. Some of you are even deducing new techniques of cultivation while claiming it to be consistent with the Prophet. In truth, however,

> you learn how to cultivate from the Persians and the Byzantines. Show me some authentic reports narrated by trustworthy transmitters!
> Sorry, folks, the way of the Prophet can be found only in the letters. Indeed, the letters are clear enough if we know the language.

A student of early Islam should be able to recognize which historical actor or group each of these fictional characters represents. Here I am not trying to reconstruct the intellectual and social complexities that made up the first few centuries of Islamic history. To do so would do no justice to the erudition of the historians who have undertaken such a challenge.[42] My aim is simply to suggest that one way to study Islam as a sociological reality would be to look at it as an outcome of a project of cultivating an ideally growing social field that revolves around and serves as the site for the realization of norms established once upon a time by the Prophet. An emic term that denotes such a social assemblage is *jamāʿa*, which literally means a collective, but can also mean a gathering, following, assembly, congregation, or circle of followers. Here I opt for the more common term "community" to denote a *jamāʿa*. A *jamāʿa* is a concrete, embodied, and organized form of the *umma*, the latter being a Qurʾānic term for a unified community of believers, which used to also include Jews and Christians before becoming a more exclusive collective term for Muslims.[43] Historically, however, what was theologically denoted by the term *umma* was none other than a congeries of *jamāʿas*. Taking *umma* as a central term risks "theologizing the practical logic symbolized by *jamāʿa*."[44] This entails that an empirical approach to Islam would be better served by a focus on the notion of *jamāʿa*, rather than *umma*.

The norms that an Islamic community revolves around are known as *sunna*. The noun *sunna* is derived from the verb *sanna*, meaning to institute a practice that is emulated by others. Following Mr. F above, today most Muslims use the term exclusively to refer to the deeds, utterances, and spoken approvals of the Prophet Muḥammad as entextualized in the *ḥadīth*s (reports of the Prophet's words, actions, or habits transmitted over a period of decades and even centuries) to the extent that both terms have become quasi-synonyms. In the first two Islamic centuries, however, *sunna* was perceived as living, culturally embedded, and cumulative. The term referred to the exemplary practice instituted not only by the Prophet but also by those connected to him and believed to know and embody his teachings, like the Prophet's companions residing in different places.[45] The sayings and practices of the Prophet were complemented by his successors, whose distinct experiences, characteristics, and memories of the Prophet blend with local cultures to form different regional *sunnas*.[46] Subsequent development of Islamic legal theory, however, led to the canonization of a methodological framework that delineates the Prophetic past, as entextualized in the *ḥadīths*, as the exclusive fount of the *sunna*. Entextualization isolated the Prophetic past as "a clearly defined and uniquely normative category," objectifying it as "an unchanging and authoritative measuring stick" that can circulate across distance and difference.[47] Those skilled in authenticating and extrapolating the normative implications of *ḥadīths*—like *ḥadīth* verifiers and jurists—emerged as religious authorities. These actors have, in turn, continued to project the *ḥadīths* as the common and readily available transcripts of the *sunna* imbued with scriptural standing and universal significance. As a form of objectification, entextualization of the Prophetic past formed "a text (whether oral or written) that is perceived to remain constant across contexts," thereby allowing Muslims to imagine an *authentic* Islam even when that very text is the product of a historically and culturally situated labor of reconstructing, selecting, and, in some cases, translating and codifying a no longer objectively available reality.[48] As text, the *sunna* moves across contexts, allowing Muslims living in different times and places to imagine a shared and disembedded normativity independent of its particular context of production and realizations.

This definition of the *sunna*, however, is just one among several conceptions. Historians of early Islam have shown how the emergence of this scriptural approach to the *sunna* (that posits the *sunna* as stable foundational text) within the developing framework of Islamic law was the result of cultural upheaval and dislocation that followed from the expansion of the Umayyad and Abbasid Empires.[49] Consequently, such a conception ought to be recognized as merely one among many approaches to the *sunna* that has achieved a paradigmatic status. The *sunna* cannot be reduced to its particular articulation within the framework of Islamic legal tradition, notwithstanding its paradigmatic status. Nor can Islamic religious authority be limited to the figures of the jurists and other textual interpreters, or even to those who engage in prescriptive work.[50] The older conception of the *sunna* continues to exist, most notably among the Sufis.[51] For the Sufis, a Sufi master is an exemplar (*qudwa*). He is believed by his followers to be connected to the Prophet, has assimilated his characteristics, and actively transmits his teachings. As a result, his personality and conduct, as well as the practices he institutes are considered as *sunna* and normative for his followers. The recognition of the universal regulatory force of the *sunna* is not accompanied by a belief in the uniformity and finality of its content, which may be derived from Prophetic precedents corroborated by *ḥadīths*, but may also include innovations tied to specific contexts and challenges but nonetheless taken to epitomize Prophetic teachings owing to the figure of the Sufi master. In this conception of the *sunna*, the question of what is *essentially* Islamic in and for the present context is more important than what is *authentically* Islamic.

Sociologically, what turns a particular practice into *sunna* is its perceived connection—in whatever shapes or forms—to the Prophetic past, together with its ability to become a precedent. Scholars who compile and disseminate *ḥadīth*s can be said to institute *sunna* precisely because they do so not simply for antiquarian reasons but to help facilitate their reenactment. Such works, however, are not sufficient to ensure the social realization of the *ḥadīth*s as *sunna*. After all, authentic *ḥadīth*s may be compiled in books that nobody reads, let alone acts upon. They may become objects of a scholastic enterprise with limited social consequences. Instituting *sunna* demands that the instituted practice is doable, recognizably connected to the Prophetic past (even if its authenticity is uncertain), comprehensible to others through their particular cultural assumptions, and that it fulfills specific needs. Indeed, it requires a relationship that ties those who institute and those who follow and practice. In other words, the articulation and social realization of the *sunna* require the labor of cultivating a community (*jamāʿa*), in whatever shape, scale, or form, that is meaningfully connected to the Prophetic past.

* * *

The relationship between the *sunna* and the community is one that is not only useful to think about when we analyze Islam as a sociological reality. It is one that is also ideologically central to Muslims. Thus, it is no surprise that 85–90 percent of the world's Muslim population identify themselves as *ahl al-sunna wa al-jamāʿa* (people of the *sunna* and the *jamāʿa*), or, simply, Sunnī.[52] Of course this does not mean that Shīʿī Muslims do not subscribe to both the notions of the *sunna* and the *jamāʿa*. They certainly do. The main difference is that for Shīʿī Muslims, Prophetic *sunna* was elaborated and complemented by the *sunna*s of the Prophet's spiritual and genealogical successors—i.e., the Imams. As all Sunnī communities do, Shīʿī Muslims believe that their communities are genuinely Islamic because they revolve around the *sunna*.[53]

The question regarding the relationship between the *sunna* and the community became decisive in the first century of Islamic history, in light of several civil wars that divided early Muslims over the issue of legitimate post-Prophetic leadership, and the subsequent consolidation of the Umayyad Caliphate. Under ʿAbd al-Malik b. Marwān (r. 685–705), the Umayyads attempted to pacify several internal revolts under the banner of the *jamāʿa* principle of Muslim unity.[54] Such a principle was based on a sense of power and unity of the Arab ruling community and sustained by administrative machinery, legal standards, and economic order, most of which drew upon the heritage of the peoples they had conquered.[55] "Their palaces were decorated in the usual Hellenistic fashion, the taxes they raised were essentially the same taxes as those raised by the governments before them," the historian Marshall Hodgson describes the situation.[56] Nevertheless, Hodgson continues, "the notion of the *jamāʿa*, the unity of the community, did not suffice as a comprehensive Islamic ideal, even when it was accepted on the specific point of who should be caliph."[57] The question of what an Islamic *jamāʿa* is pertained not only to the notion of the pragmatic political unity as envisaged by the Umayyads. Among those who were perturbed by or consciously opposed to Umayyad's monopoly of sociopolitical leadership, the notion of *jamāʿa* became intertwined with the notion of the *sunna*.[58] These actors wanted Islam to be more than merely a badge of the ruling class and expected Islam to carry with it its own self-sufficient norms without any reference to pre-Islamic norms. They concluded that an Islamic community ought to be governed in accordance with the Qurʾān and the *sunna*. Thus, according to Hodgson, "the crux lay in defining the *sunna*":

> What was objected to as contrary to *sunna* was the seemingly arbitrary departure from what Muslim Arabs had expected—or hoped for. The restrictions and indignities for the privileged Arab families which were inseparable from the development of a centralized monarchy were seen as innovations, called *bidʿa*; and the seemingly more liberal days of earlier rulers—especially of the Medina caliphs and of Muḥammad himself—were recalled as models of what all could agree ought to be: as *sunna*. At the same time, it was recognized that the *bidʿa*, the deplored innovation, was not entirely a matter of the rulers; their power and arbitrariness were partly the consequence of the moral laxity and luxurious habits of the Muslims themselves—for it was in these terms that moralizers naturally saw the assimilation of the Arab ruling class into the cultural and social life of the occupied lands. Accordingly, abiding by the *sunna* would mean restoration, for both rulers and Muslims at large, of the norms of the primitive caliphate and (or, among many Shīʿīs, only) of Muḥammad's time; what did not go back to such times was *bidʿa* and ought to be eliminated from Muslim life.[59]

The *sunna* became increasingly seen to be the norms that can differentiate Muslims from other groups—like the conquered population—and their diverse ways and customs; i.e., their *sunna*s. In the eyes of these actors, the proper Islamic *sunna* should also be differentiated from the pre-Islamic Arab *sunna*.[60] This, in turn, underlined the need to recover Prophetic *sunna* as a norm that an Islamic community could inherit, grow, and embody.

Hodgson's historical reconstruction of the sociopolitical contestations of the first two centuries of Islam highlights one conceptual point that will be further developed in this book; namely, that the project of recovering the *sunna* cannot be separated from the labor of imagining and cultivating a community. The two are mutually constitutive. As such, one way to understand Islam as a historical and sociological reality would be to posit it as an outcome of what I call *articulatory labor*—that is, the labor of articulating the *sunna* and the community. Instead of subscribing to any ideological definitions of the *sunna* and the community, however, I propose that we use both terms as analytic categories. Their definitions should not be decided based solely on what particular Muslim scholars or historians have said. Instead, they need to be opened up to historical and ethnographic inquiries. Following Shahab Ahmed, anthropologists and historians should attempt to recuperate for Islam what has been "excommunicated" by Islamic legalistic or theological frameworks and Western scholarships that have followed them.[61] Adopting a capacious understanding of the *sunna* and the community will enable us to rehabilitate a range of ideas, practices, and social formations that have heretofore been seen as situated outside the purview of what has traditionally been defined as Islamic. For the anthropologists and the historians, however, the most pertinent question is not "what is Islam?" Rather, the question ought to revolve around how particular actors become authorized to define and articulate the *sunna* and the community. Thus, going further than Ahmed's focus on texts and material artifacts, this book attends to the sociological intricacies and material processes that have led to the diversification of Islam. In doing so, it uncovers the competitive and persistently expanding social terrain in and through which the question of "what is Islam?" has been raised, addressed, and contested in socially efficacious ways.

* * *

Like the vanished common ancestor of both date and coconut palms, the *sunna* can be grasped only by retrospective reconstruction of the Prophetic past from the vantage point of a particular present. Reconstruction involves acts of definition, selection, delineation, and comparison, all of which have precipitated endless agonistic and antagonistic debates and disputes down to the present day. Is the *sunna* the embodied practice of the Medinans or of the Prophet's descendants no matter where they reside? Is the *sunna* limited to what can be deciphered from the *ḥadīth*—i.e., oral and textual reports of the *sunna* with clear chains of transmission to the Prophetic past? Does it include teachings conveyed posthumously by the Prophet through dreams and visions? Can an innovation that purportedly encapsulates the spirit of Prophetic teachings be considered *sunna*? Should the *sunna* be understood and projected as ethics, law, mystical path, or a combination of all?

Every reconstruction of the Prophetic past occurs in a specific *problem-space*—that is, a discursive and argumentative context. Problem-space, as David Scott defines it, is:

> an ensemble of questions and answers around which a horizon of identifiable stakes (conceptual as well as ideological-political stakes) hangs. That is to say, what defines this discursive context are not only the particular problems that get posed as problems as such . . . but the particular questions that seem worth asking and the kinds of answers that seem worth having.[62]

Scott's notion of problem-space is helpful to keep in mind in understanding how different articulations of the *sunna* and the community came to be formed. It pushes us to think about particular articulations of the *sunna* as answers to a set of questions or outcomes of disputes. The concept also helps us uncover the temporal development of the *sunna* in that problem-spaces "alter historically because problems are not timeless and do not have everlasting shapes."[63] In a novel historical context, old questions may lose their relevancy and, in turn, the *sunna* that was articulated as a response to those questions may become barren and irrelevant, even when it remains true. The *sunna* may be authentic, but it may no longer be *essential* to a changing problem-space and thus loses its mobilizing steam.

Debates have also emerged around the notion of *jamāʿa*, or the community. What is an Islamic—or *sunna*-aligned—community and what form should it take? Is it a caliphate, a sultanate, a post-Westphalian nation-state, or an informal community? Is it simply a momentary prayer gathering that takes shape five times a day in the neighborhood mosque, only to dissipate twenty minutes later? Or is it an enduring social formation like a Sufi order, political party, *madrasa*, or an immediate or extended family? Can the Taliban Emirate of Afghanistan or the Islamic State of Iraq and Syria be considered a *jamāʿa*? Or does an Islamic community need to literally describe itself as a *sunna*-aligned *jamāʿa* like the *Jamāʿat ahl al-sunna li-l-daʿwa wa-l-jihād* (*Jamāʿa* of the people of the *sunna* for preaching and Jihad), otherwise known by its Hausa moniker as Boko Haram? Historians and anthropologists need not choose which of these can be genuinely considered an Islamic community as Muslims have been arguing for centuries over that very question. In saying that all of these different social formations can be considered as diverse figurations of *jamāʿa*, I am suggesting the need for a common frame that enables us to analyze these different Islamic social formations, rather than treating each of them as analytically distinct. This common frame can accentuate the labor of articulation that lies behind all of these social formations. It also allows for fruitful comparisons among a Sufi order, a caliphate, a *madrasa*, a Jihadi network, a modern Islamic association, and a simple Friday prayer congregation, as social formations that have emerged and continue to take shape in different parts of the Muslim world. Such a common frame highlights the possibility for a particular Islamic social formation to develop into another—say, from a Sufi order to an empire—without succumbing to a historicist view that posits some form of social formation as receding with the passing of time.[64] Such a frame would deter analysts from treating some Islamic social formations as more Islamic and authentic just because they emerged in particular parts of the world, while seeing others as vernaculars. This analytic frame would also permit analysts to see how a specific Islamic social formation can mirror, or even create alliances with, dissimilar sociopolitical formations, including the modern state. Posed as an open category, the notion of *jamāʿa*/community can serve these analytic purposes.

Understanding Islam as an outcome of articulatory labor that aligns the *sunna* and the community also opens up another crucial question—namely, what connects or mediates the two and what processes are involved in their articulation. What are these connectors? If they are humans, who are they? Are they scholars, teachers, proselytizers, saints, sultans, or presidents? What kind of authority do they hold? How do they establish and maintain the relationship that allows them to effectively articulate the *sunna* to others? What infrastructure do they employ? Texts, YouTube, Twitter, Zoom? What kind of connection to the Prophetic past do they claim to have and how do they make it evident to others? Connection to the Prophetic past can be established through various means, from bloodline (*nasab*) or Sufi spiritual genealogies (*silsila*) that link an actor to the Prophet, to the mastery of textual sources that contain reports (*ḥadīth*s) of the Prophet's sayings and actions.[65] Others claim connections to the Prophet through visions and dreams, both of which are believed by some Muslims to facilitate interactions between contemporary actors and the spirit of the Prophet.[66] In the modern era, there are even Muslims who think that the *sunna* is transmittable only through its entextualized forms in the *ḥadīth* collections, thereby excusing them from the necessity of finding a living connector.

The historical and geographic circulation of the *sunna* requires constant work of building, expanding, and maintaining channels that allow for such movements.[67] Things and ideas do not just flow and circulate. They need channels and avenues, which demand constant maintenance as passages often fill with sediment and debris that required dredging. Islamic religious authorities are actors who have been able to create and sustain such channels, whether the channels linking them to the Prophetic past as the basis of their legitimacy, or those that connect them to their fellow Muslims who, in turn, can recognize their authorities and revolve around them. What we understand as Islamic religious authorities are therefore those who have taken the role of, and become recognized as, *connectors* between the Prophetic past and their fellow Muslims to the extent that they can effectively articulate and help realize the *sunna*. One does not simply connect the *sunna* and the community because one has authority. Instead, one becomes a religious authority because one is engaged in the labor of articulating the *sunna* and the community, thereby garnering the recognition of those who make up the community.

* * *

Cultivating Islam thus becomes akin to coconut and date cultivation for at least two reasons. First, it is a project of creating a growing social field involving available conceptual and material infrastructure. Secondly, what is contextually sown is something that is taken as being modeled on a common ancestor, while in actuality it becomes a model for reconstructing the vanished common ancestor. Articulating the *sunna* and the community involves mutual calibration. The *sunna*, after all, is the *sunna* only when it becomes a normative standard for others, or when it is pragmatically reproduced in daily life and in concrete interactions that make up the community. In these processes, the role of the connectors is principal. One should, therefore, ask how particular human actors become recognized as connectors. To do so demands serious consideration of the labor that constitutes Islamic religious authority.

Articulation

The triangular relationship between the *sunna*, the connectors, and the community, all of which are mutually and contingently constituted, opens up an alternative way of thinking about the transmission of Islam. Transmission of Islam has been described primarily as a linear process in which prepackaged Islamic teachings—often posited to be distinct from culture—are transmitted, disseminated, and localized or indigenized to the extent that they take root in, merge with, and shape new sociocultural contexts.[68] Following the actors who formed the vectors of that transmission, however, yields a more grounded perspective that allows us to see transmission as a far more complicated process. Such an approach shows that what we often describe as the transmission of Islam is a sporadic, highly contingent, locally grounded process of social formation that brings together diverse elements into a new assemblage that allows for the Prophetic past to be recalled, represented, and transformed into examples, or *sunna*, for present and future action. The ways in which that past becomes articulated with the present correspond to the changing proclivities of its audience, the shifting problem-space in and through which that articulation occurs, and the availability of new resources and infrastructure. Far from being a stable product of habits or transgenerational inheritance, a social formation is a fragile achievement. As Bruno Latour reminds us, a social formation is "an association between entities which are in no way recognizable as being social in the ordinary manner, *except* during the brief moment when they are reshuffled together."[69] This momentary association transforms and translates the correlated elements so that they can act in unison, facilitate movements and transmission, and mobilize. If a social formation is by definition momentary, the question becomes: what makes some social formations durable and susceptible to growth, while others are liable to contraction and succumb to ephemerality? Posing this question pushes us to think about the different labors and infrastructure—whether conceptual or material—behind any given social formation. It also leads us to the question of politics, not only because social formation involves the matter of leadership through its ability to empower actors differentially, but also because it takes shape in an unequal world filled with multiple intersecting and overlapping social formations, where limited resources—including material resources—limit or shape social processes, and where "the unpredictability of resource accumulation" constantly imposes risk on its capacity to reproduce and endure.[70]

The implications of this shift in analytic perspective are threefold. First, the *sunna* is always local because it is always produced through specific retrospective attempts of connecting to the Prophetic past using different modifying mediums and infrastructure. Secondly, there have always been multiple Islamic social formations, revolving around similar or distinct articulations of the *sunna*, which may compete with one another, forming what the historian Nile Green has called a competitive "religious economy."[71] This, in turn, underlines the need to move away from the theological notion of *umma* that for long has been imagined as the basic analytic unit of Islamic community, and to shift to its concrete and organized form—i.e., *jamāʿa*/community.[72] Thirdly, the absence of consistency in the religion's foundational source is the consequence of social formation as a process that articulates different elements, including the Prophetic past, and simultaneously translates and transforms them. One may argue that this lack of consistency is what enables Islam to be endlessly reproduced in different ways in disparate contexts. Indeed, it is what equipped Islam with the ability to become a world religion, even without the support of global institutional structures.

If every Islamic social formation is a product of *articulatory labor*, then differences among Islamic communities can be explained in terms of articulatory variation. Adopting this point permits us to develop a nonholistic and nonhistoricist reading of Islam and Islamic history, one that portrays the transmission of Islam not as a linear process, but as a discontinuous reproduction of different

Islamic communities, all of which may be interrelated without necessarily forming a whole. To clarify this point, I want to turn to Louis Althusser, whose discussion of articulation is central to the approach I am formulating here. In *Reading Capital* Althusser argues that previous readings of Marx confuse the Marxist concept of historical time with the Hegelian notion of the homogeneous temporal continuity and contemporaneity.[73] Such readings reflect Hegel's conception of synchronic and diachronic unity and wholeness, thereby presenting historical time as successions of wholeness, or total synchronicity in a temporal continuum. As a result, historical time tends to be presented as the evolution of different modes of production posited in holistic terms. In contrast, Althusser developed the notion of articulation to conceive of a more complex social totality made up of interrelationships among different modes of production that coexist alongside one another, each having its own historical existence and temporal dynamic, and may come to be conjoined with one another without forming a whole.[74] Althusser explains that, unlike the Hegelian whole, the Marxist totality is "constituted by a certain type of complexity, the unity of a structured whole containing levels or instances which are distinct and relatively autonomous, and co-exist within this complex structural unity, articulated with one another according to specific determinations."[75] Althusser seems to point to two articulatory dynamics operating on two levels. The first is articulation that makes up a mode of production, one that combines productive forces and relations of production.[76] Being an outcome of articulation, each mode of production has its own temporal dynamic and is relatively autonomous, although it may also suffer from internal contradictions that can lead to its disintegration. The second is articulation that makes up a complex totality, one that ties different modes of production without altering their own internal structures, thereby generating contradictions that may eventually result in revolutionary change.[77] One important implication emerges from Althusser's reading of Marx, one that renders the Marxist theory of history radically antievolutionist. Each mode of production is by definition a combination of elements, which are only notional elements unless they are articulated with one another according to a determinate articulatory mode. Similarly, what we call a totality or whole is also an uneasy, if not contradictory, interrelationship among different modes of production. Consequently, transition from one mode of production to another, and by the same token transition from a totality to the next, should not be understood in terms of continuity or evolution, but as perpetual *reproduction of the combinations* through various articulatory modes. The reproduction of the combination that occurs in each mode of production affects the interrelationship that makes up the social totality. As Étienne Balibar succinctly puts it, Althusser's reading of Marx shifts the central analytic problem of history and the social to the question of articulatory variation.[78]

Subsequently, several scholars have attempted to refine Althusser's conception of articulation. Stuart Hall, for example, critiques Althusser's positing of articulation as a process that produces variation among *invariant* elements.[79] Ernesto Laclau and Chantal Mouffe, in their turn, underline how articulation may involve a qualitative transformation of the conjoined parts, in that "their identity is modified as a result of the articulatory practice."[80] In their rendering, articulation is an active practice of negotiation pursued by different actors and parties and involves "the construction of nodal points which partially fix meaning" among its constitutive and often contradictory parts, thereby allowing the entanglement and possible alignment of meaning and agendas.[81] Such a reconceptualization allows us to underline successful articulation as the outcome of concrete negotiations and contingent labor of human actors that otherwise are not at all apparent, or are even disregarded as systematic delusions, in Althusser's structuralist schema.

Drawing judiciously on these theoretical insights, I propose that the notion of articulatory labor allows us, first of all, to break down the holistic unit of Islam or *umma*, which, after all, is a contradictory ensemble or an imaginary reconstruction that "gives legitimacy to the small group pretending to speak in its name."[82] Instead, the notion of articulation as developed in this book enables us to focus on divergent itineraries and social and literary networks, as well as varieties of articulatory labors that generate different Islamic *jamāʿas*/communities.[83] It permits us to conceptualize each Islamic community—even those claiming to speak on behalf of the *umma*—as a locally embedded assemblage made up of a combination of particular elements that are brought together according to a specific articulatory mode. Instead of historical continuity and linear transmission, this approach enables us to think about Islamic history in terms of combinatory variation that (re)produces different forms of Islamic community (or different Islamic modes of production). Each Islamic community is the outcome of articulatory labors that calibrate its diverse constitutive elements. Such labors are concrete and contingent by nature. They may become efficacious in some relational contexts, while failing to do so in others. Nevertheless, some modes of articulatory labor and the forms of authority they engender may become paradigmatic, forming what I call *articulatory paradigm*, which shapes the labors of subsequent generations. Ultimately, positing articulatory labor as a central problematic means maintaining a commitment to the microcontext, even of the biggest world and history-making schemes like religion.

Secondly, positing Islam as an outcome of articulatory labors enables us to see how, despite their differences or even contradictions, distinct Islamic social formations may become articulated with one another. In fact, an Islamic social formation—like a Sufi order or a modern Islamic association—can create alliances with other similar and dissimilar formations, including the state, by partially fixing meanings despite their pursuance of diverse and often conflicting objectives. The complex and plural social terrains in which articulatory labors take place means that articulations are realizable only momentarily. Nonetheless, when a temporary efficacious alignment takes shape, it may produce results that endure long after the relationship disintegrates. The proliferation of actors, entanglements, and associations, and their attempts to transmit and realize contending *sunnas*, ultimately means that the complete dominance of an Islamic community and the Islamic teachings it instantiates will remain an unachievable aspiration. This pushes us to think about the social life of Islam as a set of exchanges, interactions, conflicts, and perpetual transactions among different communities, thereby avoiding linear models of transmission or historicist explanations of religious development.

Finally, the notion of articulation accentuates how the "religious" may articulate with other domains such as politics, bureaucracy, business, and the military. Recent anthropological works on Islam have turned away from the messiness of social life to study schools, mosques, revivalist groups, and Islamic courts.[84] These works relegate as peripheral what Samuli Schielke describes as the "complex logic of lived experience"—that is, the multiple and contradictory ideals and aspirations expressed by different actors; the complexity, ambiguity, and openness of everyday lives; and the tension among the local, national, and global connections that actors locate themselves in or are contingently entangled with.[85] This book suggests that the notion of articulation allows us to think about how an Islamic community in whatever shape or form may become articulated with other social formations, including the state. It accentuates how actors belonging to an Islamic community are constantly in dialogue with other social milieus. This, in turn, enables us to think more critically about areas that cut across the dichotomy of the religious and the secular.

Islam thus stands—sociologically speaking—as an outcome of a particular form of labor, that of articulating the *sunna* and the *jamāʿa*/community.[86] These two notions have taken different forms and possibilities, even when they share the Prophetic past as a common and foundational reference point. Adopting this approach does not mean that we are back to the notion of multiple Islams that operate in a zero-sum game—that is, positing that one either take Islam as a predefined religion or as a relational ongoing and plural production of meaning. Rather, thinking about Islam through the prism of articulation permits us to identify the concrete invariant dynamics in historically evolving, open configurations, thereby generating diversity of Islamic teachings, practices, communities, and forms of authority.

Narrating Islam

In a notable article, the historian Shahzad Bashir questions the usefulness of the notion of "Islamic history" as a unifying historiographical category. Reviewing the works of Marshall Hodgson, Ira Lapidus, and Jonathan Berkey, Bashir observes how these scholars presume the unity of Islam, despite the presence of data within their works that can attest to the historical reality of Islam "as a fundamentally fractured and conflicted tradition, not susceptible to representation by an internally coherent narrative."[87] In Bashir's view:

> The ultimate impetus for the unifying approach comes from commitment to the idea that a religion such as Islam must be a factor of cohesion. . . . [T]hese scholars presuppose that persons professing belief in "Islam" must share a core in common even though there is no shortage of data to suggest that the meanings and implications of such belief can vary radically from context to context . . . [T]his is a theological view of history that invests a particular geographical locality with *longue durée* patterns claimed as eternal constants despite radical change in circumstances.[88]

This unified perspective, Bashir continues, derives from "placing the essence of Islam in a vision of the essentials of a timeless Middle Eastern culture," thereby "casting Islamic perspectives produced outside the Middle East as being forever derivative on the one hand and encumbered with accretions from 'other' cultures on the other."[89] Bashir concludes his critique by emphasizing that:

> An Islam divided between an essence and additions is made possible by imagining Islamic history as a single timeline that begins in pre-Islamic Middle Eastern religions, consolidates in the Middle East in the "classical" Islamic age, and then eventually flows out from there to other regions to constitute weaker, diluted, or deviant versions.[90]

Bashir's critique poses a challenge to think about alternative ways of narrating the history of Islam that does not reproduce the tendency to posit the religion as the factor that unites historical differences or one that comprehends Islamic historical geography along a core-periphery model. There is a resonance between the problem that Bashir highlights and that faced by art historians. In art history, Islam has long been posited as "a historicized civilizational category distinct from that of living production." This, in effect, produces "a universal Islam in a manner that never existed in the absence of the epistemologies of positive classification that aimed to define it."[91] For Bashir, whose works focus on hagiographical and historiographical texts, the solution lies in "untying the consideration of texts and other materials from the standardized timeline of

Islamic history" and recovering human agency in manufacturing different conceptions of time.[92]

Building on Bashir's intervention, this book proposes a narrative approach to Islam that does justice to the religion's polyphonic reality—one that does not presume Islam to be an explanatory paradigm. Instead, it situates Islam as a sociological product, a contingent achievement that needs to be explained. Rather than taking Islam as a given or positing it as a unifying factor that can explain contending itineraries and social formations, this narrative approach seeks to trace the articulatory processes that produce particular realizations of Islam. It does this by adopting what the Czech novelist Milan Kundera describes as polyphonic narrativity. In music, polyphony is "the *simultaneous* presentation of two or more voices (melodic lines) that are perfectly bound together but still keep their relative independence."[93] Polyphony in the novel, according to Kundera, begins with a unilinear composition, which opens up to rifts in the continuous narration of a story. Take Cervantes's *Don Quixote*, for example, which begins with Quixote's unilinear travel story. As he travels, Quixote meets other characters, who narrate their own stories, thereby diversifying the novel's linear framework by introducing different voices and stories that enrich and transform the overall narrative structure of the novel.

Similarly, the narrative of Islam can be fruitfully constructed by taking the actuality and metaphoricity of travel seriously. This narrative begins as a single itinerary, only to encounter forks along the road that lead it in different directions, where it encounters different voices and stories that enrich and transform the overall narrative. While these particular itineraries may constitute the overarching narrative of Islam, such a grand narrative becomes visible only when we take a God's-eye view, or *panorama*, to use Latour's term.[94] Yet, whatever the global and universal picture actors—whether Islamophobes or Pan-Islamists—have attempted to conjure of Islam, some of whom are informed by desires for an expansive wholeness and centrality, such a representation is always assembled, maintained, and sustained in concrete localities through different technological mediations, where it becomes susceptible to political vicissitudes and sociological variabilities.[95] The reality remains that Islam materializes in divergent ways. Muslims live and will continue to live in differentiated societies. They engage in different genres of discourse, subject to contending language games, linked to multiple contexts of communication and practice, and participate in different practices of world making that often generate tensions among members of the same community as well as among different communities. We therefore need to take seriously Michael Gilsenan's proposition that a historical or anthropological approach to Islam should be concerned with "sociological questions of social and cultural variations in very different societies."[96] That is, it should attempt to identify "varying relations of practice, representation, symbol, concept and worldview within the same society and between different societies."[97]

Rather than pretending that we can offer a panoramic view of Islamic history, historians and anthropologists should limit their work to tracing one itinerary by following the actors who traversed it, while allowing the encounters with other itineraries along the road to complicate it. There is no one single, overarching narrative of Islam apart from these itineraries. No particular itinerary can be raised to a higher level and used to make sense of other itineraries, let alone be used as a unifying paradigm. As Kundera notes, one fundamental principle of polyphonic composition is "the equality of voices: no one voice should dominate, none should serve as mere accompaniment."[98] Following the travels of scholars, saints, and leaders and their labor of cultivating diverse Islamic communities is one way of staying true to the polyphony that is Islam. There have always been many Islamic communities, which emerged from encounters between different times, voices, stories, and itineraries. Every narrative of Islam, including the one I am about to tell, is by nature incomplete.

The first part of this book follows a highly influential articulatory paradigm that emerged between the Ḥaḍramawt and Java. Pioneered by a Bā ʿAlawī Sufi scholar, ʿAbdallāh b. ʿAlawī al-Ḥaddād (d. 1720), this paradigm began as a labor of articulating the *sunna* for the tribal communities in the Ḥaḍramawt. Chapter 1 observes several pre-Ḥaddādian modes of articulatory labor that have enabled the cultivation of different forms of Islamic community with varying scale in Java and the Ḥaḍramawt. Each of these communities revolved around particular figures of authority—whether saints or sultans—and their successors, who were recognized as connectors to the Prophetic past and living embodiments or purveyors of Prophetic teachings. The first chapter thus serves to acquaint readers with the notion of articulatory labor while providing the history behind the emergence of the Ḥaddādian paradigm. Chapter 2 focuses on al-Ḥaddād and his attempt to formulate a new mode of articulatory labor that shifts the emphasis of Islam away from the inimitable achievements of living figures to text-based Prophetic teachings accessible to the commoners (*ʿawāmm*). The chapter then follows the spread of this paradigm in Java in the early nineteenth century. Chapter 3 looks at the Islamic communities established by Ḥaddādian scholars in late nineteenth- and early twentieth-century Java. While assembled in accordance to the Ḥaddādian articulatory paradigm, these communities gradually developed into saintly dynasties. Focusing on the Bā ʿAlawī saintly dynasty of Pekalongan, Central Java, the chapter shows how behind the transformation of a Ḥaddādian community into a saintly dynasty is a changing mode of articulatory labor that adjusted the way the *sunna* is imagined and generated a novel form of authority that has remained influential down to the present day. The first three chapters touch on several topics, including mobility, objectification, purification, colonial encounters, and modernity, each of which deserves its own monograph. My treatment of them here is not meant to be a thorough or definitive demonstration. Instead, my purpose is to accentuate the larger framework that informs the ethnography presented in the second part of the book.

The second part of the book continues the narrative by following the emergence of a growing Islamic community in contemporary Java. This community is cultivated by a Bā ʿAlawī scholar who has risen to become Indonesia's leading Sufi master, Habib Luthfi Bin Yahya (b. 1947) of Pekalongan, with whom this introduction begins. Believed by his followers to be a living saint, Habib Luthfi is considered an eminent Islamic authority and his counsel is widely sought not only by his devotees but also by prominent politicians, generals, scholars, and business people. While influenced by the Ḥaddādian paradigm, the *habib* has sought to transcend this dominant Bā ʿAlawī articulatory paradigm by drawing upon and synthesizing different articulatory modes that have been historically present in Indonesia. Chapter 4 follows the biographical becoming of Habib Luthfi. Unlike the scions of the Bā ʿAlawī saintly dynasties, Habib Luthfi does not come from an established scholarly or saintly background. Consequently, he had to form new connections and embed himself in established genealogical channels to be recognized as a credible connector to the Prophetic past. The chapter then describes the *habib*'s rise to prominence and rivalries with competing religious leaders, including the scion of the saintly dynasty of Pekalongan. Chapter 5 focuses on Habib Luthfi's mode of articulatory labor. It observes how the infrastructure that makes up a Sufi order enables him to create a durable community that centers on the hierarchical relationship between a Sufi master and his disciples. Such a relationship, in turn, allows Habib Luthfi to adjust and augment the *sunna* by introducing new teachings and practices to suit the changing proclivities of his disciples without being perceived as deviating from Prophetic teachings.

The penultimate chapter focuses on Habib Luthfi's relationships with different actors and institutions of the Indonesian state. It observes how different articulatory labors have allowed the *habib* to establish alliances with the state and, in turn, employ the state as an infrastructure of religious authority. These relations enabled him to organize religious events in and through which he performs the labor of articulating the *sunna* to a broader audience, often at the expense of other Muslim leaders. Alliances with the state have also permitted Habib Luthfi to enact consequential interventions on behalf of others. The final chapter observes the *habib*'s labor of recovering Indonesia's saintly past. Much of this labor has been devoted to the hagiographical composition of his own little-known and unrecorded forefathers. Such a hagiographical composition presents Habib Luthfi as a lineal successor of an old, but forgotten, Bā ʿAlawī saintly dynasty closely linked to the Ḥaddādian scholars on the one hand and the Javanese royal dynasty on the other. In Habib Luthfi's hand, hagiography works to articulate historically competing genealogies and itineraries of Islamic transmission discussed in the first part of this book. The convergence of multiple genealogies of Islamic transmission in Habib Luthfi allows him to situate himself as the living terminus of diverse historical itineraries that connect contemporary Java to the Prophetic past. Being an embodiment of several genealogies of authority, in turn, affords the *habib* the possibility to authoritatively nest himself in different Islamic communities in Java and articulate the *sunna* for them, albeit without necessarily determining its success.

The book closes with a short epilogue that discusses the implications of the analytic approach proposed in this book to the way we understand Islam's universality. In attending to the articulatory labor that produces Islam as a social reality, the book critiques the common tendency to equate Islam with a consistent supracultural package of precepts, values, and practices distinct from local particularities. By asserting the existence of a "pure" Islamic tradition, scholars have consistently misrecognized Islam as a premade universal project. In contrast, this book proposes a way of thinking about Islam's universality as a *concrete universality*. This entails that what is universal about Islam is not ideational commonality, but the concrete labor of articulating the *sunna* and the community that has generated doctrinal and practical diversity.

Readers may be struck by the near absence of socioeconomic class and gender as analytic categories in this book. Scholars have drawn attention to the intersection between religious authority and socioeconomic class. To give one example, Richard Bulliet's classic work, *The Patricians of Nishapur*, observes how the power and prestige of medieval Nishapur scholarly elites were derived from land ownership and commerce as much as religious knowledge.[99] While recognizing the importance that socioeconomic class may play in the formation of religious authority, both the textual sources and the people I work with have drawn my attention to other forms of stratification that have played more critical roles, at least for the actors discussed in this book. This includes a genealogically based system of social stratification among the Ḥaḍramīs that differentiates people on the basis of descent, generating a hierarchy of groups beginning with Bā ʿAlawī *sayyids* (descendants of the Prophet), the *mashāʾikh* (non-*sayyid* scholarly families), the *qabāʾil* (tribesmen), and the *masākīn* (unarmed town and city dwellers who cannot trace their descent to a prominent historical figure).[100] Another form of stratification distinguishes people based on knowledge. Shahab Ahmed aptly described it as "a class hierarchy constituted not by material wealth or political power, but relative to the capacity to *know Truth*."[101] This form of stratification has generated categories like the commoners (*ʿawāmm*), the elect (*khawāṣṣ*), and the elect of the elect (*khawāṣṣ al-khawāṣṣ*). Both genealogical and knowledge-based stratification do not necessarily map onto one another, let alone onto socioeconomic status, although there are also cases in which they do, owing to the historically contingent control of economic resources and educational institutions.[102] For example, a Ḥaḍramī tribesman and a successful Bā ʿAlawī *sayyid* merchant may be considered as commoners based on their religious learning, notwithstanding the latter's high genealogical status. The same tribesman, for example, may have migrated to Java where he amassed extraordinary wealth, which makes him economically higher than an impoverished *sayyid*. While the impoverished *sayyid* may be financially dependent on the tribesman, the former is still, genealogically speaking, higher than the latter. Similarly, affluent Ḥaḍramī tribesmen and *sayyids* may yet be categorized as commoners compared with a penniless Javanese scholar, from the perspective of knowledge-based stratification. All of this is to say that different social hierarchies are often at play and *may* form contingent relationships to one another, although they should not be treated as derivatives of socioeconomic class.

In this book I do not deploy gender as a central analytic category. The Ḥaḍramī textual materials I work with—including genealogical tomes (*kitāb al-ansāb*), hagiographies (*manāqib*), biographical dictionaries (*tarājim*), travelogues (*riḥla*), and letters (*mukātabāt*)—were written by men and seldom contain any reference to women. Even the legal abridgments (*mukhtaṣar*) discussed in chapter 2 do not contain specific legal or ethical teachings for women. This absence is not surprising considering that such texts, as Zahra Ayubi has argued in her work on gender in classical Islamic ethics, "construct their entire ethical framework around a normative elite male."[103] Thus, "from the individual to the home to society and cosmos, ethics unfolds as a process of creating ethical men."[104] Even when women are discussed, such texts portray them as either dependents who ought to assist men's ethical becoming or threats to men's ethical integrity. Consequently, these texts do not help me comprehend the formation of female religious authority, although at times they provide hints of women's participation in the formation of male religious authority. As Ayubi's work has demonstrated, however, these texts can be analyzed to understand the gendered logics of exclusion. Nevertheless, such a project is not what this book is about. The task that I have set myself here is to formulate a basic analytic model to understand religious authority: how it works, the politics and infrastructure it involves, and the social processes—involving both men and women followers or detractors—that enable certain individuals to gain enduring recognition as religious authorities.

Historically, Islamic religious authority has been predominantly the domain of men, although there are, of course, exceptions.[105] Asma Sayeed's study of female *ḥadīth* transmitters, to give one example, has shown how "evolving social use of religious knowledge throughout Islamic history dramatically impacted women's roles, alternately promoting or inhibiting their religious participation in the public arena."[106] Among the second generation of Muslims, "a mere eight women are commemorated in the classical Sunnī collections for narrating more than just one of two *ḥadīth* and for doing so in a relatively broad transmission network," followed by a decline in the second and third Islamic centuries.[107] The professionalization of the religious sciences required aspiring scholars to embark on extensive journeys to encounter venerable teachers directly. Such a practice inadvertently disadvantaged women, who had to fulfill domestic duties and faced restrictions on unaccompanied travel. The advent of written transmission of *ḥadīth*s and the development of the *ʿulamāʾ* as a socioreligious elite in the fourth and fifth Islamic centuries, however, "positively impacted women's *ḥadīth* participation," which continued for the next three centuries.[108] Women who succeeded in becoming recognized *ḥadīth* transmitters were, by and large, those who came from elite scholarly families. They were able to establish connections to the Prophetic past through written transmission or through their fathers, husbands, brothers, or visiting scholars and *ḥadīth* transmitters who graced their homes. Their authority, however, was to a large extent contingent on the recognition of male family members and biographers. In contrast to this historical dynamic, the ethnography presented in this book underlines the participation and recognition of both men and women—including those who do not come from the scholarly elites—in the formation of (male) religious authority. Nevertheless, I must admit that conducting fieldwork among women in Pekalongan was a challenge. For a male fieldworker to sit and chat with unrelated women would have invited frowns if not outright reprimand. The only chance for me to observe female disciples and followers of Habib Luthfi was either during mass ritual gatherings or when they were interacting with their Sufi master. These ethnographic limitations aside, the pivotal point remains that women in contemporary Indonesia, like men, actively evaluate male claimants to religious authority, a dynamic that has also been evinced in several recent works.[109] Nevertheless, my ethnographic experience among Muslims of Pekalongan has limited my ability to further analyze how gender difference shapes and complicates such evaluations. It is my hope that future scholarship can further develop the analytic model presented in this book by taking other variables, including gender differences, that may complicate the processes of evaluation and recognition of Islamic religious authority.

Finally, I need to recognize my own background and relation to my interlocutors. I am a Muslim and a Bā ʿAlawī born in Indonesia. My own background makes the research and writing of this book an endeavor that is close and, to a certain degree, personal. The extended time I have spent outside Indonesia since I was fourteen and the historical and anthropological training that I have received have created some measure of critical distance to the tradition and culture that I was born into. I am fully aware that the production of knowledge—particularly in the humanities and the social sciences—in Western universities cannot be divorced from the identities of the researchers and the ways in which they formulate their research questions. I am also aware that the question of insider versus outsider has generated a long debate in Western academia.[110] At the same time, our increasingly globalized world has continued to produce complex interweaving of identities. More and more anthropologists and historians today are "halfies," straddling two—or more—identity borders.[111] Having said this, I strongly believe in the inherent weakness of a scholarly project that presupposes the existence of a single and complete story and pretends to be able to recount such a story, whether it is produced by a stranger and distant observer or by an intimate or native analyst. In my view, the best anthropological research is one that maintains, rather than ignores or suspends, the tension between estrangement and intimacy and uses it to sketch a simultaneously objectifiable and personal, but nevertheless incomplete, picture of human sociality that "arises from within human sociality."[112]

PART I

Authority in Motion

1

Figures

IT IS REPORTED that among the earliest acts executed by the Prophet Muḥammad following his migration from Mecca to Medina in 622 was the construction of a mosque, which is recognized today as Islam's second holiest site after the Grand Mosque of Mecca.[1] The building of the mosque, as a communal place of worship, marked the crystallization of a religious community. A mosque is a site where members of the community can assemble and interact with one another. At the very least, they congregate every Friday to listen to a sermon that elaborates Prophetic teachings and pray, although ideally they are supposed to assemble five times a day for the obligatory prayers. Apart from being a site of worship and social interaction, a mosque also serves as an infrastructure of regimentation. While praying collectively, Muslims ought to stand behind a prayer leader and follow his lead. They are supposed to face one, and only one direction (*qibla*), that of the Kaaba, the stone cube edifice at the center of the Grand Mosque of Mecca believed by Muslims to be built by Abraham. Thus, every mosque is built in a way that the *miḥrāb*—the semicircular prayer niche where the imam stands as he leads the prayer—faces Mecca.

Emulating the Prophetic precedent, the *wali sanga*—the nine saints believed to be among the earliest Muslim missionaries in Java—also built a congregational mosque, following the establishment of the first Islamic sultanate in Java. Erected in 1498, the grand mosque of Demak served as an infrastructure that facilitated the materialization of Java's newly organized Islamic community.[2] Assembling a new community regimented toward a fixed *qibla*, however, was apparently not that simple for the early Muslims of Java. A nineteenth-century Javanese court annal, the *Babad Joko Tingkir*, tells a story of the mosque's resistance to the saints' attempt to orient its *qibla* toward the Kaaba:

> The mosque nudged to right and left
> swinging to and fro from north to south
> still never came to rest. Then did the Lord Sunan Bonang and the First
> Among Kings [Sunan Giri]

drawing in their breaths will the world condensed
in a flash accomplished was the sovereign *wali*'s [saint] miracle
Condensed the world was tiny
And Mecca shone close by
Allah's Ka'bah was nigh, manifest before them
To estimate its distance but three miles off it loomed
The Celibate Lord did beckon Sèh Malaya [an alias of Sunan Kalijaga],
ware to the subtle sign
Lord Sunan Kali [Jaga] rose to his feet
From north he did face south
One leg he did extend to side
Both legs did stretch forth
Long and tall, their stance astride
His right foot reaching Mecca came just outside the fence of Allah's
Ka'bah there
His left foot did remain behind
Planted to the northwest of the mosque
Allah's Ka'bah did his right hand grasp
His left hand having taken hold of the uppermost peak of the mosque
Both of them he pulled
Stretched out and brought to meet
The Ka'bah's roof and the peak of the mosque
Realized as one being were
Perfectly straight strictly on mark.[3]

This anecdote alludes to the historical difficulty that marked Java's conversion to Islam. It portrays the saints as living connectors who labored to assemble an autochthonous community oriented toward a new religion, sacred space, and foundational past, all of which were foreign. In performing such arduous tasks, the saints had to overcome various challenges, symbolized in the anecdote by the mosque's resistance. The anecdote describes how Sunan Kalijaga finally surmounted the mosque's obduracy not by forcing the mosque to orient itself toward the Kaaba, but by adjusting the position of both edifices so that the two could form a perfect alignment.

In this chapter, I want to use the preceding anecdote to think about the transmission of Islam. At the heart of such a process is the formation of Islamic communities—that is, social formations that serve as sites for the social realization of Prophetic teachings. The anecdote draws our attention to the *articulatory labor* that lurks behind a seemingly smooth and linear transmission. Thinking about transmission as the outcome of articulatory labor foregrounds the messy and oftentimes conflictual process of community building. It accentuates the work of reproducing the Prophetic past in light of the community's cultural assumptions to represent that foundational past as a comprehensible, relevant, and doable model, or *sunna*, for present and future action. Articulating the *sunna* and the community thus involves mutual calibration and qualitative transformation of the conjoined parts. It entails a cultural modulation of the Prophetic past that is required for its social realization as *sunna*. Focusing on articulatory labor, in turn, highlights the agency of actors who perform the labor and in the process come to be recognized as holding some form of authority. Thus the anecdote portrays Sunan Kalijaga as someone who successfully performed articulatory labor to the extent that Islam has been able to take root and flourish in Java. His success in forming such an alignment, in turn, constituted—or, at the least, reinforced—his religious authority.[4]

To illustrate this dynamic, the chapter observes several modes of articulatory labor that have constituted divergent forms of Islamic community with varying scale in Java and the Ḥaḍramawt. Examining different modes of articulatory labor permits us to conceptualize each community as a contingent assemblage made up of a combination of elements that are brought together according to a determinate articulatory mode, and, in turn, generate divergent forms of religious authority. Instead of historical continuity, this approach pushes us to envisage Islamic history in terms of multiple itineraries of transmission and combinatory variation that (re)produce different forms of Islamic community and authority. The boundary of an Islamic community, however, is porous to the influence of, and entanglements with, other networks, itineraries, and social formations, which may lead to its expansion, contraction, or even dissolution. This chapter also provides historical background for the development of the Ḥaddādian paradigm, a highly influential mode of articulatory labor that has become paradigmatic in the Ḥaḍramawt and Java, discussed in the next two chapters.

Regulators of Religion

On one sunny morning in May 2012, I found myself navigating the narrow alleys of the Arab quarter of Surabaya, East Java. The winding pathways were overcrowded with merchants selling various religious commodities, from prayer beads and mats to scarves and sarongs. The sweet scent of incense burnt by shopkeepers selling nonalcoholic perfumes infused the air. A fiberglass canopy protected passersby from the sweltering sun. Up ahead I could see the unassuming minaret of the Ampel mosque. Behind the mosque lies the tomb of Sunan Ampel, one of the nine saints of Java. The tomb has continued to draw thousands of pilgrims from across Indonesia and beyond, bursting the alleys leading to the mosque with unending shoppers. A shopkeeper from whom I bought a poster depicting the nine saints told me that the constant stream of pilgrims that makes local businesses thrive is a "sociological testament" (*bukti sosiologis*) to the persisting spiritual potency of the deceased saint. Although long gone, the saint still provides for the livelihood of the locals, he said. Sunan Ampel's hospitality continues to welcome pilgrims and ensures a thriving economy.[5]

As one of the so-called nine saints, Sunan Ampel is widely believed to have played a major role in the preaching of Islam in Java that led to the establishment, in 1475, of the island's first Islamic polity, the Sultanate of Demak.[6] Javanese Muslims hold that the sultanate was founded by Raden Patah (d. 1518) in cooperation with eight of the nine saints. They maintain that the saints coronated Raden Patah and that both parties agreed to divide authority into the interrelated spheres of the religion and the state.[7] The agreement stipulates that the ruler is answerable to the saints, who also acted as arbitrators between feuding ruling elites. The saints tasked the sultan with the responsibility to manage, defend, and enforce Islamic norms in his realm.

Gus Zayn, one of the caretakers of Sunan Ampel's tomb, explained to me that the political structure of the Demak Sultanate was founded on medieval Sunnī political theories. Such theories posit sovereignty as stemming from coercive force—that is, raw military and disciplinary power that is legitimated and restricted by Islamic law as extrapolated from the Qurʾān and the *sunna* by the scholars. In this capacity, the scholars are known as "the people who loosen and bind" (*ahl al-ḥall wa-l-ʿaqd*).[8] Theoretically speaking, in consideration of the changing public interest, temporal rulers are also able to establish, under the juristic principle of *siyāsa sharʿiyya* (*sharīʿa*-sanctioned governance), their own customs or rulings as they see fit, "even if no authority is found for them in divine revelation and the *sunna* of the Prophet."[9] Such a prerogative made the sultan a complement to but also a potential competitor of the scholars.

Existing autonomously alongside the royal court, or *kraton* as it is called in Java, were the *perdikans*, or free villages. These were autonomous Islamic communities that served as the seats of the religious authorities. A *perdikan* status was given by a ruler through a royal decree (*piagem*) to villages or people who were considered by the monarch to be deserving in religious matters, such as Muslim scholars who had established institutions of religious learning. Some villages were declared as *perdikan* due to the existence of saintly graves within their vicinity. These villages were exempted from taxes and compulsory labor but were expected to watch over royal or saintly graves and provide religious education.[10] The *perdikans*, Ann Kumar explains, were distinguished from ordinary villages:

> by their manners and morals (according to Dutch observers, by a "holier-than-thou" attitude) and often enforced prohibitions on the enjoyment of,

> for instance, *wayang* and *gamelan*; some even proscribed common objects and actions not usually considered offensive to Islamic law or morality.[11]

Several of these *perdikans* were believed to have been founded by the nine saints and their disciples, some of which were established under the auspices of the pre-Islamic Hindu kingdoms of Majapahit and Pajajaran respectively. Each of these communities revolved around the religious authority of its founding scholar/saint and his descendants.[12] Several of the *perdikans*, like Cirebon and Giri, even developed to become semipolities in their own right.

The existence of the *perdikans* alongside the *kraton* resulted in the emergence of royal and saintly dynasties, whose relationship to each other was often fraught with turbulence, although it was also marked by complex overlaps and intermarriages. Intermarriages between scions of royal and saintly dynasties facilitated the entry of Islamic culture and literature from the *perdikans* into the court, while adding further legitimacy to the sultan.[13] The rulers of the Javanese Mataram Sultanate (founded in 1586), for instance, claim descent from both the rulers of the Hindu-Buddhist Majapahit kingdom and the mythic kings of the Mahabharata, and from the nine saints (in particular Sunan Kudus), that ultimately goes back to the Prophet Muḥammad.

The emergence and consolidation of the Mataram Sultanate in the sixteenth century was marked by the pacification of several influential *perdikans*.[14] The founder of the sultanate, Panembahan Senapati (d. 1601), claimed the title of *khalīfatullāh* (caliph of God) and worked to expand Mataram's territory, partly by subsuming the *perdikans* into his dominion. The reign of Amangkurat I (r. 1646–77) witnessed a huge number of "Mohammedan popes"—the term used by Dutch writers to describe the masters (*Ki Ageng*) of the *perdikans*—executed following their involvement in the rebellion of the king's younger brother.[15] In 1679 and 1680 respectively, the influential *perdikans* of Kadjoran and Giri—both of whom refused to submit to Mataram's power—were ransacked and destroyed by the army of Amangkurat II (r. 1677–1703).[16] The redrawn political geography signaled Mataram's attempt to capture undivided political power and religious authority, and secure Javanese kingship as supreme spiritual and temporal sovereignty. The rulers of Mataram claimed the title of *panatagama*—that is, the regulator of religion. In 1755, the war of succession between the ruler of Mataram, Pakubuwana II (r. 1726–49), and his brother Prince Mangkubumi concluded in the signing of the treaty of Giyanti, which divided the sultanate into two.[17] Subsequently, Pakubuwana III (r. 1749–88) became the ruler of Surakarta, ruling over the eastern half of Mataram's dominion, and Mangkubumi (r. 1755–92) became the sovereign of Yogyakarta with suzerainty over the western half, and took on the regnal title of Hamengkubuwana I. Both assumed the mantle of caliph of God and *panatagama* in their respective dominions.

The *kraton* thus emerged as a religiopolitical institution that materialized a sovereign Islamic community in Java under the power and religious authority of the *panatagama*. Sovereignty allowed the *panatagama* to align his subjects to his articulation of the *sunna*. Unlike the *perdikan*, the *kraton* demanded the allegiance of its subjects, if necessary by force. Consequently, it emerged as an independent center of Islam that recognized no single absolute temporal or spiritual authority.[18] One can compare the notion of the Javanese ruler as the *panatagama* with the notion of "millennial sovereign" claimed by some of the Mughal emperors, a conception of sovereignty that combines the notion of absolute kingship with that of Sufi sainthood.[19] Indeed, the regnal title of both rulers of Mataram, whether Pakubuwana (axis of the world) or Hamengkubuwana (he who holds the world in his lap), resonate with the Sufi notion of *quṭb*, or the axial saint of the age, on whom the world metaphysically depends.[20]

* * *

The historian M. C. Ricklefs describes the form of religiosity that developed in the *kraton* as *mystic synthesis.* This, in his view, rested on three constitutive elements: (1) a strong sense of Islamic identity; (2) observation of the five pillars of Islamic ritual; and (3) acceptance of the reality of local Javanese spiritual forces such as Ratu Kidul (the Goddess of the Southern Ocean), Sunan Lawu (the spirit of Mount Lawu), and other, lesser supernatural beings.[21] The notion of mystic synthesis, as Ricklefs defines it, denotes a unique combination of what some would describe as the more purified elements of Islam (elements 1 and 2) and non-Islamic elements (element 3). Indeed, he presents the former as Islam and the latter as Java, as if positing Islam as external to Java. For him, mystic synthesis was a historical achievement that resulted from the maintenance of Javanese philosophy and the adoption of "the outer symbols, rituals, and (rather selectively) the law" of Islam.[22] On the one hand, Ricklefs's point of using the notion of mystic synthesis is to affirm a two-way negotiation between two entities, in contrast to the notion of syncretism, which involves value judgment in terms of what is authentic and what is derivative. Nevertheless, his use of such an agglomerative term leaves the impression that Islam, as one of the two constituents of mystic synthesis, was already a prepackaged entity that could actually exist without the other. In other words, the basic assumption at work is that of Javanese importation and subsequent localization of Islam, rather than autochthonous (re)production.

Perhaps one could retain the term "Islam" to denote this particular *kraton*-based religiosity. As one among multiple instantiations of Islam that have developed historically in different parts of the Muslim world, this particular *kraton*-centered Islam became increasingly seen as *mystic, synthetic,* or even problematic only because of the modern promotion and acceptance of a particular historically/geographically situated instantiation of Islam as normative, thereby measuring other instantiations on its terms.[23] One might perhaps begin by asking whether the *kraton* ever distinguished the three pillars of Ricklefs's mystic synthesis as distinct elements at all. If not, then one would indeed have to ask from what point of view they become perceivable as such. When one particular—and often culturally purified and abstracted—Islamic normativity is accepted, then other more complex and culturally bound instantiations of Islam are seen as "Islam + *y*," where *y* points to the various elements deemed to be different from Islam, such as Javanism, Hinduism, or local cultures. To assume that culture is extrinsic to Islam, however, is to miss the complex and culturally situated articulatory labors that align and modulate the Prophetic past and the community, determine the alignment between the two, and, as a result, produce Islam as an autochthonous but monophyletic social reality. This entails the need for an approach that can account for the "process of production" that generates this "complex and challenging cultural and religious interaction."[24]

To illustrate this, I want to turn to the figure of Prince Dipanagara, the leader of the Java War (1825–30) against the Dutch colonial regime, and an aspirant to the mantle of the *panatagama*, who, in the words of his biographer:

> drew inspiration from the ancestral spirit world of the Javanese heartland just as much as from his devotion to Islam and the esoteric teachings of the Shaṭṭāriyya, precisely the type of "mystic synthesis" which Ricklefs has described as reaching its epitome in early nineteenth-century Java.[25]

As many historians of Java have noted, the Java War that ended with the victory of the colonial forces marked the twilight of the *kraton*-centered sociopolitical order in Java, a process that brought about the gradual withering of the *kraton*-based Islam.[26] Drawing on Dipanagara's own memoir, together with a critical rereading of Peter Carey's exhaustive biography of the prince, I want to situate this enigmatic figure as one of the last emblematic embodiments of the form of Islamic authority that I have described as the *panatagama*, or regulator of religion. Observing the history of this mystifying character highlights the centrality of articulatory labor that produces Islam as a historically and culturally situated, but monophyletic social reality.

* * *

Prince Dipanagara was born in the *kraton* of Yogyakarta in 1785. His father was the eldest son of the second sultan of Yogyakarta, who briefly held the throne between 1812 and 1814. Dipanagara himself also claimed that he was maternally descended from the nine saints, thereby embodying both the royal and saintly genealogies.[27] Unlike other princes who grew up within the walls of the *kraton*, Dipanagara was brought up by his pious great-grandmother, the widow of the first sultan, in her estate of Tegalrejo in the outskirts of Yogyakarta. There, he grew up in an atmosphere of Islamic piety and devotion.[28] Living in an area of farmland enabled him to become familiar with the livelihood of the peasants and developed his sensitivity toward their plight. Whilst growing up, Dipanagara mixed with the *santri*s (pious Muslims) and studied Islamic texts under Muslim scholars who frequented the estate. He immersed himself in Islamic theology and law, Arabic grammar, Qurʾānic exegesis, Sufism, and history, as well as edifying works including the *Naṣīhat al-mulūk* (Advice for princes). At the same time, he delved into pre-Islamic Javanese classics like the *Serat Rama* and *Arjuna Wiwaha*.[29] Here is Peter Carey describing the prince's religious outlook:

> As regards Dipanagara's doctrinal position as a Muslim, it can be seen from his writings that *he was more a typical Javanese mystic than an orthodox Muslim reformer* [my italics]. This was recognised early in the Java War by his principle religious adviser, Kyai Maja, himself a possible adherent of Shaṭṭāriyya mystical brotherhood (*tarekat*), who pointed out that the prince seemed to be striving for the mystical unity of the Sufi. Despite an impressive display of quotations from the *Qurʾān* in his Makassar notebooks, Dipanagara laid the greatest stress on the use of *dhikr* (short prayers for the glorification of Allah which are endlessly repeated in ritual order) and on various forms of meditation. . . . [H]e took a mystical view of the fundamental dogma of Islam, namely *tokid* (Arabic *tawhīd*), the profession of Allah's unity and uniqueness. He considered that all man's efforts should be directed towards living up to this profession of unity by denying being to all that exists, inclusive of himself, and striving after union with the Eternal and Only Being (*Kang Jati Purbaning Sukma*).[30]

Instead of describing the prince as "a typical Javanese mystic" in contrast to "an orthodox Muslim reformer," one can perhaps comprehend Dipanagara as a proponent of a distinct conception of the *sunna*. Dipanagara was familiar with the Prophetic past, which he deemed to be foundational. Indeed, Lieutenant Julius Heinrich Knoerle, a German officer who accompanied the prince on his journey into exile after the conclusion of the Java War, described the prince as "very closely acquainted with the spirit which pervades the religious system of [the Prophet]."[31] Nevertheless, akin to the Sufis, his interest in the Prophetic past was mainly concerned with the role of the Prophet as the ultimate prototype of a mystic. Sufis posit the Prophet's night ascension to the divine presence, the *miʿrāj* (as well as his descent back to the sensible realm), as their central paradigm for emulation. In their view, the *sunna* is first and foremost a set of physical and spiritual disciplines directed toward remaking the self in the image of the Prophet in the hope of attaining spiritual ascent. Sufi metaphysicians have elaborated such a conception of the *sunna* in numerous works, including *Al-Tuḥfa al-mursala ilā rūh al-nabī* (*The Gift Addressed to the Spirit of the Prophet*) of the Gujarati Shaṭṭarī scholar Muḥammad b. Faḍlallāh al-Burhānpūrī (d. 1620), which according to Carey was amongst the prince's favorite readings.[32] A work of Sufi metaphysic, the *Tuḥfa* presents the ontology of seven grades of being.[33] While the notion of *sunna* as presented in Sufi texts like the *Tuḥfa* may differ from that preached by "an orthodox Muslim reformer" (whatever that term means), it should nevertheless be considered a *sunna* precisely because it centers on the figure of the Prophet, taken as an object of emulation.

When he was twenty years old, Dipanagara embarked on a spiritual wandering, or what is known in Java as *lelono*, akin to the Islamic conception of *riḥla*, or travel as a means for "seeking advanced learning in religious matters and spiritual fulfillment."[34] The practice of *riḥla* is premised on the Qur'ānic story of Moses traveling in search of the wise al-Khiḍr, which, according to the eminent Sufi Rūzbihān Baqlī (d. 1209), establishes the "*sunna* in following the masters."[35] Dipanagara began his peregrination by visiting several *perdikan*s and *pesantren*s (Islamic boarding schools). He then visited and meditated at places of crucial historical connection to his royal ancestors, including caves (like the Prophet) and graves.[36] During these meditations he beheld several spiritual visions and encountered important historical and mythical figures, including the aforementioned Sunan Kalijaga and Ratu Kidul (the Goddess of the Southern Ocean), both of whom prophesied the upcoming ruin of Java and the prince's future as the divinely anointed *ratu adil* (just ruler).[37] The goddess proposed to help Dipanagara in facing his future enemies, an offer that the prince rejected, "for in religion there is only the assistance of the Almighty."[38] Dipanagara's spiritual wandering and his imaginal meetings with both the spirits of Muslim saints and pre-Islamic deities highlight an imaginal world that dynamically combines the Prophetic past as refracted through the Sufi teachings of the Shaṭṭāriyya and the ancestral spirit world of Java.[39] It is a cultural context that paradoxically contains and combines several foundational pasts, from the foreign Prophetic past to Java's more local pre-Islamic and saintly pasts, thereby opening up the possibility for a distinct articulation of the *sunna*.

* * *

Between 1809 and 1810, Dipanagara witnessed an unprecedented colonial intrusion into his homeland. The colonial state annexed the eastern territories of the Yogyakarta Sultanate. The new Governor-General, Herman Willem

Daendels (d. 1818), acting on behalf of the Napoleonic Empire, enforced several crippling and humiliating treaties on the sultanate. One year after the British invasion of Java in 1811, the British Lieutenant-Governor Sir Thomas Stamford Raffles (d. 1826) turned decidedly against the Sultanate of Yogyakarta and ransacked the *kraton*, adding more humiliations to prior injuries.[40] The return of the Dutch in August 1816 resulted in further radical changes in Java, the most important of which was the absorption of Java into the global market and the expansion of foreign capital into the Javanese hinterlands. Here is Carey describing the situation:

> The combination of the land tax, poor harvests, the 1821 cholera epidemic, the tollgates and the renting of estates to Europeans had turned south-central Java into a powder keg. . . . The desire for regeneration and the reestablishment of the old political order governing relations with the European government had begun to fuse with messianic expectations of a golden age of justice and plenty. What was now required was for a leader of sufficient stature to proclaim himself and bind the discontented to his cause.[41]

That awaited leader was Dipanagara, whose twin genealogy and eclectic upbringing enabled him to speak to diverse elements of Javanese society, including royalty and aristocrats, Muslim scholars and their students, and the peasants. The prince, whose vision of a normative social order had been shattered by the violent and humiliating colonial expansion, was determined to unite these diverse elements under the banner of holy war (*prang sabil*) against the Dutch.

As Carey has meticulously reconstructed the details of the Java War, there is no need to discuss them further. What I want to suggest, however, is that one way to understand the enigmatic prince and his significant success in assembling a composite force is to see it as a project of cultivating an Islamic community that revolved around his notion of the *sunna*. Dipanagara, as I have mentioned earlier, subscribed to a Sufi conception of the *sunna*. He was deeply influenced by Prophetic history, the teachings of the Shaṭṭāriyya, older Javanese imaginations, and Javanese court culture, all of which coalesced without being necessarily reconciled in his very person.[42] This allowed Dipanagara to offer his own version of the *sunna*, one that drew on Prophetic teachings and Javanese traditions communicable to the composite community he was cultivating. He was able to simultaneously embody several recognizable leadership roles, including those of heroic commander, Sufi warrior, and *ratu adil*, the just messianic king as foretold in old Javanese prophecies. By embodying these diverse and sometimes contradictory forms of authority, the prince was able to assemble a composite martial community that could maintain an extended war effort.

The project of cultivating a composite community that revolved around different forms of authority, however, generated misunderstandings from different segments of the community, thereby threatening it with the prospect of failure:

> Dipanagara reinforced this image of a court by conferring titles on his close family . . . , marrying key supporters to members of his family, distributing traditional largesse to his supporters at the time of the Garebeg ceremonies, having one of his *santri* advisers act the court jester . . . , and giving yellow *payung* (state umbrellas) to his princely followers and military commanders as a mark of their status in the holy war. The fact that these quintessential *kraton* symbols of office were described in the Javanese sources as "signs of the holy war" (*pratandha prang sabil*) is a measure of the confusion which seems to have prevailed about what Dipanagara was doing. Was he establishing a *kraton* or fighting for something entirely different—a new moral order in Java in which the high state of the Islamic religion would be restored?[43]

Ultimately, such inherent tensions undermined Dipanagara's project of cultivating a durable community. The configuration of the Islamic community envisaged by Dipanagara was one that modeled itself on the customs, honor system, and hierarchical structure of the *kraton*. This ultimately did not fare well with some of his supporters from the *perdikans*.[44] After all, the history of Islam in Java was marked by oftentimes uneasy tensions between the *kraton* and *perdikan*.[45] Some of the Prince's *santri* followers began to perceive Dipanagara as seeking worldly goals, violating the *sunna*, and "too taken up with Javanese superstitions and beliefs."[46] This conflict over the actual shape of the community shows that in the labor of cultivating an Islamic community, configuration matters. It matters whether or not the shape and infrastructure an Islamic assemblage takes on are recognized and appreciated by its members. It also matters whether or not the articulated *sunna* is recognizable and relevant. What is clear, however, is that Dipanagara was aspiring to the mantle of the *panatagama*, a position that would have allowed him to use force, if necessary, to realize his version of the *sunna*. His principal aim, as Carey made clear, was "the restoration of an idealized Javanese past and the establishment of a new moral order in which the teachings of Islam, especially its legal codes, would be enforced."[47] Up to the very conclusion of the peace negotiation with the Dutch in 1830, the prince refused to settle on any position except to be recognized as the "royal maintainer and regulator of religion in Java (*ratu paneteg panatagama ing Tanah Jawa sedaya*).[48]

Dipanagara spent the last years of his life under house arrest in Makassar, Sulawesi. Living in solitude and stranded from most family members and followers, the exiled prince, who had witnessed more glorious days, decided to inscribe his version of the *sunna* into two texts, written "in a curious Javanese style with many Arabic words and phrases."[49] The texts were composed for the last remaining members of his *jamāʿa*/community—namely, his children. In one of the books, Dipanagara still refers to himself as the *panatagama* and caliph of the Prophet in the land of Java. Its contents, according to Carey:

> deal with the prince's understanding of Islam, his own religious experiences, Sufi prayers used by the Naqshbandiyya and Shaṭṭāriyya mystical brotherhoods . . . and various meditation techniques most of which involved the control of the breath. Diagrams (*daérah*) for the utterance of Arabic words and breathing exercises during prayers as well as local Javanese mystical traditions (*ngèlmu*) are frequently referred to. Indeed, the whole book is rather reminiscent of a Javanese divination manual or *primbon*.[50]

If Carey sees the text as akin to a Javanese divination manual, his description seems to resonate more with what I have described as Dipanagara's distinctive version of the *sunna*. Confronted by the failure to maintain an enduring community that could serve as a locus for the transmission and social realization of this particular conception of the *sunna*, the aging prince turned to the pen, inscribing the *sunna* in textual forms, hoping that they could guide his offspring and, perhaps, a future community.

There is a similarity between Dipanagara's *sunna* text with other kinds of *sunna* texts that are often not recognized as such. Among Ḥaḍramī scholars, for example, there is a textual genre known as *safīna*. While in codicology the term *safīna* (literally, vessel) refers to a specific kind of oblong-shaped notebook used in a vertical position and small enough to be carried, among Ḥaḍramī scholars the term refers to personal notebooks (not necessarily oblong) in which scholars record religious teachings, Prophetic *ḥadīth*s, poems, prayer formulas, and litanies that they heard from others or found in books. The six-hundred-page *safīna* of the scholar ʿAlī b. Aḥmad al-ʿAṭṭās of Pekalongan—who we will encounter in chapter 3—for example, also contains information on his personal and family histories, chains of Sufi initiation, advice for his children, letters he received from saints and scholars, and significant dreams he witnessed.[51] A *safīna* serves not only as an aide-mémoire to its owner, but, more importantly, as a personally curated *sunna* text that can be bequeathed to his progeny as a book of religious and moral guidance. Other kinds of *sunna* texts not recognizable as such include the tradesmen's *risāla* (treatise) that used to be popular among the Uighurs. According to Rian Thum, these are "talismanic handbooks dedicated to particular trades and crafts for which they are named."[52] Such texts prescribe proper ritual actions and present "the history of the trade's origin, in which God teaches the trade to its first master, most often an old-testament prophet such as Moses, along with a genealogy of famous masters."[53] There may be different kinds of Islamic prescriptive texts that fuse multiple genealogies of knowledge and function as customized or personalized *sunna* texts, alongside those compiled by *ḥadīth* scholars who work under the discipline of *ḥadīth* criticism.

As Dipanagara was concluding his textual project, however, other and less intricate—certainly less composite, customized, and personalized—*sunna* texts had begun to proliferate in Java, brought by, among others, the increasing number of Arab migrants from the Ḥaḍramawt. Amidst such a rapid change, the Dipanagaran *sunna* texts became increasingly seen as "syncretic" and even problematic. Indeed they began to be perceived as "Javanese divination manuals," or a textual expression of a Javanese "mystic synthesis," instead of *sunna* texts.

Saintly Planters

Notwithstanding its prominence, the tomb of Sunan Ampel represents only one of the many historical itineraries of Islamic transmission in Java. Each of these itineraries continues to exist alongside the others, offering its version of the *sunna*, which may have some similarities with the other versions, but also differences. The confluence of these itineraries has made Java a thriving Islamic religious marketplace. Perhaps no place on the island better epitomizes this reality than the Arab quarter of Surabaya. The many bookshops that grace the neighborhood stand as a testimony to the polyphony that is Islam. Considered a mecca for Muslim bibliophiles, the neighborhood hosts an array of bookshops selling Islamic texts in Arabic, Javanese, and Indonesian. All kinds of texts are on offer, from medieval theological, exegetical, juristic, and hagiographic treatises to the works of modern Islamic revivalist authors. Books on Islamic medicine and magic can also be found. These bookshops cater to Muslims not only of various religious orientations but also of different socioeconomic classes by selling books of different qualities, ranging from the expensive, leather-bound books imported from Cairo and Beirut to cheap, lithographic, loose-leaf books with often illegible print produced by local presses.

Aside from the tomb of Sunan Ampel, the Arab quarter of Surabaya also boasts another saintly mausoleum, which stands for an alternative itinerary of Islamic transmission. The number of pilgrims who visit this mausoleum on a daily basis certainly pales in comparison with that of Sunan Ampel, although the annual commemoration of the saint's death continues to draw thousands of people. Situated behind the bazaar that leads to the mosque of Sunan Ampel, this domed mausoleum is encircled by high whitewashed walls that make it easy to miss. A large iron gate serves as the entry to the compound where the mausoleum is located. An official plaque—erected in 2008 by the

Culture and Tourism Board of Surabaya—proclaims in bold font that "the mausoleum of al-Ḥabīb Muḥammad b. ʿAydarūs al-Ḥabashī (d. 1919)" is a protected heritage site.

Constructed in the empire style, the mausoleum was originally built by an affluent mercantile Ḥaḍramī family in the mid-nineteenth century to house the tombs of their departed relatives. Only later did it serve as the burial place of a saint. In its architecture, the mausoleum resembles the tomb of the Ottoman Sultan Mahmud II (d. 1839) in Istanbul.[54] The building is constructed on an octagonal plan and is supported by columns and eight large, semicircular open arches, forming a circular arcade that surrounds the burial space. One arch serves as the gate through which visitors enter the burial chamber. Each arch is adorned with decorative golden iron railings in the form of arrows and long spears. Ornate turquoise tiles bearing an eight-pointed-star design frame the interior of the arches. The walls of the mausoleum are about eight meters high and are covered in grayish marble. The upper part of the interior wall is lined with a white marble band that runs horizontally, encircling the burial chamber, and engraved with calligraphic verses of salutation to the Prophet Muḥammad. The tombs are situated at the center of the chamber, forming two rows, with that of the saint on the furthest right, followed by the tombs of the members of the mercantile family.[55]

The saint buried in the mausoleum, Muḥammad b. ʿAydarūs al-Ḥabashī, was born in 1849, in Khalʿ Rāshid, Ḥaḍramawt, a sacred sanctuary (*ḥawṭa*) established by his saintly great-grandfather Aḥmad b. Zayn al-Ḥabashī (d. 1731). As a scion of a saintly lineage, al-Ḥabashī was immersed in religious learning from childhood. He studied with prominent scholars of Ḥaḍramawt and in 1864, traveled to the Hejaz, India, and Singapore before settling down in Batavia (Jakarta).[56] In Java, al-Ḥabashī became a successful merchant and was known for his philanthropic activities.[57] While traveling for work, he also held religious gatherings attended by Ḥaḍramī migrants and sponsored by the diasporic community's mercantile elites, like the family whose bodies now lie buried next to his. Combining saintly lineage, scholarship, wealth, and philanthropy, al-Ḥabashī rose to become one of the most influential Ḥaḍramī religious leaders of early twentieth-century Java. He stands for an itinerary of Islamic transmission that connects Java to the Ḥaḍramawt through the articulatory labor of mobile actors known collectively as the Bā ʿAlawīs.

* * *

Recognized as the direct descendants (Ar. *sayyid*, pl. *sāda*) of the Prophet Muḥammad, the Bā ʿAlawīs have lived in the Ḥaḍramawt valley of the south Arabian peninsula since the tenth century. Almost all surviving *sayyid*s in the

Ḥaḍramawt trace their descent from ʿAlawī b. ʿUbaydillāh (d. beginning of the eleventh century), and hence are known as Bā ʿAlawī or Banī ʿAlawī (children of ʿAlawī). It was ʿAlawī's grandfather, Aḥmad b. ʿĪsā (d. 956), who first migrated to the Ḥaḍramawt from Basra, in 931.[58] Upon arriving in the Ḥaḍramawt, Aḥmad and his descendants invested the wealth they brought with them from Iraq in agriculture, reviving fallow lands and cultivating date-palm plantations.[59] The combination of Prophetic bloodline, religious learning, and agricultural enterprise became the foundation of Bā ʿAlawī religious authority for centuries to come.

In the thirteenth century, a Bā ʿAlawī scholar, Muḥammad b. ʿAlī (d. 1255), instituted his own Sufi order, which became known as the Ṭarīqa ʿAlawiyya, or Ṭarīqa Sāda Banī ʿAlawī (The way of the children of ʿAlawī). The name of the *ṭarīqa* itself seems to indicate that it was initially conceived as a family order of the Bā ʿAlawī *sayyids*, most of whom were based in the city of Tarīm. In the writings of its early Tarīmi masters, the *ṭarīqa* is presented as a path of spiritual wayfaring (*sulūk*) that involves the establishment of a formal contract (*taḥkīm*) between a disciple (*murīd*) and a spiritual mentor or master (*murshid*).[60] The kind of educational relationship that developed between the master and the disciple is one that is usually described in Sufi circles as *ṣuḥba*, or companionship, whereby a disciple lives with and serves a master for a protracted amount of time. Apart from learning the Qurʾān and *ḥadīth* texts that contain descriptions of the Prophetic *sunna*, disciples take their master as the living embodiment of the *sunna*. The master trains his disciples to ascend from one spiritual station (*maqām*) to the next, culminating in the highest station, wherein the disciple develops intimacy with the divine and becomes endowed with gnosis (*maʿrifa*). Disciples who attain gnosis can then be authorized by their master to act as masters in their own right. They can then perform the labor of cultivating the spiritual growth of a subsequent generation of disciples. The practical underpinning of this Sufi tradition is articulated in the doctrine of emulating the Prophet's *sunna*, both inwardly and outwardly, by emulating the Bā ʿAlawī masters. Here, revolving around the *sunna* means imitating the masters, who are genealogically connected to the Prophet.

Being initiated into the Sufi tradition provides disciples with tangible links that tie them to their master and the previous masters all the way back to the Prophet, while also creating bonds with fellow disciples. The Ṭarīqa ʿAlawiyya was not sustained by the elaborate economic and institutional infrastructure that characterized large, organized Sufi orders found in some areas of the Muslim world. Like other South Arabian Sufi orders, this *ṭarīqa* remained as a spiritual lineage built on family ties and sporadic master-disciple relationships. This may be attributable to a "lack of resources on the part of Yemeni ruling elites" that barred them from endowing Sufi lodges and prevented the economic foundation of more elaborate infrastructure.[61] Nevertheless, symbolic and conceptual infrastructure like the bond of allegiance (*ʿuqda*) between master and disciples and chains of Sufi initiations (*silsilas*) was able to generate a sense of vertical and horizontal solidarity among the initiates.

The Ṭarīqa ʿAlawiyya facilitated the emergence of a community of elect (*khawāṣṣ*). Members of this community posit Bā ʿAlawī masters as the transmitters and embodiments of the *sunna*. Claiming direct descent from the Prophet, the Bā ʿAlawīs professed intimate knowledge of the *sunna* through a genealogy of knowledge transmitted internally through the family, from father to son, without external mediation. Their descent from the Prophet afforded them the ability to present themselves as the inheritors of the Prophet superior to other claimants.

* * *

An urban-based community of elect was not the only Islamic social formation cultivated by the Bā ʿAlawīs in the Ḥaḍramawt. Hagiographical sources retrospectively display a pattern in the formation of Bā ʿAlawī religious authority outside the city of Tarīm as one that involves the migration of Bā ʿAlawī scholars to new territories, proselytization, agricultural enterprise, and the establishment of ties with local tribes, all of which enabled these mobile actors to cultivate new Islamic communities in the tribal hinterlands.[62] The Bā ʿAlawī scholars are portrayed as saintly planters who preoccupied themselves with the labors of cultivating two living entities: plantations and congregations.

Proselytization usually began prior to the decision of a Bā ʿAlawī scholar to settle in an area. Thus ʿUmar b. ʿAbd al-Raḥmān al-ʿAṭṭās (d. 1661), to give one example, was said to have frequented the valleys of ʿAmd and Dawʿān to proselytize among the tribesmen and gain their trust, before finally settling in the nearby town of Ḥurayḍa.[63] In these tribal territories, ʿUmar could not transmit the *sunna* in the same way as his Tarīmi masters. The tribesmen were not interested in his ability to explain intricate scholastic discourse. Nor were they keen on his capacity to serve as a guide in the systematic discipline of spiritual wayfaring. Instead, they were more attracted to his ability to act as a rainmaker, healer, and warder of evils.[64] A hagiographical anecdote succinctly describes this dynamic. One day, ʿUmar's pupil, ʿAlī b. ʿAbdallāh Bā Rās (d. 1683), asked his master:

> "Master, you often travel to these valleys, but no one benefits from your presence" (*lam yantafiʿ bika aḥad*). He [ʿUmar] replied: "O ʿAlī if only they see me with the eyes through which you see me, I will bring them to Allāh in an instant (*la awṣalathum ilā Allāh fī laḥḍa*). Unfortunately, they do not

> utter a word except for '*Ḥabīb* comes' and '*Ḥabīb* goes.' Even if some of them came to me, it is because they were asking me to supplicate for rain or to ask Allāh to give them children."[65]

To be recognized as a religious authority among the tribesmen, however, ʿUmar had to supersede previous authorities recognized by the locals:

> Before ʿUmar's arrival, the people of Hurayda went for advice and assistance to the al-ʿAfif family in al-Hajaryn, a village in Wadi Dawʿan. According to an anecdote, one day, ʿUmar b. ʿAbd al-Rahman, who was not famous yet, had a conversation with ʿAbd Allah b. Ahmad al-ʿAfif, a famous *waliy* [saint] who visited Hurayda to pray for rain. ʿUmar told him that he had just come to the town. On hearing this, ʿAbd Allah al-ʿAfif stopped visiting Hurayda on account of ʿUmar's presence in that town. One day, ʿUmar cured a person who could not walk by striking his back. Because of this miracle, he acquired a high status among the locals. Since then, the al-ʿAttas family has been acting as the almost sole religious authority in the town.[66]

Through his ability to perform a miraculous act, ʿUmar was able to replace the authority of the ʿAfif family in Hurayda. This anecdote illustrates how the triumph of a new religious authority simultaneously hinges on tapping into the inroads of previous authorities and the ability to supersede them.

Upon settling in a new area, these migrating scholars began to cultivate plantations. Agriculture was central because the ability of a scholar to provide hospitality to others was key to his success in cultivating an Islamic community that cut across tribal ties. There were at least two reasons for this. First, the tribes' acceptance of the authority of these Bā ʿAlawī scholars was propelled, as Evans-Pritchard has shown in the case of the Sanusiya of Cyrenaica, by their need for some authority "lying outside their segmentary tribal system which could compose intertribal and intersectional disputes."[67] These scholars were "*among* tribes but not *of* them."[68] This entails that part of these scholars' authority was built on the externality of their own selves and teachings from tribal kinship structures and moral systems, thereby giving them the ability to mediate intra- and intertribal disputes. Peace negotiations, however, were often lengthy and expensive. During the process, the scholar had to extend hospitality for each disputing party, as well as inviting all of them to joint feasts. Secondly, to be recognized as an authority, the scholar also had to provide room and board for visitors, pilgrims, travelers, and scholars. The hagiography of the founder of the settlement of ʿInāt, Abū Bakr b. Sālim (d. 1584), for instance, portrays his kitchen as baking a thousand loaves of bread for the poor, not including the food prepared for his incessant guests.[69]

His son and successor, Ḥusayn (d. 1634), was also known to provide lavish hospitality. He could do so precisely because he was said to own a vast date plantation and exported its produce as far as Iraq.[70] The notion of *karam* (generosity), central to the Arabian tribal ideology, thus became pivotal to the formation of religious authority in the tribal hinterlands. To be recognized by the tribes, the migrating Bā ʿAlawī scholars had to equal or exceed the generosity exhibited by the tribal chiefs. Agricultural enterprise provided them with a stable source of income that allowed them to extend hospitality.

Once a migrating Bā ʿAlawī scholar succeeded in gaining the trust and recognition of the local tribes, he could then try to negotiate with them for the establishment of a *ḥawṭa* or *ḥaram* (sacred sanctuary). Establishing a *ḥawṭa* could either mean founding a new settlement altogether or declaring an already existing settlement where the scholar lived as a sanctuary. Thus Aḥmad b. Ḥusayn al-ʿAydarūs (d. 1578) and Abū Bakr b. Sālim (d. 1584) founded the new sanctuary settlements of Thibī and ʿInāt, respectively, while ʿUmar b. ʿAbd al-Raḥmān al-ʿAṭṭās (d. 1661) and ʿAlī b. Ḥasan al-ʿAṭṭās (d. 1759) declared the already existing settlements of Ḥurayḍa and Ghaywār as *ḥawṭa*s. Declaring a territory as a *ḥawṭa* required the consent of the local tribes. Such agreements stipulated that the local tribes recognize the suzerainty of the *ḥawṭa* founder over the newly carved territory. Both the *ḥawṭa* founder and the local tribes guaranteed the neutrality and security of the *ḥawṭa* and its inhabitants.[71] Arms and violence were strictly prohibited in the *ḥawṭa*s. The neutrality and security of the *ḥawṭa* enabled these Bā ʿAlawī scholars to host markets and intertribal meetings, organize religious gatherings, and cultivate plantations. Upon declaring a *ḥawṭa*, the scholar demarcated his newly established territory with whitewashed pillars before building more permanent infrastructure like a mosque.[72]

The notion of a sacred sanctuary is one that can be found in different parts of the Muslim world. The Prophet himself worked to declare Medina (Yathrib) as a *ḥaram* following his migration to that oasis settlement, and for that reason establishing a sanctuary can be considered a *sunna*.[73] Such a social formation bears similarities to the previously discussed *perdikan*s of Java. Scholars have shown that in Arabia, this social formation predates Islam and is closely linked to the genesis of the religion.[74] Robert Serjeant explains that:

> in a society where war is the norm of existence, a neutral territory is a necessity for reasons religious, political, and economic. The *ḥawṭah* is such an area, often situated at a natural road junction, where tribes meet, perhaps an important market. . . . The essential political factor herein is that the saint induces the tribes or [in Islamic times] *sulṭāns* to contract agreements

> with him to maintain the inviolability of the *ḥawṭah* and define penalties for its infringement.[75]

Upon the death of a *ḥawṭa*'s founder, his hereditary successor—referred to by the term *manṣab*—continued to administer the sanctuary. He built a mausoleum on top of the founder's tomb and established an annual commemoration.[76] He continued to perform the daily labor of maintaining the community. His responsibilities included resolving local conflicts, propagating the *sunna*, and extending hospitality.[77] The spiritual authority of the *ḥawṭa*'s founder—believed to be stronger after his death—became the foundation upon which the *manṣab* established his religious and political influence over the tribes.

Hagiographical sources further illustrate how these saintly planters set themselves as living embodiments of the Prophetic *sunna* from whom the mostly illiterate members of the community could learn. One ethnographic example can help illustrate how these Bā ʿAlawī scholars transmitted the *sunna* to their tribal followers. In 2006, I visited the mausoleum of ʿAlī b. Muḥammad al-Ḥabashī (d. 1914) in Seiyun, Ḥaḍramawt. Every Monday evening, the *manṣab*—who was al-Ḥabashī's great-grandson—leads a two-hour ritual of singing al-Ḥabashī's poems accompanied by drumming, a practice known as *ḥaḍra* (presencing). Before the *manṣab* concluded the ritual with the final supplication, he led the congregation to collectively rehearse what Muslims usually recite during *ṣalāt* (Muslim prayer), beginning with the intention, the inaugural *takbīr*, the opening prayer, the *fātiḥa*, all the way to the final *salām*, all of which were recited whilst the congregants were sitting and facing the tomb rather than the *qibla*. Following the ritual, the *manṣab* explained to me that in the olden days, Bā ʿAlawī scholars like his great-grandfather had to teach illiterate tribesmen how to pray in accordance to the *sunna*. So they held recitations of poems and drumming to attract tribesmen and used the occasion to teach them what to recite during *ṣalāt*. When I asked the *manṣab* why such rehearsals continue when most people already know how to pray, he responded that such a practice is the *sunnat salaf* (the *sunna* of the predecessor) and thus, as a *manṣab*, he has to maintain ritual regularity. Note how while the invocations recited by the congregants were initially taught by the Prophet and as such are considered Prophetic *sunna*, the practice of rehearsing them while sitting in a congregation during the ritual of *ḥaḍra* is the *sunna* of ʿAlī al-Ḥabashī and was initially devised to instruct his tribal followers. This practice can be described as a *sunna* precisely because it is connected to both the Prophetic past—through the community's more recent saintly past—and the tribal members of the community who perform and realize it.

This example shows how the *ḥawṭa*s represented a particular form of Islamic community born out of a specific mode of articulatory labor performed by Bā ʿAlawī scholars in dialogue with tribal cultures and realities. Such communities serve as sites for the transmission and social realization of the *sunna* as articulated by the *ḥawṭa* founders and their descendants. These scholarly actors labored to present themselves to their tribal followers as connectors to the Prophetic past and living embodiments of the *sunna* in a culturally recognizable and relevant manner, using the means and infrastructure that were available to them. While in reality the *sunna*s that were socially realized in the *ḥawṭa*s contained innovations and elements derived from tribal culture, they were nonetheless recognized and revered as *sunna*.

* * *

Writing in the early twentieth century, the modern reformist Ḥaḍramī historian Ṣalāḥ al-Bakrī (d. 1993) criticized the Bā ʿAlawīs for establishing what he described as *sulṭa rūḥiyya* (spiritual power) among the tribes of Ḥaḍramawt. In al-Bakrī's view, this "power" was created not through force or military might, but through showcasing piety and claiming descent from the Prophet.[78] Each Bā ʿAlawī family, al-Bakrī explained, exercised "power" over a particular Ḥaḍramī tribe, like "the āl-Shaykh Abī Bakr over the Yāfiʿīs, the āl-ʿAydarūs over the Kathīrīs, and the āl-ʿAṭṭās over the Jaʿda."[79] The power relation was instantiated in everyday practices, including in the special sitting arrangements reserved for the Bā ʿAlawīs in rituals and gatherings, the prescribed acts of kissing their hands, and their practice marrying the women of the tribes while prohibiting their womenfolk from marrying the tribesmen.

Despite its polemical nature and misconstrual of authority as power, al-Bakrī's *Tārīkh ḥaḍramawt al-siyāsī* (Political history of Ḥaḍramawt) illustrates how the Bā ʿAlawīs' migration into tribal hinterlands and their labor of establishing *ḥawṭa*s generated multiple Islamic communities that revolved around different religious authorities. Each tribe adhered to the *sunna* only as articulated by a religious authority it recognized. These *ḥawṭa* founders embodied and instituted specific versions of the *sunna* that were born out of pragmatic negotiations with their followers, and were subsequently institutionalized and maintained by their hereditary successors. What this points to is precisely the development of multiple Islamic communities that revolved around and socially realized divergent *sunna*s as articulated by the saintly planters. Islam, in other words, "*is* what they do. They *are* Islam."[80]

The labor of cultivating a new Islamic community involves a culturally situated modulation of the *sunna*. It requires mutual calibration, whereby not only is the community subjected to the *sunna*, but also the latter is reconfigured to suit the needs and demands of the former. One result of this is the emergence of multiple connectors and multiple articulations of the *sunna*. While rejected by modernist readings of Islam, such as those offered by al-Bakrī, similar dynamics can still be found in different parts of the Muslim world. In the Comoros, Michael Lambek observes how to exercise a degree of authority over their followers, local Islamic scholars had to master not only Islamic knowledge (*ʿilim fakihi*) but also other ideological systems operating in their localities, including astronomy (*ʿilim dunia*) and spirit possession (*ʿilim ny lulu*).[81] Similarly, Dale Eickelman shows that in Morocco, a *qāḍī* (Islamic judge) has to master local customs and tribal genealogies for his authority to be accepted. Eickelman documents how at times, the ruling of a *qāḍī* is rejected by his tribal followers on account of its being too distinct from the *ʿurf* (tribal custom).[82] These cases illustrate how the labor of cultivating an Islamic community requires the ability, on the part of the scholars, to negotiate with local regimes of knowledge. In articulating the *sunna*, these scholars had to maintain the balance between conservation and relevance.[83] Indeed, unfamiliarity with local knowledge can very well lead to the failure of a scholar to gain recognition.[84]

Conclusion

As I bade farewell to the Arab quarter of Surabaya, I began to realize that saints and sultans are two similar, often interchangeable, but different figures of authority that emerged from various labors of articulating Prophetic teachings and assembling an Islamic community. Such labors attempt to ensure growth, whether individual spiritual growth through a set of disciplines or a collective growth. These articulatory labors involve the cultivation of a community or collective, a *jamāʿa*, that revolves around, and serves as the locus for the transmission and social realization of the *sunna*, whether in the form of a *ṭarīqa*, *ḥawṭa*, *perdikan*, or *kraton*. Both the contours of the *sunna* and the *jamāʿa* are historically situated and culturally specific. Aligning a cultivated community to the *sunna* involves subjecting both to mutual calibration. It requires a degree of wisdom in reconfiguring the latter to suit the concrete needs of the former, although much, of course, depends on what one takes to be "concrete" and what one considers to be a "need." Such dynamics led to the emergence of multiple, distinct, yet often overlapping Islamic communities. Each community is linked to a particular articulation of the *sunna* through one or more connectors to the Prophetic past, whose authority is formed through their ability to forge connections with the locals and maintain the cohesion of the community through various techniques and strategies. *Ṭarīqa*, *ḥawṭa*, *perdikan*, and *kraton* are different configurations of Islamic community, each involving distinctive infrastructure and hinging on the authority of one or several connectors, whether royal regulators of religion, Sufi masters, or saintly planters. Indeed, a single individual can take on more than one of these roles if he is involved in the labor of cultivating different communities. Thus ʿUmar al-ʿAṭṭās founded a *ḥawṭa* and was involved in cultivating an Islamic community that cut across tribal lines, while simultaneously performing the role of a Sufi master to several elect disciples. Prince Dipanagara, on the other hand, tried to assume different garbs of authority in the process of assembling a composite community.

Casting religious authority as a relationship engendered by a particular mode of articulatory labor enables one to grasp its contingent and precarious character. It allows us to inquire into the labor and infrastructure that can facilitate recognition and establish perduring bonds. As connectors to the Prophetic past, the effectiveness of these figures of authority hinges on their ability to transmit Prophetic teachings and constitute a community. They need to be accepted and recognized as being connected to the Prophetic past. Concurrently, they have to negotiate a functioning connection between the *sunna* and the community, whether by force and military might in the case of the regulators of religion, or by provision of guidance and hospitality in the case of the saintly planters. At the same time, an Islamic community may expand or contract, as in the case of Dipanagara, who commanded an extensive martial community at one point of his life, and was left with only his children at another.

By focusing on several modes of articulatory labor that led to the emergence of different forms of Islamic authority and community, this chapter suggests an alternative way of narrating the history of Islam that does not posit the religion as the factor that unites historical differences. Instead, it proposes a narrative approach to Islam that highlights the religion's polyphonic reality and situates Islam as a historically contingent, locally situated, and culturally embedded sociological achievement. Multiple itineraries of transmission and distinct modes of articulatory labor produce various social realizations of Islam, although some—like the modern reformist historian al-Bakrī—view such a polyphony as a problem that needs to be transcended. But al-Bakrī was not the first to perceive this polyphonic reality as somewhat problematic. In the eighteenth century, a Bā ʿAlawī scholar conceived a new mode of articulatory labor to minimize Islam's sociological indeterminacy. Subsequently, this mode of articulatory labor became paradigmatic not only in the Ḥaḍramawt, but also in Java, thereby connecting both regions through a single but increasingly influential itinerary of Islamic transmission. The advent of this mode of articulatory labor in Java occurred at a time when the *kraton* ceased to be the dominant center of Islam. It is to this development that I now turn.

2

Texts

IN A SERMON delivered in 1964 to six thousand worshippers gathered for the *ʿĪd al-Fiṭr* prayer, the former governor of Indonesia's Aceh province, Daud Beureu'eh (d. 1987), enthused over global Muslim unity:

> The entire community must, five times a day, face towards Mecca and, at the proper time, engage in worship. So too, for the whole Islamic community, we must come together. We are with God, we face toward Mecca. When we pray in assembly (*berdjema'ah*), we are face to face with each other after prayer. The poor face the rich, the evil the learned, the weak the firm, and the humble face the proud.[1]

Beureu'eh's imagination of a global Islamic community regimented toward Mecca is at variance with that encapsulated by the anecdote of the building of the Demak mosque, with which I began the preceding chapter. In Beureu'eh's words we are confronted with a pan-Islamic vision of global unity that posits the existence of localized Islamic communities with divergent *sunnas* as a problem to be surmounted. Lurking behind Beureu'eh's discourse is a conception of objectified Islam as an ideological force that can unite Muslims by transcending cultural, historical, and even class differences.[2] Such an outlook is often attributed to the proponents of Islamic modernism, a term used to describe a variety of intellectual movements that emerged toward the end of the nineteenth century and sought to reconcile Islam—posited to have an objective existence separate from its sociocultural realizations—with modern values.[3] Consequently, modernist Muslims tend to imagine culture as extraneous to Islam. Indeed, culture is often dismissed as an impediment to the social realization of a genuine Islam, one that is nevertheless imagined to be harmonious with the purportedly neutral modernity.

This vision of a culturally disembedded and objectified Islam became quite commonplace in Indonesia from the twentieth century. Its emergence is usually attributed to Muslims' encounters with colonial modernity in the Dutch East Indies and with forms of Islamic modernity elsewhere, like in Cairo. Such a vision was able to materialize and take root thanks to the advent of modern infrastructure, including new educational institutions, novel transportation technologies, print capitalism, and the rise of literacy.[4] While Islamic modernism is largely responsible for its preponderance, it is not the only itinerary of Islamic transmission that facilitated the crystallization of the idea of an objectified, culturally disembedded Islam believed to be socially realizable in different contexts. Long before the appearance of the modernist movements, a vision of an objectified Islam was already taking shape in Java, one that was promulgated by those who today are usually described as *traditionalist Muslims*. Such a vision emerged from a particular mode of articulatory labor that is less tied to authoritative figures as in the cases discussed in chapter 1. Instead, this articulatory mode hinged on novel textual technologies and a standardized curriculum that prepackage a curated *sunna* in an accessible format geared for an imagined general Muslim audience. Instead of a malleable product of ongoing interactions between a localized present and the Prophetic past, the *sunna* is in this way presented as being contained in texts that ought to remain constant across contexts and as impervious to culture and other localizing forces.[5] Owing to its modularity, this articulatory mode has become paradigmatic not only in Java but in many different places across the Indian Ocean. Its preponderance helps to project and sustain the imagination of an objectified Islam distinct from cultural particularities and socially realizable everywhere.

Taking such ideological projections at face value, anthropologists have too often fallen into the trap of presupposing the existence of a decontextualized, text-based global or scriptural Islam, which is usually posited in opposition to local Islams or local cultures. Many have even reproduced such an ideological product as an analytic category or explanatory paradigm, whether by asserting Islam as a "blueprint" or as "core symbols" that shape and thus can explain social order, instead of recognizing it as a contingent product of ongoing social negotiations that needs to be explained.[6] Critiquing this tendency, the late Abdel Hamid el-Zein argued that anthropologists should focus more on Muslims and less on Islam, while questioning the utility of Islam as a theoretical object and analytic category.[7] A more useful critique was offered by Talal Asad, who argued that Islam ought to be approached as a discursive tradition that includes and dynamically relates itself to the scriptures and to the changing forms of social practice.[8] While agreeing with Asad, one should also recognize that historically Muslims have exhibited different ways of relating to Islam beyond those provided by scripture or textual traditions, as recently demonstrated by the late Shahab Ahmed.[9] A salient example that Ahmed provided pertains to the once widespread belief in the knowability of the unseen world posited to be the source of divine revelation, or what he calls the "Pre-Text of revelation." This, he suggested, allowed Muslims to produce a myriad of Islamic discourses and practices deemed to be authoritative beyond what is typically regarded as Islamic scripture or scripture-based prescriptive texts.[10] Similar but not identical to Ahmed, in this book I focus on the centrality of the Prophetic past as a vanished but nevertheless foundational past that Muslims have oriented themselves toward in their attempt to derive religious meanings and norms. Temporal estrangement from the Prophetic past necessitates articulatory labor—that is, the attempt of connecting to that past, along with reconstructing and representing it as a realizable model, or *sunna*, to others. Such labors are historically and culturally situated, involving different infrastructure and technologies, with texts—including *ḥadīth* texts—being merely one among the many forms employed to perform these labors. These cultural and technological variabilities modulate the Prophetic past, thereby diversifying and particularizing the articulation and social realization of the *sunna*. Consequently, as a social reality Islam is always embedded in and modulated by cultural and infrastructural particularities.

The fact remains, however, that scriptures and texts have become the increasingly dominant form through which the majority of Muslims derive meanings and norms in their attempt to live a religious life. Ahmed himself recognized this reality when he wrote that in the modern era Muslims had "begun conceiving of and living normative Islam primarily as hermeneutical engagement with Text of Revelation"—i.e., the scriptures.[11] Many Muslims even go as far as foreclosing the possibility of knowing the Pre-Text of Revelation. Similarly, one may suggest that Muslims began envisaging their relationship with their foundational past primarily as an engagement with a set of texts assumed to contain reliable accounts of that past. Some even foreclose the possibility of accessing the Prophetic past and deriving normative teachings from it through other means. This development gradually resulted in the crystallization of the ideological notion of a disembedded global or scriptural Islam, sustained by the circulation of religious texts. Consequently, we need to ask how this shift occurred and what mode of articulatory labor enabled this development. Whatever the global and universal picture people have attempted to conjure of Islam, such a representation, and the scalar imagination it entails, is always produced and sustained in concrete localities where it becomes subject to sociological vicissitudes and infrastructural constraints.[12]

To say that one needs to focus on the mode of articulatory labor is to go against the—rather simplistic, one must add—tendency to attribute the crystallization of the ideological notion of a disembedded, text-based global or scriptural Islam to the transition from orality to textuality. While such a transition was certainly important, one should not assume that textuality is synonymous with standardization. One fascinating example that goes against such assumption is a once popular text known as the *One Thousand Questions* that has been translated into Persian, Tamil, Malay, Javanese, Turkish, Urdu, Sundanese, Buginese, and Latin from the original Arabic since the beginning of the tenth century. The book tells the story of the Prophet's encounter with a Jewish scholar, ʿAbdallāh b. Salām. Ibn Salām posed questions to the Prophet, who responded to each and every one of them—spanning the topics of history, mysticism, belief, and ritual—to the satisfaction of the Jewish scholar. In her study of the *One Thousand Questions*, Ronit Ricci shows how the Prophet's words in the text "were clearly later, and so less authentic, than the very early accounts."[13] In fact, different translations of the text contain different questions posed by Ibn Salām and answers to those questions given by the Prophet. As Ricci describes it, "Muḥammad as a teacher and prophet was redefined through the *One Thousand Questions*, in time and place to suit different cultural contexts."[14] While the text has been seen as problematic since the nineteenth century, due to the absence of *isnād* (chain of narrators) that can attest to the authenticity of the Prophet's words, the *One Thousand Questions* was for a long time an important source from which Muslims across time and space could learn the normative teachings of their religion, or the *sunna*, in ways that were essential to their cultural surrounds and suitable to the changing problem-space. What is essentially Islamic seems to be more crucial than what is authentically Islamic. The case of the *One Thousand Questions* should be adequate to deter us from attributing the crystallization of the ideological notion of a disembedded, text-based global or scriptural Islam to textuality. Instead, one needs to focus on the mode of articulatory labor that allowed for such a projection. Ultimately, texts are technologies that can be employed to realize different projects.

In this chapter, I trace the development of an influential mode of articulatory labor that was partly responsible for the emergence of a vision of an objectified universal Islam in Java. Its origin can be traced to a late seventeenth- and early eighteenth-century Bā ʿAlawī scholar, ʿAbdallāh b. ʿAlawī al-Ḥaddād (d. 1720), and his work of social reform in the Ḥaḍramawt. Faced with prolonged political instability, lawlessness, and ongoing tribal conflicts in the Ḥaḍramawt, al-Ḥaddād sought to construct a common text-based Islamic authority that could transcend tribal particularities and minimize normative indeterminacy. He achieved this by objectifying Prophetic teachings into accessible theological, legal, and liturgical texts posited to be universally applicable. The simplicity and modularity of these texts allowed for their rapid circulation among both urban dwellers and rural tribes of the Ḥaḍramawt, and beyond. In the second half of this chapter, I follow the gradual crystallization of the Ḥaddādian articulatory mode into an established articulatory paradigm. I trace the spread of this articulatory paradigm in the Indonesian Archipelago in the early nineteenth century through the labors of traveling Ḥaḍramī scholars. These mobile actors were sponsored by the prosperous Ḥaḍramī commercial diaspora to assuage what they saw as a crisis of religiosity among their locally born children. Moving between thriving port cities of Southeast Asia allowed these actors to cultivate new Islamic communities that could serve as sites for the transmission and social realization of the *sunna* as encapsulated in the Ḥaddādian texts. In Java, the spread of this articulatory paradigm correlated with the pacification of the Javanese Islamic sultanates at the hands of the Dutch colonial state. The downfall of the *kraton*s accelerated the fragmentation of Islamic religious authority, turning Java into a competitive religious marketplace where the Ḥaddādian paradigm complemented, but also competed with, other text-centered articulatory paradigms brought by pilgrims returning from Mecca. The convergence of these itineraries of Islamic transmission led to a significant transformation in the way Muslims in Java conceive and live Islam.

Ḥaddādian Labor

Langgar al-Ḥusayn is a small prayer hall situated not far from the grand congregational mosque of Pekalongan, Central Java. Owned and maintained by the Bā ʿAlawī *sayyid*s of the āl-Shahāb family, the *langgar* holds only the five obligatory prayers usually attended by members of the family and their neighbors. Every evening, following the twilight prayer, the imam of the *langgar* leads the congregation to recite a short litany and creedal text composed by the Bā ʿAlawī scholar ʿAbdallāh b. ʿAlawī al-Ḥaddād. Both texts are written in simple formats to facilitate memorization and are meant to be recited individually and collectively.

At the time of my fieldwork, the late Rahman (d. 2018) was the imam of the *langgar*. A pleasant and jovial man who was then in his early sixties, Rahman owned a shop selling sarongs at the local market. When the time for prayer came, he closed his shop, rode on his timeworn motorcycle, changed into a clean sarong, white shirt, and prayer cap, and rushed to lead the prayer. Oftentimes he found the congregation already waiting. Being a prayer leader of a small *langgar* is a voluntary occupation. Rahman took on the role when the health of the previous imam, his father's paternal cousin, was deteriorating. "I am not a scholar, nor do I know much about Islam although I did learn basic Islamic law [*fiqh*] from one or two elementary legal abridgments [*mukhtaṣar*s], so at least I know how to teach children how to perform ablution, pray, and recite the litany of Imam al-Ḥaddād," Rahman admitted.

Although not a scholarly family, the āl-Shahābs of Pekalongan were once a wealthy landowning family. In the mid-nineteenth century, a member of the āl-Shahāb family of Tarīm, Ḥaḍramawt, migrated to Pekalongan and married the daughter of a wealthy Ḥaḍramawt-born Bā ʿAlawī entrepreneur, a local sugar baron. The migrant learned the tricks of the trade from his father-in-law and local language from his Pekalongan-born wife. Following the death of his father-in-law, he took on the family business and developed it further. He began investing in properties in Batavia (Jakarta) and Pekalongan, including the compound of Ledok where the *langgar* stands and where most of his descendants still live in their airy bungalows. The days of wealth and ostentation, however, are long gone. Rahman told me how later generations of the family had been overindulged with wealth and no longer possessed the business acumen of their ancestors. "My ancestors were buying lands, now their descendants are selling them," he lamented. Despite the elegiac tone of his recollections, Rahman was proud that the *langgar* remained fully operational. "If you sit here and observe the way we do things, you will think that you are sitting in Tarīm," he said, although he himself never had the chance to visit his ancestral homeland.

The story of the āl-Shahāb family fits into a recognizable pattern of the rise and decline of the Ḥaḍramī diasporic families in Southeast Asia recounted by historians and anthropologists like Ulrike Freitag, William G. Clarence-Smith, Engseng Ho, and Kazuhiro Arai, to name a few.[15] Such narratives usually begin with a young Ḥaḍramī crossing the Indian Ocean, seeking his fortune. In the host country, the migrant works for an already established Ḥadramī entrepreneur and marries his daughter. Unlike his wife's brothers, who are born into wealth, the migrant is a hard worker and is determined to succeed, thereby making him the most suitable heir to the family business. Three generations later, the family business can no longer cope with the changing economy, and the migrant's descendants begin selling family assets to cover living expenses. What is missing from these narratives of docks, mansions, and shophouses, however, is the story of the *langgar*s and the mosques built by these mercantile elites.[16] What went on inside them? How is it that they remain steady and fully operational when the mansions are decaying, and not much remains of the ships and shophouses except for their phantom traces in the soporific bedtime stories told by Ḥaḍramī grandmothers to their grandchildren?

Observing Rahman's daily labor of leading prayers and recitation of al-Ḥaddād's litany and creedal texts made me cognizant of the *langgar* as an infrastructure that sustains a modest but subsisting Islamic community. Such a community is an assemblage made up of people, infrastructure, and textual technologies that come together punctually thanks to the articulatory labor of a determined, but not necessarily learned, prayer leader. Textual forms like the creedal texts, abridged legal manuals, and litanies, all of which curate and codify Prophetic teachings into accessible and user-friendly forms, allowed someone like Rahman, who was neither a saint, a scholar, nor a sultan, to perform the labor of articulating Prophetic teachings to others through curricular-based instruction. Such an articulatory mode opened up the possibility for the formation of new, identical, but simultaneously autonomous Islamic communities across contexts. Indeed, there are innumerable actors in Java today who perform a role similar to that of Rahman. One way to understand how this came to be is to start from the author of the texts recited at the *langgar* al-Ḥusayn and at many other prayer halls scattered throughout Java: ʿAbdallāh b. ʿAlawī al-Ḥaddād.

* * *

Living between the mid-seventeenth and the early-eighteenth centuries, al-Ḥaddād is today remembered as an Islamic renewer (*mujaddid*) (see figure 2.1). He lived at the beginning of a period described by Ḥaḍramī historians as "chaotic" (*fawḍawī*), marked by the decline of the Kathīrī dynasty that ruled the Ḥaḍramawt from the late fourteenth century.[17] The descendants of the Yāfiʿī mercenaries—initially brought to the Ḥaḍramawt from the mountainous Yāfiʿ region close to Aden to help the Kathīrī state repel the Northern Yemeni Qāsimī expansion into its territory—were becoming stronger and harder to control. Factional rule and misrule together with prolonged struggles for power among the Kathīrīs, their former Yāfiʿī lieutenants, and other tribes divided the Ḥaḍramawt, generating political instability that devastated the livelihoods of the city dwellers who had to deal with shifting political alliances and with the exaction of protection money. Dissatisfied with the rampant lawlessness in the Ḥaḍramawt and the absence of a strong state, the aggrieved al-Ḥaddād came to the conclusion that Islam ought to become a vehicle for social transformation.[18]

For al-Ḥaddād, the chronic instability that befell Ḥaḍramawt was due to the failure of Islam as socially realized in his homeland to provide a common and accessible normative code that could help structure everyday life and shape inter- and intratribal sociality. He described how "so many of those who are included in the circle of Islam do not have any knowledge of the kinds of devotion divinely ordained for them and the kinds of vice prohibited for them."[19] Widespread ignorance, in his view, had led to the proliferation of *bidʿa* (innovations) and *muḥdathāt* (novelties) foreign to the Qurʾān and *sunna*.[20] Al-Ḥaddād blamed his fellow scholars for this state of affairs. He was dissatisfied with the exclusivist bent of the Ṭarīqa ʿAlawiyya—the Bā ʿAlawī Sufi order he was brought up in—that had engendered an Islamic community of elect (*khawāṣṣ*; see chapter 1), leaving the commoners (*ʿawāmm*) to

FIGURE 2.1 The tomb of ʿAbdallāh b. ʿAlawī al-Ḥaddād in Tarīm, Yemen. (Photo by the author)

spiritual and moral degeneracy.[21] He was also critical of the *manṣab*s, the lords of the sanctuaries, positions that, due to their hereditary nature, were often filled with unlearned individuals whose only concern was perpetuating the asymmetrical relations they had established vis-à-vis their tribal followers, instead of instructing them on proper religious knowledge as their saintly ancestors had done.[22] "Catastrophe has befallen the population," al-Ḥaddād anguished over this state of affairs:

> The disease has spread. The tongues of the reminders have become mute. Ignorance and absent-mindedness have engulfed the general population, to the extent that one without knowledge can fantasize that he has the spiritual states of the people of truth and guidance of the past. . . . Oh, but how far! how far![23]

The solution, for al-Ḥaddād, lay in Islam, which in his view ought to edify the character of every member of the society, notwithstanding their scholarly, tribal, or modest artisanal background.

To this end, he reformulated the Ṭarīqa ʿAlawiyya from its earlier form as a kind of patrician mysticism into a more accessible and attainable spiritual discipline accessible to every Muslim. For al-Ḥaddād, the *ṭarīqa* should realistically focus on helping people from all walks of life fulfill their essential religious obligations, rather than stressing strenuous devotional exercises (*riyāḍa*) and retreat from society (*ʿuzla*).[24] Furthermore, he contended that the personified authority of the Sufi masters and the *manṣab*s, who are taken as connectors to the Prophetic past and embodiments of Prophetic teachings, should be significantly downplayed as it only subjects the *sunna* to sociocultural indeterminacy, leaving Ḥaḍramawt without a common and uniformed normative code. Instead, al-Haddād contended that Prophetic teachings as objectified in the *ḥadīth*s and codified into a defined set of creedal, legal, and devotional texts, ought to be recognized as the source of the *sunna* to be transmitted and socially realized everywhere, notwithstanding sociocultural heterogeneities. This entails that religious authority ought to be displaced from individuals recognized as connectors to the Prophetic past to a set of standardized texts that contain consistent and realizable Prophetic teachings. In other words, Islam should not be understood as what those figures of authority do. Islam is what the texts say. Only then can the *sunna* serve as the moral foundation for the creation of a stable economy and society.[25]

Inspired by the twelfth-century polymath Abū Ḥāmid al-Ghazālī (d. 1111), al-Ḥaddād redefined the role of Muslim scholars as preachers (Ar. *dāʿī*, pl. *duʿāt*).[26] Even jurists, whose role traditionally consisted of issuing legal opinions and teaching students (most of whom hailed from scholarly families) aspiring to be legal experts, should be engaged in the labor of calling people to God.[27] They ought to actively eradicate erroneous innovations and reorient the masses to the *sunna*. Scholars who failed to do so "are not the leaders of guidance" but are "partners of the ignoramuses in futility and apathy . . . and cannot be distinguished from them save by the images and appearances of knowledge."[28] Al-Ḥaddād further argued that religious authority does not stem from kinship ties, nor from being the biological or spiritual inheritors of deceased scholars or saints. Neither does it arise from leading an ascetic life or from the persistent performance of devotional acts. Religious authority, in his perspective, emerges from the active labor of transmitting what he described as "beneficial sciences" to the commoners.

Al-Ḥaddād described what he meant by beneficial sciences in his final work, *Al-Daʿwa al-tāmma wa-l-tadhkira al-ʿāmma* (The complete call and the general reminder), completed in 1702. He defined beneficial sciences as those that introduce people to God and his commandments relevant to their everyday life. He divided beneficial sciences into two branches: the sciences of *īmān*, or faith (*ʿulūm al-īmān*), which deal with belief, and the sciences of *islām*

(ʿ*ulūm al-islām*), which revolve around practical knowledge. Regarding the first, he wrote that for most Muslims:

> it is sufficient to learn the creeds [ʿ*aqīdas*] composed by the imams whose knowledge, trustworthiness, and devotion have been agreed upon, like the Proof of Religion [*ḥujjat al-islām*] [al-Ghazālī]. His creed, written in the beginning of the chapter "Foundation of Belief" in the book *Iḥyāʾ ʿulūm al-dīn* [*Revivification of Religious Sciences*], is adequate and final for this purpose. We have also presented an abridged but thorough creed in the beginning of *Itḥāf al-sāʾil* and in the epilogue of *Al-Naṣāʾiḥ al-dīniyya*. These are sufficient.[29]

As for the second branch, al-Ḥaddād maintained that:

> it is adequate to learn what has been conveyed by the Proof of Religion [al-Ghazālī] in *Bidāyat al-hidāya* [*The Beginning of Guidance*], except that this book does not discuss the needed knowledge pertaining to alms and hajj. Nevertheless, he [al-Ghazālī] discussed them in the *Iḥyāʾ ʿulūm al-dīn*. It is sufficient for the devout to learn from what has been discussed by the most learned jurist ʿAbdallāh b. ʿAbd al-Raḥmān b. al-Ḥāj Abī Faḍl in *Al-Mukhtaṣar al-laṭīf* [The delicate abridgment]. . . . Deepening and widening of one's grasp of the sciences is not considered as an indispensable duty for everyone. Rather, it is specific to those who have the time and skill for it, like the leaders and the learned.[30]

From this description, it is clear that al-Ḥaddād was envisioning a new mode of articulatory labor. At the heart of this articulatory mode is an accessible curriculum that would allow for the social realization of a standardized and doable *sunna*, both doctrinal and practical, among all Muslims, notwithstanding their tribal or class backgrounds. As al-Ḥaddād made clear in the above passage, two textual technologies were central to this articulatory mode: creedal text (ʿ*aqīda*, Ar. pl. ʿ*aqāʾid*) and the legal abridgment (*mukhtaṣar*).

* * *

The significance of the creed as a semiotic form that aligns theological propositions and social formation through the performance of individual assent (what Muslims call *taṣdīq*) has been discussed in the case of Protestantism by Webb Keane.[31] The creed, Keane suggests, is a portable and intimate mode of objectification that ensures the portability and circulation of religion—at least its propositional content—allowing it to be extracted from one context and inserted into others. Creed gives theological doctrine an explicit form, making it "impressive, morally commanding, and above all, part of an inhabitable world."[32] Its circulation brings together elites and laypersons and works against localizing forces. By articulating public doctrine and subjective experiences, the creed challenges believers to be responsible for aligning their words with their thoughts, thereby making it a model for a publicly perceivable notion of sincerity. Keane's work suggests how the creed reinforces globality as an ideology of scale and a standardized notion of religious community made up of free and self-conscious agentive subjects, while reaffirming, quite paradoxically, these subjects' reliance on material objects like texts.

If creed conjoins a standardized theological doctrine and subjective belief, the legal abridgment, or *mukhtaṣar*, mediates the emergence of a common standard of practice. An abridgment usually denotes either a condensation of a larger legal text or a synopsis of authoritative legal positions of a particular school of law. Apart from their concise and synoptic format, a key characteristic of abridgments is their univocality. Unlike the larger heteroglossic legal tomes consulted by the jurists and studied in the institutions of higher learning, there are no juristic disagreements in the abridgments. These texts simply consist of one definite legal ruling for each matter of concern, presented in an accessible and straightforward manner. This particular genre arose in the thirteenth century to address the problem of legal indeterminacy in Islamic law. It does so by facilitating *taqlīd*, or imitation, whereby an individual follows the legal views or opinions of an established school of law codified in the abridgments, rather than following the opinion of a qualified *mujtahid*, a scholar able to perform legal inferences from the scriptures. Owing to the abridgments, Islamic law became less reliant on the discretion of legal officials like judges.[33]

Al-Ḥaddād's project can thus be perceived as an attempt to constitute an Islamic community that can be replicated globally, one that is aligned to and serves as the site for the social realization of the *sunna* as codified into a common and consistent theological doctrine and legal codes.[34] On top of the two textual forms discussed above, al-Ḥaddād also composed two litanies (*rātib*): *Al-Rātib al-shahīr* (The renowned litany) and *Al-Wird al-laṭīf* (The gentle invocation). Each of these litanies is a compilation of Qurʾānic verses, prayers, and invocations prescribed by the Prophet, to be recited on a daily basis. The two litanies are compact and susceptible to memorization. Normal recitation takes only fifteen to twenty minutes, thereby allowing people to recite them once or twice a day without disturbing their daily chores. The objective of compiling a litany is to facilitate a guided recitation that enables the commoners to memorize and practice invocations prescribed by the Prophet and derive spiritual benefits, without burdening them with the daunting task of finding such invocations from the Qurʾān or the voluminous *ḥadīth* compendia. Al-Ḥaddād's litanies, as Anne Bang has suggested, are also uniquely understood as something accessible, standardized, and easy that can be recited collectively, and simultaneously as texts that contain esoteric and mystical meanings that can be accessed only by the elect.[35] This allows the litany to become a textual technology that can bring together those who are considered as the elect and the commoners through collective ritual recitation, while still differentiating the potential of meaning-making based on one's capacity to know.[36] Subsequently, the two litanies became the defining liturgical text of the reformed Ṭarīqa ʿAlawiyya and are recited in different places across the Indian Ocean, from Southeast Asia to South Africa.[37]

* * *

The Ḥaddādian mode of articulatory labor is, therefore, an attempt to assert the consistency of Islamic norms and minimize normative indeterminacy by codifying the *sunna* into uniform and accessible theological, legal, and devotional texts accessible to self-conscious agentive subjects. Such an articulatory mode projects a vision of an objectified *sunna* posited to be consistent, autonomous, and purified from the particularities of local cultures, in which the *sunna* has often been embedded. The creed, the legal abridgment, and the litany became the means for constituting a community of standardized belief, practice, and liturgy. These texts work against localizing forces by allowing doctrines and teachings posited to be universally applicable to be extracted from one context and inserted into others. Concurrently, they generate asymmetrical relations by opening up a space for the emergence of actors who can explain, translate, or even simply lead the recitation of these texts in diverse interactional settings. Al-Ḥaddād refers to such an actor as a *shaykh al-taʿlīm* (teaching master)—that is, someone who provides instruction by following an established curriculum of study.[38] He differentiated a *shaykh al-taʿlīm* from a *shaykh al-riyāḍa* (training master) or a Sufi master.[39] In contrast to the latter, pedagogical interaction with the former centers on the content of the texts that compose a curriculum. One does not need to be a scholar, a spiritual athlete, or virtuoso to become a *shaykh al-taʿlīm*. What is required is simply the ability to teach the texts. After all, the texts recommended by al-Ḥaddād are accessible and written for the most general Muslim audience. They can be taught easily by someone who has studied them with another *shaykh al-taʿlīm*. As such, al-Ḥaddād invented a new but enduring pathway to constituting text-based religious authority that can reproduce itself for generations. It has done so by opening the way to the widespread participation of persons who were neither Arab nor highly literate but could nevertheless rise to become socially recognized religious authorities by mastering and transmitting these straightforward texts. Al-Ḥaddād himself trained a group of devoted disciples who were then sent off to live, preach, and cultivate Islamic communities in different parts of the Ḥaḍramawt. These disciples inspired subsequent generations of Ḥaḍramī *shaykhs al-ta ʿlīm*, who cultivate communities aligned to the Ḥaddādian curriculum not only in the Ḥaḍramawt but also in distant places, including the Swahili and the Malabar coasts, and the Malay-Indonesian Archipelago.

Ḥaddādian Paradigm

The Ḥaddādian mode of articulatory labor began to take root in the Malay-Indonesian Archipelago around the early nineteenth century. Its success in becoming paradigmatic correlated with the pacification of Java's Islamic sultanates at the hands of the Dutch colonial state following the Java War (1825–30) discussed in the last chapter. This was a time when Java's old Islamic order was falling apart. The established articulatory mode that centered on the *kraton* was disintegrating. Not unlike in al-Ḥaddād's Ḥaḍramawt, it was an era when the religiopolitical center—the *kraton*, as embodied in the figure of the regulator of religion (*panatagama*)—no longer held. It was also, however, an era of economic prosperity for the Ḥaḍramī entrepreneurial diaspora of British Malaya and the Dutch East Indies. To present a contextualized glimpse of this historical development, the remainder of this chapter follows the itinerary of a traveling Bā ʿAlawi scholar, ʿAbdallāh b. ʿUmar Bin Yaḥyā (Ibn Yaḥyā; d. 1849) and his attempt to introduce the Ḥaddādian mode of articulatory labor.

* * *

Ibn Yaḥyā was born in Ghuraf āl-Shaykh, a town located at the opening of the Masīla valley not far from Tarīm, in 1794. He studied under his two maternal uncles—Ṭāhir (d. 1814) and ʿAbdāllāh b. Ḥusayn Bin Ṭāhir (d.1855)—and other Bā ʿAlawī scholars of the Ḥaḍramawt. By the time Ibn Yaḥyā was born, the Ḥaddādian mode of articulatory labor had become paradigmatic, at least among the Bā ʿAlawīs. All of Ibn Yaḥyā's teachers were students of al-Ḥaddād's disciples. Available biographical accounts further show how Ibn Yaḥyā's education primarily revolved around developing mastery of a set of legal, theological, and Sufi texts, particularly those authored by al-Ḥaddād.[40]

We don't know exactly what drove Ibn Yaḥyā to travel to the Malay-Indonesian Archipelago, as he himself never made it clear. One can only suggest a combination of both push and pull factors. The first was the protracted political instability in Ḥaḍramawt, which drove his uncle Ṭāhir to lead a failed armed insurrection against the Yāfiʿīs.[41] In the aftermath of the uprising, Ṭāhir was exiled from the Ḥaḍramawt valley. It may be the case that his nephew, who was implicated in the conflict, suffered a similar fate. Concurrently, there was a pull factor from the archipelago in the form of increasing demand for Ḥaḍramī scholars to take on the position of religious instructors for the wealthy Ḥaḍramī diasporic community. For Ḥaḍramī scholars influenced by the Ḥaddādian emphasis on the urgency of calling people to God, the archipelago presented itself as a new mission field.

Since at least the seventeenth century, the Ḥaḍramīs had been emigrating in increasing numbers to the Malay-Indonesian Archipelago. Internal strife and limited opportunities in Ḥaḍramawt, together with the ample economic opportunities abroad, drove many Ḥaḍramīs to leave their homeland. Thriving port cities including Malacca, Kutaraja (Aceh), and several Javanese port cities were the preferred destinations for many. These cities became the bases where the migrants established trading ventures. Advances in maritime transportation in the early nineteenth century resulted in an increasing presence of Ḥaḍramīs in the region.[42] The sphere of Ḥaḍramī mercantile activities was, for the most part, centered on the sea and the littorals.[43] This expanding world of Ḥaḍramī economic diaspora generated an increasing demand for *shaykh*s *al-ta ʿlīm* from the homeland, who could provide religious instruction for the merchants and their families. Estranged from their homeland, the Ḥaḍramīs abroad were aspiring to form moral communities and educate their locally born children. In order to do that, they needed actors who could articulate the *sunna* for them. Such demands provided the impetus for the expansion of the Ḥaddādian paradigm in the diaspora.

Ibn Yaḥyā's first destination in Southeast Asia was Singapore, where he arrived in 1832. Since its establishment in 1819, Singapore had attracted merchants from various ethnic communities, including Ḥaḍramīs from all over Malaya and the Indonesian Archipelago. Among them was the wealthy Bā ʿAlawī merchant ʿUmar b. ʿAlī al-Junayd (d. 1852), with whom Ibn Yaḥyā stayed. Al-Junayd had come to Singapore from Palembang shortly after Raffles established Singapore as a British trading port. He brought his accrued wealth from Sumatra and invested in Singapore, buying land and developing properties, which led to the substantial growth of his family's fortune. In 1820, he built what is today known as Singapore's oldest mosque.[44] Al-Junayd frequently invited and sponsored Ḥaḍramī scholars to come and impart religious knowledge to his family and the community. Among them was the jurist Sālim b. ʿAbdallāh Bin Sumayr (d. 1853), who had migrated to Singapore several years before Ibn Yaḥyā and begun teaching there. As a proponent of the Ḥaddādian paradigm, Ibn Sumayr authored his own legal abridgment, *Safīnāt al-najāḥ* (*Ark of Salvation*), which gradually became a popular legal and doctrinal primer taught in the Islamic boarding schools of Indonesia and Malaysia.[45]

During his stay in Singapore, Ibn Yaḥyā taught at al-Junayd's house. He also led the recitation of al-Haddād's litanies at al-Junayd's mosque. Several letters addressed to his son in Ḥaḍramawt, however, indicate that Ibn Yaḥyā was disappointed with the state of Islamic learning exhibited by the children of the Ḥaḍramī mercantile elites. In one letter, Ibn Yaḥyā lamented how Bā ʿAlawī children in Singapore were commoners (ʿ*awāmm*) and not interested in learning about Islam. They "developed the manners of the transgressors [*al-fāsiqūn*] and took pride in sins and lusts."[46] Proper education for the children of these merchant elites was a central concern for Ibn Yaḥyā. In a poem written during his stay in Singapore, he implored al-Junayd to send his children to the Ḥaḍramawt for proper education.[47] He also insisted that al-Junayd familiarize the children with al-Ḥaddād's litanies by holding communal recitations. He feared that without proper education and ritual socialization, the children of these wealthy merchants would lose their attachment to the *sunna*.

From Singapore, Ibn Yaḥyā traveled to Java and visited the Ḥaḍramī mercantile elites there to impart religious instruction. He was proud of the fact that these wealthy Ḥaḍramīs were building infrastructure of religious worship like mosques and *langgars*, as illustrated in a poem he wrote in 1833 commemorating the opening of a prayer hall in Batavia built by one Ḥasan b. ʿAfīf.[48] Whilst important, built infrastructure alone was not sufficient in the larger scheme of cultivating Islamic communities. Mosques and *langgars* need to serve as sites for imparting religious instruction. Thus, aside from holding classes at such sites, Ibn Yaḥyā—following the Ḥaddādian precedent—also attempted to facilitate religious learning by authoring a simple creed, entitled *ʿAqīda jāmiʿa nāfiʿa* (*Complete Beneficial Creed*), and several thematic legal abridgments, including the still popular *Safīnāt al-ṣalāh* (Ark of prayer).[49] He also issued legal responsa (*fatwā*) on various issues he witnessed in the Malay-Indonesian world.[50]

* * *

While the estates and the prayer halls of the Ḥaḍramī entrepreneurs formed the itineraries of traveling Ḥaddādian *shaykhs al-taʿlīm*, these sites also afforded them the ability to interact with a broader audience. After all, the Ḥaḍramīs were living in buzzing port cities like Singapore, Betawi (Jakarta), Gresik, and Surabaya, where exchanges of merchandise, commodities, and ideas took place. In these emporiums, the itineraries of the Ḥaḍramī instructors intersected with other itineraries of Islamic transmission, generating synergies, but also confrontations. To give a concrete example of how this worked, let us turn to Surabaya, where Ibn Yaḥyā stayed for a period of time at the opulent homes of the Ḥaḍramī merchants and shipowners in the Arab quarter.

As discussed in the previous chapter, the Arab quarter of Surabaya was built around the mosque and tomb of Sunan Ampel, an important pilgrimage site that has continued to draw many visitors from different places, making it into a node where diverse networks intersect. Being in close geographic proximity to the mosque allowed Ibn Yaḥyā to visit it regularly. There he interacted with various people, not only his fellow Ḥaḍramīs but also Javanese scholars, pilgrims, and students. Fortunately, we do have a trace of such interactions in the form of a *tadhkira* (reminder/memorandum) written by Ibn Yaḥyā upon the request of several Javanese pilgrims (*ḥujjāj*) who studied with him at the mosque of Sunan Ampel.[51] This document provides a glimpse into Ibn Yaḥyā's attempt to introduce the Ḥaddādian articulatory mode to the broader Javanese population. What follows is my translation of the *tadhkira*:

> In the name of God most Gracious, most Merciful:
>
> *O ye who believe! Fear Allāh and be with those who are true* [Q. 9:119]. All praise be to Allāh who has made piety [*taqwā*] as a cause for goodness in this world and the next. God's salutation be upon our master Muḥammad, His prophet and His chosen one, and his elevated family and companions. This is a reminder from him who is in need of God's mercy, ʿAbdallāh b. ʿUmar, to our brethren, the pilgrims [*al-ḥujjāj*] residing in Surabaya. [They have] requested [from] me this [reminder]. I have seen their commitment to goodness, their acceptance of the truth, and their assistance in reviving the symbols [*shaʿāʾir*] of the religion. May God further them and us in this, and lead them and us to the best path.
>
> Know, O brothers, that this religion is built on five things:
>
> First, beneficial knowledge, that which introduces you to your Lord and His commandments and prohibitions; and [teaches] abstention from the world, desire for the hereafter, and humility; and discourages you from great sins, jealousy, envy, the desire for respect in the hearts of men, and being removed from the truth. Any knowledge that results in these [spiritual/psychological] states is beneficial knowledge to our condition and possessions. Any knowledge that does not result in what we have described is harmful knowledge. It will not result in anything in the two abodes except disgrace and decay. This [beneficial] knowledge is divided into two: exoteric and esoteric. As for the exoteric: [it is] the knowledge of the law [*fiqh*]. And among its sources are beneficial books for every seeker: *Mukhtaṣar bā faḍl* and *ʿUmdat al-sālik, Mukhtaṣar al-anwār*, and the *Minhāj* of Imām al-Nawawī. As for the esoteric: the *Bidāyat al-hidāya* of al-Ghazālī, the *Al-Naṣāʾiḥ al-dīniyya* of al-Ḥabīb ʿAbdallāh b. ʿAlawī al-Ḥaddād, also *Risāla al-muʿāwana* and *Risāla al-mudhākara* by the same author, and the *Minhāj al-ʿābidīn* of al-Ghazālī.

Second, teaching this knowledge to those who are ignorant, especially the creed of al-Ghazālī, and other abridged treatises on theology such as the *matn Jawharat al-tawḥīd* and *Ta'līm al-'ishrīn al-ṣifa*, without learning the [*Umm*] *al-barāhīn*. As for the last book, it is forbidden to learn it, except for those who have mastered several sciences and have the intelligence and acumen as cautioned by the imams, such as al-Ghazālī and Shaykh Ibn Ḥajar. They asserted the interdiction of teaching the book to the commoners [*'awāmm*]. And the people of this age are commoners. We have mentioned earlier the selections of books in the legal sciences and Sufism. However, the novice should start by learning short and gentle abridgments. Of particular importance is the *Sullam al-tawfīq* of our master and shaykh my maternal uncle 'Abdallāh b. Ḥusayn Bin Ṭāhir Bā 'Alawī. Our devotee [*muḥibbunā*] Ḥajji Muḥammad Ḥāshim has received this text and we have read it in the Ampel mosque in the presence of our devotee Ḥajj Muḥammad Arshad for the most part. Beware, and beware of occupying oneself with learning any knowledge before learning these short manuals, as these texts have collected a lot of important things that have to be put before the others.

Third, being truthful to God with sincerity in knowledge and work. Truthful to God's creations in advising, teaching, and instructing them in the good, while prohibiting them from any evil, first with gentleness and soft speech, then with warnings and reminders, and finally with pressure and anger freed from whims and debased passions.

Fourth, leaving any pretension of being a man of knowledge and positioning oneself as a teacher to the ignorant while having no ability on such matters. As it will only bring calamities to the person and his followers. The Prophet, may peace and blessing be upon him and his family, said:

> God does not snatch away knowledge from the chests of His servants, but He takes away knowledge by the death of scholars, until, when there are no more scholars remaining, the people take ignorant leaders [as scholars]. And these leaders will be asked [by the people], and they will respond without any knowledge, and they will be misguided and misguide others.

This is narrated by al-Bukhārī and Muslim. There seem to multiply in this land those whom the master of all masters [*sayyid al-sādāt*] had warned. Many occupy themselves with teaching and giving legal opinion [*fatwā*] without the necessary knowledge and mastery, resulting in destruction and catastrophe. Many people are led astray because of them, and the sins that result from such confusions remain continuously and accrue upon them even after their death. And among the disasters of those phony men is their preoccupation with learning great tomes that no one has the ability to master except the *ʿulamāʾ* and the erudite sages [*jahābadha al-mubarrizīn*], and as a result they make mistakes in comprehending their intended meanings. This has led to the obfuscation of [legal] boundaries. Thus, what is suitable for them is to occupy themselves with abridgments [*al-mukhtaṣarāt*] so that they can gain some knowledge that will lead them to its conclusions. As such, they will learn what is obligatory for them. And among the calamities is their preoccupation with uncommon problems without any finality. There is no benefit in learning about every situation. They hope that, in discussing such matters in their gatherings, they will be seen as illustrious *ʿulamāʾ*. They do not know that the Prophet—may God and peace and blessings be upon him—prohibited [them] from irresolvable questions of doctrine [*al-aghlūṭāt*]. So beware, and beware [of occupying oneself with] such matters, as it constitutes something without benefits, which only results in anger and discord. It is an approach by which Satan led people to pride and arrogance.

Fifth, inviting [people] to the collective performance of the five obligatory prayers, calling [people] to it in the markets and streets, and reverberating the call to prayer [*adhān*]. Such acts are among the symbols [*shaʿāʾir*] of Islam and faith [*imān*]. Commit to it with perseverance, and invite every Muslim to it. When they gather, teach them interactively, and summarize for them the commandments of the religion. This is because the commoners do not benefit from the reading of books. They do not fully understand the arguments and explanations [of these books]. And those who are teaching them [the commoners] should approach them in their gatherings, their congregations, their fathers, and their mothers. By doing so, they will revive Islam, and they will gain God's mercy.

I ask the almighty God to secure you and us in all goodness, and to protect us from all evils. May God's salutation and blessing be upon our master Muḥammad, his family, and his companions. And all praise belongs to God the lord of the two universes.

In the *tadhkira,* Ibn Yaḥyā defines "beneficial sciences" as the foundation of Islam. Echoing al-Ḥaddād's exposition in *Al-Daʿwa al-tāmma,* he describes beneficial sciences as those that equip Muslims with the knowledge of God's commandments and prohibitions, and induce humility and desire for the hereafter. He then divides beneficial sciences into doctrinal and practical, while detailing the texts that need to be studied and propagated. Ibn Yaḥyā's curriculum mirrors that of al-Ḥaddād. It consists of straightforward creeds and legal abridgments, many of which were authored or recommended by al-Ḥaddād, like the works of al-Ghazālī. Ibn Yaḥyā also prohibits the teaching of intricate theological texts, like *Umm al-barāhīn* (Mother of proofs) of Muḥammad b. Yūsuf al-Sanūsī (d. 1490). After describing the content of the curriculum, Ibn Yaḥyā provides a practical strategy of proselytization. In his view, what were needed in Java were *shaykhs al-ta ʿlīm* who could "summarize the commandments of the religion" for the commoners, rather than scholars working on labyrinthine theological and legal theories.[52] Ibn Yaḥyā himself led by example. From the *tadhkira* we learn that he taught *Sullam al-tawfīq* (Ladder of success)—a text that combines simplified creed, legal abridgment, and ethical teachings, written by his maternal uncle and teacher, ʿAbdallāh b. Ḥusayn Bin Ṭāhir—at the mosque of Sunan Ampel.[53] It is highly likely that Ibn Yaḥyā was the first person to bring this now popular text to Southeast Asia, considering that the author was still alive when Ibn Yaḥyā was teaching this text at the Ampel mosque.

From the *tadhkira,* we get a sense of how Ibn Yaḥyā was preoccupied with redefining the canon of permissible texts for Javanese Muslims, consisting of several key texts authored or recommended by al-Ḥaddād and those written by scholars influenced by the Ḥaddādian paradigm. This curriculum functioned as a conceptual infrastructure that facilitated the reproduction of a standardized and duplicable Islamic community with shared doctrine and practice. Ibn Yaḥyā strongly disapproved of communities that revolve around figures who "occupy themselves with teaching and giving religious opinions without the necessary knowledge and mastery."[54] Instead, he envisioned an identical and duplicable Islamic community based on the authority of the texts he prescribed. Displacing authority to the texts, however, does not collapse the hierarchy that characterizes a relationship of authority. Rather, it generates another form of authority, that of the *shaykh al-ta ʿlīm,* whose authority is based on the ability to transmit, translate, and expound these straightforward texts.

* * *

Places like the mosque of Sunan Ampel served as strategic sites of knowledge transmission that enabled mobile Ḥaḍramī scholars like Ibn Yaḥyā to introduce and perform the Ḥaddādian articulatory labor to a broader audience. Owing to the works of these actors, the Ḥaddādian articulatory mode began to take root in Java and gradually became paradigmatic. The spread of this articulatory mode was enhanced by two forms of mobility that intersected with the itineraries of the Ḥaḍramī *shaykh*s *al-ta ʿlīm* like Ibn Yaḥyā, especially in places like the Ampel mosque. These were the rise of the Javanese pilgrimage to Mecca and the movement of Muslim scholars away from the *kratons*.

The increase in the number of Javanese making pilgrimage to Mecca was made possible by, among other things, the monetization of the agricultural economy. Left with no serious competitors following its victory in the Java War, the Dutch colonial state was able to focus on profit acquisition. The governor-general, Johannes van den Bosch (d. 1844), enacted an agricultural reform plan to facilitate the extraction of agricultural products from Java in quantities and at prices that would make the Netherlands Europe's biggest supplier of tropical commodities, especially coffee.[55] The monetization of the agricultural economy allowed more Javanese to afford the cost of travel to Mecca.[56] By the 1850s and 1860s, an average of approximately 1,600 pilgrims were setting out from the Dutch East Indies annually, despite the colonial authority's attempts to discourage them from going.[57] In Mecca, they were exposed to diverse scholars teaching different texts. By the early 1800s, the works of al-Ghazālī and his commentators, including the Egyptian ʿAbd al-Wahhāb al-Shaʿrānī (d. 1565), which like those of al-Ḥaddād stress the dissemination of simplified texts on legal and ethical guidance, had begun to replace the earlier Shaṭṭārī-oriented Medinese tradition of Sufism with its emphasis on intricate metaphysical teachings.[58] Indeed, the Shaṭṭārī Sufism that was once so dear to Prince Dipanagara (see chapter 1) was becoming unfashionable in the Hejaz, and Javanese pilgrims began to flock to the more law-oriented Sufi orders like the Sammāniyya, the Naqshbandiyya, and the Qādiriyya-Naqshbandiyya. Upon returning to Java, many of these pilgrims challenged the social positions of established rural teachers—many of whom were affiliated with the older Shaṭṭāriyya—and attempted to carve their own community by teaching the texts they had learned in Mecca. This development turned Java into a competitive religious marketplace, where multiple communities vied against one another, and more so when state patronage and resources began to rapidly diminish.[59]

The second form of mobility, that of the movement of Muslim scholars away from the *kratons*, was the result of the colonial state's attempt to distance the royal courts from the scholars. During the Java War, the Dutch witnessed the devastation wreaked by the coalition of the Javanese princes, Muslim scholars, and the peasantry. In its aftermath, the Dutch worked to isolate the *kratons* from both the masses and the influence of Muslim scholars. This was accomplished by cultivating a sense of "cultural remove" among the royals of the *kratons* by identifying "high Javanese culture as an entity standing in opposition to Islam and as the exclusive and conservative preserve of a hyper-refined elite class."[60] Nancy Florida describes this purification project as a form of conceptual denial of Islamic elements in the *kraton*. It was an enterprise of rendering the *kraton* more akin to a European royal court than a sovereign Islamic community aligned to the Prophetic past through the mediation of the regulator of religion. The mantle of the *panatagama* proudly worn by the rulers of Surakarta and Yogyakarta was becoming no more than a fancy title. One consequence of this colonial project of purification was the movement of Muslim scholars—many of whom were involved with Prince Dipanagara—away from the royal court into the countryside and the littoral.[61] This movement resulted in the proliferation of new *langgars* (prayer halls) in the countryside, some of which gradually developed—owing to the popularity of the presiding scholar—into a *pesantren*, or Islamic boarding school.[62] Infrastructure like the Great Post Road linking the western to the eastern tip of Java, completed in 1808, facilitated greater movement and communication these sites of learning.[63] Being among the commoners meant that these scholars had to adjust to more straightforward pedagogical texts. Consequently, their educational institutions served as sites of learning where new Islamic curriculums began to take shape. Influenced by the works of the Egyptian, Hejazi, and Ḥaḍramī scholars, these emerging curriculums emphasized the dissemination of simplified theological creeds, legal abridgments, and Sufi treatises dealing with ethical guidance, while restricting the circulation of the once desired speculative Sufi treatises—like the Shaṭṭārī *Tuḥfa* favored by Prince Dipanagara—to the elects (*khawāṣṣ*).

The intersection between the two aforementioned forms of mobility and the itineraries of Ḥaḍramī *shaykhs al-ta ʿlīm* resulted in both the proliferation of Islamic communities on the one hand and their gradual standardization on the other. By the time L.W.C. van den Berg compiled a list of fifty texts studied in the *pesantrens* of Java and Madura in 1887, a clear and consistent program of study was already discernible, albeit with slight variations from one institution to the next.[64] These *pesantrens* had become sites of learning where simplified creed and legal abridgment, together with several texts on Arabic linguistic sciences, made up the core elementary curriculum.[65] Included in the curriculum were the texts recommended by both al-Ḥaddād and Ibn Yaḥyā, including the *Sullam al-tawfīq* that the latter had brought to Java. Absent from the nascent curriculum were Sufi philosophical works like the Shaṭṭārī *Tuḥfa*.[66] While not included in the core curriculum, devotional works like al-Ḥaddād's litanies also circulated in the *pesantrens*, where they were regularly recited individually or collectively. Run almost exclusively by *shaykhs al-ta ʿlīm*—some of whom performed the extracurricular role of Sufi master or *shaykh al-riyāḍa*—and geared towards equipping students with mastery over these textual canons, the *pesantrens* became the premier sites for producing future *shaykhs al-taʿlīm*.

Over time an increasing number of *pesantren* graduates spread all over Java and beyond, cultivating new Islamic communities in different places. Their mastery of the creedal texts and the legal abridgments enabled them to constitute their own communities. Albeit sporadic and autonomous, these communities are aligned to a standardized notion of belief, practice, and worship as codified in the canonized texts. These *shaykhs al-taʿlīm* and the *langgar*s or *pesantrens* they preside over are the acephalous capillaries that make up a living and interlinking sociodiscursive assemblage that in the early twentieth century became known and objectified by its modernist critics as *traditional Islam*. The traditionalist Muslims themselves, however, prefer to identify themselves as the *ahl al-sunna wa al-jamāʿa*, the people of the *sunna* and the community.[67]

* * *

So far I have shown how the Ḥaddādian mode of articulatory labor became paradigmatic in Java as part of a broader reconfiguration of Islam brought about by the synergies of different itineraries of Islamic transmission. The crisscrossing of itineraries, however, can also lead to competition and confrontation between Islamic community leaders. During such moments, a community may face a disconcerting trial that may well lead to its disintegration. No matter how well formed, a community is a precarious assemblage, a social achievement made up of heterogeneous elements and ties prone to the risk of disentanglement. At the same time, a community may be impacted by external actors, networks, and forces, which may jeopardize its delicate existence. To illustrate this point, I turn to Ibn Yaḥyā's eventful final days in Java, which he spent in the place where this chapter began: Pekalongan.

Since the early nineteenth century, Pekalongan has had a significant and prosperous Ḥaḍramī population. Among them was the Bā ʿAlawī family of Bin Yaḥyā—Ibn Yaḥyā's own family—who had married into the Javanese aristocracy.[68] So it is not surprising that Pekalongan was among Ibn Yaḥyā's destinations. There he preoccupied himself with the labor of cultivating a community by employing the Ḥaddādian articulatory mode. It was in Pekalongan that Ibn Yaḥyā's itinerary became competitively entangled with other itineraries of Islamic transmission, leading to a confrontation that brought about the involvement of the colonial state and resulted in the disintegration of his own community. Unfortunately, we do not have any documentary trace of his activity in this coastal town save one letter written by Ibn Yaḥyā to his uncle ʿAbdallāh b. Ḥusayn Bin Ṭāhir, the author of the aforementioned *Sullam al-tawfīq*. Written from Trengganu, on the eastern coast of Malaya, on the first of March 1835, the letter provides a glimpse into what Ibn Yaḥyā described as "the Pekalongan affair" (*qaḍiyat fakalunghān*). He informed his uncle that some people in Pekalongan were envious of his ability to attract followers and began:

> planting fear in the heart of the infidels with seduction and exaggeration. And so I became perceived as a complete army—a full infantry—frightening the infidels and worrying the hypocrites. They accused me of the greatest offense. They spoke of me as an unjust sower of discord. . . . [T]he infidels attempted to imprison us, and so we turned to the *sayyid*s [*sāda*] and the Arabs who were there. But we found great fear in their hearts. They convinced us to turn ourselves in. So we excused them from any assistance or victory, but we refused to turn ourselves to imprisonment. No one remained with us except the boy Aḥmad b. ʿAlī Bāfaqīh, who refused to part from us. We did not have weapons, and yet the leader of the infidels in that land mobilized around a thousand people to lay siege on the house. They remained there for seven days, while we were inside. Every night they attempted to attack the house, but every time they came close, they suddenly retreated. There were no boats belonging to the Arabs on the pier until the arrival of a boat belonging to the āl-ʿAṭṭās family. So we traveled on it to Semarang, and when we arrived there, they said: he [Ibn Yaḥyā] will not get off from that boat onto this land, for we fear mischiefs from him. And so we stayed [on the boat] for days and finally sailed to Singapore and Trengganu.[69]

Ibn Yaḥyā's ambiguous description invites some speculation. It alludes to the hostility exhibited by certain actors toward his activities. Ibn Yaḥyā's travel to Java certainly fits into an established history of religious divines coming from elsewhere and criticizing established Islamic communities and their practices. Perhaps it was his critical evaluation of these practices that angered some people, who then attempted to agitate the colonial authorities into perceiving him as a security threat.[70] As sinister rumors began to spread, the mercantile Ḥaḍramī elites of Pekalongan chose to disassociate themselves from Ibn Yaḥyā, for fear of repercussions from the colonial authorities. This incident, after all, took place only five years after the conclusion of the Java War, a period marked by a heightened sense of colonial anxiety, especially toward the devout Muslim populations, many of whom had been involved with Prince Dipanagara. Various local skirmishes under the banner of Islam and messianic movements continued to haunt the colonial state in the years following Ibn Yaḥyā's departure from Java.

The Pekalongan affair illustrates the risks associated with the labor of cultivating an Islamic community, and more so in a thriving and competitive religious marketplace made up of contending itineraries of Islamic transmission. A community, after all, is a volatile assemblage made up of networks that are subject to expansion and contraction. Entanglement with the colonial state or with other communities may force members of a community to withdraw and disassociate themselves from it. When this happens, the community may be left with resources inadequate to secure its durability. This was what happened to Ibn Yaḥyā. While the texts he brought and authored and the curriculum he helped to formulate have remained popular in Indonesia to the present day, Ibn Yaḥyā did not leave behind an enduring community or an institution that immortalizes his name. But perhaps such is a characteristic of the Ḥaddādian paradigm as a mode of articulatory labor that centers less on figures than on texts deemed to be authoritative.

Conclusion

This chapter began with an infrastructure of Islamic worship and learning, a modest *langgar* that stands proudly surrounded by the decaying bungalows of a once prosperous Ḥaḍramī mercantile family of Pekalongan. The prayer hall serves as a site in and through which a humble but durable Islamic community punctually materializes five times a day. Members of this community come together to perform obligatory prayers, recite al-Haddād's creed and litanies, and periodically listen to the recitation of legal abridgments. The leader of the community at the time I was there was not a scholar skilled in the scholastic sciences. Nor was he a Sufi master learned in spiritual subtleties. Rahman was simply a prayer leader who made ends meet by operating a small shop at the market. In the eyes of the scholars he was just an enthusiastic commoner, albeit one with a strong determination to maintain the Islamic community bequeathed to him by his forefathers. The dynamic I witnessed at the *langgar* al-Ḥusayn, however, was not unique. While traveling around Java, I visited numerous *langgar*s built by Ḥaḍramīs or non-Ḥaḍramīs, where I found very similar prayer leaders, young and old, performing comparable labor using identical texts. How did these autonomous, but clearly connected, communities come to be formed? What kinds of subtle and supple tissue bind them? How did this particular form of religious authority come about?

Tracing the itineraries of Islamic transmission responsible for this development prompted me to move across time and space to eighteenth-century Ḥaḍramawt—more specifically, to ʿAbdallāh b. ʿAlawī al-Ḥaddād and the mode of articulatory labor he envisaged and popularized. At the heart of this articulatory mode is an aspiration to assert the *sunna* as a standardized normative code that can help structure social life in a region that had suffered from prolonged sociopolitical instability. This was made possible with the help of textual technologies like the creed, the legal abridgment, and the litanies.

Being modular and accessible renders these texts susceptible to circulation across an indefinitely wide range of contexts. Their dissemination sustains a vision of an objectified and disembedded *sunna* assumed to be socially realizable everywhere. Concurrently, the transmission of these texts demands actors who can articulate the *sunna* texts to others and whose authority is contingent solely on their mastery of these authoritative texts. Described by al-Ḥaddād as *shaykhs al-taʿlīm*, these religious instructors range from graduates of *pesantrens* who are able to teach and explain the intricacies of the texts, to shopkeepers who use the texts to lead ritual recitation, help children memorize divine attributes, and teach them how to pray. The Ḥaddādian articulatory mode shifted the emphasis away from the inimitable achievements of the royal regulators of religion or the saintly planters and their descendants to teachable texts and achievable lessons accessible to the commoners.[71] This reorientation opened the way to widespread participation in the modes of Islamic learning and practice in Java and elsewhere. Although not well known in the Middle East or elsewhere in the Islamic world, this articulatory mode has become paradigmatic and struck deep roots across the Indian Ocean.

The Ḥaddādian paradigm helped to facilitate the emergence of a vision of a universal, text-based Islam purified from cultural entanglements, an imagination that was reinforced quite vehemently by modernist Muslims at the turn of the twentieth century. Despite its claim to universality, such a vision is produced and maintained in concrete sociocultural contexts. Indeed, it requires particular infrastructure and hierarchical relationalities that can inflect and undermine its purificatory aspiration. In the next chapter I look at the Islamic communities established by Bā ʿAlawī scholars in late nineteenth- and early twentieth-century Java. While cultivated in accordance to the Ḥaddādian articulatory paradigm, these communities gradually took on the particularities of tribal social relationship, such as those that characterized the sanctuaries of Ḥaḍramawt (see chapter 1) that al-Ḥaddād strived to leave behind. Indeed, particular saintly dynasties akin to those found in the Ḥaḍramawt began to emerge from within the very communities that had been founded upon the aspiration to disembed the *sunna* from figures of authority and cultural particularities.

3

Institutions

ON THE OUTSKIRTS of Pekalongan's public cemetery of Sapuro stands the mausoleum of Aḥmad b. ʿAbdallāh al-ʿAṭṭās (d. 1929), a Ḥaddādian *shaykh al-taʿlīm* who is regarded today as the city's principal saint. Every day, the mausoleum hosts devout pilgrims, who come from all over Java to pray for and seek the blessing of the deceased scholar. The number of visitors significantly increases on auspicious times such as Thursday night or Friday morning, or before Ramaḍān when Javanese Muslims welcome the onset of the holy month by visiting the graves of saints, scholars, and family members. In front of the mausoleum is a small bazaar selling local commodities like batik cloth, sarongs, prayer caps, and alcohol-free perfumes. Buses transporting pilgrims are parked along the road leading to the mausoleum, bearing license plates from all over Java. Some locals living around the mausoleum have transformed parts of their homes into modest food stalls and inns that cater to the steady flow of pilgrims.

Every year, on the fourteenth of Shaʿbān, two weeks before the beginning of the holy month of Ramaḍān, tens of thousands of pilgrims descend into Pekalongan to attend the annual commemoration (*ḥawl*) of al-ʿAṭṭās. Muslim scholars come with their families and followers from all over Java, Sumatra, and even as far as the Ḥaḍramawt and Saudi Arabia. The commemorative ritual is held at the mausoleum and led by one of al-ʿAṭṭās's descendants, recognized as his official successor or surrogate. The commemoration involves communal prayers for the saint, recitation of his hagiography (*manāqib*), and sermons by attending scholars, and concludes with a communal feast.[1]

In this chapter, I examine the processes through which a Ḥaddādian *shaykh al-taʿlīm* became posthumously identified as the principal saint of a Javanese city. Al-ʿAṭṭās was one among many migrating Ḥaḍramī scholars who cultivated Islamic communities based on the Ḥaddādian curriculum in late nineteenth- and early twentieth-century Java. Unlike the period discussed in the last chapter, this era witnessed a steep increase in the number of Ḥaḍramīs migrating to Southeast Asia thanks to the opening of the Suez Canal in 1869, the advent of direct steamer lines between Singapore and Aden, and a decrease in the cost of travel. The growing Ḥaḍramī population in the Dutch East Indies, together with the Dutch colonial policy of racial segregation, worked to intensify ethnic identity and tribal solidarities among migrants living in the legally imposed Arab quarters. Consequently, the religious communities established by these Ḥaḍramī *shaykhs al-ta ʿlīm* gradually took on the particularities of tribal social relationship, similar to those that characterized the sacred sanctuaries of the Ḥaḍramawt discussed in chapter 1. Saintly dynasties, or manṣabates (*manṣaba*), similar to those found in the Ḥaḍramawt emerged in the Arab quarters of Java, led by hereditary *manṣabs* whose religious authority stemmed from their genealogical connection to the founders of the communities, posthumously regarded as saints. While this chapter focuses on one particular case, the dynamics described here help illustrate similar processes that occurred in other parts of Java. Al-ʿAṭṭās, after all, is just one among several Ḥaḍramī *shaykhs al-ta ʿlīm* who enjoy posthumous fame as saints and whose cultivated communities developed into manṣabates. There are at least fifty-two major Ḥaḍramī saintly commemorations of varying scale in Indonesia, each organized and led by a *manṣab*, who is regarded not only as the head of his saintly family but also as a prominent local or regional religious authority.

Behind the transformation of a Ḥaddādian community into a manṣabate is a changing mode of articulatory labor that adjusted the way the *sunna* is imagined and generated a novel form of authority. As discussed in chapter 2, the Ḥaddādian articulatory paradigm champions a standardized curriculum consisting of accessible *sunna* texts geared for an imagined general Muslim audience. This articulatory paradigm has helped to sustain imaginations of a disembedded Islam distinct from cultural particularities. Instead of a malleable product of ongoing dialogue between a localized present and the Prophetic past, the Ḥaddādian paradigm advocates a purified, text-based *sunna* posited to be impervious to culture and other localizing forces. In contrast, a manṣabate revolves around a locally embedded *sunna* that crystalizes from the interactions between its founding saint—recognized as a living connector to the Prophetic past—and his followers, and subsequently institutionalized by his hereditary successors—i.e., the *manṣabs*. The manṣabate represents a vision of Islam as what the saint does, as opposed to the Ḥaddādian insistence on Islam as what the texts say.[2] If the authority of a *shaykh al-ta ʿlīm* comes from his mastery of certain texts, the authority of a *manṣab* hinges on his genealogical connection to a saintly forebear.

By charting the transformation of a Ḥaddādian community into a manṣabate, this chapter highlights how any attempt to purify the *sunna* from cultural accretions can never be completely successful.[3] This inability, as Webb Keane has shown in the case of Protestant purification projects, is "*inherent* in the very materiality of semiotic form" employed to undertake such a project.[4] Like any doctrine or ideology, Prophetic teachings "cannot exist socially or be transmitted without some semiotic embodiment, which necessarily imposes certain conditions on them (such as iterability, contingencies of form, and the hazards inherent in the processes of decontextualization and recontextualization)."[5] Notwithstanding its universalist aspiration, the Ḥaddādian articulatory paradigm depends on the particularities of semiotic forms, like texts, whose efficacy hinges on their portability and capacity to be recontextualized elsewhere. Recontextualization, however, generates new kinds of interactions, interpersonal relations, hierarchies, and infrastructures that can themselves become objects of fetishism, thereby undermining purification. The question of who transmit these texts and to whom they are communicated is also significant, as human actors are not abstract individuals. The people who make up an Islamic community come with their own historical and cultural particularities, which, in turn, may shape the way the textually mediated *sunna* is understood, transmitted, and socially realized.

While inherent, the risks of fetishism that come with any project of purification are troubling only when viewed within the values and ideas of particular semiotic ideologies that assume the possibility of separating religion from culture or deem the cultural embeddedness of religious teachings to be a problem. Despite the purificatory aspiration of the Ḥaddādian paradigm, many Ḥaddādian *shaykh*s *al-taʿlīm* were not particularly concerned with such risks, as long as the transmission of the textualized *sunna* specified in the curriculum remained steady. There were those, however, from within the Ḥaḍramī diasporic community who began to see such risks as profoundly troubling after being influenced by modern Islamic visions radiating from Istanbul, Cairo, and Beirut. The dissemination of such views, made possible by new technologies and infrastructure such as the printing press, led to the emergence of modern Islamic institutions that materialized new knowledge structures.[6] These institutions hinged on a novel mode of articulatory labor that promised to transmit and realize Prophetic teachings in a way that transcends parochial ties and cultural particularities. Consequently, the Ḥaddādian paradigm with all of its universalist ambitions became increasingly perceived as parochial and culturally polluted. In their attempt to articulate their own version of purified *sunna*, these modernists problematized what they perceived as the Ḥaddādian fetishization of specific *sunna* texts and criticized forms of hierarchy that crystallized in Ḥaddādian communities, particularly after some of them developed into manṣabates.

In charting the transformation of one type of Islamic community to another as the outcome of a changing mode of articulatory labor, this chapter problematizes the established tendency to comprehend Islamic social formations as bounded and static entities. Anthropologists have come up with contrastive typologies of Islamic community based on forms of authority and religiosity instantiated by each type, from charismatic-scripturalist, master-book, and doctor-saint to the more vulgar orthodox-heterodox. These types are usually mapped on either a temporal (traditional vs. modern) or spatial (rural vs. urban) framework.[7] More recently, however, scholars have shown how the borders demarcating different Islamic communities were historically porous, and more often than not Muslims were engaging with divergent regimes of Islamic knowledge, recognizing varying kinds of authority, and participating in multiple forms of religious practice.[8] Even communities where textual authority predominated were characterized by a "complex interplay between written and spoken word."[9] This chapter complements these correctives by showing how a type of Islamic community can evolve into different types owing to the shift in the mode of articulatory labor. Even an articulatory mode that has become paradigmatic is prone to gradual or sudden adjustments. Focusing on articulatory labor, in turn, highlights the agency of human actors in maintaining or transforming a religious community. It opens up a grounded perspective into the porosity and motility of forms of Islam that have been posited as ideal types. As such, it allows us to think more seriously about the concrete labor and processes that contribute to the transformation or resilience of a particular sociological realization of Islam.

Parochialized Communities

"There is no collection of *ḥadīth*, except that I am connected to it and there is no book in all branches of knowledge, except that I have received a license [*ijāza*] for it," declared Aḥmad b. ʿAbdallāh al-ʿAṭṭās.[10] The scholar who posthumously became recognized as the principal saint of Pekalongan was "proclaiming the bounty of the Lord" (*taḥadduth bi-l-niʿma*) in front of a group of Ḥaḍramī scholars and students who came to see him during his brief return to the Ḥaḍramawt in 1894. The declaration alludes to how al-ʿAṭṭās and his audience perceived religious authority as being based on texts, whether *ḥadīth* collections or other books, and the ability to transmit and teach them. Connection to the Prophetic past is imagined as a connection to *ḥadīth* texts and, hence, articulating the *sunna* becomes synonymous with articulating *ḥadīth*s or *ḥadīth*-based prescriptive texts. This, as I discussed in the preceding chapter, is one of the hallmarks of the Ḥaddādian paradigm that has engendered Islamic communities that revolve around the labor and authority of a *shaykh al-taʿlīm*.

Indeed, *shaykh al-taʿlīm* was how al-ʿAṭṭās perceived his principal role, as someone learned in the religious sciences. Born in the village of al-Hajarayn, Ḥaḍramawt, in 1839, al-ʿAṭṭās came from a scholarly Bā ʿAlawī family and was educated under the guidance of leading scholars of the Ḥaḍramawt who were trained under the by then dominant Ḥaddādian paradigm.[11] Many of his teachers were the students of Ibn Yaḥyā whose itinerary we traced in chapter 2. After studying with the scholars of Ḥaḍramawt, al-ʿAṭṭās traveled to Mecca in 1865 to continue his education. Among his teachers in the holy city was the Shafiʿī *muftī* Aḥmad b. Zaynī Daḥlān (d. 1886), who also taught many Southeast Asian scholars.[12] Daḥlān himself studied with and was closely connected to several Bā ʿAlawī scholars and was influenced by the Ḥaddādian paradigm.[13] Like al-Ḥaddād, he stressed the importance of proselytization and instructed his students, including al-ʿAṭṭās, to go and live among the bedouins to teach them how to live in accordance with the *sunna*.[14] Daḥlān prepared his students not only to become scholars skilled in scholastic sciences but, more importantly, to become *shaykhs al-taʿlīm* and community builders.

After living in Mecca for almost twelve years, al-ʿAṭṭās traveled to Java. Like Ibn Yaḥyā before him, he had all the credentials required to take on the much-needed position of *shaykh al-taʿlīm* among the Ḥaḍramīs of Java. He settled in Pekalongan, the town where Ibn Yaḥyā once failed to cultivate a durable community. Soon after his arrival in 1876, he took up the position of prayer leader of a mosque in the Arab quarter (*kampung Arab*) of Pekalongan built by a wealthy Ḥaḍramī migrant.[15] He held daily classes at the mosque where he taught the creed and the legal abridgments authored and recommended by al-Ḥaddād and led the collective recitation of the litanies following the dawn and twilight prayers.[16] Al-ʿAṭṭās also organized weekly gatherings of worship, as described by his son ʿUmar:

> Among the practices of my father was that every Thursday night and Friday morning he occupied himself with the remembrance of Allāh, praising the Prophet, and reciting Qurʾānic *sūra*s that have been specified by the *sunna* to be recited on Thursday night and Friday morning. . . . He recited them at the mosque and used them to substitute for the regular litanies. He recited them collectively with those who were present with a beautiful voice. When reciting the verses, he made quick stops at the prescribed places as the Prophet did as reported in the *ḥadīth*s. If you look at his congregation, you will see them forming a gradated ring [*mudawwira madrūja*] like a beautifully shaped circle. No one sat ahead or behind the others. He chided those whose sitting position ruffles that beautiful form.[17]

Aside from these daily and weekly routines, al-ʿAṭṭās also instituted two one-month-long annual gatherings: the ritual recitation of the Bukhārī collection of Prophetic *ḥadīth*s during the month of Rajab and the recitation of al-Ḥaddād's book *Al-Naṣāʾiḥ al-dīniyya* (Religious advice) during the month of Ramaḍān.

These routine gatherings served to constitute a stable, mosque-based Islamic community. At the heart of this community was a hierarchical relationship premised on the recognition of al-ʿAṭṭās's ability to articulate the *sunna* through his mastery of the *ḥadīth* and other *ḥadīth*-based prescriptive texts. Owing to al-ʿAṭṭās's ongoing labor, the community continued to grow. To accommodate his growing numbers of followers, in 1913 he led a project of enlarging the mosque, securing funds from wealthy Ḥaḍramī entrepreneurs.[18] He also built an elementary school called Salafiyya next to the mosque, where he and some of his advanced students taught legal abridgments and basic creedal texts to local children.[19] The term *salafiyya*—meaning followers of the predecessors (*salaf*)—encapsulates the school's outlook as, for the Bā ʿAlawīs, *salaf* refers not only to the earliest generation of Muslims but also to the preceding Bā ʿAlawī masters, including al-Ḥaddād.

* * *

By the time al-ʿAṭṭās arrived in Java in the late nineteenth century, the Ḥaḍramī diasporic community was significantly larger than in the days of Ibn Yaḥyā. The unstable political condition in the Ḥaḍramawt and the decrease in transportation costs following the opening of the Suez Canal in 1869 and the advent of direct steamer lines between Singapore and Aden resulted in a significant increase in Ḥaḍramī migration to the Dutch East Indies. In Java alone, the Ḥaḍramī population rose from 6,133 in 1860 to 18,051 in 1900.[20] By 1900, the Arab population of the entire Dutch East Indies had increased to around 27,000.[21] This alarmed the Dutch, who feared that the presence of "the Arabs" would exacerbate anti-European, anti-Christian, and Pan-Islamic sentiments.[22] Under the rubric of protecting the economic interests of the natives, the Dutch divided the population into four legal categories: the Europeans; those equated with the Europeans, like the Japanese; the foreign Orientals (*Vreemde Osterlingen*), like the Arabs and the Chinese; and the natives (*inlanders*).[23] By the 1860s, the Dutch were enforcing a policy of segregation and had introduced the pass and quarter systems (*pass- en wijkenstelsel*), which meant that foreign Orientals such as Ḥaḍramīs—now collectively termed "Arabs"—had to live in separate quarters away from the indigenous population and were required to carry a pass to travel.[24] The policy proved effective in distancing the Ḥaḍramīs from the Javanese, particularly the nobility and the administrative elites.[25] Along with the Chinese, the Ḥaḍramīs in Pekalongan formed bounded commercial networks, centered in their respective quarters. Established Ḥaḍramī families financed batik production and provided jobs for the more recent migrants, while Ḥaḍramīs in other urban centers like Batavia (Jakarta), Surabaya, Solo, Cirebon, and Palembang constituted the expanding distribution chain.[26] As a result, the Ḥaḍramīs rose to become a wealthy but bounded, if not racialized, group.[27] Complementing the existing scholarship on the political and economic developments that led to the intensification of a racialized group consciousness among the Ḥaḍramīs, here I draw attention to the impact of these developments on the Islamic communities cultivated by Ḥaḍramī *shaykhs al-ta ʿlīm*.[28]

While today the annual commemoration of al-ʿAṭṭās draws the participation of thousands of people—the majority of whom are Javanese—the community he cultivated during his life consisted almost exclusively of Ḥaḍramīs. All of his classes were conducted in Arabic. Al-ʿAṭṭās did not speak Javanese or Malay fluently. He lived amongst his fellow Ḥaḍramīs in the Arab quarter of Pekalongan and did not travel much. Even in Pekalongan, he was not generally known to non-Ḥaḍramīs.[29] His hagiographies do not mention any Javanese disciple, and all of his existing correspondence is addressed to fellow Ḥaḍramī scholars.[30] This parochial character of al-ʿAṭṭās's community and networks is not unique. A similar feature is evident in Islamic communities assembled by other Ḥaḍramī *shaykh*s *al-ta ʿlīm* of this period.[31]

The development of strong Ḥaḍramī characteristics is further attested by the architecture of religious infrastructure built in the Arab quarters during this period. While religious infrastructure constructed by Ḥaḍramī families in the early nineteenth century took on Malay, Javanese, or even Ottoman architecture, that built in the early twentieth century exhibited Ḥaḍramī character.[32] For example, when al-ʿAṭṭās renovated the mosque in the Arab quarter of Pekalongan in 1913, he redesigned its interior to resemble the mosques in Ḥaḍramawt and added an iconic Ḥaḍramī-style minaret (figure 3.1). The Ḥaḍramī-style mosques and minarets that began to appear in the Arab quarters of this period attest to the intensification of connections between Java and Ḥaḍramawt, facilitated by novel technologies. While in the eighteenth and early nineteenth centuries most Ḥaḍramī migrants who traveled to Southeast Asia did not return to the Ḥaḍramawt, the advent of the steamship facilitated the oscillation of Ḥaḍramīs between Java and the Ḥaḍramawt. This, together with the circulation of photographs, enabled a preservation of memories of Ḥaḍramī landscapes and architecture among the diaspora that had not previously been possible.

* * *

While earlier Ḥaḍramī migrations were made up almost exclusively of the Bā ʿAlawīs, the new migrants who arrived toward the end of the nineteenth century came from other genealogical strata as well, including tribesmen (*qabā ʾil*). In Pekalongan, along with members of the āl-ʿAṭṭās family came

FIGURE 3.1 The Ḥaḍramī-style minaret built by Aḥmad b. ʿAbdallāh al-ʿAṭṭās in the Arab quarter of Pekalongan in 1913. The photo was taken during the 2011 annual commemoration of al-ʿAṭṭās. (Photo by the author)

those who belonged to Ḥaḍramī tribes with time-honored ties with that *sayyid* family, like the Nahd and the Jaʿda. In Ḥaḍramawt, these two tribes reigned over the territories where the ancestors of the āl-ʿAṭṭās family had established their sacred sanctuaries, including Ḥurayḍa and Mashhad. As discussed in chapter 1, Bā ʿAlawī saintly planters have for long cultivated communities in tribal territories. These tribes, in turn, recognized the authority of those scholars and their descendants. Tribes like the Nahd and the Jaʿda, for instance, recognized the religious authority of the āl-ʿAṭṭās family. Male members of the āl-ʿAṭṭās family married into these tribes, thereby cementing such ties into affinal kinship. For this reason, when members of these tribes migrated to Java, they settled in places where members of the āl-ʿAṭṭās family already resided, like Pekalongan. Upon arriving in Pekalongan, these tribal migrants began to revolve around Aḥmad al-ʿAṭṭās, whom they recognized not only as a *shaykh al-taʿlīm* but also as a descendant of the founders of the sanctuaries of Ḥurayḍa and Mashhad. The Arab quarter of Pekalongan, populated by the āl-ʿAṭṭās, the

Nahd, and the Ja'da, thus started to look like a satellite of those sanctuaries. The relationship among these three groups began to resemble the one they had in Ḥaḍramawt, as attested by several Ḥaḍramī travelers in their travelogues.[33]

Similar dynamics also occurred in other places in Java, involving other *shaykhs al-ta'līm* from Bā 'Alawī families with tribal followers in the Ḥaḍramawt. One notable example is Muḥammad b. 'Aydarūs al-Ḥabashī (d. 1919), whose mausoleum in the Arab quarter of Surabaya I discussed in chapter 1. Al-Ḥabashī was a descendant of Aḥmad b. Zayn al-Ḥabashī (d. 1731), the founder of the sanctuary of Khal' Rāshid (thereafter known as *ḥawṭa* Aḥmad Bin Zayn). The sanctuary was carved from the territories of several Kathīrī tribes, including the Bin Ṭālib and the Bin 'Abdāt. These tribes recognized al-Ḥabashī's family as their spiritual patrons, and both his father and uncle served as *manṣabs*. When al-Ḥabashī migrated to Java in the late nineteenth century, he was regarded by the Kathīrīs who had migrated to Java as their spiritual leader.[34] Another example is Muḥammad b. Aḥmad al-Miḥḍār (d. 1926) of Bondowoso, East Java. Al-Miḥḍār's father was the founder of the sanctuary of al-Quwayra, an autonomous settlement carved out of the territory of the Yāfi'ī Qu'ayṭī Sultanate. In Ḥaḍramawt, the Yāfi'ī tribes recognized al-Miḥḍār's family as their spiritual leaders. When the Yāfi'īs migrated to Java, they began to revolve around al-Miḥḍār and recognized him as their spiritual leader.[35]

Like al-'Aṭṭās, both al-Ḥabashī and al-Miḥḍār were Ḥaddādian *shaykhs al-ta'līm* who also happened to be scions of Ḥaḍramī saintly dynasties. With the influx of Ḥaḍramī tribes that historically revolved around the authority of these dynasties, these scholars began to be regarded as *manṣabs* whose authority stemmed not only from their mastery of *sunna* texts but also from their genealogical descent from their saintly ancestors. Some practices associated with the manṣabate were reinvented in Java. For example, when al-'Aṭṭās went to visit al-Miḥḍār in Bondowoso, the latter organized a reception that resonated with the custom of a Ḥaḍramī manṣabate, as recorded by one of al-'Aṭṭās's disciples:

> He [al-'Aṭṭās] then went to Bondowoso accompanied by Habib Muḥammad b. Aḥmad al-Miḥḍār and around forty other Bā 'Alawīs. When he reached the outskirt of Bondowoso, he was received by a large welcoming party with drums and raised flags, who then accompanied him from the city limit all the way to the house. He was the guest of Habib Muḥammad [al-Miḥḍār] for eight days.[36]

To welcome a guest on the outskirts of the town is an established Arabian tribal custom observed in places like Ḥaḍramawt. To do so with drums and raised banners, however, was exclusive to either a tribal chief or a *manṣab*.[37]

This account alludes to how al-Miḥḍār was recognized not only as a *shaykh al-taʿlīm* but also as a *manṣab*. While theoretically the Ḥaddādian paradigm champions the constitution of a flattened and duplicable Islamic community that revolves around and serves as the site for the social realization of a purified and culturally disembedded *sunna*, in reality, the communities that emerged under the tutelage of the Ḥaddādian *shaykhs al-taʿlīm* like al-Ḥabashī, al-Miḥḍār, and al-ʿAṭṭās became more akin to the older, tribal-based Islamic communities that took shape in the sacred sanctuaries of Ḥaḍramawt. This dynamic prepared the ground for the emergence of manṣabates in Java.

The Manṣabate

When al-ʿAṭṭās passed away in January 1929, his role as a *shaykh al-taʿlīm* was continued by his youngest son ʿAlī (d. 1992), whose notebook (*safīna*) was discussed in chapter 1. ʿAlī studied under his father before being sent to the boarding school of Tarīm, where he stayed for almost a decade. Upon returning to Pekalongan, ʿAlī stayed with his father, assisting him in teaching and leading ritual gatherings. When al-ʿAṭṭās passed away, senior Bā ʿAlawī scholars came from all over Java to attend the funeral. While no one alive today witnessed the event, senior members of the Ḥaḍramī community of Pekalongan I conversed with explained that the initiation took place moments before the burial. The scholars took ʿAlī's hand and made him vow to continue the works of his father. ʿAlī was henceforth recognized as *al-qāʾim bi-l-maqām* (the one who stands in the station) of his father, although he was commonly referred to by his fellow Ḥaḍramīs as a *manṣab*. With ʿAlī's ascendancy to his father's position, the succession of the community leadership became hereditary and the Ḥaddādian community that al-ʿAṭṭās had cultivated became more recognizable as a manṣabate. Toward the end of his life, ʿAlī delegated his leadership role to his eldest son, Aḥmad, who also graduated from the boarding school of Tarīm. When ʿAlī passed away in 1992, Aḥmad uttered an oath to take over his father's role in front of senior Bā ʿAlawī scholars and other *manṣabs*, assembled for the funeral. When Aḥmad passed away in 1999, his eldest son Abdullah Bagir (b. 1962), who studied in Mecca, was formally invested during the funeral. Habib Bagir, as he is usually referred to, remains the *manṣab* down to the present day.

The three *manṣabs* who succeeded al-ʿAṭṭās were all trained as *shaykh al-taʿlīm* in the Ḥaddādian tradition. Nevertheless, with the hereditary succession of community leadership, their authority as offspring and designated successors of a saintly forebear became more pronounced than their authority as *shaykhs al-taʿlīm*. This came with the production of hagiographies that promote al-ʿAṭṭās as a miracle-working saint and present the historical community he cultivated as an idealized sociological realization of the *sunna*.[38] Consequently, the principal duty of the *manṣab* is to preserve what was already realized in that saintly past with all of its particularities, including the use of the Arabic language, more than to articulate the *sunna* as contained in the texts recommended by al-Ḥaddād. If, for al-ʿAṭṭās, the gatherings, ritual practices, and institutions he founded were historically contingent means to effectively articulate the *sunna*, with the idealization of his era as the community's saintly past, those historically contingent forms began to be taken as exemplary realizations of the *sunna* that should not be altered even if they were no longer efficacious for articulating Prophetic teachings.

One example of this is the communal recitation of the Bukhārī compilation of Prophetic *ḥadīths*, performed annually in the month of Rajab. Every day during that month the *manṣab* and his followers recite the text for several hours in the morning and the afternoon. The attendees carry their own copies of the text and take turns in reciting the *ḥadīths*. The *manṣab* himself listens attentively and corrects mistakes in the recitation. This practice was introduced by al-ʿAṭṭās as a way to familiarize his community with the Prophetic *sunna*. Today, however, it has become no more than a ritualized communal recitation. The whole nine volumes of the compilation are recited hastily, and the *manṣab* does not bother to translate or elucidate the recited *ḥadīths*. As a result, the attendees are usually arabophone Ḥaḍramī elders and Javanese graduates of *pesantrens* who are literate in Arabic. Most Ḥaḍramīs in Pekalongan no longer understand Arabic and do not bother to attend the daily recitation, although they still attend the concluding celebration. Many expressed to me that they no longer see the point of attending as they do not understand Arabic. Still, there are those who regularly attend the sessions even if they are not literate in Arabic for the *baraka*, or blessings, of being present in a ritual instituted by a saint. Another example is the recitation of al-Ḥaddād's *Al-Naṣāʾiḥ al-dīniyya* (Religious advice) during the month of Ramaḍān, which is also conducted in Arabic. One person impatiently asked me, "why couldn't he just translate the text he is reading into Indonesian so that we can all benefit from it?" Most Ḥaḍramīs in Pekalongan are no longer interested in attending such sessions because of the language barrier, while others do so to partake in the blessings of the saint. In regard to actually learning about Prophetic teachings, most have resorted to other means, like reading translations of Islamic texts published and distributed by the burgeoning Islamic publishing industry or watching Islamic programs on television and YouTube.

When I asked the current *manṣab* about his reluctance to introduce innovations to the ways the ritual practices are conducted, he responded that they are the *sunna* of the predecessors. Indeed, to introduce significant modification could incur the anger of living Bā ʿAlawī elders. For example, during the

2012 *ʿĪd al-fiṭr* prayer, the *manṣab* began the prayer at 7:15 a.m., five minutes earlier than it had customarily been performed since the days of al-ʿAṭṭās. Upon the completion of the prayer, the *manṣab*'s maternal uncle came up to him angrily and told him that he had introduced an innovation to the *sunna* of the predecessors (*salaf*). This example suggests how practices instituted by al-ʿAṭṭās have been detached from their specific context of emergence and idealized as the *sunna* of the community to the extent that they bind a reigning *manṣab*. Thus, at the heart of the transformation of a Ḥaddādian community into a manṣabate is a changing mode of articulatory labor that has adjusted the way the *sunna* is imagined and generated a novel form of authority, one that hinges on genealogical connection to the community's saintly past.

* * *

The formation of the *manṣab*'s genealogical authority went hand in hand with the sanctification of al-ʿAṭṭās. One visible mark of a *manṣab*'s genealogical authority is his possession of material objects associated with his saintly forebear, which may include prayer caps and beads, walking sticks, shawls, turbans, or rings. Upon request, a *manṣab* would usually allow visitors to wear or touch these heirlooms to seek blessings (*tabarruk*).[39] The *manṣab* of Pekalongan safeguards several objects associated with al-ʿAṭṭās, including his shawl, turban, and books. He wears the shawl during the annual commemoration and other major Islamic holidays. Another heirloom kept by the *manṣab* is an early twentieth-century lithographic copy of a *mawlid* text—i.e., a panegyric narrative of the Prophet's nativity—which al-ʿAṭṭās used to recite from when he led the *mawlid* ritual.[40] Today, this weathered copy is used only during the annual commemoration. The *manṣab* also safeguards a Ḥaḍramawt-made carpet that was used by al-ʿAṭṭās to cover the floor when he held religious gatherings. Today the old carpet is no longer used except twice a year during the *ʿĪd al-fiṭr* and *ʿĪd al-aḍḥā*, when it is brought out to cover the floor of the mosque (figure 3.2). While these objects were simply materials used by al-ʿAṭṭās in his labor of cultivating community, today they are treated as irreplaceable saintly relics. Objects associated with al-ʿAṭṭās are believed to carry his blessings. They also serve to project the historical connection to the community's saintly past upon which the *manṣab*'s authority rests.

Apart from material objects, al-ʿAṭṭās's sanctity and the *manṣab*'s genealogical authority are also inscribed in built environments. In 1933, al-ʿAṭṭās's son ʿAlī built a new annex to the front reception room of his father's house and turned it into a mosque, the Masjid al-Rawḍa. This mosque has continued to be the seat of the manṣabate. The mosque and the adjoining living quarters are where the reigning *manṣab* lives and receives guests. The mosque also serves

FIGURE 3.2 The current *manṣab* of Pekalongan, Habib Abdullah Bagir, leading the recitation of the *mawlid* on the afternoon of *ʿĪd al-fiṭr*. For the occasion, the mosque floor is covered by an old carpet used in al-ʿAṭṭās's day. (Photo by the author)

as the infrastructure in and through which the *manṣab* maintains his community by leading ongoing rituals, from the daily prayers and litany recitation to the weekly reading of the *mawlid* and the annual recitation of the Bukhārī *ḥadīth* compilation. Genealogical authority and hierarchy are physically inscribed in the built environment of the mosque. A dais (*amben*), located in one corner of the reception space, is reserved for the *manṣab*, his family and fellow Bā ʿAlawīs, and other distinguished guests. The wall facing the entrance is decorated by several framed calligraphic texts that project al-ʿAṭṭās's authority. Among them are a genealogical tree (*nasab*) and a chain of Sufi initiation (*silsila*), both connecting al-ʿAṭṭās to the Prophet. Adjoining the two charts are poems praising al-ʿAṭṭās's sanctity and extolling the virtues of the Prophet's family. During ritual events, the *manṣab* sits against the wall facing his audience, and behind him are these authority-projecting texts.

Spatial inscription of al-ʿAṭṭās's sanctity and the *manṣab*'s genealogical authority can also be seen in the former's mausoleum. Al-ʿAṭṭās was buried in private land adjoining Pekalongan's main cemetery. Apart from those of al-ʿAṭṭās and his wife, the mausoleum contains the graves of the first and second *manṣab*s and their wives. Al-ʿAṭṭās's tombstone stands on a long, rectangular, ceramic-covered plinth next to his wife's at the center of the chamber. The white marble tombstone is engraved with fading black Arabic inscriptions declaring al-ʿAṭṭās's sanctity and authority as the articulator of Prophetic teachings:

> This is the tomb of the reviver of the *sunna* and the conferrer of gifts; the flowing sea and the brilliant moon; the one who revealed the truth and dispelled with it the darkness of misguidance and repelled with its proofs the whispers of the wayward. The sublime prelate, the celebrated Imam, the knowing master, the one who is at the forefront in every clime. The prime of primes, grand in majesty, famed for his reputation, whose utterances are heard; the pride of the epochs; the radiance of the lands, the bearer of the banners of honor, the best of the pure lineage, the noble descendant of the Prophet, the knower of God, the beloved [*al-ḥabīb*] Aḥmad bin ʿAbdallāh bin Ṭālib al-ʿAṭṭās the Bā ʿAlawī [*al-ʿalawī*], the Ḥusaynī [*al-ḥusaynī*], the Ḥaḍramī [*al-ḥaḍramī*]. May God benefit us with his blessings. He passed away on Sunday, 25th of the ever-flowing month of Rajab in the year 1347 [January 7, 1929], having reached the age of ninety-one.

A poem in Arabic written by the Ḥaḍramī jurist Muḥammad b. ʿAwaḍ Bā Faḍl (d. 1950) is framed and hung on the wall inside the mausoleum. Like the tombstone, the poem projects al-ʿAṭṭās's sanctity and authority:

> O luminous mausoleum, worthy of praise
> Thou contain the grave of the pious one,
> Whose similitude no eyes have ever witnessed
> Truly he was the best in austerity and piety,
> Who has traversed the finest life story.
> He, the son of Ṭālib al-ʿAṭṭās, a pure and clean soul
> Aḥmad, the reviver of the *sunna*, a real treasure
> Say to those who visit this tomb: You are the best flock.
> Felicitous are those who visit it,
> to honor the rising light from the beam of the aiding sun [the Prophet],
> Allāh's blessings upon him and his family, the best of all lineages

Beneath the poem is a chronographic phrase that dates the mausoleum's construction. The phrase simply states: "and it [the mausoleum] is a piece of Ḥurayḍa" (*wa hiya qiṭʿa min ḥurayḍa*), referring to the sanctuary settlement established by the eponym of the al-ʿAṭṭās family, ʿUmar b. ʿAbd al-Raḥmān, in Ḥaḍramawt (see chapter 1). Declaring the sanctity of al-ʿAṭṭās's mausoleum while positing it as a piece of Ḥurayḍa means aligning the former with the latter, thereby projecting a continuity with a saintly and, ultimately, a Prophetic past. In contrast to the Ḥaddādian insistence on specific *ḥadīth*-based texts as the reliable links to the Prophetic past, the infrastructure of the manṣabate projects a genealogical cartography that leads to that foundational past, made up of specific places and human bodies, living and entombed.

Al-ʿAṭṭās's sanctity and the *manṣab*'s genealogical authority are performed on a grand scale during the annual commemoration, first instituted by ʿAlī to honor of his father. The commemoration is a ritual performance that reproduces the manṣabate as a social formation beyond its locality. A few weeks before the event, the *manṣab* receives gifts and votive offerings from his followers, including money, goats, rice, fruits, and vegetables, which are then used to prepare the feast for the guests. No ritual performed during the commemoration instantiates the *manṣab*'s authority better than the *madkhal*—the *manṣab*'s ritualized entry into al-ʿAṭṭās's mausoleum. During the day of the commemoration, thousands of pilgrims flock to the area surrounding al-ʿAṭṭās's mausoleum. The mausoleum's door, however, is kept locked and is opened only upon the arrival of the *manṣab*. The *manṣab* and his entourage—consisting of other *manṣab*s and senior scholars from different places—arrive at the site heralded by drums, banners, and the singing of praises to the Prophet and his family.[41] The *madkhal* marks the commencement of the commemoration.

The commemoration is a public performance of the *manṣab*'s authority. Such an authority hinges on the *manṣab*'s connection with a saintly and, ultimately, Prophetic past. His authority also depends on carefully maintained networks that tie him to other *manṣab*s and scholars from different localities. During the two-day event, the *manṣab* meets and greets other Bā ʿAlawī *manṣab*s, who usually arrive in Pekalongan with their followers. In return, when those *manṣab*s organize the commemoration of their saintly predecessors, the *manṣab* of Pekalongan attends, bringing his followers along. The maintenance of ties between *manṣab*s—which in some cases are further cemented by intermarriages—helps to ensure that each of these saintly commemorations is well attended by people from various places.

Many attendees I conversed with related that, usually a month before the commemoration, an oral invitation would be read during the Friday prayer in their village. Some reported how their local *shaykh al-taʿlīm* told them about the event. Senior scholars with large followings usually receive telephone invitations from the *manṣab* and bring a bus or two of their followers to attend the commemoration.[42] The commemoration thus momentarily expands the *manṣab*'s following by bringing people—including prominent scholars—from different places, before contracting again after the event. The commemoration, however, should not be seen merely as benefitting from these networks. As a site that cements horizontal solidarity while reinforcing hierarchy, the commemoration also extends, strengthens, and consolidates the networks.[43]

As the biggest religious gathering in Pekalongan, the commemoration reinforces the *manṣab*'s prestige in his hometown. His ability to draw people to Pekalongan benefits local businesses. The commemoration also attests to the wide recognition of the *manṣab*'s authority to the people of Pekalongan, who, consequently, have to take him seriously. Thus, the mayor of Pekalongan personally delivers a welcoming speech at every commemoration. The city council also lists al-ʿAṭṭās's mausoleum as one of the city's heritage sites on its website. Every time new mayors, police chiefs, or army commanders are elected or appointed, they visit and introduce themselves to the reigning *manṣab*. The *manṣab*'s ability to stage the large annual gathering that draws people from elsewhere into the city enables him to become recognized as a major, if not preeminent, religious authority in Pekalongan, and not just the spiritual leader of the Ḥaḍramīs like his saintly forebear.

* * *

The gradual transformation of a Ḥaddādian community into a manṣabate highlights how the project of purifying the *sunna* from cultural accretions is never completely successful. The materiality of semiotic forms like texts that are employed to undertake purification may become objects of reverence, and their recontextualization generates new interactional contexts and hierarchical relationships, which may be idealized and institutionalized as part of the community's *sunna*. While inherent, such risks are troubling only when viewed from the perspective of particular semiotic ideologies that deem the cultural embeddedness of the *sunna* to be a problem. The Ḥaddādian *shaykh*s *al-taʿlīm* discussed above, for instance, did not seem to be perturbed by such risks as long as the transmission of the textualized *sunna* specified in the Ḥaddādian curriculum remained steady. But there were those from within the Ḥaḍramī diasporic community who began to perceive them as highly problematic after being influenced by modern Islamic ideas radiating from Egypt and the Levant. Born out of the interactions between Muslim scholars and European modernity, such visions spread into Southeast Asia thanks to new infrastructure and technologies such as print and steam travel.[44]

Modern Muslim reformists argued for bypassing the authority of established scholars and their particular articulation of the *sunna*, including the creed, the legal abridgments, and the litanies. They insisted on the need for Muslims to directly access the scriptures and reinterpret the Qurʾān and the *ḥadīth*s in light of modern developments in the natural and social sciences.

Equally important is their adoption of a style of writing about Islam in "universalistic and systemic terms as a 'system' (*niẓām*)" seen not "from within a specific legal tradition, not for a particular people, and not with respect to any period."[45] One semiotic form used to transmit this objectified Islam was the periodical, which, as Michael Warner suggests, "allow[s] participants in its discourse to understand themselves as directly and actively belonging to a social entity that exists historically in secular time and has consciousness of itself, though it has no existence apart from the activity of its own discursive circulation."[46] The circulation of modern Islamic periodicals—like the Cairo-based *Al-Manār*—gave existence to a public consisting of readers from different places throughout the Muslim world, including Southeast Asia, who were abstractly addressed by the periodicals, thereby allowing them to imagine themselves as members of a broad and unlocalizable social entity.[47] Such a social entity is conceived to have a kind of temporal durability owing to the punctuality of the periodicals. Following the footsteps of the modern reformists of Egypt and the Levant, Ḥaḍramīs in Java began to publish Arabic-language newspapers, creating an Arabic reading public through their circulation, fueling a Java-wide Arabic collective imagination.[48]

One institution that attempted to materialize the new reading public into a concrete community was the *jam ʿiyya*, or modern association.[49] Inspired by modern European clubs and Chinese diasporic voluntary associations, the Ḥaḍramī entrepreneurial elites of Batavia (Jakarta) established the Jamiat Kheir (Ar. Jam ʿiyyat al-Khayr, "The Benevolent Association") in 1901.[50] In 1919 they established a modern Arabic-based school under the same name.[51] While Salafiyya, the school that al-ʿAṭṭās founded in Pekalongan, was strictly grounded on the Ḥaddādian curriculum, the Jamiat Kheir school combined traditional religious subjects with natural sciences and languages. Natalie Mobini-Kesheh describes the school:

> The students were divided into graded classes, sat at desks, and used modern textbooks with illustrations (taboo in traditional Islamic schools). They studied arithmetic, geography, Islamic history, and English language, along with Arabic and more traditional Islamic subjects. The underlying philosophy of the schools emphasized the importance of understanding, Arabic language being viewed as the means by which students would be able to read and comprehend the Scriptures for themselves. Apart from formal classes, informal discussions or *majlis* were conducted in which problems of the reform of Islam were discussed, based on articles from the Middle Eastern press including the Egyptian publication *Al-Manār*.[52]

The Jamiat Kheir school was designed to produce a modern intelligentsia, and not *shaykhs al-ta ʿlīm*. It materialized new knowledge structures—based on a modern understanding of rationality and informed by an ideology of progress—which attempted to move people from parochial ties to a common standard of practice and ethics susceptible to modern urban sociality. The curriculum was geared toward producing modern subjects who would be able to actively participate in the *jamʿiyyas*. The success of the Jamiat Kheir school in Batavia led to the emergence of similar Arabic schools in other parts of Java, including Pekalongan, Solo, and Surabaya.[53]

One significant consequence of this modernizing current was the strengthening of critical attitudes, particularly among the tribesmen who had achieved economic success in Java, toward genealogical or descent-based status. Such sentiments had been building up, although they lacked an articulative framework. Modern ideas of egalitarianism, propounded by modern Muslim reformists like Muḥammad ʿAbduh (d. 1905) and Muḥammad Rashid Riḍā (d. 1935) in the pages of the *Al-Manār* as part of their articulation of the Prophetic *sunna*, finally provided them with such a framework.[54] In 1915, several Ḥaḍramī modernists established the Jamʿiyyat al-Iṣlāḥ wa al-Irshād al-ʿArabiyya (The Arab Association for Reform and Guidance), better known as al-Irsyad.[55] This *jamʿiyya* called for progressive educational reforms and social equality for all Muslims, as well as a return to what it perceived as the pristine *sunna* based on the scriptures.[56] While there were several Bā ʿAlawīs who initially supported al-Irsyad's agenda, the *jamʿiyya*'s insistence on social equality and its demand for the eradication of practices deemed as erroneous innovations (*bidʿa*)—including grave visitation and veneration of saints—drove many of them away. Among the primary objects of al-Irsyad's criticism were institutions and practices associated with the manṣabate, including the genealogical authority of the *manṣabs*. Such practices became increasingly seen as *bidʿa*, betraying a significant difference in the way the *sunna* was coming to be understood. These criticisms enraged senior Bā ʿAlawī scholars and *manṣabs*, leading to high-profile public polemics and intense clashes between the Irsyadis and the Bā ʿAlawīs that tore apart the Islamic communities assembled by the Ḥaḍramīs.[57]

While there is no source that points to how al-ʿAṭṭās personally responded to this rift, there are those that describe the reaction of his fellow Bā ʿAlawī scholar and scion of a saintly dynasty, the aforementioned Muḥammad al-Miḥḍār of Bondowoso (East Java). Al-Miḥḍār actively dissuaded non-Bā ʿAlawī Ḥaḍramīs from joining al-Irsyad. He wrote letters to the Yāfiʿīs of Bumiayu, Central Java, warning them that affiliating with al-Irsyad "would cut their ties to the Prophet's family."[58] Al-Miḥḍār discouraged the Yāfiʿī elders from accommodating a preacher from Tegal who was visiting Bumiayu to propagate Irsyadi ideology to the Yāfiʿīs. According to the Yāfiʿī historian and Irsyadi ideologue Ṣalāḥ al-Bakrī, upon receiving the letter, the Yāfiʿī elders laughed and ridiculed al-Miḥḍār.[59] While, traditionally, the Yāfiʿīs recognized the authority al-Miḥḍār's family, it seems that by this time, the family's authority was no longer deemed sacrosanct by the group that was formerly under its influence. Al-Miḥḍār's aggressive stance against the Irsyadis was pivotal in both uniting the Bā ʿAlawīs in Java and intensifying the conflict with the increasingly anti–Bā ʿAlawī Irsyadis. Two years after al-Miḥḍār's death in 1926, the Bā ʿAlawīs founded their own exclusive *jamʿiyya*: the Rabithah Alawiyah (Ar. al-Rābiṭa al-ʿAlawiyya, "the Bā ʿAlawī League").

The Irsyadi–Bā ʿAlawī conflict reflected a broader trend that was happening throughout the Muslim world at the turn of the twentieth century.[60] The internal Ḥaḍramī conflict, for instance, mirrored the contestation that erupted between Javanese Muslim modernists and traditionalists (for the latter, see chapter 2) that paved the way for the emergence of Indonesia's two biggest Islamic *jamʿiyya*s: the Muhammadiyah and the Nahdlatul Ulama (NU) founded in 1912 and 1926, respectively. Central to Muhammadiyah was the project of purifying Islamic practices from what were seen as *bidʿa*, specifically understood as religious practices that have no precedents in the Qurʾān or the *ḥadīth*s.[61] It posited the Qurʾān and the *ḥadīth*s as the only authoritative legitimating references for acceptable religious practice. Both the Qurʾān and the *ḥadīth*s should, in turn, be subjected to rational interpretation in light of modern developments. NU, on the other hand, has been committed to the preservation of "traditional" Islamic practices, including the celebration of the Prophet's birthday, saintly commemoration, and visitations (*ziyāra*) to the graves of scholars and saints. NU scholars follow the teachings and precedents of past scholars, and emphasize scholastic learning involving the study of classical Arabic texts in Ashʿarite theology, linguistic sciences, Shāfiʿī legal texts, and Sufism. NU's traditionalism has similarities with and has been influenced by the Ḥaddādian paradigm, as discussed in chapter 2.

* * *

The modernizing currents among the Muslims of Java led to the contraction of the community that made up the manṣabate. In the course of the Bā ʿAlawī–Irsyadi conflict, many non–Bā ʿAlawī members of al-ʿAṭṭās's community—including those from the Nahd and the Jaʿda tribes—began to disassociate themselves from the community and joined al-Irsyad. Some even criticized al-ʿAṭṭās and his successors openly, using modernist ideas to question their authority. While most of the Bā ʿAlawīs remained respectful of the manṣabate, they also began to be more attuned to modern articulations of the *sunna* disseminated through the periodicals. After the founding of the Rabithah Alawiyah, many Bā ʿAlawīs perceived the *jamʿiyya* as their principal institution and took an active part in it. The Pekalongan branch of the *jam ʿiyya* was founded in 1929 under the leadership of young Bā ʿAlawī intelligentsia educated in modern Arab schools. The *manṣab* played only an advisory role in the Rabithah Alawiyah.

The second development that led to the contraction of the *manṣab*'s community was the dissemination of modern reformist ideas among Javanese Muslims of Pekalongan. While during al-ʿAṭṭās's lifetime the community consisted of Ḥaḍramīs, by the time ʿAlī became the *manṣab*, Javanese Muslims in the city began to revolve around him. This, however, did not last long, for in 1946 a West Sumatran Muhammadiyah activist by the name of Abdul Gaffar Ismail (d. 1998) was exiled to Pekalongan. Born in 1911, Ismail was educated in the Sumatra Thawalib, the most influential reformist school in Sumatra, led by the charismatic Abdul Karim Amrullah (d. 1945), also known as Haji Rasul, who was one of the leading propagandists of the Muhammadiyah.[62] In Pekalongan, Ismail settled in a house less than a block from the *manṣab*'s al-Rawḍa mosque and organized a weekly gathering there. In his gatherings, Ismail did not read from a particular Islamic text, nor did he perform any devotional service. The gatherings consisted of simply orations, delivered by Ismail in clear and eloquent Indonesian. He actively criticized religious practices that have no grounding in the scriptures, including those frequently performed at the al-Rawḍa mosque. One of my interlocutors recalled how in the early 1960s, Ismail used to reprimand the *manṣab* for maintaining practices that contradict the *sunna*. His speeches were amplified using modern technology (considered taboo by *manṣab* ʿAlī), thereby enabling people in the neighborhood to hear, including the *manṣab*, who lived only a few houses away. Gradually, more and more people attended Ismail's weekly gathering. The sharp political and social commentaries of his speeches—which stood in marked contrast to the *manṣab*'s obtuse recitations of Arabic texts—and the simple, modern, and more egalitarian character of the gathering drew the interests of the city's Javanese Muslims who had been educated in the modern schools. As Ismail's community drew more and more members, that of the *manṣab* was shrinking.

The third development that led to the contraction of the *manṣab*'s community was the establishment of a modern Islamic school, the Ma'had Islam, in 1942. The school was established by Abdullah Hinduan, a Bā ʿAlawī graduate of Cairo University. Unlike the Ḥaddādian Salafiyya school established by al-ʿAṭṭās, Ma'had Islam was bilingual. In contrast to the former, its curriculum included the study of natural sciences, geography, mathematics, and history. In teaching the *sunna*, the school relied not on the creed, the legal abridgments, and the litanies, but on Indonesian translations of modern Egyptian school textbooks. Using a modern standardized curriculum meant that students of the school could continue their study to public high schools and universities, an educational trajectory that was almost impossible for Salafiyya students. Ma'had Islam did not identify itself as a Ḥaḍramī, let alone a Bā ʿAlawī, institution. The teachers and staff included Bā ʿAlawīs and Javanese Muslims. Ever since its establishment, the school has been the preferred institution of elementary learning for Muslims in Pekalongan, forming social bonds among Arab (both Bā ʿAlawī and non–Bā ʿAlawī) and Javanese children. While there were other modern Islamic schools run by al-Irsyad and the Muhammadiyah, only staunch supporters of the two *jamʿiyya*s sent their children there. The popularity of these modern schools led to the decline of enrollment in the Salafiyya. In the final years of its existence, only children from the *manṣab*'s immediate and extended family composed its student body. In the early 1980s, *manṣab* ʿAlī finally closed down the school.

The three developments that resulted in the contraction of the *manṣab*'s community did not mean that he was left without followers. After all, these developments involved only those living within the city of Pekalongan. The annual commemoration that draws thousands of people from all over Java, for instance, continues to attest to the *manṣab*'s gravitas. At the same time, the modernizing currents within the city drove *manṣab* ʿAlī, and subsequently his son and grandson, to focus on cultivating followings amongst those living south of the coastal city, in the hinterlands that make up the district (*kabupaten*) of Pekalongan. Most towns and hamlets in the district have continued to be a bastion of the traditionalist Nahdlatul Ulama. There, the role of traditionalist *shaykh*s *al-taʿlīm* remains central in people's daily lives down to the present day. Unlike al-ʿAṭṭās, or most Ḥaḍramīs for that matter, the three succeeding *manṣab*s have been active in the hinterlands, where they have presided over weddings and funerals and led other ritual practices. In a single day, the *manṣab* might conduct religious ceremonies in three different villages in different parts of the district, receiving remuneration for the service. The *manṣab*s succeeded in establishing cordial relations with local *shaykh*s *al-taʿlīm*, entrepreneurs, landlords, and village leaders. In return, people from the district would flock to the events held at the al-Rawḍa mosque. The manṣabate might have lost many followers within the city of Pekalongan; nevertheless, the *manṣab*s have been able to forge new connections and ties with the inhabitants of the district, who long for a living link to Pekalongan's saintly past and the more distant Prophetic past. The *manṣab*'s influence in the district, however, has more recently been challenged by a Bā ʿAlawī scholar who has succeeded in cultivating an expansive following in Pekalongan and beyond. The second part of this book tells that story.

Conclusion

In this chapter, I have traced the emergence of the Bā ʿAlawī manṣabate in Java, a new type of Islamic community that resonates with those that had historically developed in the tribal territories of Ḥaḍramawt. I have argued that the growth, segregation, and diversification of the community of Ḥaḍramī migrants in late nineteenth-century Java led to the emergence of exclusive and self-consciously Ḥaḍramī communities marked by a heightened sense of ethnic identity. Members of Ḥaḍramī tribes—many of whom had long lived under the spiritual authority of different Bā ʿAlawī manṣabates in the Ḥaḍramawt—were also populating the Arab quarters of Java. This resulted in the reproduction of older relationships akin to those that materialized in the sacred sanctuaries of Ḥaḍramawt, as opposed to the ideally flattened Ḥaddādian community solely bound by a standardized, *sunna*-derived theological, ethical, and devotional code. Despite the Ḥaddādian assertion of the universality of its objectified *sunna*, universals are, to draw on Anna Tsing, "effective within particular historical conjunctures that give them content and force."[63] Indeed, all universals are embedded when we think about them as practical projects involving concrete labors performed and accomplished by particular actors in a heterogeneous world.[64]

The manṣabate, however, was not the only new form of Islamic community that emerged among the Ḥaḍramīs of Java at the beginning of the twentieth century. The same period also witnessed various attempts to redefine the *sunna* in light of modern scientific progress and new ways of aligning it to individual Muslims inspired by modern Islamic reform movements in the urban centers of Egypt and the Levant and transmitted to the Dutch East Indies through the circulation of periodicals. This, in turn, led to the emergence of new Islamic institutions—namely, the *jamʿiyya* and modern schools founded on a different mode of articulatory labor.

It is essential to note that both the manṣabate and the *jamʿiyya*s developed almost concurrently. Like the latter, Ḥaḍramī manṣabates in Java were, to some extent, also products of colonial modernity. Each, however, was premised on a different mode of articulatory labor involving different semiotic forms, technologies, and infrastructure that, in turn, facilitated the emergence of contending Islamic communities, although their members may overlap. As such, one should refrain from adopting a teleological perspective that concludes with the triumph of the "modern" over the "traditional" institutions, as many scholars have explicitly stated or implicitly insinuated.[65] The fact that the *jamʿiyya*s subscribe to a teleological view of history, or "a moral narrative of modernity," to use Webb Keane's term, does not mean that we need to reproduce such an ideological vision in our analysis.[66] This chapter shows how the manṣabate and the *jam ʿiyya* are best understood as two dissimilar but overlapping Islamic social formations that emerged from different modes of articulatory labor, both of which have continued to grow and remained significant for Indonesian Muslims down to the present day. The notion of articulation thus allows us to develop a nonhistoricist reading of Islam and Islamic history. It enables us to think about the history and social life of Islam as a set of exchanges, interactions, conflicts, and perpetual transactions among Islamic communities assembled through different articulatory practices. While these communities are relatively autonomous, each is nevertheless articulated with others through interactions or contestations. It is such relations, whether amicable or adversarial, that make these Islamic communities meaningfully different from one another.

PART II

Assembling Authority

4
Itineraries

IN NOVEMBER 1997, amidst the financial crisis that devastated the Indonesian economy, a modest ground-breaking ceremony was held in Pekalongan's neighborhood of Noyontaan. Such celebrations were almost unheard of during the crisis. The significant devaluation of the Indonesian currency had halted most construction projects. Yet it was precisely during that time of economic and political uncertainty that a Bā ʿAlawī scholar, who today has risen to become Indonesia's most influential Sufi master, embarked on a major building project. That man was Habib Muhammad Luthfi b. Ali Bin Yahya and he was laying the foundation for a congregational center to cater for his growing community. The building of the congregational center marked a critical stage in the consolidation of Habib Luthfi's religious authority in Pekalongan. Having a physical space and built infrastructure where people can assemble regularly is crucial for the stabilization of a religious community. Congregational centers are sites of hospitality that have the potential to foster new social relations and intimacies.[1] They facilitate knowledge transmission and ethical cultivation.[2] Such centers have taken on different forms throughout the history of Islam, from mosques and prayer halls to Sufi centers (*zāwiya*) and lodges (*khānaqā*). Historically, they have also functioned as military camps, administrative centers, treasuries, courts of justice, inns, and marketplaces.[3] They often served as burial sites for religious leaders, thereby turning them into shrines and pilgrimage destinations.[4]

This chapter follows the biographical becoming of Habib Luthfi Bin Yahya. It observes the labors performed by Habib Luthfi in his attempt to cultivate an Islamic community. Unlike the *manṣab*s discussed in the last chapter, Habib Luthfi does not come from an established scholarly or saintly background. He may be a Bā ʿAlawī *sayyid*, but his father was not a scholar who could bequeath him an already-cultivated community. Consequently, he had to form new connections and embed himself in established genealogical channels to be recognized as a credible connector to the Prophetic past. He achieved this by traveling across Java in search of teachers who could connect him to the Prophetic past. The case of Habib Luthfi suggests how an aspiring scholar may assume a position of authority by tapping into different genealogies, networks, and itineraries of Islamic transmission. As such, it highlights the practical and ideological centrality of *genealogy* and *mobility* in the formation of Islamic authority. Different genealogies and itineraries of mobility, and the contingent relation between the two, may, in turn, open up new articulatory possibilities and engender distinct forms of religious authority.

Genealogy works to identify, authenticate, and limit the communicative channels in the transgenerational transmission of Prophetic teachings. It also operates ideologically as a recognizable basis of religious authority, allowing others to perceive its bearer as a credible connector to the Prophetic past.[5] Two different forms of genealogical relation are considered important among traditionalist Muslims: *nasab* and *silsila*. If *nasab* (Ar. pl. *ansāb*) means "pedigree" or "bloodline," *silsila* (Ar. pl. *salāsil*) denotes a continuous string of Sufi initiation and transmission of spiritual knowledge. *Silsila* connects disciples to their master (*murshid*, shaykh, or *pīr*), all the way to the founder of the Sufi order, and ultimately back to the Prophet Muḥammad. In charting genealogical connection to the Prophet, a *silsila* works like a Prophetic *nasab*, although the former is, theoretically speaking, accessible to any Muslim compared with the exclusivity of the latter. If one has to be born into a *nasab*, one has only to attach oneself to a Sufi master over a protracted period to be initiated into a *silsila*. This functional similarity may turn *silsila* into a competitor of Prophetic *nasab*, particularly when both are understood as channels of knowledge transmission and spiritual blessings (*baraka*) constitutive of religious authority. Thus the *sayyid*s have persisted in emphasizing the centrality of Prophetic *nasab* as a channel that facilitates the inheritance of Prophetic teachings and blessings, thereby making it a prerequisite of authority and leadership of the Muslim community.[6] Nevertheless, *nasab* and *silsila* may also work together in augmenting the authority of Muslim leaders, forming family Sufi-order or saintly dynasties (like the manṣabate), and establishing hereditary successions of community leadership.[7]

If genealogy serves as a channel that links the present to the Prophetic past, mobility allows aspiring scholars to embed themselves in different genealogies of knowledge transmission. Traveling in search of teachers is a central trope in traditional Islamic education.[8] The *ḥadīth* literature reminds Muslims that "the search for knowledge is intimately tied to the physical act of travel."[9] Mobility and travel for the pursuit of knowledge and proselytization are also stressed in saintly hagiographies.[10] Travel confers distinction, expands social spaces, and shapes networks, thereby allowing the traveling actor to borrow the authority of others.[11] The importance of travel to the constitution of Islamic authority helps to explain why, traditionally, there are a disproportionate number of male religious authorities, compared with female.[12] While there are many explanations for this gender imbalance, one reason has to do with the ability to travel. Until the recent era, travel was seen by many Muslims as a dangerous endeavor not befitting a woman. The limitations on women's travel disadvantaged many of them from achieving positions of authority compared to men.

Those who completed a journey in search of knowledge and returned to their homeland are perceived by others to have expanded religious knowledge and broader social ties. Certain itineraries—say, traveling to Mecca, Cairo, or the Ḥaḍramawt—are deemed more prestigious than traveling to local educational institutions. It is perhaps partly for this reason that recent scholarship has focused on transregional travel as the most important and socially consequential form of religious mobility.[13] The work of Magnus Marsden, however, diverges from this trend by drawing attention to local and regional practices of mobility.[14] Working among the Chitralis of northern Pakistan, Marsden highlights how local tours serve to "cultivate in young village minds a sense of curiosity about their region and diverse influences found therein."[15] Such trips afford the Chitralis with "broader insights into the complexity of collective and personal forms of Muslim self-understanding" and shape "complex forms of emotional and intellectual attachment to their region and a curiosity about its heterogeneity."[16] Marsden further suggests that the cultivation of such a critical mode of perceiving the self and the world diverges from recent anthropological depictions of Islamic ethical practices amongst urban-based piety-minded Muslims.[17] In contrast to the active habituation of textual or discursive moral norms practiced by the latter, Chitrali tours hinge on "the appreciation of a mindful, if often sceptical, curiosity about heterogeneity."[18] Congruent with Marsden's findings, this chapter demonstrates how Habib Luthfi's educational mobility in Java not only allows him to tap into different genealogies of Islamic transmission by encountering numerous teachers and connectors to the Prophetic past, but also formed his sensitivity toward local sociocultural heterogeneity. This, in turn, has shaped his understanding of Islam. The experience accrued from travel has afforded Habib Luthfi the ability to envision the *sunna* as culturally embedded norms that are mindful of, and dialogically entangled with, local sociocultural particularities.

The case of Habib Luthfi pushes us to think about the contingent relationship between genealogy and mobility in the constitution of religious authority. Genealogy, as Engseng Ho has shown in his work on the Bā ʿAlawīs, may serve as a theory of ethical mobility. Genealogy encapsulates discourses that mobilize places, texts, and persons in meaningful narratives of travel.[19] The temporally structured genealogy, Ho suggests, functions to direct the spatial mobility of the bearer of the genealogy. This imperative to synchronize mobility and genealogy is the primary reason why most Indonesian Bā ʿAlawīs are sent to study under Bā ʿAlawī teachers—whether in Indonesia or Arabia—instead of attending institutions headed by non–Bā ʿAlawī teachers. In light of Ho's work, the case of Habib Luthfi becomes interesting owing to the divergence of his mobility from the directive of his own genealogy. Habib Luthfi's divergent itinerary, however, allowed him to tap into other non–Bā ʿAlawī genealogies through what I call *genealogical adoption.* Divergent mobility and adoptive genealogy thus constitute both the spatial and temporal foundations of Habib Luthfi's religious authority, one that is at variance with his fellow Bā ʿAlawīs, but which nevertheless opens up new articulatory possibilities. This is by no means unique to Habib Luthfi. James Hoesterey's work on Abdullah Gymnastiar, a highly successful contemporary Islamic self-help guru in Indonesia, illustrates how the ability to tap into non-Islamic genealogies of knowledge such as "New Age sciences and [the] self-help circuit popular in the United States during the 1970s–1980s" enabled Gymnastiar to position himself as a "dispenser of the practical wisdom that can help Muslims overcome problems in their everyday lives."[20] In articulating Prophetic teachings, Gymnastiar and other "Muslim trainers" like him "summon the perceived legitimacy of Western academics and self-help gurus," thereby allowing them to cultivate Islamic communities comprising the urban-based, secular-educated Indonesian middle class.[21] One should note, however, that Gymnastiar's ability to tap into non-Islamic genealogies of knowledge to produce novel Islamic discourse has a long precedent. The notion of "Prophetic medicine" that emerged in the fourteenth century, to give one example, was, after all, a new synthetic medical discourse that resulted from "a critical evaluation of Greek medical traditions alongside relevant Prophetic *ḥadīth*."[22] If the case of Gymnastiar points to the ability of Muslim trainers to tap into non-Islamic genealogies of knowledge to produce novel Islamic discourses, that of Habib Luthfi attests to the heterogeneous genealogies of Islamic knowledge that an aspiring scholar can tap into to open up new articulatory possibilities. Both the case of Habib Luthfi and that of Gymnastiar provoke us to think about how the contingent relationship between mobility and genealogy of knowledge can engender different forms of religious authority.

Divergent Mobility

Warung Bang Hoody is a modest café in South Jakarta owned by Hood Segaf, a middle-aged second-generation Bā ʿAlawī. In the evenings, the outdoor seating area is frequented by young Bā ʿAlawī men, who gather to converse all night long until Hood decides to turn off the lights and kick them out. The café is a place where one hears the latest gossip on Indonesian Bā ʿAlawīs. It is also a place to meet elusive individuals who are otherwise difficult to encounter, like Saleh. A native of Tegal, Central Java, Saleh is a rather controversial character, who first became known as a psychic. In Indonesia, such an ability can take its possessor to high places. In the 1990s he developed a close relationship with the family of President Suharto and several leading army generals, including the then-commander of the armed forces, General Wiranto. In 1998, Saleh's name surfaced in the national media when he assembled a militia to support the newly installed President Habibie—the handpicked successor of Suharto—against the proreform student activists. In that same year, Saleh introduced a young and relatively unknown Bā ʿAlawī schoolteacher, Rizieq Shihab, to his military friends, leading to the establishment of the now notorious vigilante organization the Islamic Defenders Front (Front Pembela Islam, FPI). In 2000, his name once again became the talk of the town when then-president Abdurrahman Wahid publicly accused Saleh, together with Suharto's youngest son, Tommy, of being the masterminds behind the bombing of the Jakarta Stock Exchange.

One evening in December 2011, as I was conversing with Hood at the café, Saleh walked in and sat with us. We talked and joked about Indonesian politics until he said, rather unexpectedly:

> I heard from people you are doing your research on Luthfi? Why do you bother with him? He is just a *dawir*, not a scholar who graduated from an institution [*maʿhad*]. Why would someone who studies in America spend his time writing about Luthfi?

Saleh remained dismissive when I explained my research project to him. Minutes later, he lost interest in the topic altogether and decided to talk to Hood about the property market. What is interesting from my brief conversation with Saleh was his use of the term *dawir* to characterize Habib Luthfi. As used by Indonesian Bā ʿAlawīs, the term *dawir* comes from the Arabic *dawr*, which in its verbal form means "to go around, to circulate." One may think that *dawir* is an apt adjective to describe the Bā ʿAlawīs, whose long history has been characterized by transregional mobility. In contemporary Java, however, the term is used derogatorily to refer to Bā ʿAlawīs—or other Ḥaḍramīs pretending to be Bā ʿAlawīs—who frequent the rural areas to profit from the respect shown toward them by the locals. A *dawir* is usually an itinerant peddler who brings a variety of merchandise to be sold at exorbitant prices, knowing that the villagers will never dare to bargain. Often, he plays the role of a wandering holy man, reciting prayers and invocations in exchange for monetary gifts.

This practice of preying on the rural population has exasperated many Bā ʿAlawī scholars and *manṣabs*. As a result, forms of mobility that involve traveling to rural areas have been increasingly viewed with suspicion among the urban-based Bā ʿAlawīs. One form of itinerancy that has suffered from this changing perception of mobility is *lelono*, or wandering in search for knowledge. *Lelono* is a time-honored educational rite of passage practiced by Javanese seekers of spiritual knowledge, including Prince Dipanagara, discussed in chapter 1. For the Javanese, *lelono* means "to find wisdom in the sense of finding a teacher who could guide one's development."[23] The practice resembles the Islamic tradition of *riḥla*—that is, traveling to seek "advanced learning in religious matters and spiritual fulfillment."[24] While *riḥla* is a central trope in the hagiographies of leading Bā ʿAlawī saints and scholars, the practice has now gone out of fashion. Literally speaking, however, Saleh is right in characterizing Habib Luthfi as a *dawir*, for central to his biographical becoming were the years he spent wandering around the rural areas of Java in pursuit of knowledge.

* * *

Habib Luthfi was born in 1947 in Pekalongan. Unlike most Ḥaḍramī families, his did not live in the Arab quarter, but in a narrow alley in the neighborhood of Kwijan, among the less well-off Javanese. His father, Ali, was a violinist playing for a local musical troupe. His mother, Nur, looked after her six children. Both Habib Luthfi's paternal and maternal families have been in Java for at least six generations. The future Sufi master grew up playing with Javanese boys in Kwijan. Unlike most Ḥaḍramī boys of the Arab quarter, who went to private Islamic schools like the Ḥaddādian Salafiyya or the modernist Ma'had discussed in chapter 3, Habib Luthfi went to a government school. He did, however, attend the classes held by the then *manṣab* of Pekalongan, ʿAlī b. Aḥmad al-ʿAṭṭās, which familiarized him with the Ḥaddādian tradition. Upon graduating from the primary school in 1959, his father sent him to the old *pesantren* (Islamic boarding school) of Benda in the village of Benda Kerep, Cirebon (West Java). Established by Kyai Saleh Zamzami (d. 1727) in the early eighteenth century, Benda is an ultraconservative institution known for prohibiting the use of electricity and other modern innovations in its vicinity. The *pesantren* was also a center of the Shaṭṭāriyya Sufi order.[25] It was at Benda that Habib Luthfi became acquainted with non-Ḥaddādian Sufism as practiced by his Javanese teachers.

Traditional Javanese *pesantrens* like Benda concentrate on producing *shaykhs al-taʿlīm* who can provide Islamic theological and legal education to their fellow Muslims. Education is geared toward developing a mastery of Ashʿarite theological and Shāfiʿī legal texts, particularly the ability to translate them into Javanese. Being at Benda allowed Habib Luthfi to hone his mastery of the Javanese language, especially the high register not commonly used by people in Pekalongan. Living in Cirebon also enabled him to learn Sundanese.

Concurrently, studying in a Javanese *pesantren* exposed Habib Luthfi to traditionalist Javanese scholars and students who subsequently became community leaders in various places. Competency in local languages and contact with traditionalist Javanese and Sundanese scholars were two crucial foundations of his future career. His subsequent popularity as a preacher is due to, among other things, a competency in different Javanese and Sundanese linguistic registers rarely exhibited by other Bā ʿAlawī scholars.

Habib Luthfi's formative education diverged from the educational trend of most Bā ʿAlawī scholars. While, generally, Bā ʿAlawī scholars in Indonesia have studied under older Bā ʿAlawī scholars, Habib Luthfi learned Islamic sciences under Javanese scholars. As an illustration, let us compare Habib Luthfi's education to that of the current *manṣab* of Pekalongan, Habib Bagir. As a scion of a saintly dynasty, Habib Bagir has been immersed in the Ḥaddādian tradition since his childhood. He studied with both his father and grandfather before enrolling in a *pesantren* in East Java run by the charismatic Bā ʿAlawī scholar Husein b. Abu Bakar al-Habsyi (d. 1994).[26] Known as the Yayasan Pesantren Islam (Islamic Pesantren Foundation, YAPI), the *pesantren* was one of the preferred educational destinations for aspiring Bā ʿAlawī scholars of Habib Bagir's generation. Classes were conducted not in Javanese, but in Arabic. Unlike traditionalist *pesantrens* and their emphasis on the mastery of classical texts and the ability to translate them into Javanese, YAPI stressed Arabic language acquisition, which would allow students to continue their study abroad. For al-Habsyi and most Bā ʿAlawī scholars, Islamic education in Java is considered inadequate. Consequently, local Islamic educational institutions should be geared toward preparing students to continue their education in what they perceive to be "the central lands" of Islam. Al-Habsyi had developed close connections with several major Muslim scholars in the Middle East, including the eminent Meccan scholar Muḥammad b. ʿAlawī al-Mālikī (d. 2006). Al-Mālikī had agreed to take on and financially support promising YAPI students. Toward the end of the 1970s, dozens of young Indonesian Bā ʿAlawīs, including Habib Bagir, were sent to Mecca for further education.

The disparity in the educational trajectories of Habib Luthfi and Habib Bagir shaped their respective communication skills and social circles. While Habib Bagir speaks flawless Arabic, he does not speak any local language except for the low Javanese spoken in Pekalongan. His interactions with his Javanese followers tend to be conducted in formal Indonesian, rather than Javanese, which in most cases creates a distance between him and his audience. Unlike Habib Luthfi's vast networks among Javanese scholars, Habib Bagir's social network revolves mainly around his fellow Bā ʿAlawīs and several Javanese scholars who studied under al-Mālikī in Mecca. His fluency in Arabic and his experience of living in Mecca, however, have allowed Habib Bagir to develop connections with scholars from the Hejaz, the Ḥaḍramawt, and other parts of the Muslim world. Habib Luthfi, on the other hand, often found it difficult to communicate with foreign scholars as Arabic conversational skills were never part of the curriculum of the traditionalist Javanese *pesantren*. While graduates of Javanese *pesantrens* may master Arabic grammar down to the last detail, most lack adequate conversational skills to allow them to converse effectively in Arabic. Nevertheless, growing up outside the Arab quarter, attending a state school, and enrolling in a traditionalist Javanese *pesantren* shaped Habib Luthfi's ability to engage and interact with the broader Javanese society, which usually lies outside the parochialized social circle of most Ḥaḍramīs in Java.

* * *

After being at Benda for five years, Habib Luthfi wandered around the rural areas of Java in pursuit of knowledge. Among the teachers he studied with were Muhammad Bajuri (Indramayu, West Java), Said b. Armiya (Tegal, Central Java), Abdullah Hadziq (Jepara, Central Java), Aḥmad Bafaqih (Yogyakarta), Dimyati Kedawung (Comal, Central Java), Utsman al-Ishaqi (Surabaya, East Java), Ali Bafaqih (Negara, Bali), Noer Durya (Moga, Central Java), and Umar Bin Yahya (Arjawinangun, West Java). In Javanese traditionalist circles, these individuals tend to be referred to as *kyai khos*—from the Arabic *khāṣṣ* (pl. *khawāṣṣ*, "elect")—meaning scholars who are known primarily for their mastery of Islamic esoteric knowledge, like Sufism. Most *kyai khos* belong to a Sufi order, although not all perform the role of a Sufi master (*murshid*) who guides initiated disciples. Many did not even establish a *pesantren*, opting to teach a few students from the privacy of their own homes. Apart from teaching, *kyai khos* usually perform other roles in their localities, such as mediating village conflicts, curing illnesses, exorcism, and writing amulets.

In his speeches and conversations, Habib Luthfi often points to how the years of peregrination shaped his appreciation of the dynamic and contingent relationship between the *sunna* and the community. Here I quote two excerpts taken from his sermons, both of which discuss some of the things he learned during his wandering years. These sermons, which I recorded, were delivered in his congregational center in January and October 2012, respectively:

> Whenever the villagers of Balongan [Indramayu, West Java] held a *slametan* [thanksgiving ritual feast], they would put a cup filled with a mixture of tea and coffee at the center of where people were sitting. They called it *wedang jembawuk*, and it was meant as an offering to the ancestral spirits [*arwah leluhur*]. My teacher, Granpa Bajuri, did not discourage them from doing

> so. He was invited by the villagers to attend the *slametan*, and he attended without saying anything. One day, Granpa Bajuri told the village elders that one cup is not adequate as an offering. They should add six more cups and that each should contain different sweetened liquid. He himself started to put seven cups during a *slametan* that he held, each containing coffee, tea, Fanta, orange juice, milk, Coca Cola, and coconut water. When the villagers asked him as to the significance of the seven liquids, he told them that when the Prophet Muḥammad was dying, he asked for seven cups of waters taken from the seven springs of Medina. As to their sweetness, Granpa Bajuri explained that the Prophet used to like sweet things. So today the *sunna* of having seven sugary liquids has persisted in Balongan and what Granpa Bajuri did was to make what used to be an offering to the ancestral spirits into a way to remember and emulate the Prophet.

> When I was living with Granpa Arwani in Kudus [Central Java], I asked him, "Granpa, why is it that in Kudus, no one slaughters a cow during the *ʿĪd al-Aḍḥā* [Festival of the Sacrifice]?" Granpa Arwani explained to me how this had been the way people of Kudus practice Islam. They forbid the slaughtering of cows, although it is *ḥalāl* [lawful]. This rule was introduced by the Lord Sunan Kudus [one of the nine saints of Java] when he noticed that most people living in Kudus were Hindus and he did not want to offend them by slaughtering cows. So he made a new rule that forbids the slaughtering of cows during the *ʿĪd al-aḍḥā* and asked his followers to slaughter water buffalos instead. This has remained the *sunna* of the people of Kudus.

From both excerpts, one can see how Habib Luthfi's experience of living in several localities, encountering problems that arose from the messiness of social life, and seeing his teachers handling such situations, formed his sensitivity toward cultural and societal differences that demand different approaches. In both cases, scholars articulate localized *sunna*, rather than imposing one version of the *sunna* on the local people. They were less interested in applying categorical legal concepts like *ḥalāl* or *ḥarām*, and instead, were more attentive to producing new meanings out of old practices and maintaining communal harmony. Not unlike the traditional Moroccan judges (*qāḍī*s) and Yemeni jurisconsults (*muftī*s) observed by Lawrence Rosen and Brinkley Messick, in the hands of these scholars, religious norms become organically linked to the surrounding cultural processes.[27]

Habib Luthfi once told me how living in the villages made him realize how the models of Islamic societies that he learned from studying Islamic legal texts in the *pesantren*—most of which are taken from medieval Baghdad, Damascus, or Cairo—cannot be realized in a place like Java, where people are facing dissimilar problems. Such a sensitivity toward cultural differences and social complexities was gained through *lelono/riḥla*. This is not to say that *lelono/riḥla* is not geared toward the acquisition of spiritual knowledge. Nor does it negate the fact that the objective of *lelono/riḥla* is the cultivation of embodied virtues through face-to-face contact with virtuous individuals.[28] It is simply to suggest a need to pay more attention to the sociocultural dimension of *lelono/riḥla* beyond the master-disciple relationship. At least in the case of Java, where scholars and spiritual masters live among local populations and play important social roles, *lelono/riḥla* does not negate social space and time, contrary to what an anthropologist has suggested regarding the tradition of Sufi wandering in Morocco.[29]

* * *

It was two in the morning, and we were on the road from Surabaya to Pekalongan. Habib Luthfi was sitting next to the driver, finishing his cigarette. I was in the back seat with two of the *habib*'s aides. The car was moving fast. The road was empty except for two or three lorries, which we were able to overtake easily. Usually, we would spend the journey conversing, while Yanni—Habib Luthfi's favorite composer—plays in the background. Being in the car for nine hours provided me with the rare opportunity to converse with Habib Luthfi without interruption. On that particular journey, however, everyone seemed to be too exhausted to chat. We had just left Pekalongan the night before, arriving in Surabaya just before dawn. After lunch, Habib Luthfi gave talks at three different venues. After the last event, which ended at 11 p.m., we immediately drove back to Pekalongan. From the rear-view mirror, I could see that the *habib* was about to fall asleep. He put out his cigarette, covered his head with a white cotton scarf, and closed his eyes. He must have fallen asleep, I thought, and so I decided to rest my eyes. But all of a sudden, I heard him speak:

> In the *pesantren*, I learned dead knowledge [*ilmu mati*]. Again and again, we studied text, text, and text. When I traveled, however, I learned wisdom [*ḥikma*]. The scholars I encountered were not known for their textual knowledge. Yet from them, I learned living knowledge [*ilmu hidup*]. It is true that the knowledge of the saints is living knowledge.

Puzzled by this offhand comment, I asked him what he meant by "living knowledge." "You are the anthropologist," he replied, "You study human life. You of all people should know." Not knowing how to respond, I waited for the *habib* to say more. But nothing was forthcoming and before long, we all took the gift of sleep.

It took me a few months to realize what Habib Luthfi meant by living knowledge. That moment of realization presented itself one afternoon when I arrived at the *habib*'s house to find him sitting with eight recent graduates of a *pesantren*, all men in their early twenties. They had come to visit the *habib* to seek his blessing and advice. "You have learned all the necessary books in the *pesantren*," Habib Luthfi told them,

> What remains for you is to try to gain wisdom. Remember what Allāh said to the Prophet: *Allāh had sent down the book* [*al-kitāb*] *and wisdom* [*ḥikma*] [Q. 4:113]. Knowing the book without wisdom freezes your knowledge. But if you have wisdom, the knowledge of the book that you have within you will spread and move others. You learn wisdom not from the books. You learn it from the people, by being with them and understanding their culture [*kultur*]. I understand that you have a strong zeal [*himmah yang kuat*] to teach others what you have learned, especially when you see practices that go against the *sunna*. But you should also learn that life is complex. Do not try to make people change their habits if you want them to hear and follow you. Instead, learn from them. By understanding their habits, you will be able to attract them. The Prophet prescribed different things to different people according to their capacities. To a companion, he prescribed an invocation be repeated one thousand times. To another, he prescribed the same invocation be repeated only thirty-three times. So do not just impose one particular *sunna* on everyone. You should strive to act as the Prophet did.

Habib Luthfi's advice to the *pesantren* graduates sums up his mode of articulatory labor. It made me realize that what he meant by living knowledge is a knowledge that moves and mobilizes, thereby creating a difference in the world. While the mobility of knowledge requires infrastructure, channels, and pathways, its ability to mobilize demands that the knowledge is comprehensible to others through their particular cultural assumptions and fulfills their specific needs. For Habib Luthfi, the *sunna* is not singular. The Prophet prescribed different things to different people because he was aware of individual variations. Thus, in the *habib*'s view, a one-size-fits-all religious approach will not work because of the complexity of human social life. The ways in which Prophetic teachings are selected and articulated ought to depend on the particularity of the context where those teachings are to be socially realized. For Habib Luthfi, wisdom mediates the tensions between prescription and freedom that characterize human ethical life.[30]

What the case of Habib Luthfi accentuates is precisely how *lelono*/*riḥla* exposes students, particularly those who were trained in scholastic settings, to the complexity and heterogeneity of social life. As a dialogical process, *lelono*/

riḥla teaches a wandering student that a productive alignment between the *sunna* and the community requires their mutual calibration. Such activity, however, has become increasingly rare in the Islamic educational tradition in Java. In most cases, students finish their studies at a single *pesantren*. While there are still students who move from place to place, they do so only to advance from one *pesantren* to another.[31] In the case of most Indonesian Bā ʿAlawīs, religious education has become even more detached from the localities, in that education in Java is concerned primarily with preparing students to go to places that are perceived to be the fount of genuine knowledge of the *sunna*, like the Hejaz or the Ḥaḍramawt. Consequently, what is understood as the *sunna* becomes increasingly detached, objectified, and estranged from the dialogical entanglements with the sociocultural particularities that make up a community.

Genealogical Adoption

Habib Luthfi's final destination in his wandering days was the village of Kedungparuk, Purwokerto (Central Java), the home of the Naqshbandī-Khālidī Sufi master Abdul Malik b. Muhammad Ilyas (d. 1980). He spent a total of twelve years in the company of Abdul Malik and was initiated into the Naqshbandī-Khālidī Sufi order. The Naqshbandiyya-Khālidiyya is a "suborder" of the Naqshbandī order instituted by an Ottoman Sufi master of Kurdish origin, Khālid al-Shahrazūrī (d. 1827). Driven by a desire to invigorate Islam in the face of the Ottoman decline, al-Shahrazūrī introduced three additional ritual practices into the established Naqshbandī spiritual discipline, which turned his community into a fast-growing, highly organized religious movement. These consisted of:

> the *khalwa arba'iniyya*, a concentrated seclusion of forty days which allowed him to authorize with great speed deputies to spread his message; the *rabita*, a mystical binding to his image designed to centralize their activity under his leadership; and *ghalq al-bab*, the closing of the door during the *dhikr* ceremony, which helped him to stress the uniqueness of his path.[32]

Within few decades, the Naqshbandiyya-Khālidiyya had spread all over the Ottoman lands and become a significant social force.[33]

The Naqshbandiyya-Khālidiyya became widespread in Java from the 1850s with the return of Javanese pilgrims who had been initiated into the order by the Daghestan-born master of Mecca Sulaymān Zuhdī. Among Zuhdī's pupils was Abdul Malik's father, Muhammad Ilyas. Upon returning from Mecca, Ilyas established himself in Sokaraja (Central Java) and began initiating people into the order.[34] His son Abdul Malik studied in Mecca for fifteen years and was initiated into the Naqshbandī-Khālidī and the Shādhilī orders. Upon his return to Java, Abdul Malik succeeded his father and inherited his community. Subsequently, he established himself in the village of Kedungparuk. Abdul Malik combined the teachings and litanies of the Naqshbandiyya-Khālidiyya and the Shādhiliyya that he received from his masters, creating his own "suborder," which he called the Naqshbandī-Khālidī-Shādhilī order (NKS). By following the Khālidī method of swift induction, Abdul Malik was able to rapidly produce deputies (*badal*), who could lead NKS rituals in different villages.

The NKS community was hierarchically organized. The community revolved around one master. Only the master was authorized to initiate people into the order. Members of the community could generally be separated into those who studied with the master intimately and those who only attended the weekly *dhikr* session. Those who studied with the master usually came to Kedungparuk from different places in Java. After performing the forty days' seclusion, they were appointed as deputies of the master and were sent back to their places of origin. The deputies were given the task of initiating people and leading weekly classes and worship sessions in their localities. Several times a year, the deputies brought the members of their respective communities for an audience with the master. The master also traveled to visit the communities assembled by his deputies. While deputies are permitted to initiate people into the order, they can do so only in the name of the master. Thus, when a deputy initiates people, he asks them to swear an oath of allegiance to the master and not to himself.

To aid his deputies in assembling their communities, Abdul Malik composed a prayer manual entitled *Al-Tarqīb al-uṣūl li tashīl al-wuṣūl* (Guarding the fundamentals to assist the communion).[35] The booklet begins with a *tawassul*, a supplication for a blessing on behalf of the Prophet, his companions, and their families, and continues with a list of the names of individuals who make up Abdul Malik's *silsila* (spiritual genealogy). The text instructs the readers to recite the *fātiḥa* (the first *sūra* of the Qur'ān) for the spirits of those who are named, while requesting their intercession. Naming the individuals that make one's *silsila* all the way back to the Prophet helps to cement the community's genealogical identity. As a gateway to a ritual session, the *tawassul* serves to anchor the gathering in a temporal framework that connects it to the Prophetic past, while projecting the *silsila* as the secure and authoritative channel through which Prophetic teachings are transmitted to the community. The bulk of the booklet consists of Qur'ānic verses and Prophetic prayers and invocations, some of which are to be recited multiple times. As an anthology of prayers and invocations organized in a specific order, the text constitutes the prescribed liturgy of the NKS. While most of the specific verses and prayers can be found in other prayer manuals, and are even recited by Muslims who do not belong to a Sufi order, what gives this anthology its specific NKS identity is the opening *tawassul*, its genealogical transmission, and its particular ordering, including the specific numbers in which Prophetic invocations should be recited. Like the Ḥaddādian litany, the *Al-Tarqīb al-uṣūl* is a particular articulation of the Prophetic *sunna* projected as credible and authoritative through the *silsila* of the master. Such a manual, in turn, allows the master's deputies to set up and lead their own congregations in their respective localities.

* * *

To be an initiated disciple of a Sufi master is to be adopted into the master's *silsila*. Being a disciple of a Sufi master involves submitting oneself to the master. In exchange for the disciple's loyalty and attachment, the master adopts him as his spiritual child, providing him with support, protection, and a *silsila*.[36] If *nasab* denotes bloodline, *silsila* designates spiritual genealogy—that is, a chain of transmission of spiritual knowledge and initiation that links a Sufi master to the Prophet Muḥammad through the founder of a Sufi order. *Silsila* has been a potent discursive and symbolic tool that has held together adherents of a Sufi order over the generational and geographic distances that divide them from the eponymous founder of the order. While *silsila* may or may not point to concrete bonds of connectivity, it nevertheless provides adherents of an order with a conceptual infrastructure that allows them to imagine themselves as belonging to an inherited religious tradition that ultimately goes back to the Prophet. As Nile Green explains, *silsila* "offered a way for initiates to conceive themselves as being meaningfully connected to the teachings and power of a Prophet who had lived centuries ago."[37] Equally important is how *silsila* works to declare an eponymous founder of a Sufi order as a successor of the Prophet who can impart Prophetic teachings and guidance to the community.[38]

Silsila endows disciples of a Sufi master with a spiritual genealogy in addition to their *nasab*. In doing so, it provides a recognizable link to the Prophet even when its possessor is not his descendant. *Silsila* and *nasab*, however, often intersect, creating tensions owing to the different ethical imperatives entailed by the two genealogical relations. Having two parallel genealogies may invoke questions regarding the primary locus of the disciple's ethical responsibility. What should the disciple do when the demands of the master conflict with those of the parents? Indeed, candid competition between a disciple's parents and his master is a persistent trope discussed in many hagiographical texts.[39] A disciple may frequently feel conflicted about his ethical obligations toward his parents and master, as the following story told to me by Habib Luthfi makes clear:

> Once, when I visited Granpa Ahmad Bafaqih in Tempel [Yogyakarta], he told me to stay and forbade me from leaving. I felt awful, as, at the time, I was the sole breadwinner of the family, and my mother's livelihood depended on me. I stayed for ten days with Granpa Ahmad and could not work. You see, I was selling *sarongs* at the time, which meant that I had to bring them to different markets and try selling them. Another week went by, and Granpa Ahmad still refused to grant me leave. I was constantly thinking about my mother. How is she going to eat next week? The next day, Granpa Ahmad called me and told me to return to my mother. On the one hand, I was relieved, but on the other hand, I did not have any money with me as I still had the *sarongs* that I was supposed to sell. But before leaving, Granpa Ahmad gave me Rp. 100,000 which in the seventies was a large sum of money. He told me, "no need to sell the *sarongs*; just go back to your mother."

While in this particular case, the master resolved the disciple's ethical dilemma, such an easy resolution does not always happen.

The entanglement between *nasab* and *silsila* is also discernible in the case of the so-called family *ṭarīqa*. A family *ṭarīqa* is a Sufi order in which the *nasab* of the master also functions as his *silsila* and where transmission of spiritual knowledge and leadership of the order are passed down within the family.[40] An example of a family *ṭarīqa* is the Bā ʿAlawī Sufi order the Ṭarīqa ʿAlawiyya, where *nasab* plays a crucial role in securing the transmission of knowledge and succession of leadership. Adoption of another *silsila* by a Bā ʿAlawī may, in turn, be seen as a form of disloyalty to one's *nasab*. Stories exchanged in informal conversations among Indonesian Bā ʿAlawīs or recounted in sermons during exclusive Bā ʿAlawī gatherings discourage them from following another Sufi order by presenting it as an act that would incur the anger of the ancestors. One popular anecdote tells of the arrival in Ḥaḍramawt of a Sufi master from Samarkand, who attempted to attract the Bā ʿAlawīs to his order. In a dream, the preacher encounters the spirit of the founder of the Ṭarīqa ʿAlawiyya, Muḥammad b. ʿAlī, who indignantly orders the preacher to leave *his children* alone. Another story presents the bleak eschatological future of a Bā ʿAlawī who entered another Sufi order:

> There was once a Bā ʿAlawī who joined another order and became attached to it. One night, he dreamt that he found himself in the Day of Resurrection when humans gather to await the divine verdict. He saw how all humans went and sought solace in their respective groups. So he went to the

gathering of the order that he had joined. The masters of that order, however, told him that there is no place for him there as he belongs to the Bā ʿAlawīs. So he looked for those who were gathering under the banner of the Ṭarīqa ʿAlawiyya. When he found them, the Bā ʿAlawī masters told him to leave, saying "you were once our son, but you have rejected us and joined another family." The man was thus left with no group to provide support.

Both anecdotes conflate *silsila* with *nasab*, which explains why Indonesian Bā ʿAlawīs can easily dismiss those among them who have joined another Sufi order. The poetic verses of the Bā ʿAlawī scholar-poet ʿAlī b. Muḥammad al-Ḥabashī (d. 1915), repeatedly evoked by Indonesian Bā ʿAlawī preachers in their sermons, capture the importance of synchronizing *silsila*, *nasab*, and mobility:

> Whoever does not tread the path [*ṭarīq*] of his family
> will become confused and lost
> O offshoots of the Prophet, trudge and emulate
> on the straight path [*al-ṭarīq*] and avoid innovations [*al-ibtidāʿ*].[41]

The imperative to synchronize mobility and genealogy is the primary reason why most Indonesian Bā ʿAlawīs have continued to question Habib Luthfi's authority.

* * *

Shortly before his death, Abdul Malik appointed Habib Luthfi as a master of the NKS order. The ninety-nine-year-old master instructed his family and followers to pledge their allegiance to Habib Luthfi. While Abdul Malik appointed his eldest grandson to continue and lead the community in Kedungparuk and initiate people into the order, the old master specified that he do so on behalf of Habib Luthfi. In other words, Abdul Malik's grandson was appointed a deputy of Habib Luthfi. When the nonagenarian master passed away in 1980, Habib Luthfi became the sole master of the NKS. From Abdul Malik, he inherited a considerably expansive community that had been assembled and maintained for more than a century, since the days of Abdul Malik's father, Muhammad Ilyas. Those who had pledged their allegiance to Abdul Malik renewed their pledge to Habib Luthfi. Unlike the internal conflicts that occur in many Sufi orders following the death of a master, the succession of the NKS leadership went smoothly. This was perhaps due to the fact that Abdul Malik did not have a son. Another reason was that both Abdul Malik and Habib Luthfi left the control of Kedungparuk to the children of the former's daughter. Thus, votive offerings and monetary gifts brought to the house and grave of

Abdul Malik, as well as the profit accrued from the sale of the prayer manuals, were left to Abdul Malik's family. In many cases, internal contestations over leadership succession are sparked by the question of who gets to control resources and income.

Genealogical adoption enabled Habib Luthfi to become the leader of an established social assemblage with multiple branches in different localities. Unlike the *manṣab* of Pekalongan, Habib Luthfi did not inherit a community leadership position from his father. By diverging from genealogically directed mobility, however, Habib Luthfi made himself available to be genealogically adopted by another father, who had his own community. Adopting a Bā ʿAlawī *sayyid* can become a source of pride for a Javanese master, as in a place like Java it implies a role reversal. It is quite uncommon for a Bā ʿAlawī to study under a Javanese teacher. In contrast, studying under a Bā ʿAlawī scholar allows an aspiring Javanese scholar—particularly one who does not come from an illustrious saintly or scholarly lineage—to be adopted into the Bā ʿAlawī *silsila*. Perhaps genealogical adoption was what attracted Javanese scholars to pledge allegiance to different Sufi orders, precisely because genealogy operates ideologically as a recognizable basis of religious authority, allowing others to perceive its bearers as credible connectors to the Prophetic past. Nevertheless, the genealogical adoption that allowed Habib Luthfi to become a leader of a mature community also came with a price, particularly after his return to the coastal city of Pekalongan.

The Return

When Habib Luthfi returned to Pekalongan, he had to face a society that was not well-disposed toward him. The Bā ʿAlawīs were under the authority of the *manṣab*. Other Muslim scholars were preoccupied with cultivating their own communities. There was not much room to maneuver, let alone to cultivate an Islamic community, without affronting other Muslim leaders. People close to Habib Luthfi recalled how he used to keep a low profile in Pekalongan. Although he was a Sufi master with a significant following outside of Pekalongan, Habib Luthfi carried himself like a commoner, dressed in jeans, T-shirt, and a leather jacket. With time, however, many began to notice that, at certain times, the dandy young man known to his friends as Upik would receive a busload of guests coming from out of town. One Bā ʿAlawī friend of Habib Luthfi recalled those days:

> Both Upik and I are from Pekalongan, but we did not know each other before the eighties. That was because I lived in the Arab quarter and he lived in Kwijan, so we did not play together. Plus, he was away for a long time.

> God knows where he went. I got to know him around the early eighties. We used to spend a lot of time together. I used to go with him to the cinema. He used to play the guitar. But then I noticed that every now and then, there would be a lot of people from the villages at his house. The house was tiny, and those guests would sit outside. I also noticed that they brought bottles of water and asked him to bless the water. When I asked Upik about it, he just smiled and said that they were his old friends. I gradually realized that he was a Sufi master. That is why he was always traveling. Again, God knows where he went.

While Habib Luthfi kept a low profile in Pekalongan, he maintained his role as a Sufi master by regularly visiting his followers in different villages across Java. Concurrently, his reputation as a preacher who spoke the language of the people was rising outside of Pekalongan.

Two controversies caused Habib Luthfi's name to surface in Pekalongan. The first concerned the printing of a text composed by Abdul Malik, entitled *Al-Miftāḥ al-maqāṣid li ahl al-tawḥīd* (The key to the aspirations of the people of unicity). The text is an anthology of poetic salutations to the Prophet Muḥammad (*ṣalawāt*) composed by different Muslim scholars and saints that Abdul Malik had received from his teachers in Java and the Hejaz. The printed version includes an epilogue by Habib Luthfi. Written in Arabic, the epilogue begins by discussing the merits of *ṣalawāt*, but moves to a personal testimony regarding the significance of Abdul Malik's anthology:

> On the afternoon of Sunday 17 Rabīʿ II 1397 [April 6, 1977] I was sitting in the house of Muhammad Sutiman in the village of Jenggot. With me was our master, the knower of Allāh [*al-ʿārif billāh*] Abdul Malik and several other brothers-in-Allāh, including Haji Abdul Adhim b. Abdul Qadir and the host, Muhammad Sutiman. The master was reciting the *ṣalawāt* that he had compiled, entitled *al-Miftāḥ al-maqāṣid*, and we were reciting with him. During the recitation, I suddenly witnessed the Master of the Sharīʿa [*ṣāḥib al-sharīʿa*, the Prophet] may peace and blessing be upon him. He was sitting on a throne, situated on an elevated dais. On his right was our master Abū Bakr al-Ṣiddīq and the Imam ʿAlī b. Abī Ṭālib, may Allāh be pleased with them both. Next to them were five of the ten companions promised with heaven [*khamsa min al-ṣaḥāba al-ʿashra al-mubashshara bi-l-janna*]. On his left was our master ʿUmar b. al-Khaṭṭāb and our master ʿUthmān b. ʿAffān, may Allāh be pleased with them both. Next to them were five of the ten companions promised with heaven. The master and I were standing in front of the Prophet, God's peace and blessings upon him. This was due to the blessing of the *al-Miftāḥ al-maqāṣid* written by our master Abdul Malik.[42]

The epilogue is signed by Habib Luthfi. Below his signature is a short paragraph, also in Arabic, written and signed by Abdul Adhim b. Abdul Qadir, a resident of Buaran, Pekalongan, that says:

> It should be known that this gnostic Habib [*al-ḥabīb al-ʿārif*], Muḥammad Luṭfī b. ʿAlī b. Hāshim b. ʿUmar b. Ṭāhā Bin Yaḥyā Bā ʿAlawī, has been blessed with many visions [*kathīr al-ruʾya*] of the Prophet, God's peace and blessings upon him, both in waking and sleeping states [*yaqaẓatan wa manāman*].[43]

The circulation of the printed *Al-Miftāḥ al-maqāṣid* sparked controversy in Pekalongan. Initially, a local senior scholar got hold of a copy and began duplicating the epilogue and sending it to other scholars. They met to discuss the issue and agreed to reject the validity of the testimony and sent a written warning to Habib Luthfi. At issue is the claim of sainthood coming from a relatively young and unknown person. While Habib Luthfi clearly states that the vision was the result of reciting Abdul Malik's anthology, yet the only person who witnessed the vision was Habib Luthfi (and perhaps Abdul Malik, although this is unclear from the text). Implicit in his testimony of the merit of the *ṣalawāt* anthology is an indirect claim regarding his own spiritual station. In many parts of the Muslim world, the ability to see the spirit of the Prophet either in a dream or in a waking state is understood to index the sanctity of the dreamer/seer.[44] It was this implicit claim to sainthood, or having direct access to the spirit of the Prophet, that angered local scholars. In their view, such a public claim could lead to the proliferation of similar claims, which in turn, may cause widespread confusion.

* * *

The second controversy concerned Habib Luthfi's involvement with the ruling New Order regime. From the early 1970s, the Indonesian government had been active in promoting Islamization programs at the grassroots level. Such programs were devised to bring Muslim scholars, most of whom were more disposed toward the Islamic political party—the Partai Persatuan Pembangunan (PPP)—into the orbit of the regime and to purge the society of what the government saw as the remnants of communism. In 1971, the government initiated the Religious Mentality Promotion Project (Proyek Pembinaan Mental Agama, P2A), aimed at strengthening public religiosity.[45] The ruling political party, Golongan Karya (Golkar) also instituted an Islamic Mission Council (Majelis Dakwah Islamiyah, MDI) for a similar purpose.[46] For most traditionalist scholars, the activities of the MDI were perceived as a direct threat to their own sphere of influence. Backed by the government and local military apparatus, the MDI organized Islamic activities in both urban and rural areas without heeding the authority of local scholars, and actively campaigned for Golkar during general elections. The MDI also supported scholars who joined its campaigns and disregarded the social standing of those who refused to do so. Despite the efforts of the uncooperative scholars to discourage their followers from attending events organized by the MDI, many chose to do so, particularly when the organization was able to bring in popular preachers and celebrities from Jakarta. Through initiatives like the P2A and the MDI, the state involved itself in shaping the religious lives of its citizens and intruded into the traditional domain of village- and neighborhood-based *shaykhs al-taʿlīm*. The MDI also became an effective vehicle for new and less-influential scholars to cultivate their communities. With the financial support of the government and the backing of the local state apparatus, these scholars were able to build their own mosques and schools, organize events, and print booklets and pamphlets in their effort to expand their regime-friendly Islamic communities.

Not long after his return to Pekalongan, Habib Luthfi became affiliated with the MDI and was subsequently appointed as the advisor for Islamic affairs to the local branch of Golkar. This involvement allowed him to establish connections with the leading members of local government, including the mayor, the police chief, and the commander of the district military command. Formal entry into Golkar allowed Habib Luthfi to gain resources and protection from the local government. It was during this time that the *habib* began to organize his own annual *mawlid* (the birth of the Prophet) celebration. Financial support and protection from local government helped him to host the annual event. The *mawlid* drew the participation of all of his NKS deputies and their followers. Previously, the yearly *mawlid* of the NKS order had been staged in Kedungparuk, and Habib Luthfi himself had to travel there for the occasion. From the mid-1980s, however, Habib Luthfi has been able to host his own *mawlid*. This marked a crucial step in the relocation of the center of the NKS order from Kedungparuk to Pekalongan.

Habib Luthfi's formal entry into Golkar further aggravated the traditionalist scholars of Pekalongan, who were already irritated by his claim to Prophetic vision. Most traditionalist scholars of Pekalongan were not willing to associate themselves with him. They forbade members of their community from attending his *mawlid*. One senior scholar of Pekalongan and an active functionary of the PPP, Kyai Tolha (d. 2005), even delivered a speech in front of an assembly of local scholars, warning them from associating with Habib Luthfi. One elderly scholar recounted to me parts of Kyai Tolha's speech:

> Yes, Habib Luthfi is an offspring of the Prophet [*putro wayahe kanjeng nabi*]. And we love him for that. But, at this moment, he is not in the

condition of ritual purity. He is akin to a woman during menstruation. Just as we do not touch our beloved wives during their menstrual cycles, we should not touch Habib Luthfi. God willing [*insha Allāh*] soon, his menstruation will come to an end, and we can embrace him again.

* * *

Most Bā ʿAlawīs of Pekalongan were also dismissive of Habib Luthfi, although this was primarily because of his divergent educational mobility and spiritual genealogy. To make it worse, his Sufi order, the Naqshbandiyya-Khālidiyya, had been severely criticized by Ḥaddādian scholars for its tendency to liberally initiate people into the order. In the late nineteenth century, for example, an eminent Bā ʿAlawī Ḥaddādian scholar and self-proclaimed *muftī* of Batavia, Uthmān b. ʿAbdallāh Bin Yaḥyā (d. 1914), criticized the Naqshbandī-Khālidī masters for initiating people who were yet to learn the basics of Islam.[47] To the present day, ʿUthmān's criticisms of the Naqshbandiyya-Khālidiyya are often invoked by the Bā ʿAlawīs to criticize Habib Luthfi. Not only did Habib Luthfi adopt another *silsila*, but he chose one that had been reprimanded by a Bā ʿAlawī scholar whose authority is generally recognized by the Bā ʿAlawīs. Committed to the Ḥaddādian paradigm, most Bā ʿAlawīs were of the opinion that the notion of an organized Sufi order is superfluous. In their view, it is sufficient to stick to learning the Ḥaddādian legal abridgments, creeds, and litanies without having to pledge allegiance to a Sufi master.

In the early 1990s, the tension between Habib Luthfi and the Bā ʿAlawīs of Pekalongan weakened, owing to the emergence of a Bā ʿAlawī Shīʿī community. While there were a handful Bā ʿAlawī actors in the past who had become Shīʿī and preached Shīʿism in their own ways, the 1979 Iranian revolution sparked a growing interest in Shīʿism among Indonesian Bā ʿAlawīs in an unprecedented way. In the 1980s several young Indonesian Bā ʿAlawīs went to the *hawzeh* (seminary) of Qom (Iran) and, upon their return, disseminated Shīʿism to their fellow Bā ʿAlawīs and other Muslims.[48] One graduate of the Iranian *hawzeh,* Salim of Pekalongan, established his own Shīʿī *pesantren* in the Arab quarter in 1989. The *pesantren*'s curriculum was inspired by those used in the *hawzeh.* In fact, the aim of the institution is to provide preparatory education to help its pupils gain admission into the *hawzeh.*[49] From my conversation with Salim, I gathered that, aside from the success of the Iranian revolution, what drew him and his fellow Bā ʿAlawīs to Shīʿism was its recognition of the *ahl al-bayt*—that is, the Prophet's family—as the most authoritative articulators of Prophetic *sunna.* Shīʿī Bā ʿAlawīs were highly critical of the Sunnī *ḥadīth* collections, which in their view are replete with fabricated reports and downplay the importance of the *ahl al-bayt.* In contrast, Shīʿī Bā

ʿAlawīs assert that one can learn the Prophetic teachings only from the Prophet's progeny—that is, the twelve infallible imams believed to be the divinely designated successors of the Prophet and articulators of his *sunna*. Shīʿism as taught and practiced in Iran, in turn, is posited to be the authentic continuation of the Imams' teachings.

Salim explained to me that the Bā ʿAlawīs were originally Shīʿīs. They had to practice *taqīyya* (religious dissimulation) for fear of their safety when they migrated from Iraq to the Ḥaḍramawt, and gradually forgot their true religious orientation. However, Salim continued, the situation is changing:

> God be praised that with the help of modern technology and media He guides us back to the original teachings of our ancestors. From the television, we learned of the great Islamic revolution. Iran is the land of Salmān, a companion most beloved to the Prophet. He said, "Salmān is from us the family of the Prophet." The Prophet counted Salmān as his family, even though he was Persian. Now, we, the offspring of the Prophet are being reconnected again to our grandfather through the Persians.

Note the similarity between Habib Luthfi and Salim in that both were able to assume a position of authority and assemble their own Islamic communities through divergent itineraries of mobility and adoptive genealogy. Traveling to Iran and studying under Shīʿī scholars enabled Salim to be adopted into the genealogy of his Persian teachers. Salim, however, does not posit his adoption into the *silsila* of his Persian teachers as a betrayal of his *nasab*. Rather, adopting Shīʿīsm was considered to be a form of "ancestral allegiance."[50] For Salim, it was his Persian teachers who had been adopted into the Prophetic genealogy, while the Sunnīfication of the Bā ʿAlawīs had broken the confluence of the *nasab* and the *silsila*. Consequently, those with Prophetic *nasab*, like him, had to regain their true *silsila* from the Iranian scholars.

Through his active proselytization, Salim was able to win converts from among his fellow Bā ʿAlawīs. Those who converted to Shīʿīsm stopped recognizing the *manṣab* as a credible religious authority. The growth of the Shīʿī community created a rift among the Bā ʿAlawīs of Pekalongan. Many Bā ʿAlawī families were divided, including that of the *manṣab*. When Manṣab ʿAlī passed away in 1992 and his eldest son Aḥmad took over, the latter was no longer the unitary spiritual leader of the Bā ʿAlawīs of Pekalongan. One result of this rift, however, was the strengthening of the connection between Habib Luthfi and the Sunnī Bā ʿAlawīs of Pekalongan. In the face of a growing Shīʿī community, Sufi affiliation ceased to be a decisive issue. Up to the mid-1990s, Habib Luthfi and Habib Bagir—who was to succeed his father Aḥmad as the third *manṣab* in 1999—were working hand in hand to halt the spread of Shīʿīsm among young Bā ʿAlawīs. They jointly organized classes on "the danger of Shīʿī deviations" (*bahaya kesesatan Syiah*) utilizing heresiological texts like that authored by the medieval Sunnī theologian al-Shahrastānī (d. 1153). The liaison, however, did not last long.

* * *

In 1997, Habib Luthfi began the construction of his congregational center. Before the establishment of the center, the Sufi master was interacting with his disciples—most of whom came from elsewhere—in his small house in a narrow alley in Pekalongan's Noyontaan neighborhood. Having neither a mosque nor a prayer hall, he had to be content with holding rituals at his house. His followers flocked and congested the alley, generating complaints from the neighbors. Thus there was an excitement among Habib Luthfi's disciples when they heard that their master was finally building a proper place of assembly. Others were skeptical of the project's feasibility, considering the financial crisis. Still, there were others who saw the move as a provocation against the manṣabate of Pekalongan.

During the ground-breaking ceremony, Habib Luthfi unveiled the name of the future building: the Kanzus Shalawat (*Kanz al-ṣalawāt*), the treasury of *ṣalawāt* (salutation to the Prophet Muḥammad). Since its completion, the Kanzus Shalawat has become a thriving congregational center where Habib Luthfi's followers assemble regularly (see figure 4.1). The center serves as a site where the bonds between Habib Luthfi and his disciples are reproduced through different interactions and ritual events. The center also hosts weekly classes on Islamic law, which help to establish it as an Islamic congregational center for local Muslims and not solely for Habib Luthfi's initiated disciples. While the texts are recited in Arabic, they are translated into Indonesian, thereby making their content available to a broader audience. Many of those who frequent the Islamic law class, for instance, are not interested in Sufism or Sufi orders. One lady who hailed from the Mandailing cultural group of North Sumatra and has lived in Pekalongan for thirty-odd years confessed to me that she is an active member of the modernist organization Muhammadiyah, and that she attends the class simply because she wants to learn Islamic law. Habib Luthfi occasionally hosts cultural performances at the center, like the traditional Javanese shadow puppet (*wayang kulit*) or the Sundanese wooden puppet (*wayang golek*), which attract the wider public. The variety of events and classes, as well as the usage of the national language, have allowed the Kanzus Shalawat to become a more open congregational center. This contrasts with the al-Rawḍa mosque—the seat of the manṣabate—and its pedantic commitment to the Arabic language and Bā ʿAlawī rituals. The Kanzus Shalawat, on the other hand, was consciously configured as an Indonesian rather than a Ḥaḍramī or Bā ʿAlawī congregational center.

FIGURE 4.1 Habib Muhammad Luthfi Bin Yahya addressing the congregation at the Kanzus Shalawat. (Photo by the author)

The establishment of the Kanzus Shalawat reignited the tension between Habib Luthfi and the third *manṣab* of Pekalongan, Habib Bagir, which remains to the present day. At stake is the existence of two congregational centers in close proximity to each other, each headed by a Bā ʿAlawī scholar who is actively cultivating Islamic communities. The tension intensified in 2000 after Habib Luthfi was elected—through a conclave of senior Sufi masters representing different Sufi orders—as the chairman of the Association of Recognized Sufi Orders (Jamʿiyyah Ahlith Thoriqoh al-Mu'tabarah an-Nahdliyyah, JATMAN). JATMAN is an autonomous body under Indonesia's largest Islamic organization, the traditionalist Nahdlatul Ulama.[51] As the leader of a nationwide organization, Habib Luthfi enjoys considerable media attention, which he has used partly to call on Indonesian Muslims to join a recognized or authoritative (*muʿtabar*) Sufi order.

While Habib Bagir does not directly criticize Habib Luthfi, he often openly questions the authority of those who claim to be Sufi masters, without naming names. For example, during a ritual event I attended at the al-Rawḍa mosque in April 2012, Habib Bagir gave a short impromptu talk about the role of a Sufi master:

> A real master is almost impossible to find these days. Many claim that they are Sufi masters, but there are heavy prerequisites for becoming a Sufi master. A master has to act in full accordance with the Prophetic *sunna*. A real master guides by acts [*bi-l-ḥāl*] and not merely by speech [*bi-l-maqāl*], let alone ceremonies [*upacara-upacara*] or organizations. . . . What is more important is to follow the *sunna* as elucidated in the texts of Imam al-Ḥaddād. These texts are accessible to all and are realizable in our daily lives. These texts already encapsulate Islamic law, theology, ethics, and Sufism. As such they are more than adequate.

It is unclear whether Habib Bagir had Habib Luthfi and his community in mind when he delivered the talk. The relationship between the two has certainly not been ideal. Note, however, that both Habib Luthfi and Habib Bagir belong to a Sufi tradition. Nevertheless, they differ in how the *sunna* ought to be articulated and the community organized. As discussed in chapter 2, since the eighteenth century, the Ṭarīqa ʿAlawiyya has been reconfigured by al-Ḥaddād into a more accessible and attainable spiritual path through the propagation of a common theological, ethical, and devotional code. Such an articulatory mode demands connectors who can mediate between the *sunna*—as entextualized in the Ḥaddādian creeds, abridgments and litanies—and individual Muslims. Such connectors need not be Sufi masters. In fact, many Bā ʿAlawī scholars rooted in the Ḥaddādian paradigm—including the *manṣab* of Pekalongan—tend to be suspicious of organized Sufi orders like Habib Luthfi's NKS, opting to stress the importance of learning and striving to realize the *sunna* as encapsulated in the Ḥaddādian texts. This view was most famously articulated by the aforementioned Bā ʿAlawī scholar Uthmān Bin Yaḥyā, to the extent that one historian mistakenly described him as someone with "strong reservations about Sufism."[52] What is at stake is not Sufism, but how the *sunna* (including its mystical dimension) ought to be articulated, and the community organized.

Conclusion

This chapter began and ended with the establishment of the Kanzus Shalawat, which marked the emergence of a new center of Islamic authority in Pekalongan. It moved backward to trace the biographical becoming of Habib Luthfi Bin Yahya and argued that the case of Habib Luthfi illustrates the centrality of genealogy and mobility, as well as the contingent relationship between the two, in the formation of Islamic religious authority. Genealogy identifies diachronic channels that link the present to the Prophetic past and serves as a conceptual infrastructure that allows for the transmission of Prophetic teachings. Genealogy also performs ideological work by allowing its bearer to be perceived by others as an authoritative articulator of the *sunna*. Mobility, in its turn, enables aspiring scholars to tap into genealogies of knowledge transmission, disseminate their own articulation of the *sunna*, and expand their communities. Mobility permits actors to either retrace their lineage or become entangled with other genealogies and itineraries of Islamic transmission. For the Bā ʿAlawīs, genealogy and mobility ought to work in tandem, in that the former ought to direct the latter. The cases of Habib Luthfi and Salim, however, point to the divergence of mobility from the directive of genealogy. Divergent mobility facilitates the adoption of these actors into alternative genealogies, which, in turn, opens up different articulatory possibilities and enables them to cultivate alternative Islamic communities. As such, divergent mobility and adoptive genealogy may serve as the foundation of new forms of religious authority. For others, however, divergent mobility and adoptive genealogy are adequate grounds for rejecting the legitimacy of a religious authority.

This chapter has also highlighted the importance of travel or wandering as a mode of perceiving the self, the world, and the religion. Travel or wandering in pursuit of knowledge may shape heightened sensitivity towards sociocultural heterogeneity, which, in turn, can fashion an actor's understanding of religious norms and how they ought to be socially realized. This mode of ethical self-becoming stands in contrast to—but may indeed complement—the text- or discourse-based Islamic ethical practices found among the urban piety-minded Muslims who have been discussed in recent anthropological works on Islam. In the case of Habib Luthfi, traveling experience afforded him the ability to envision an embedded notion of the *sunna* that is mindful of, and dialogically entangled with, local sociocultural particularities. The next chapter focuses on Habib Luthfi's mode of articulatory labor that serves to transmit and socially realize such a notion of the *sunna*. It observes how the infrastructure that makes up a Sufi order enables Habib Luthfi to create a durable community that centers on the hierarchical relationship that ties him to his disciples. Such a relationship, in turn, allows Habib Luthfi to adjust and augment the *sunna* by introducing new teachings to suit the changing proclivities of his disciples, without being perceived as deviating from Prophetic precedent.

5

Infrastructure

THE CONSTRUAL OF authority as a form of power or violence is among the most common traits that overshadow philosophical treatments of authority. This perception stems from the ways in which authority, like power, requires obedience.[1] Diverging from this portrayal, the philosopher Hannah Arendt proposes that authority is a hierarchical relationship that is defined in contradistinction to coercion by force and persuasion through argument.[2] Arendt arrives at this conclusion through an insightful observation of the Roman political tradition. The term "authority," Arendt explains, comes from the Latin *auctoritas*, which is derived from the verb *augere*, meaning "to augment." What is being augmented is a foundation built by others in the past and deemed to be sacred. For the Romans, that foundational past was the founding of the city of Rome. Those endowed with authority were "the elders, the Senate or the *patres* who had obtained it by descent and by transmission (tradition) from those who had laid the foundations."[3] Significantly, Arendt highlights that those in authority did not have power (*potestas*). Instead, their task was solely to augment the foundation and transform it into an example, or model for present action, by imparting advice and effecting obedience without coercion. Resorting to power in articulating such a model, in turn, signals the failure of authority.

While Arendt's account may be historically specific and relies on a rather restricted conception of power compared with what we are now accustomed to after Foucault, it nevertheless can help us develop an alternative framework to comprehend Islamic religious authority, one that highlights the peculiarity of authority as a relationship distinct from other forms of power relation. Her observation accentuates how authority "rests neither on common reason nor on the power of the one who commands," but on the recognition of the hierarchy deemed by all parties involved to be right and legitimate.[4] Moreover, her treatment highlights three constitutive elements that make up authority: the notion of, and connection to a foundation; the capacity to transform that foundation into examples; and the ability to effect obedience without coercion. In this chapter, I want to think through these elements by observing Habib Luthfi's role as a

Sufi master (*murshid*) and his labor of cultivating a durable community that revolves around his articulation of the *sunna*. The case of Habib Luthfi, I suggest, allows us to further complicate Arendt's theorization of authority by foregrounding the question of infrastructure, which did not receive adequate treatment in her essay, but nevertheless plays a central role in the formation and diversification of religious authority. As I have repeatedly argued over the course of this book, different infrastructures shape divergent contours of hierarchical relationship and open up distinct articulatory possibilities.

In this chapter, I focus on an institution that has long helped to enact stable hierarchical relationships and facilitate the transmission and social realization of the *sunna*—namely, the Sufi order (*ṭarīqa*). While recent scholarship has questioned the analytic purchase of the notion of "religious order" for making sense of non-Christian religious institutions, I argue that the concept can be retained provided that we refine its definition. In the first half of this chapter I propose an analytic definition of the Sufi order as an *ordering mechanism*—that is, an ensemble of conceptual and material infrastructure that works to transform volatile networks into a durable religious community that centers on the hierarchical relationship between a Sufi master and his disciples. Through the master's skillful orchestration, an array of new and inherited infrastructure that makes up a Sufi order can work to crystallize, stabilize, centralize, and expand a religious community.[5] This infrastructure also allowed for the duplication of a religious community elsewhere, while helping people to recognize a Sufi master as a connector to the Prophetic past and living embodiment of Prophetic teachings. In the second half of the chapter, I show how the hierarchical relationship engendered by a Sufi order enables a Sufi master to adjust and augment the *sunna* by introducing new teachings to suit the changing proclivities of his disciples without being perceived as deviating from Prophetic teachings. Articulated in and through the master-disciple relationship, the *sunna* becomes a living and socially embedded norm with the capacity to accommodate and adapt to cultural particularities, individual needs, and the vicissitudes of the everyday. Comprehending the dynamics of the living *sunna*, in turn, allows us to transcend a major division in the anthropology of Islam that posits a putative opposition between Islam as normative moral codes and "the everyday."[6]

Ordering Mechanism

Recent works on Sufism have questioned the notion of the "religious order" employed by earlier scholars, who analyzed Sufi orders in relation to their perceived similarities with Christian monastic institutions.[7] Mark Sedgwick, to give one example, warns against the supposition of institutional continuity that Christian models of religious orders may promote when observing Sufi orders. Sufi orders, Sedgwick argues, have historically reconfigured themselves in diverse shapes through cyclical dynamics of disruption and stabilization.[8] Similarly, Shahzad Bashir suggests that the notion of order "has led scholars to misapprehend the type of internal cohesion and discipline that can be attributed to the Sufi communities."[9] Instead of order, Bashir argues that "network" is a more useful and neutral concept in understanding Sufi forms of sociality on their own terms.

Although network captures the complex, nebulous, and historically contingent horizontal relations among adherents of a particular Sufi order, it does not capture the modes of hierarchical interaction and temporal relationship that allowed Sufi orders to produce a sense of coherence across time. The term does not do justice to the mechanisms of reproduction and authentication that have enabled each Sufi order to formulate a genealogy that sustains a distinct identity vis-à-vis other Islamic communities, as discussed in the last chapter. The informal connotation of the term "network" downplays the various techniques of boundary making that have historically been deployed by the adherents of a particular Sufi order to distinguish themselves from others. While Bashir's argument for the importance of embodied beliefs and practices as mechanisms that unite people into a moral community devoted to living exemplars is well taken, it is also important to remember that religious communities assume a more complex and institutionalized form "when the group finds it needs to acquire a representation of itself that can incorporate the idea of its continuity beyond the immediate context of its members' interrelating."[10]

Instead of abandoning the notion of order, I suggest that we refine it. One reason for this has to do with the utility of the term for comparative purposes. The term *order* allows constructive comparison across religious traditions—like Islam, Christianity, and Buddhism—which can shed light on the similarities and differences in the features of these traditions. Such features include infrastructure, conception of affinities, and mechanisms of reproduction, self-representation, authentication, and lineage making.[11] The following ethnography illustrates that a Sufi order is best understood as an ordering mechanism made up of networks and infrastructure. Networks are not stable over time, but they can be organized and stabilized with the help of conceptual and material infrastructure. This infrastructure can work to establish shared historical lineage and corporate identity, and facilitate steady transmission of ideas and practices. The shape of a Sufi order at a particular moment in time is related to the available infrastructure that can be utilized by a Sufi master to stabilize networks into a durable community. Historians of Sufism have noted how the development of Sufi orders could not be separated from the organizational frameworks that were available, such as the *futuwwa* (chivalrous) fraternities—exclusive and esoteric societies of crafts and professions found in medieval Persian towns. These historians have shown how varying organizational forms and disciplinary techniques were employed by Sufi masters as mechanisms to create a durable hierarchical relationship.[12] One of the most important labors of a Sufi master like Habib Luthfi lies precisely in orchestrating this infrastructure so that its components may work together to function as an ordering mechanism. Even within a single religious tradition like Islam, these ordering mechanisms and the infrastructure they rely on may differ significantly across time and place. Instead of conceiving a Sufi order as a rigid institution, I suggest we see it as an ongoing ordering activity that aspires to produce, without necessarily attaining, a durable and cohesive religious community.

* * *

"I have seen with my own eyes how his following grows," Idrus told me as he sipped his coffee. It was an hour past midnight on February 3, 2012, and we were chatting on the balcony of Habib Luthfi's house. The master of the house had not yet returned from a speaking engagement in a mountain village south of the city. A short and stocky Javanese man in his early sixties, with a thick, carefully groomed mustache, Idrus has been a disciple of Habib Luthfi since the mid-1980s. He first encountered the *habib* in his hometown of Pasuruan, East Java, at an event hosted by his neighborhood mosque to commemorate the Islamic new year in which Habib Luthfi was the guest speaker. Idrus recalled how he felt drawn to him after listening to the sermon. Back then, the *habib* had not achieved the celebrity status he now enjoys. It was quite easy, Idrus explained, to meet him after a speaking engagement. A few weeks after that initial meeting, Idrus was on his way to Pekalongan in the hope of becoming more acquainted with the *habib*. That trip turned out to be the first of what has become, at the very least, a monthly routine. "That is what a disciple ought to do. . . . [A] disciple maintains his relationship to his master just as the companions maintained their relationship with the Prophet," Idrus said as he savored the last sip of the saccharine black coffee.

Every now and then, Habib Luthfi would ask Idrus to accompany him on his travels. Together, they have visited different parts of Indonesia, from big cities to rural hamlets. That night, as we sat on the balcony, Idrus reminisced about his traveling experiences with his master:

> We used to travel to different villages using an old Toyota Hiace that Habib rented from a Chinese guy who lived near his house. It was an uncomfortable car with no AC. But we were younger then and we used to joke a lot during those long trips. So we were able to have fun. Habib has always been

> generous. Whenever he receives *amplop* [envelope—i.e., monetary gift] after a speaking engagement, he always shares it with me and his other traveling companions. Many times, he did not receive *amplop*. Some villages would give him fresh produce instead. They were peasants, you know, and they did not have much cash. I had never heard Habib Luthfi complain, although I knew that once we reached Pekalongan, he would have to borrow some money to pay for the rented car and the driver. . . . Gradually Habib Luthfi's name became famous in different parts of Java. He began to receive speaking invitations not only from villagers, but from mayors, *bupatis* [district heads], and district military commanders.

Idrus's recollection provides an aperture into the processes that have led to the growth of Habib Luthfi's following. His narrative does not depict a sedentary Sufi master who receives his guests whilst seated in a divan draped with Persian rugs and velvet cushions, but a mobile preacher, who over several decades has indefatigably visited many and varied localities and interacted with a highly diverse audience.[13] Such encounters have allowed Habib Luthfi to be known by many different people, and some, like Idrus, have decided to become disciples.

Being a disciple of a Sufi master establishes a different kind of hierarchical relationship from the one taking shape between preachers and their audience. The relationship between preachers and their audience is that of speakers and their public. It is constituted solely through attention, and its temporality depends on the duration of the speech event.[14] Having seen Habib Luthfi speak on numerous occasions, I have come to realize that, despite the thousands of people who flock the gathering, not all are attentive to his sermon. Children play during the sermon and elderlies snore, while testosterone-driven adolescents try to catch glances of the village beauty. Sometimes, when the noise level gets high, Habib Luthfi himself would discipline the audience by raising his voice and instructing the audience to concentrate. Only those who are paying attention to the sermon are, strictly speaking, the preacher's public. Even then, once the event concludes, all return to their respective homes and that momentary relationship gradually evaporates.

Discipleship, on the other hand, is a hierarchical relationship that endures beyond the fragility and fleeting temporality of a public. As Idrus's recollection makes clear, being a disciple involves the continuous effort of maintaining connection to the master, notwithstanding the geographic distance that separates them, which, of course, not everyone has the luxury of being able to do. Modeled on the paradigmatic relationship between the Prophet Muḥammad and his companions, Sufis posit discipleship as the privileged site of religious learning and spiritual growth.[15] While Habib Luthfi's mobility has certainly worked to expand his networks, such associations are not durable on their own. There need to be some further mechanisms that stabilize them into a durable community.

* * *

"You need to talk to Husen for he has tasted the sweetness of discipleship," Idrus said before bidding me farewell. That was not the first time I had heard of Husen. His name had been recommended to me by many of Habib Luthfi's followers, who see him as the ideal disciple. Finding time to sit with Husen, however, was challenging and that was not simply because he lives in Solo, Central Java. By the time I arrived in Pekalongan, Husen had become a famous preacher with his own *pesantren* (Islamic boarding school) and was constantly on the move. While he came to Pekalongan at least once a month to meet with Habib Luthfi, he usually only stayed for a few hours. I finally managed to sit with Husen during the month of Ramaḍān, when his students were away on vacation. All through the holy month, Husen stayed in Pekalongan to attend his master's daily class. For Husen, Ramaḍān is a time when he suspends his hectic life and declines any speaking invitation to reconnect with Habib Luthfi.

Before his successful preaching career, Husen led a life of intellectual peregrination, studying under several renowned scholars in Java. As a teenager, he studied the Qurʾān, Arabic grammar, theology, and Islamic law with the venerable Kyai Arwani (d. 1994) of Kudus, Central Java. Granpa (*mbah*) Arwani, as he is usually described, was known not only for being a master of the Naqshbandiyya Sufi order, but also for his famed school of Qurʾānic memorization. Upon graduating from the school, Husen continued his study at other *pesantrens* before attaching himself to the saintly Naqshbandī master Kyai Shobiburrahman of Jepara, Central Java, otherwise known as Granpa Shobib (d. 2009). When Husen expressed his desire to become a disciple, however, Granpa Shobib refused to initiate him, pointing out that his real teacher is Habib Luthfi. Following Granpa Shobib's instruction, Husen traveled to Pekalongan. Not knowing anyone there, he had to wait for several days before being able to meet the *habib*.

"Habib Luthfi did not even look at me," Husen recalled after we broke our fast. "When I told him that I wanted to be a disciple, he just pointed to Pak Bambang's house and told me to wait there." Belonging to a wealthy disciple from Solo, the house was empty most of the time, as its sole purpose was to accommodate disciples from out of town. Husen reminisced:

> I stayed at Pak Bambang's house for two years, with only two sarongs and two shirts. I only had Rp. 100.000 [$14], enough to cover my food for a few

> days and buy my return bus ticket. But Habib told me to wait. So I waited . . . [*pause*] . . . for two years. Sometimes I thought Habib had totally forgotten about me. But every now and then he would see me and smiled at me, but he continued to ignore me. For two years I stayed at Pak Bambang's, eating from the leftover food that Habib and his family consumed. I offered massage to Habib Luthfi's visitors and made some money from it, enough to buy detergent, soap, toothpastes. Sometimes those visitors would give me gifts. Most of the time I recited the Qur'ān and different litanies [*awrād*]. Then one afternoon, one of the boys working at Habib Luthfi's house came by to tell me that Habib was looking for me. You can't imagine how elated I was. So I went to see Habib Luthfi. I was very shy and nervous. I did not dare to look at his face. He asked me whether I wanted to be a disciple, and I nodded. And that was how I became Habib Luthfi's disciple. Habib personally inducted me into the Naqshbandī order.

A few months after the initiation, some disciples of Habib Luthfi from Jakarta's upper class whom Husen had interacted with over the waiting period asked him to go with them to Jakarta and become their private Qur'ān tutor. They needed someone who could teach them how to recite the Arabic scripts and explain their meaning. Being a graduate of Granpa Arwani's *pesantren,* Husen was well positioned for the job. Habib Luthfi, however, refused to grant him permission, telling him to go to Solo instead. "He told me that I am needed in Solo and that Solo needs a lot of work," Husen explained. He obeyed his master and moved to Solo. Pak Bambang, whose house Husen had stayed in, and other Solo-based disciples of Habib Luthfi helped Husen to get settled. Together they formed a weekly study group. More and more people attended the group and Husen's popularity as a preacher gradually soared. He began to receive speaking invitations. Before long, the once impoverished disciple was able to buy a huge tract of land and build a *pesantren.* Over the years, Husen has brought countless people to Pekalongan and introduced them to Habib Luthfi, many of whom have been initiated as disciples.

A Sufi order, Husen explained, turns devotees (*muḥibbūn*) into disciples (*murīdūn*). The first connotes followers of a religious scholar or "untutored enthusiasts."[16] They can be those who have merely developed affection for a Sufi master and regularly attend his gatherings. Devotees go beyond mere members of the public whose relationship to the master is based solely on attention. They may regularly visit the master, recite litanies prescribed by him, and participate in Sufi rituals. Nevertheless, devotees are not formal disciples in that they are not legally obligated to maintain ongoing relationships with the master.

What transforms devotees into disciples is the initiation ceremony, which involves the taking of an oath of allegiance (*bay'a*) to a Sufi master. Habib

Luthfi organizes this ceremony once a month, during the monthly gathering held at his congregational center, the Kanzus Shalawat. One of Habib Luthfi's deputies (*badal*) presides over the ceremony. There are usually fifty to seventy-five initiates each month, of diverse ages and economic backgrounds, around one-third of whom are females. Female initiates form a separate group and sit beside the males. The initiates are asked to fill in their personal details on a computer-generated form distributed by the officials of the Kanzus Shalawat.

The deputy begins the ceremony by explaining to the audience the meaning of joining a Sufi order. He describes how pledging allegiance to a Sufi master is a *sunna*, just as the Prophet's companions did to Muḥammad. He warns them that an oath is legally binding under Islamic law and that once initiated, they will have to obey the master unconditionally. The deputy then teaches the *dhikr*s (invocatory phrases or prayers) that every disciple has to recite daily. "All of the *dhikr*s I have described were taught by the Prophet, and we are connected to them through Habib Luthfi's *silsila* [chain of spiritual descent]," he explains. He then reads from a prepared text:

> A Muslim should perform *dhikr* in accordance to the ways prescribed by the Prophet Muḥammad. This is why in the Sufi order, disciples perform *dhikr* by emulating the master. This means that in performing *dhikr,* disciples admit that the *dhikr* they perform is a result of emulation and not something they make up themselves. By pledging allegiance to a master and emulating his *dhikr,* one enters his *silsila.*

Note how joining a Sufi order is presented as facilitating the establishment of a connection between disciples and the Prophet through the mediation of those who compose the master's *silsila.* The oath of allegiance to the master itself is construed as iconic of the oath made by the companions to the Prophet. The oath allows for the creation of a legalized hierarchical relationship that is perceived to mirror, and is simultaneously connected to, the historical relationship between the Prophet and the companions.

The deputy then holds the hand of one of the male congregants and asks those sitting directly behind him to put their right hands on his shoulder. This continues with those sitting behind the first row of people, thereby forming an unbroken physical chain to the deputy. He also holds one end of a set of prayer beads, while asking one of the female initiates to hold the other end, thereby forming a parallel chain to the female initiates without involving direct bodily contact. The deputy then asks the congregants to repeat the Islamic creedal sentence after him, and to repeat, in Indonesian:

> I am content with Allāh as my God, our master Muḥammad as my Prophet, and Habib Luthfi as my master. I promise to obey the law of Allāh as

> revealed to the Prophet Muḥammad and which I have received from Habib Luthfi. I ask for Allāh's forgiveness, and I promise not to perform major sins and to try, as much as possible, to refrain from minor sins.

Pronouncement of the oath concludes the initiation ceremony.

Becoming a disciple is a voluntary act. While in his sermons Habib Luthfi often talks about the importance of joining a Sufi order, he himself does not try to persuade, let alone coerce, people to become his disciples. I have seen Habib Luthfi discourage younger people from becoming disciples for fear that they may not be ready to honor the obligations entailed. While becoming a disciple is a voluntary act, the oath serves to formalize the hierarchical relationship between the master and the initiate. Thereafter, initiates are legally obligated to follow their master. This legal status is what differentiates disciples from devotees.

* * *

Once initiated, disciples are required to keep the company of the master, a practice known as companionship (*ṣuḥba*). Traditionally, this means living with the master for a protracted period, as Habib Luthfi had done with his master, Abdul Malik. Habib Luthfi, however, has reduced this obligation to the minimum requirement of a once-monthly companionship, to ease the burden on his disciples, particularly those who live far away and are preoccupied with work. This monthly companionship takes the form of a mass gathering he organizes at the Kanzus Shalawat. The gathering was initially held at Habib Luthfi's house, but was relocated to the more spacious and publicly visible Kanzus Shalawat after it opened (see chapter 4). As a result, the gathering began to be attended not only by Habib Luthfi's disciples but also by neighbors and other residents of Pekalongan. People who have heard Habib Luthfi speak in their localities travel to Pekalongan and attend. Over time, the gathering has become larger, to the extent that the main road in front of the center has to be closed for the occasion. Today, the gathering is attended by around ten thousand people.

The gathering begins at seven in the morning with the arrival of Habib Luthfi—dressed in white robe and turban—at the Kanzus Shalawat. He enters the already-packed congregational center through the back door, walks past the densely filled main chamber, and sits on the front porch of the building overlooking the main road, where the majority of the congregants are sitting. From that position, Habib Luthfi is able to see and be seen by those who sit inside and outside the building. The *habib* begins the ritual by invoking the names of the individuals who make up his *silsila* from the Prophet Muḥammad to the eponyms of several Sufi orders and down to his own teachers. He prays for their souls, while asking God to grant blessings to the congregation through the intercession of the named individuals. Aside from naming an elite group of intercessors, the invocation also serves to anchor Habib Luthfi in a genealogy of interpersonal relationships that goes back to the Prophetic past.[17] Such a ritualized projection situates Habib Luthfi as an immediate access point in the transgenerational transmission of Prophetic teachings, presenting him as an authorized purveyor of the *sunna*. While the invocation is conducted in Arabic, the fact that it consists mainly of proper names serves well the apprehension of listeners who cannot comprehend Arabic. In contrast to comprehension, apprehension is concerned more with the situated practice of reading, such as ritual recitation, where one can grasp what there is to know—such as substantive nouns—without necessarily knowing how to subject it to predications. The foreignness of a language, for instance, does not obstruct apprehension of proper names as they lie "outside of the semantic conventions of a synchronically structured language."[18]

Following the invocation, Habib Luthfi leads the congregants in *dhikr*. After the *dhikr*, one of the *habib*'s senior disciples recites and translates into Javanese one or two paragraphs from the *Jāmiʿ al-uṣūl fī-l-awliyāʾ*, a Sufi text authored by the Turkish Naqshbandī-Khālidī scholar Aḥmad Ḍiyāʾ al-Dīn b. Muṣṭafā al-Kumushkhānawī (Gümüşhanevi) (d. 1893).[19] The recitation usually takes less than fifteen minutes. Habib Luthfi then begins his thirty-minute sermon in Indonesian, elaborating what has just been recited. On most occasions, the sermon describes a particular Prophetic saying discussed in the text. At other times, Habib Luthfi uses the sermon to discuss the idea of belonging to a Sufi order, as in the following excerpt from a sermon delivered in November 2011:

> What differentiates someone who belongs to a Sufi order from those who do not? First of all, we have to understand that Sufism means turning and fleeing to God. Turning to God means turning to the *sunna* of the Prophet, following his teachings, norms, and manners. Each Sufi order has a continuous chain that connects our teachers to the Prophet. Sufi orders, whether Naqshbandiyya, Qādiriyya, Shādhiliyya, are not the inventions of the Sufi masters. For example the Qādirī Sufi order is named after Shaykh ʿAbd al-Qādir al-Jīlānī. This simply means that Shaykh ʿAbd al-Qādir was the leader of the order. But the practices and teachings were not invented by him. He merely systematized and elaborated them. He received them from his teachers all the way back to the Prophet Muḥammad.

Observe how Habib Luthfi presents Sufi orders as consisting of conceptual infrastructures that link the present to the Prophetic past, thereby facilitating the stable transmission of Prophetic teachings through time and space. While

Prophetic teachings can be found in entextualized forms in the anthologies of Prophetic sayings (*ḥadīths*), Sufi orders seek to reproduce the very mode of transmission that materialized between the Prophet and his companions—namely, discipleship and companionship. Hinging on physical contact, discipleship forms an embodied chain that links the present to the Prophetic past. It is for this reason that disciples ought to maintain companionship with their masters.

For the disciples, attending the monthly gathering is understood to fulfill the minimum requirement of companionship. If noninitiates attend the gathering to learn something about their religion by listening to Habib Luthfi, for the disciples, the substance of the sermon itself is secondary to the actual activity of being in the presence of their master and establishing bodily contact with him. Brian Silverstein has noted the centrality of companionship as a "discipline of presence" believed by the Sufis to constitute "ethically structured dispositions oriented toward the Good."[20] Companionship, Silverstein explains, is undergirded by a metaphysic of influence that posits being with morally upright individuals as productive of desires to become a virtuous person. Thus, while the sermon concludes the gathering, for the disciples what subsequently takes place is equally important. Following the sermon, Habib Luthfi remains sitting on the porch of the Kanzus Shalawat. Guarded by security personnel, the Sufi master avails himself to his disciples. Each disciple comes forward in turn to kiss Habib Luthfi's hand. While kissing his hand, the disciples also give him an envelope containing a monetary gift. An attendant sitting next to Habib Luthfi puts the envelopes into a big bag, to be counted later by officials of the Kanzus Shalawat. Aside from Habib Luthfi's personal use, the money collected is used for the maintenance of the congregational center and to pay the salaries of the center's officials.

* * *

Aside from the monthly companionship, disciples are still required to maintain their connection to the master at other times through the recitation of the daily litany. Entitled *Awrād al-ṭarīqa al-shādhiliyya al-ʿalawiyya* (Litanies of the Shādhilī-ʿAlawī Sufi order), this series of prayers was compiled and systematized by Habib Luthfi and entextualized in the form of a privately printed prayer manual sold during the monthly gathering at the Kanzus Shalawat. Disciples are obligated to buy the manual and recite the litany on a daily basis. The litany is written in Arabic with Roman-alphabet transliteration, thus making it accessible for people who cannot read Arabic script.

Aside from the short Qurʾānic verses and invocations that make up the litany, the prayer manual also contains Habib Luthfi's *silsila*, which connects him to the Prophet, presented in a schematic form. What are important to note for our present purposes are the intercessory prayers at the beginning of the manual, one of which is specifically directed to Habib Luthfi. It begins:

> To the presence of our teacher, our master, the educator of our spirits, the most knowledgable, Habib Luthfi bin Yahya. May Allāh grant him long life in health and abundant blessings. May Allāh ennoble his stature and expand his honor.[21]

Note how this intercessory prayer is informed by a logic of gift exchange that connects the disciples and the master. Disciples ought to reciprocate the guidance and prayers of their master by sending a daily prayer to him. This form of reciprocation parallels the gifting of money during the monthly companionship. These reciprocal acts of giving serve to constitute and further stabilize the hierarchical relationship that ties the disciples to their master even when they are physically separated.

Another means for maintaining a connection with the master is the practice of bonding (*rābiṭa*). The term refers to a technique of visualization involving keeping the image of the master in the disciple's heart. Such a practice has historically been aided by various technologies that serve to evoke visual imaginations, including hagiographical texts, paintings, sketches of shrines and relics, or photographs of modern-day saints and Sufi masters.[22] Many disciples have told me how they recite the daily litany whilst gazing at a photo of Habib Luthfi. Others confessed that at times they would converse with a hung portrait of their master, particularly when they wanted to complain about something. An elderly man even reminded me that if one has a portrait of the master in one's bedroom, one should cover it when one is engaging in sexual intercourse. Even though Habib Luthfi's photos are mechanically mass-produced and can easily be purchased from street vendors during the monthly gathering, for the disciples they are "vanishing mediators" that can facilitate transparent connection to the master by erasing their own mediatory traces and interferences.[23]

Among the new infrastructure that complements other, older infrastructure discussed thus far are social media. Today, Habib Luthfi has an official website, a Facebook fan page, and a Twitter account.[24] These platforms are used to disseminate his sermons. Many disciples also use these new virtual interfaces for the purpose of bonding. This development was facilitated by the availability of affordable Chinese-made smartphones and the decreasing price of internet data plans due to increasing competition among service providers. One disciple explained to me that the portability of smartphones had increased the immediacy of the master's presence, enabling him to bond whilst commuting to work. Another disciple said that her decision to become an active user of Facebook and Twitter was due to what she described as "spiritual disturbance," by which she meant the intrusions of Muslim televangelists into her living room through the television. This, in her view, had distracted her from bonding with her master. Following Habib Luthfi on Facebook and Twitter afforded her the ability to maintain her focus on her own master. Social media have thus acted as new infrastructure that allow for novel ways to perform bonding.

* * *

Pledging allegiance to a Sufi master involves recognizing him as a spiritual father whose duty it is to look after his spiritual children and nurture their spiritual growth. In return, disciples ought to follow, obey, love, and respect the master, just as they ought to do to their biological parents. Such a hierarchical relationship allows the Sufi master to unilaterally interfere in the personal lives of the disciples. This ability to interfere marks one of the major differences between a Sufi master and other kinds of Islamic authority. For example, a *muftī*—a jurisconsult who produces Islamic legal opinions—also plays the role of a religious or moral guide, just like a Sufi master. Through his legal opinions (*fatwā*), a *muftī* "puts the questioner on a *journey* of ethical cultivation," as Hussein Agrama points out in his ethnography of the Egyptian Fatwa Council.[25] Nevertheless, a *muftī* can do so only when he is asked by a questioner and even then, his *fatwā* is not binding.

While Habib Luthfi hardly micromanages the affairs of his disciples, there are times when he explicitly invokes his authority as a Sufi master to interfere, as in the following case. One afternoon in July 2012, I was sitting and conversing with Habib Luthfi in the library of his house when the district head (*bupati*) of Purwokerto (Central Java) suddenly appeared, accompanied by another person. The *habib* stood up to welcome them and invited them to sit. After a brief opening conversation, the companion of the district head, whose name was Ali, began complaining to the *habib* regarding a problem faced by the Muslims of a particular area of Purwokerto: the absence of a Muslim cemetery. Ali told Habib Luthfi how Muslims living in the area are buried with people of different faiths in a public cemetery. Several people in the community had come up with an idea of collectively buying a large piece of land, roughly two hectares, and endowing it as a Muslim cemetery. A committee was formed with Ali as its head, and the land was successfully purchased. Yet there remained a problem of access to the land from the main road. The only way to obtain access to the land was by buying a small and narrow piece of land owned by a local scholar (*kyai*), who happened to be Habib Luthfi's disciple. After being approached several times, however, the scholar had persistently refused to sell the land. He told them that he would sell the land only if they were willing to buy his whole property, a total of twenty thousand square feet. Knowing that the committee was in need of the land, the scholar was charging an astronomical price for it. The scholar explained to the committee that having a cemetery next to his property would decrease the value of his own land. The committee then tried to persuade the scholar using religious language, enticing him with the promise of great rewards that God would grant him in heaven if he were willing to give up a bit of his land for road access to the Muslim cemetery. In response, the scholar simply rebuffed the committee by saying that "heaven is not cheap!"

Habib Luthfi listened attentively to Ali's story. He then told both visitors that he would try to deal with the situation. When the visitors left, Habib Luthfi called one of his attendants and told him to ring one of his deputies in Purwokerto. On the phone, Habib Luthfi told the deputy to visit the scholar and let him know that he had been summoned to Pekalongan. Two days later, the scholar came to Pekalongan. When he entered the library, Habib Luthfi was sitting with several guests. He welcomed the scholar warmly, asked about his family, and told him that he wanted to have a private conversation. Both went into Habib Luthfi's bedroom, and around half an hour later they came out. The scholar kissed Habib Luthfi's hand and left. One week later, Ali returned to Habib Luthfi's house. Looking jubilant, he told the *habib* that the scholar had agreed to sell a small piece of his land for road access to the planned cemetery. Ali thanked Habib Luthfi for his intervention. The *habib* modestly responded by saying that he had not taken any action owing to his preoccupation with other matters. I do not know what transpired between Habib Luthfi and the scholar. What is clear, however, is that as an ordering mechanism, a Sufi order enables the formation and maintenance of a hierarchical relationship that allows a Sufi master to summon and unilaterally intervene in personal matters of his disciples.

The ability of a master to intervene, however, is not always as simple and straightforward. During my fieldwork there was a moment when a joint business venture between Habib Luthfi's son and one of his disciples turned sour. Each blamed the other for the failure and both took the case to the father/master. Each conflicting party saw the *habib* as a (biological/spiritual) father. In such a case, the line separating biological and spiritual family becomes blurred, and Habib Luthfi simply refused to interfere. In fact, I have heard more than once the *habib* admonishing his children, asking them to refrain from involving themselves in commercial activities with his disciples. As a Sufi master, Habib Luthfi has to constantly maintain the boundary separating the family and the community, the spiritual and the biological children, although such lines have been transgressed multiple times, leaving him in difficult positions.

* * *

On several occasions, Habib Luthfi confided in me how since becoming a master, he had witnessed many disciples failing to honor their discipleship by not reciting the daily litany or following his instruction and advice. Such failures are due to various reasons, some of which are construed as ethical, like preoccupation with work and the need to provide for one's family. In his younger days Habib Luthfi would discipline his disciples by admonishing them, albeit to limited success. Many disciples have simply drifted away. Significantly, Habib Luthfi sees such cases as pointing to his own failure to be a good master. He gradually realized that he has to accommodate his disciples if their relationship is to work and endure.

Recent scholars of Sufism have rightly observed how the success or failure of a Sufi master in assembling a durable community depends largely on his creativity and leadership. A Sufi master may inherit followers from his deceased master. To preserve and maintain them, however, demands creativity and resourcefulness.[26] As Alexander Knysh points out, the language of routinization of charisma that previous generations of scholars of Sufism adopted from Max Weber fails to capture the ways in which a Sufi master does not simply "inherit his authority and prestige to enjoy for the rest of his life."[27] Failures to maintain an inherited community are as common as successes, although they are usually not recorded.[28] Interestingly, Habib Luthfi's own recollection suggests that a self-conscious perception of failure is central to his own personal development of becoming a better master. That is, his sense of past failures has actually helped him to become a more successful religious authority. Such an explanation points to what David Kloos and Daan Beekers describe as "the productive potential of moral failure" in religion.[29] Beekers and Kloos observe how "the recognition of, and response to, failure takes a central place in core doctrinal traditions in both Islam and Christianity," although it has received minimal attention in anthropological studies of lived religion.[30] While Beekers and Kloos focus their attention on the failures that individuals experience in becoming moral subjects, the case of Habib Luthfi draws our attention to how a sense of failure also plays a significant role in the production of religious teachings and the modification of religious practices.

This is the very logic that lies behind Habib Luthfi's composition of a new prayer manual, different from the manual of his own master. As discussed in chapter 4, Habib Luthfi was appointed a master of the

Naqshbandī-Khālidī-Shādhilī (NKS) Sufi order by his master Abdul Malik. Until 2006, Abdul Malik's prayer manual was used in Habib Luthfi's own circle. Thereafter, Habib Luthfi decided to present himself as a master of the Shādhilī-ʿAlawī Sufi order (SA), a combination of the Shādhiliyya that he received from Abdul Malik and the Ṭārīqa ʿAlawiyya that he inherited from the Bā ʿAlawī scholars. This, however, does not mean that Habib Luthfi disowned the NKS. He remains a master of the NKS and still appoints NKS deputies. When I asked the *habib* regarding this shift, he explained that the NKS teachings have become too demanding for the current era:

> It is more difficult to become a good Naqshbandī-Khālidī disciple as it requires practices like the forty-days seclusion, which is less realizable in today's society. That is why the Shādhiliyya-ʿAlawiyya demands less from the disciples. The daily litany is brief so that even if you work in an office or factory, you can still strive to become a responsible disciple. We have to understand that times are changing, people are changing. What was doable thirty years ago is no longer feasible for most people today.

Through the master's acumen, a Sufi order has the capacity for innovation.[31] Understanding this point enables us to consider distinctions among different Sufi orders, or among different masters of the same order, not only in terms of varying *silsila*, but also in terms of variation in the substance of the ordering mechanism deployed to maintain the community. Even a single order with a shared genealogy may turn out to consist of masters who institute diverging practices. In some cases such differences have led to schism, the birth of a new order, or the development of a suborder.[32] For the most part, however, disciples do not see such innovations as problematic because of their recognition of the master's legitimacy and connection to the Prophet. A stable hierarchical relationship thus allows the master to introduce new measures that can help disciples maintain that very relationship. As we will see in the next section, such a relationship also allows for dynamic articulations of the *sunna*.

Living *Sunna*

As an ordering mechanism, a Sufi order shapes and reinforces the disciples' recognition of the master as someone who is genealogically connected to the Prophet, has assimilated his characteristics, and actively transmits his teachings. His personality and conduct, as well as the practices he institutes, are considered normative for his disciples.[33] He is, as one disciple of Habib Luthfi told me, an exemplar (*qudwa*) and a purveyor of the *living sunna*. Here, the recognition of the universal regulatory force of the *sunna* is not accompanied by the belief in the uniformity and finality of its content, which may be derived from Prophetic precedents corroborated by texts, but may also include innovations tied to specific contexts and challenges that are nonetheless taken to epitomize Prophetic teachings owing to the figure of the master. The hierarchical relationship that links a Sufi master to his disciples enables the former to augment the *sunna* by evaluating and adjusting inherited teachings or introducing new practices to suit the changing proclivities of his followers without being perceived as deviating from Prophetic teachings. Such a relationship enables a Sufi master to transform the foundational Prophetic past into individualized and customized models for action, thereby assisting him in effecting obedience without coercion. Here is where wisdom (*ḥikma*; see chapter 4) comes to play a central role.

Treating the *sunna* as a living and socially embedded norm allows us to think beyond a major division that has taken shape in the anthropology of Islam. This division has in part arisen over long-standing anthropological questions regarding the conceptualization of agency. Several influential works have come to favor approaches that focus on authoritative practices, piety, and the embodiment of Islamic moral norms.[34] Influenced by the late Foucault, these works argue that the constitution of an Islamic ethical subject is a process of subjectivation or self-cultivation involving reflective consciousness and freedom.[35] In doing so, they highlight a style of agency hitherto undervalued in anthropological literature and allow us to think about morality beyond the practice of conforming to, or resisting, moral codes.[36] Such approaches, however, have been criticized by other anthropologists for privileging coherent and programmatic modes of religion rather than the contradictions, incoherencies, ambiguities, and "moral pluralism" of "the everyday."[37] For these scholars, the "everyday" acts as a site that allows for critical evaluation of and even creative resistance to (religious) norms.[38]

In this section I problematize the juxtaposition, and the opposition, of normative moral and ethical codes and "the everyday" by exploring the ways in which both are constituted by and constitutive of Islam. I use the dynamics of the living *sunna* to question the contrast between allegedly hypercoherent Islamic norms and the messiness of the everyday by observing the former as a site of instability that allows for creative explorations demanded by the latter.[39] I contend that the dynamic of the living *sunna* accentuates Islamic norms as the products of articulatory labor. This, in turn, allows us to see Islamic norms as embedded, immanent in, and modulated by cultural particularities and the vicissitudes of the everyday.

* * *

"I have seen the Prophet Muḥammad in Habib Luthfi," Husen whispered to me. He explained to me how, in the beginning, God created the Muḥammadan Reality (*ḥaqīqa muḥammadiyya*). The Muḥammadan Reality reflects the beauty and perfection of the divine. It then manifested itself in diverse forms and in varying intensity, including in the forms of different prophets and saints. The Prophet Muḥammad was its most perfect human manifestation. The Prophet is the prototype of the perfect man (*al-insān al-kāmil*), a human who has succeeded in adorning himself with divine names and attributes. The perfect man, Husen explained, continues to exist in different shapes and forms at different times. These are the inheritors of the Prophet Muḥammad and the manifestations of the Muḥammadan Reality. "Just as the companions recognized the Prophet Muḥammad as the perfect man, I too, with an absolute positive thought have come to recognize Habib Luthfi as the perfect man," Husen concluded.

In making sense of his relationship with Habib Luthfi, Husen unapologetically shows his indebtedness to the works of the Iraqi Sufi theoretician ʿAbd al-Karīm al-Jīlī (d. 1428). Elaborating the metaphysical ideas of the great Andalusian Sufi Muḥyī-l-Dīn Ibn al-ʿArabī (d. 1240), al-Jīlī's notion of the perfect man describes a human being who has succeeded in becoming the manifestation of divine attributes and becomes the point for the community to establish contact with the divine, akin to the role of the prophets, but in post-Prophetic era. Al-Jīlī's ideas, as Alexander Knysh suggests, reflect a "gnostic-individualistic" interpretation of Islam that, whilst accepted by many Sufis, scandalized many others (Sufis and non-Sufis) who upheld the primacy of the "communal-legalistic" religious framework.[40] Although the latter group did not doubt the existence of mystical experience, they did disagree over "its role in, and practical implications for, a society based on the revealed law."[41] Different from Knysh, I prefer to read al-Jīlī's notion of the perfect man as an attempt to resolve the problem of temporal estrangement from the Prophetic past by pointing to the existence of living Prophetic inheritors. Read in this way, the notion of the perfect man is not necessarily individualistic. Instead, it opens up the possibility for the formation of an Islamic community that revolves around a living *sunna*.

Al-Jīlī's notion of perfect man has a long history in the Malay-Indonesian Archipelago. Its transmission was aided by its rendering into poetic forms by the likes of the sixteenth-century Aceh's mystical poet Hamzah Fansuri. The notion was meticulously studied in the Muslim royal courts of Java, Aceh, and Sulawesi, and was used to construct the concept of Islamic kingship as universal mystical sovereignty.[42] Today, however, such a notion has been identified as "deviant teachings" (*aliran sesat*). In Fansuri's own homeland of Aceh, for instance, to describe *Al-Insān al-kāmil* as the main text of reference for a particular group is tantamount to calling that group heterodox.[43] Husen recognized the dangerous potentials of al-Jīlī's perfect man. Indeed, he told me that he does not discuss such an intricate concept in an open forum for fear of generating misunderstanding. The concept may give the impression of undermining Islamic law, for if humans have access to the perfect man, why do they need the law? Such a conclusion is erroneous in Husen's view, for the perfect man does not abrogate the teachings of the Prophet Muḥammad. Rather, the perfect man is the concrete embodiment of Prophetic teachings. He is the purveyor of *living sunna,* and through him people can come to understand the *sunna* as it relates to their particular context. Through the perfect man, the *sunna* ceases to exist solely as objectified reports of the Prophet's life, and instead becomes a living reality to be witnessed and emulated:

> I am convinced that Habib Luthfi's words, actions, and mannerism are the concrete enactment and elaboration of the Prophet. He is a *living sunna,* a *sunna* that lives among us. I simply follow Habib Luthfi. It is like having the Prophet guiding me in the 21st-century Java. So I treat the *habib* just as the companions treated the Prophet. *Whatever the Prophet gives you, take it. Whatever he forbids, abstain from it* [Q. 59:7]. This is the essence of discipleship.

Far from being a mere metaphysical conundrum, for Husen, the concept of the perfect man has practical implications and serves as a theoretical foundation for his understanding of discipleship. The concept gives grounds to the existence of Prophetic inheritors, from whom Muslims of every generation can learn. Through the perfect man, the *sunna* becomes a living phenomenon and Muslims can once again learn it from a living exemplar, just as the companions once did when they lived with the Prophet. For Husen, the living *sunna* is not simply a replication of the Prophetic *sunna* as entextualized in the *ḥadīths*. Rather, by virtue of living in a time and place different from the Prophet, a purveyor of the living *sunna* elaborates Prophetic teachings—both pedagogically and performatively—in culturally specific idioms and actions, thereby augmenting those teachings.

Husen recognizes the universal regulatory force of the *sunna,* without, however, assenting to the uniformity or finality of its content. Embodied in living individuals, what is posited as the *sunna* no longer exists on its own, but is always in motion, bundled with and augmented by other particular qualities that make up the individual, thereby creating a surplus.[44] Such an understanding has allowed Husen to envision the *sunna* as a universal norm that is also concretely Javanese and contemporary.

* * *

The notion of the Sufi master as the purveyor of living *sunna* is one that I have repeatedly encountered in my conversations with Habib Luthfi's disciples, although not all were able to express it in a sophisticated manner as Husen did.

Indeed, there is variation in how this dynamic is understood. Many disciples I conversed with noted how being a disciple allows them to entrust their religious affairs to their master. One medical doctor from Jakarta explained how she does not have the time to think about what religious practice she needs to do or litanies she needs to recite. Consequently, having Habib Luthfi prescribing what to do helps her tremendously in practicing her religion in the midst of her professional and personal life. For another disciple, having a master assists him in coming to terms with his own personal developments. "Habib always provides guidance on a case by case basis, he prescribes litanies and practices based on my current needs," he explained. A lecturer from a university in Semarang, Central Java, described how having a master is like buying a suit from an experienced tailor: "Different from buying a ready-made suit, a suit from a tailor is made especially for me; its size and dimension fits perfectly."

Being a disciple provides many of the people I talked to with a sense of trust and certainty that what the master prescribes is the *sunna* curated for their particular needs. There is certainly the minimum requirement of reciting the standardized daily litany to be a disciple, which, as I discussed in the previous section, is pivotal to the maintenance of a steady master-disciple relationship. Nevertheless, having a master allows each disciple to consult and receive individualized guidance and prescriptions. "Habib Luthfi knows the *sunna* well, he is connected to the Prophet. . . . I believe he knows which *sunna* can be applied to me and not to others, and I trust him on that, as after all I don't even have the time nor the capacity to dive into the *sunna*," said the CEO of a major advertising company. Another disciple complains about the increasingly difficult work of choosing whom to follow when "different scholars are saying different things on television and Youtube, which is why when I met Habib Luthfi and felt at ease with him, I just entrusted my religion to him." Speaking to the disciples made me realize how the increasing complexity of life and the rapid social change that has led to the fragmentation of Muslim lives have actually increased the appeal of the guidance of a Sufi master. What attracts many of the middle-class professionals and the "newly pious"—to use Robert Hefner's term—to become Habib Luthfi's disciples is the ability of the master to provide guidance adapted to their individualized needs (see figure 5.1).[45]

Habib Luthfi often compares his role to that of a medical doctor, who diagnoses his patients individually and prescribes different medications for each. Unlike that prescribed by modern Islamic organizations, his guidance is not directed toward rectifying the social and political ills of society. Rather, it is directed toward helping individual disciples to practice their religion amidst the complexity of modern life. In order for it to work, such a relationship

FIGURE 5.1 A female disciple in consultation with Habib Luthfi while other disciples and visitors wait for their turn. (Photo by the author)

requires trust and willingness to obey. Concurrently, it demands from the master some degree of practical wisdom that can effectively mediate prescription and practice. As an ordering mechanism, a Sufi order thus engenders a hierarchical relationship that allows the master to transform the Prophetic past into individually customized models for action, thereby assisting him in effecting obedience without coercion.

* * *

One afternoon in March 2013, an octogenarian Naqshbandī-Khālidī Sufi master from Damascus came to visit Habib Luthfi. Alongside other guests, he sat quietly, accompanied by two of his Indonesian students, whilst waiting for the appearance of Habib Luthfi at the reception chamber of the Sufi master's house. As usual, the Indonesian guests were smoking, joking, and laughing to help pass the waiting time. The Damascene master was shocked and was clearly upset by what he saw. He suddenly clapped his hands, recited four Qur'ānic verses, and asked his students to translate them into Indonesian:

> Believers, do not raise your voices above the Prophet's, do not raise your voice when speaking to him as you do to one another, or your [good] deeds may be canceled out without you knowing. It is those who lower their voices in the presence of God's Messenger whose hearts God has proved to be aware—they will have forgiveness, and a great reward—but most of those who shout to you [the Prophet] from outside your private rooms lack understanding. It would have been better for them if they had waited patiently for you to come out to them [Q. 49:2–5].

He then told the other guests that one should treat a master just as one treats the Prophet, for a master is a successor of the Prophet. Expressing his bewilderment at their conduct, he rhetorically asked, "what kind of disciple smokes, jokes, and laughs in his master's house?" He concluded his short impromptu lecture by stating that "being in a Sufi order means following the *sunna*." The room became silent, and those who were waiting for Habib Luthfi lowered their heads. They evidently felt embarrassed.

For the Damascene master, what he saw at Habib Luthfi's house was a foundering hierarchical relationship that necessitated disciplinary intervention. He disciplined Habib Luthfi's disciples and guests by drawing on the Qur'ān. The verses he quoted were revealed in response to a quarrel between two companions of the Prophet, Abū Bakr and 'Umar, in the presence of Muḥammad. The verses also spoke to new followers "who had taken an attitude of excessive familiarity with the Prophet."[46] By quoting these verses, the Damascene master mapped what the verses originally denoted, an event that occurred in the Prophetic past, to a new interactional situation, thereby transforming a foundational past into a model, or *sunna*, for present action.

Habib Luthfi's approach is starkly different from that of the Damascene master, despite the fact that both hail from the Naqshbandiyya-Khālidiyya. The former's approach has been described to me by many of his followers as *ngemong*, a Javanese term that means "gentle care." The term is generally used to refer to the practice of childcare whereby the chaperone follows and pays attention to the movement of children without attempting to control, steer, or stop them, except when they are faced by imminent danger. *Ngemong* entails tolerating improper behavior, as long as it is within clearly defined limits, and abstaining from open criticism. Often, my interlocutors compared *ngemong* to *ngangon*, or shepherding, in that shepherds supervise their herds while providing them with the freedom to roam around the grazing ground.

In conversations with his deputies or other scholars, Habib Luthfi often stresses the importance of *ngemong* in dealing with people. Significantly, he presents *ngemong* as a *sunna*. Many times he has described the Prophet Muḥammad as an effective community leader because he practiced *ngemong*. Here is Habib Luthfi speaking to two scholars who visited him from Bandung, West Java:

> Prophets were shepherds before they receive revelation. Attending to herds (*ngangon*) enabled them to develop patience. It also teaches them that to be a leader, one should learn how to *ngemong*. Look at how the Prophet practiced *ngemong*. The result was that people felt close to him, enabling him to fulfill his Prophetic mission effectively. That is why Allāh says to the Prophet: *Out of Mercy from God, you were gentle in your dealings with them, had you been harsh, or harsh-hearted, they would have dispersed and left you* [Q. 3:159]. Here in Java we know this very well. We know how to practice *ngemong* well.

Note how Habib Luthfi endorses a Javanese cultural practice—*ngemong*—as a *sunna* by mapping it onto the Prophetic past. In describing the foundational past by using a culturally specific term, Habib Luthfi in effect augments that foundation.

Both Habib Luthfi and the Damascene master agree that discipleship is a hierarchical relationship that ought to resemble and be connected to the relationship between the Prophet and his companions. Interestingly, both return to the foundational past only to come up with contrasting *sunnas*. Key to understanding this is the nature of the *sunna* as what the philosopher Bernard Williams calls a "thick ethical concept" that involves both evaluative and nonevaluative description, making it not only "action-guiding" but also "guided by the world."[47] Williams contrasts thick ethical terms like *courage* and *generosity* with "thin" ones like *right* or *wrong, good* or *bad*. If thin concepts are solely evaluative, thick terms also involve nonevaluative description and "express a union of fact and value."[48] For example, when one evaluates a person as courageous, one also describes what courage is like; for instance, by how Achilles behaves. Such descriptions are, strictly speaking, nonevaluative. Similarly, the prescriptive force of the *sunna* as a model for action lies in its descriptive character, in that it is supposed to recount the life and teachings of the Prophet Muḥammad. Muslim scholars, preachers, and Sufi masters retrospectively describe the Prophetic past in their attempt to transform it into examples for the present. The choices of what in that past to describe and how to do it occur in response to, and seeking response from, the everyday. Such descriptions incorporate culture- and context-specific information, concepts, and considerations that help comprehension. Consequently, these acts of description retrospectively enrich the foundational past and augment the *sunna*.

* * *

To sum up, there are at least three ways of comprehending the phenomenon of the *living sunna*, as illustrated in the foregoing ethnography. First, the notion may refer to the ways in which disciples of a master regard the very being of their teacher as an exemplar, a living, culturally specific, and embodied elaboration of Prophetic teachings. Secondly, it may point to the augmentation of the foundational past through the master's act of describing the Prophet using culturally specific idioms, thereby retrospectively incorporating them into the Prophetic past. This allows people to perceive their specific cultural practice as a *sunna*—that is, as something commensurate with Prophetic practice. Thirdly, it may allude to the ability of the master to curate Prophetic teachings, including those taken from *ḥadīth* texts, and prescribe them to others. Such prescriptions can be either generally valid for all disciples or specific to the needs of particular disciples. All these cases highlight how articulating the *sunna* is a deliberative and reflectively critical action. It involves exploration, selection, and judgment on what to prescribe, how to do so, and for what short- or long-term purpose. As an outcome of articulatory labor, the *sunna* is not hermetically sealed from cultural particularities and the vicissitudes of the everyday. This means that the putative contrast between hypercoherent Islamic norms and the messiness of the everyday does not do justice to the dynamics through which articulatory labors allow the former to be modulated by the latter.

Conclusion

The Sufi master–disciple relationship has often been comprehended through the paradigm of power.[49] This construal of authority through the lens of power has a long precedent in philosophical treatments of authority. In this chapter I draw upon Arendt to suggest that authority rests "neither on common reason nor on the power of the one who commands," but on the recognition of a hierarchy deemed by all parties involved to be right and legitimate.[50] The authority of an Islamic religious leader hinges on a hierarchical relationship that allows him to articulate Prophetic teachings for others. Such a relationship is premised on the recognition of the leader's connection to the Prophetic past. This entails that the formation of authority demands the labor of building and maintaining conceptual and material infrastructure that can facilitate transmission over time and space. This infrastructure connects a leader to the foundational past and helps solidify his connection to his followers, thereby affording him the ability to render that past as a model for action—or *sunna*—to others.

I further argue that a Sufi order is an ordering mechanism made up of various conceptual and material infrastructures that are skillfully orchestrated by a Sufi master to transform networks into a durable religious community under his leadership. At the heart of this religious community is the hierarchical relationship that ties the master and his disciples. Such a relationship is premised on the recognition, which the apparatus of a Sufi order helps to frame and maintain, of the master's connection to the Prophetic past. This recognition, in turn, affords the master the ability to articulate that foundational past as a model for action for his followers. Involving more than a simple attempt at replicating the foundation or applying the *sunna* to new domains, such articulatory labors entail acts of curation, description, exploration, and innovation that augment the foundation. Produced in and through such relationships, the *sunna* becomes a living, socially embedded, and cumulative model that guides and is simultaneously guided by the world.

The foregoing ethnography illustrates the capacity of the *sunna* to accommodate and adapt to cultural particularities, individual needs, and the vicissitudes of everyday life. Far from being simply a set of common, consistent, and disembedded norms posited to be globally applicable, the *sunna* may outwardly express itself equally well through differences and even opposites. To a certain extent, there is a resonance between the *sunna* as embedded in social relationships and what Caroline Humphrey describes as "ethics of exemplars." In her study of Mongolian morality, Humphrey argues that what distinguishes ethics of exemplars from a morality based on a code is that "there is no requirement that exemplars be consistent with one another or that they be coherent with regard to society in general."[51] This form of ethics relates to "assumptions of individual difference" and "contributes to the crystallization of a variety of different 'ways of life,'" thereby rendering moral discourse as "open-ended and unfinished."[52] Similarly, the fact that the Prophetic past as the foundation upon which the *sunna* rests is not objectively available means that the *sunna* becomes available only through contextually specific retrospective attempts of connecting to, capturing, describing, embodying, and transforming that past into a practicable model for the present. These attempts generate a plethora of particular contents that do not simply exemplify the *sunna*, but struggle with it and give specific shape and form to it. Through such articulations, the *sunna* as a universal becomes "fully engaged in the process of its particular exemplification," which, in a way, may "decide the fate of the universal notion itself."[53]

A Sufi order is simply one among many different forms of ordering mechanism. Muslim leaders employ different ordering mechanisms and rely on distinct infrastructures to assemble religious communities. This difference opens up multiple articulatory possibilities. It follows that there are manifold articulations of the *sunna,* all of which may be perceived as correct and authoritative by members of the various communities by virtue of their connection to the Prophetic past. This generates a competitive religious marketplace in and through which different Muslim leaders strive to maintain and expand their communities. At the same time, the capacity of a Sufi order to provide networks with a conceptual and organizational social framework that—at least theoretically—demands absolute allegiance to a living leader who can unilaterally interfere in the personal affairs of his followers may generate tensions with another sociopolitical formation with similar ambitions and claims—namely, the state. Addressing these two dynamics, the next chapter looks at Habib Luthfi's relationships with other Muslim leaders and with the Indonesian state.

6

Politics

ON THE EVENING of june 18, 2012, a celebration of the Prophet's birthday (*mawlid*) was held at the main public square of Central Java's capital of Semarang. Jointly organized by Habib Luthfi and the Army Regional Command (Kodam) of Central Java, the event attracted thousands of Muslims from around the city and beyond, who were joined by approximately five thousand army personnel. The attendees sat quietly, facing an enormous stage set up for the occasion. On stage were Habib Luthfi and the Kodam commander, flanked by other senior Muslim scholars, government functionaries, and high-ranking military officers. Following the ritual recitation of the Prophet's nativity story, Habib Luthfi stood up to deliver a sermon. His topic was the history of Prince Dipanagara, the leader of the Java War discussed in chapter 1. The topic of choice could not be more apt, as the Kodam of Central Java is named after the heroic prince. "We need to learn from the history of the Java War," Habib Luthfi told the congregants:

> and remember how our national hero, Prince Dipanagara, was able to turn the Dutch topsy turvy due to his ability to unite Muslim scholars and generals for the glory of the nation. But when the Dutch succeeded in sowing disunity, the great force of the Prince was defeated. We should not let this happen again. Indonesia will stand glorious when we work together with our brothers in the military.

The event concluded with a ceremony to mark the beginning of a journey being undertaken by a contingent of ten disciples of Habib Luthfi and ten soldiers from the Kodam. Habib Luthfi tasked the group with producing what he described as flags with supernatural power (*bendera keramat*). The Sufi master and the Kodam commander handed six pieces of the Indonesian national flag, the red and white, to members of the group. Habib Luthfi instructed them to travel to the mausoleums of the nine saints of Java, scattered in different parts of the island. In each of the mausoleums, the flags were to be placed by the saint's tomb for one whole night while the disciples recited the entirety of the Qurʾān. After repeating the process in nine different mausoleums, the group were to divide the flags and return them to Habib Luthfi and the Kodam commander. Sacralized through both their proximity to saintly remains and the voicing of the Divine speech, the flags are now kept in the Kodam headquarters and in Habib Luthfi's congregational center.

For more than three decades, Habib Luthfi has actively worked to establish relationships with different institutions of the Indonesian state. Such connections have allowed him to assume the role of religious advisor to various state actors, from mayors and district heads, governors and generals, all the way to cabinet ministers. In 2019 the Indonesian President Joko Widodo appointed Habib Luthfi as one of the nine members of the Presidential Advisory Council (Dewan Pertimbangan Presiden, Wantimpres). In return for his advisory work, the *habib* enjoys the state's patronage, which helps him to maintain and expand his religious community. In performing this role, Habib Luthfi fits into a long tradition of Islamic religious leaders acting as mediators between communities of Muslims and the state. The history of organized Islam in different parts of the Muslim world has shown not only tensions and confrontations, but also alliances with the state. The nineteenth-century Javanese court chronicle *Babad Joko Tingkir*, for example, describes the annual state-sponsored *mawlid* celebration held at the capital of Java's first Islamic sultanate, Demak, as an event made possible by the cooperation of saints, Sufis, scholars, princes, and the lords of the realms:

In the capital Demak with the coming
Of the month Rabīʿ I
Assemble did the saints all
And the *muftī* and *sulakha*
The *ulama*, the wise and the ascetics
The great and mighty pundits
With all the ascetics too
Assembled in Demak, together one and all
And all the princes-regent
The nobles and high courtiers
The princes-regent of the outer realms
All assembled in Demak
As was customary
Every Rabīʿ I
They came; thus it came to pass
On the twelfth of the month
They recited *The Prophet's Nativity*.[1]

There is a long-held tendency, however, to explain alliances between the state and religious leaders and communities in terms of the former's co-optation of the latter.[2] As an explanatory paradigm, co-optation does not adequately capture the subtle dynamics at play in the establishment and maintenance of such alliances as that illustrated in the preceding account. It privileges the logic of the state and downplays the agency of religious leaders and their work in maintaining such alliances for reasons that may be different from statist agendas.[3] Moreover, as several anthropologists have shown, religious communities may embody excesses of meaning that cannot be thoroughly co-opted by the state.[4]

This chapter proposes an alternative way of thinking about alliances between religious communities and the modern state, and the role of religious leaders and state actors in mediating them. I argue that such alliances can be more fruitfully comprehended using the notion of articulation. If co-optation points to the subsumption or acculturation of nonstate entities into the more-powerful state, articulation involves "the construction of nodal points" that allow for the displacement, entanglement, and regular dispersion of meaning between the state and religious communities.[5] Consecrating national flags through devotional practice performed at saintly mausoleums, for example, turns the flags into meaningful artifacts for both the state and the religious community. Articulation can produce shared objectives, which, notwithstanding their momentariness or instability, may result in significant social consequences.

To comprehend alliances between religious communities and the state not as state co-optation, but as the outcome of articulatory labors performed by state and nonstate actors is not equivalent to saying that state power is in decline, leading to a need for it to work with nonstate entities. Instead, it is to acknowledge that the dominance and power of the state cannot "be referred to the specific logic of a single force."[6] Inspired by the works of Michel Foucault, anthropologists have come to recognize power as a dynamic field constituted by multiple contradictory forces, as opposed to a concentrated phenomenon with an identifiable center.[7] This shift in the treatment of power has led several anthropologists to conceive modern state governmentality as an ensemble of contradictory processes with creative and generative potentials. State power is reproduced and felt differently at various sites and levels, where its effects appear without clear institutional boundaries or geographic fixity.[8] This entails that any illusion of a center of power called the state should be analytically unmasked to uncover the reality of micro- and disparate relations of power.[9] Institutions like schools, churches, clinics, prisons, and factories serve as sites of disciplinary power that do not simply constrain but produce individuals as civil political subjects. These sites reproduce the state as objects of fear, desire, love, trust, attachment, or disavowal. The state, Begoña Aretxaga reminds us, "cannot exist without this subjective component, which links its form to the dynamics of people and movement."[10]

Anthropological critiques of the modern state have succeeded in charting complex geographies of governmentality made up of unequal relations, discourses, institutions, and modes of subjectivation in and through which different "faces of the state" become visible in public life and affective relationships to them are produced and maintained.[11] Less obvious from these accounts, however, is the question of how the state came to be immanent in the different relations that make up public life. As Bruno Latour inquisitively puts it, "people talk of force, power, structure, habits . . . sure, but how can they be put into action here, there and now?"[12] What processes, we may ask, allow for the state to be reproduced in distinct social formations, like religious communities, to the extent that they serve as sites in and through which state power is exercised? The notion of articulation, I suggest, helps us comprehend the diffusion and modulation of state power. To speak of immanent state power as an outcome of articulatory labor is to pay attention to the ongoing processes through which state and nonstate actors establish and maintain relations that open up the possibility for the exercise of power. Such articulatory processes impregnate the state with nonstate elements, and vice versa.

This chapter focuses on Habib Luthfi's relationships with different actors and institutions of the Indonesian state. It observes how different articulatory labors have allowed the *habib* to establish alliances with the state and, in turn, employ "the state" as infrastructure of religious authority. These relations have enabled him to organize religious events in and through which he performs the labor of articulating the *sunna* to a broader audience, often at the expense of other Muslim leaders. Alliances with the state have also allowed Habib Luthfi to rechannel state power to enact consequential interventions on behalf of others. Such relations were made possible owing to the need of state institutions to work with religious leaders and their communities to maintain their presence, pursue particular goals, and exercise certain forms of power. As such, examining the articulatory labor that aligns state institutions and religious communities enables us to trace the concrete processes that have allowed the state to be reproduced in distinct social formations that then serve as sites in and through which state power is exercised. By working with an Islamic leader, however, state actors become ensnared in competition between Islamic communities. In the second half of the chapter, I look at how different state actors work with diverse religious communities in pursuit of varying agendas, often against other state actors or religious leaders. These cases further destabilize our understanding of the state and state power, while illustrating how the lines separating the state, society, and religion are empirically fuzzy and analytically ineffectual, notwithstanding their ideological reality.[13] Instead, these cases accentuate how state actors and institutions are among the many actors and infrastructures that constitute the thriving and competitive Islamic religious marketplace of contemporary Indonesia.

Militarized Mawlid

The resignation of President Suharto in May 1998 marked the end of the New Order regime that had ruled Indonesia for thirty-two years. Suharto's departure ushered in an era of extraordinary sociopolitical transformation. Referred to as the Reformation Era, this period witnessed the gradual overhaul of Indonesia from a centralized authoritarian state into a decentralized democracy. During his brief term as Indonesia's third president, Suharto's immediate successor B. J. Habibie laid the foundation for the country's experiment with democracy by arranging for free and fair national elections and allowing for the proliferation of political parties. Throughout the New Order period, only three parties had been allowed to exist, one of which was the Islamic-oriented United Development Party (PPP). In the lead-up to the 1999 general elections, up to forty-eight new parties were declared, including the National Awakening Party (PKB) founded by the traditionalist Muslim scholar and future president, Abdurrahman Wahid (d. 2009). The emergence of the PKB divided traditionalist Muslim scholars and their followers, who during the New Order were, to a certain extent, united in their support of the PPP.

Pekalongan was one of the hotbeds of the new partisan politics. Traditionalist Muslims, who form the majority of the population, were divided between those who remained loyal to the PPP and those who joined the newly formed PKB. Scholars loyal to the PPP began verbally attacking their colleagues who had joined the new party from the pulpits, and vice versa. During the May 1999 campaign season, seventeen clashes were reported in Pekalongan between supporters of the PPP and the PKB. On May 29, 1999, a major violent confrontation erupted between the two camps, involving the use of hydrochloric acid, stones, and air rifles.[14] Eleven people were injured, and several homes and motorcycles were put to fire. The police and the military had to be deployed on the streets of Pekalongan to maintain order.

The May 1999 incident shattered the political unity of the traditionalist scholars of Pekalongan. This momentum provided Habib Luthfi with the opportunity to mediate between the opposing camps, particularly between local scholars who had long perceived him as a political adversary owing to his cordial relations with the New Order regime, as discussed in chapter 4. Habib Luthfi disassociated himself from Golkar and refused invitations to join any political party. Instead, he chose to work closely with the military, particularly following the abolition of the "dual-function" (*dwifungsi*) doctrine in 2004, which marked the end—at least formally—of the military's political involvement.

During the New Order period, the Indonesian Armed Forces—particularly the army—were directly involved in national politics. Justified by the doctrine of the dual function, the military saw its role not only as preserving internal and external security but also as overseeing and arbitrating government policies. The military reserved seats in parliament. Its interference in politics trickled down to the smallest territorial units, forming a hierarchy of army area commands based on the German *Wehrkreise* system that parallels civilian governmental structure.[15] On each territorial level, army commanders extended their influence over the governing of the territory under their command. While the dual function of the military was abolished in 2004 and the military vacated their seats in parliament, the Army Area Command structure remains in place.[16] On the ground, the commanders still exercise symbolic, if not real, power in the daily life of the community.

Habib Luthfi has had a close connection to the military since the 1980s. After 2004, he began to actively mediate the relationship between the military and the traditionalist Muslims of Pekalongan, who had been traumatized by more than thirty years of military repression. This was done partly through the Sufi master's adoption of nationalist discourse. In his sermons, Habib Luthfi consistently spoke about the danger of "party fanaticism," which has divided Indonesian Muslims. He called for Muslims to mend their relationship with the military, while presenting the latter as the apolitical warden of the nation. Every time Habib Luthfi was invited to speak at a religious event, he brought at least one military officer with him and asked him to address the congregation. He also invited local army commanders to join the executive board of his congregational center. Gradually, the military began to see Habib Luthfi as an important ally, because of his ability to remedy its fractured relationship with Muslim scholars and their followers.

* * *

In 2005, Habib Luthfi instituted a big festival celebrating the Prophet's birthday (*mawlid*), which combines the ritual recitation of the Prophet's nativity story and religious sermons with a military parade. Held at his congregational center, this militarized *mawlid* festival has been organized annually. The festival conforms to military aesthetics. Habib Luthfi and other dignitaries sit on a grandstand, receiving the salutes of the parading soldiers, police, and army veterans, who sing Islamic and patriotic songs to the accompaniment of marching bands (see figure 6.1). Every year, Habib Luthfi invites government ministers and generals from Jakarta for the occasion. Two sitting presidents of

FIGURE 6.1 Habib Luthfi receiving the salute of a local sub-district military commander during the military parade that marked the beginning of the 2012 annual *mawlid* festival. (Photo by the author)

Indonesia have attended the festival since its inception. To complement the military parade, Habib Luthfi asks local communities to stage cultural performances, including the Chinese community of Pekalongan, who performed the lion dance for the occasion. Subsequently, similar militarized *mawlids* have begun to be organized in different localities in Pekalongan and other parts of Java, albeit on a smaller scale. Each of these recurring events is prepared by Habib Luthfi's disciples together with army commanders and government functionaries from their respective localities. Habib Luthfi himself actively attends these events and delivers the final sermon.

The proliferation of militarized *mawlids* allows Habib Luthfi to travel and speak at various venues. These events attract people who do not traditionally attend a *mawlid*, like secular nationalists, modernist Muslims, and military personnel. Concurrently, they provide opportunities for Habib Luthfi's disciples and other Muslim leaders to interact with local military officers and government functionaries. These recurring festivals provide common, nonpartisan platforms of interaction for Muslim leaders affiliated with different political parties. By organizing these festivals, Habib Luthfi has been able to establish himself among different Muslim communities that were previously hostile to him. Indeed, many Muslim leaders affiliated with different political parties began to see Habib Luthfi as an important nonpartisan intermediary.

By the time I arrived in Pekalongan in 2011, there were around 150 militarized *mawlids* of varying scale organized annually, including the one in Semarang with which I opened this chapter. All of these localized festivals are affiliated with Habib Luthfi's festival cycle. The *habib*'s disciples organized some of these *mawlids*. The majority, however, are held by Muslim leaders not formally linked to Habib Luthfi but who want to host a local *mawlid* celebration that can attract a large turnout. Being affiliated with Habib Luthfi's *mawlid* festival cycle ensures that the local event gains the support of the local military officers and attracts Habib Luthfi's disciples and followers. The mere presence of a nationally renowned religious leader like Habib Luthfi alone would draw a large crowd.

While these militarized *mawlids* are held all over Java, most of them take place in the district (*kabupaten*) of Pekalongan, a territory that had been quite antagonistic to Habib Luthfi owing to his affiliation with the New Order regime. As discussed in chapter 3, the district had been under the *manṣab*'s sphere of influence and had provided him with an important source of income. Some Muslim leaders in the district saw the militarized *mawlid* as an expansionist maneuver on the part of Habib Luthfi. For example, the family of Kyai Tolha of Buaran, who once publicly denounced Habib Luthfi following his decision to join Golkar (see chapter 4), perceives these *mawlid* festivals as impinging on its religious community. Kyai Tolha's son, who took over his father's leadership position following the latter's death in 2005, denounced the *mawlid* festival as resembling the New Order Golkar-military-MDI project discussed in chapter 4. Other Muslim leaders have criticized the festivals as an ostentatious waste of money. Being funded by each hosting locality, the festivals burden local populations with the responsibility of fundraising. Several Muslim leaders also disparage the use of bass drum during the *mawlid*, a new addition to the *rebana* (a large tambourine akin to the Arabic *riq* drum) traditionally used to accompany the singing of praise songs for the Prophet. The low booming sound of the bass drum is favored by the young attendees of Habib Luthfi's *mawlid* festival, who move their bodies and dance while singing the paeans. In the words of one critical local scholar, the bass drum "turns the *mawlid* into disco" and "violates the *sunna*."

Local Muslim leaders who oppose the festivals rallied around the *manṣab*, Habib Bagir, whose position in the district has been directly challenged by Habib Luthfi's expansion. Indeed, many Muslim leaders and wealthy entrepreneurs from the district have begun to frequent Habib Luthfi's congregational center instead of the *manṣab*'s al-Rawḍa mosque. Previously, they would invite the *manṣab* whenever they organized religious events in their localities. Today, many of them affiliate their annual local *mawlid* event with Habib Luthfi's *mawlid* cycle. For these local actors, hosting a *mawlid* as part of Habib Luthfi's cycle ensures a large turnout, festivity, and direct assistance from local military personnel.

Faced with this reality, in 2010 the *manṣab* and several Muslim leaders close to him, including the son of Kyai Tolha, began to organize their own *mawlid* cycle. In contrast to Habib Luthfi's festivals, these events are much more modest. There is no military parade, lion dance, or singing of patriotic songs. These festivals consist of simply the recitation of the Prophet's nativity story and one short sermon discussing Prophetic *sunna* held at the mosque or *pesantren* headed by a scholar loyal to the *manṣab*. Only 30 events are held annually in the district of Pekalongan, as opposed to the 150 events that Habib Luthfi holds all over Java. The existence of two *mawlid* festivals, however, has generated a new problem for local Muslim leaders, who now have to choose between affiliating their local *mawlid*s with Habib Luthfi or with the *manṣab*. Those affiliating with Habib Luthfi know that the *manṣab* will not attend the gathering, and vice versa. Kyai Masruri of Warungasem, along with some of the other wealthier scholars, chooses to remain neutral by organizing two events during the annual *mawlid* at his boarding school: a morning *mawlid* with the *manṣab* and an evening one on the same day with Habib Luthfi. The bifurcation becomes blurred in cases where the host of the *mawlid* is a government functionary or a local magnate who financially supports both Habib Luthfi and the *manṣab*. Although the *mawlid* events are held as part of Habib Luthfi's festival cycle, the *manṣab* usually attends them, albeit briefly, to maintain his relationship with the host.

Not all events that comprise both *mawlid* festival cycles have continued annually. Some actors who previously hosted a *mawlid* may desist from doing it the following year owing to financial constraints. Hosting a *mawlid* may cost a village or a person up to Rp. 40 million (close to $4,000). This includes the cost of providing food and beverages for the attendees and monetary gifts for the scholars, preachers, and drummers. Holders of public office like the mayor or the chairman of the city council also tend to stop hosting a *mawlid* upon leaving office. Nevertheless, other individuals, villages, or subdistricts usually fill in the vacancies left by those who withdraw from participating in the *mawlid* cycle.

* * *

Apart from the military, local government has also played an important role in facilitating Habib Luthfi's expansion in the district of Pekalongan. The support of the local government, however, is largely contingent on Habib Luthfi's relationship with the district head (*bupati*), which may improve or deteriorate depending on the *habib*'s stance during local elections, as illustrated in the following case. In 2006, a lecturer at the Pekalongan State College of Islamic Studies (STAIN), Siti Qomariyah, decided to run as a candidate for district head against the incumbent, a veteran public servant by the name of Amat Antono. Being the daughter of a senior Muslim scholar, Qomariyah was able to garner the support of the traditionalist Muslims who form the majority of the district population. Habib Luthfi went all out in supporting and campaigning for Qomariyah, who, in turn, succeeded in defeating Antono.

Qomariyah's term as district head marked the peak of Habib Luthfi's expansion into the district. Similar traditionalist background, religious grammar, and social vision allowed regular dispersion of meaning across the state and the religious community personified by Siti Qomariyah and Habib Luthfi. Under Qomariyah, the district government funded several *mawlid* events. She even hosted an annual *mawlid* at the office of the district head. The government also provided Habib Luthfi with an expansive piece of land in the district for a planned Islamic boarding school. During Qomariyah's term, Habib Luthfi embarked on a project of rebuilding the mausoleum of an obscure local saint known to the locals as *Mbah Angsono*. The tomb is situated in the hamlet of Geritan, not far from the district capital of Kajen. I will discuss the tomb's identity in the next chapter. Suffice it to say at this point that the rebuilding of the tomb was made possible with the permission and financial support of the district government, and the physical assistance of the soldiers from the nearby barracks. Qomariyah also instituted a monthly religious gathering for women under the leadership of Habib Luthfi. The gathering drew the participation of around five thousand women from villages all over the district, who came in trucks and buses, all paid for by the government. Through this recurring event, jointly organized by Habib Luthfi and the local government, many women from the district have become disciples of the *habib*.

In 2011, former district head Antono decided to once again run for office. This time, he defeated Qomariyah. Antono's return to power dealt a significant blow to Habib Luthfi. Upon taking office, Antono removed Qomariyah's loyalists and Habib Luthfi's followers from influential positions. He also cut all financial support for Habib Luthfi's events. On several occasions, Antono even publicly stated that organizing *mawlid*s is a waste of money and energy. In a phrase that has since become notorious with Habib Luthfi's supporters in the district, Antono claimed that the only achievement of his predecessor was the construction of a *rumah hantu* (ghost house), referring to the mausoleum in Geritan discussed above.

This turn of the tide, however, did not mark the end of Habib Luthfi's influence in the district of Pekalongan. Even without the support of the district government, the *mawlid* festivals still enjoy the assistance of other state institutions, like the military. Nevertheless, the fractured relationship with the district head has had its impacts. Attendees of the monthly religious gathering for women, for instance, no longer enjoy free transportation to the event. The caretaker of the mausoleum in Geritan complained to me that since Antono took office, no district government official has been willing to sit on the mausoleum's board of trustees for fear of being identified as Habib Luthfi's supporter. Since the government has withdrawn all financial support, the caretaker has had to look for donations from other sources, like local businesses and wealthy individuals. While this does not impede the caretaker's ability to host ritual events at the mausoleum, it nevertheless has impacted the hospitality he can to provide to the attendees. "In the days of Qomariyah," he recalled, "a tray of rice included six to seven large cuts of goat meat, and now we are down to four smaller pieces per tray."

* * *

Habib Luthfi's militarized *mawlids* are sites that reproduce what Aretxaga aptly describes as "the actual social and subjective life" of the state.[17] These religious events facilitate intimate encounters with the state by replicating its presence in religious rituals. They afford Muslims new ways of feeling well disposed toward and identifying with the state, particularly with the military, which for so long had been traumatically experienced as a coercive and violent force. Organizing a *mawlid* is a collective effort between state and nonstate actors, who are gathered and assembled around a shared concern. It facilitates amicable encounters between these actors and cements relationships that continue to endure long after the actual event. As such, these *mawlid* festivals allow state and nonstate actors to mirror one another in reimagining the state as an object of pious attachment and identification.[18] Observing these events and the subjective dynamics they generate provides an aperture into how the state as a reality becomes ever-present and immensely powerful in everyday life.

It is crucial, however, that we refrain from privileging the state, or the logic of the state, as the only outcome of these events. Militarized *mawlids* also serve as infrastructures of religious authority. The proliferation of such events, including those organized by Habib Luthfi's competitors, has resulted in an extended annual celebration of the Prophet Muḥammad that begins in the Islamic month of Rabīʿ I (the month of the Prophet's birthday) and continues for six months until the last day of Shaʿbān, prior to the onset of the fasting month. Almost every other evening there is a festive *mawlid* event held in one of the many neighborhoods or villages that make up the city and the district of Pekalongan. In and through these events, Habib Luthfi performs the labor of transmitting Prophetic teachings, leading to more widespread recognition of his authority. These events serve as conduits for the flow of the *sunna*, while exposing it to interpretive conflicts that cannot be isolated from the politics of congregational expansion and competition among Muslim leaders.

The State Ensnared

So far I have shown how Habib Luthfi's articulatory labors have created nodal points where meanings and agendas of his religious community intersect with those of the state. In the dense and thriving religious marketplace of contemporary Indonesia, such articulatory labors have enabled Habib Luthfi to penetrate into new territories, incorporate more people into his sphere of influence, challenge other Muslim leaders, and—as will be made clear in the following pages—rechannel state power to enact consequential interventions on behalf of others. Alliances with the state, however, are far from stable. For one thing, holders of governmental office change periodically. As discussed above, Habib Luthfi may have a good relationship with one district head, but he may not enjoy the same amicability with the subsequent holder of the position. He may easily fall into conflict with a state actor over various matters, electoral politics being one recurrent issue. As there are many religious communities competing with one another, state actors can easily turn to other Muslim leaders deemed to be more advantageous or in line with their own political or moral agendas. Consequently, the state is frequently ensnared in contestations between religious leaders and their respective communities. The following cases illustrate how different state actors have worked with different religious communities in pursuit of varying agendas, often against other state actors or religious leaders.

* * *

Pekalongan is home to a relatively small but prosperous Chinese-Indonesian community. For more than two decades Habib Luthfi has cultivated a close relationship with this largely non-Muslim community. He has continued to defend the political and cultural rights of the community members as Indonesian citizens, to protect their business interests, and to educate his followers on the immorality of racism. He has also attempted to incorporate members of the Chinese community into his circle. Every year, the *habib* delivers a speech at the local Pho An Thian temple during the *Cap Go Meh* that marks the end of the Chinese new year celebration. He has also requested the community to perform the traditional lion dance (*barong sai*) during the *mawlid* festivals. Leading members of the Chinese community, together with other non-Muslims, have continued to attend and even financially support Habib Luthfi's *mawlid* festivals.

Public performance of the lion dance was banned during the New Order until the prohibition was lifted by President Abdurrahman Wahid (1999–2001). This came together with the state's decision to recognize Chinese culture and Confucianism as constitutive parts of Indonesia's national culture. The Chinese community welcomed Habib Luthfi's decision to incorporate the lion dance into his *mawlid* festivals. In several of his sermons, the *habib* explained to his congregation that the rationale behind incorporating the lion dance into the *mawlid* celebration is to entice members of the Chinese community to attend the festivals so that they can learn more about the Prophet and his teachings. At the same time, he wanted to expose his followers to the nation's cultural varieties. Many traditionalist Muslims, however, were alarmed by the revival of Chinese culture in the country, seeing it as a visible sign of the growing economic and political power of the Chinese. The performance of the lion dance has also been used by some Muslim leaders critical of Habib Luthfi, including the *manṣab*, to justify their refusal to attend the *mawlid* festivals. In their view, the performance of the lion dance is an erroneous innovation (*bidʿa*) that contradicts the *sunna* and pollutes the *mawlid*.

In 2011, several disciples of Habib Luthfi from the village of Kebasen, in the district of Tegal (around thirty-seven miles west of Pekalongan) planned to host the lion dance during their annual *mawlid* festival. In response, several Muslim leaders from Tegal petitioned local state officials to forbid the scheduled performance. Addressed to the district head, the chief of police, and the local army commander, the petition stated that the lion dance is a theologically laden performance. The document explained that, for the Chinese, the dance is believed to be a ritual that repels misfortune (*penolak bala*) and brings luck (*pembawa keberuntungan*). The document also explained that the dancing lion is believed to be "the vehicle of the gods" (*kendaraan para dewa*).[19] The district head, the police chief, and the army commander, however, were all close to Habib Luthfi. Instead of addressing the concern of the petitioners, they traveled to Pekalongan to consult with Habib Luthfi. Stressing the importance of educating the public regarding Indonesia's cultural heterogeneity, the *habib* told his guests to support the lion dance performance, which they consequently did. Habib Luthfi's connection to the three leading embodiments of the state in the district of Tegal thus enabled him to persuade them to extend their support for his followers in Kebasen, despite the consternation of other Muslim leaders.

Unlike his cordial relationship with the three leading state actors in Tegal, Habib Luthfi's relationship with the mayor of his home city of Pekalongan has been fraught with problems. During my fieldwork, Habib Luthfi was not on speaking terms with the mayor, Dr. Basyir Ahmad (b. 1953). Habib Luthfi had supported Basyir's nomination when he first ran for office in 2005. After all, like Habib Luthfi, Basyir is of Ḥaḍramī descent, although he is not a Bā ʿAlawī. The relationship turned sour, however, when Basyir ran for a second term in 2010. The reason for this is that Basyir's deputy, Abul Mafakhir, decided to run for the mayoral office on his own. Unlike Basyir, Mafakhir is Habib Luthfi's disciple. The Sufi master thus abandoned his initial support for his fellow Ḥaḍramī and openly endorsed his disciple. Basyir was displeased with Habib Luthfi's decision. When he defeated Mafakhir in the election, Habib Luthfi lost a critical ally in city hall.

The fact that Habib Luthfi's endorsement and active support for Mafakhir failed to deliver success raises an interesting question regarding the influence of Muslim community leaders over electorate politics. Indonesian politicians have continued to befriend Muslim leaders in the hope of securing the support of their followers. Substantial donations and gifts have been distributed by politicians to woo such leaders to their camps, particularly in the lead-up to an election. Nevertheless, Muslim leaders' relationships with their followers do not automatically translate into electoral votes. In fact, an extended reportage carried out by Indonesia's *Tempo* magazine concluded that in the 2009 Indonesian general election, the influence of Muslim community leaders over electoral politics had significantly waned compared with previous elections.[20] As a result, money politics, in the form of direct distribution of money to voters on the morning of the election—a campaign strategy known in Indonesia as *serangan fajar* (dawn offensive)—has been preferred by politicians, as opposed to distributing money to Muslim leaders.

The relationship between Habib Luthfi and the mayor reached an all-time low in 2011 during the annual *mawlid* festival. While Basyir was already displeased with Habib Luthfi's decision to support Mafakhir, as a mayor, he was compelled to attend an event that brought more than a hundred thousand visitors into the city. Additionally, the presence of high-ranking government and military dignitaries from Jakarta during the festival demanded his participation as the mayor of the hosting city. It so happened that when Basyir's car approached Habib Luthfi's congregational center, a disciple of Habib Luthfi who managed parking told the chauffeur not to proceed as there was no space left ahead. Feeling entitled, the mayor's chauffeur did not heed the instruction. Not knowing that it was the mayor's car with the mayor sitting inside, the disciple smacked the hood of the vehicle. Angered, Basyir's adjutant came out of the car and punched the disciple. The two exchanged blows before the crowd finally dispersed them.

Habib Luthfi took offense at the incident and decided to take the case to court. Being the first to deliver a blow, the court sentenced the mayor's adjutant to two months' imprisonment. Humiliated by the incident and its aftermath, Basyir stopped attending Habib Luthfi's *mawlid* festival, notwithstanding the presence of the high-ranking officials from Jakarta. Even when the Indonesian president Soesilo Bambang Yudhoyono attended the festival in 2013, Basyir was strikingly absent from the stage, choosing instead to meet and welcome the president upon his arrival at the train station.

* * *

This fraught relationship with Habib Luthfi drew the mayor closer to the *manṣab*. Being a Ḥaḍramī and a long-time neighbor, Basyir had been the *manṣab*'s family doctor, providing primary care to both the first and the second *manṣabs*. The relationship between the two intensified after Basyir became the mayor. The mayor's policy of banning the sale of alcohol, as well as his ongoing plan to close down nightclubs in Pekalongan, won the support of the *manṣab*, who saw protecting public morality as central to his socioreligious role. In support of the *manṣab*, every year Basyir attends and delivers a formal speech at the annual commemoration of the *manṣab*'s great-grandfather, the principal saint of Pekalongan, Aḥmad b. ʿAbdallāh al-ʿAṭṭās. Despite his genial relationship with the *manṣab*, however, the mayor is generally known to be closer to, or at least to harbor some sympathies for, Salafi movements. Such a stance has made Basyir suspect in the eyes of many traditionalist scholars of Pekalongan. This is one of the reasons that drove Habib Luthfi to support Basyir's contender Mafakhir in the 2010 mayoral election.

In Pekalongan, the Salafi movement emerged from within the al-Irsyad, the modern Ḥaḍramī reformist *jamʿiyya* (voluntary association; see chapter 3) that Basyir is affiliated with. The movement's growth within the al-Irsyad can be traced back to the early 1980s, when several of the association's regional leaders were disappointed over the dwindling state of the organization, which in former times had been one of the precursors of Islamic educational reform in the country. While al-Irsyad is known for running kindergartens, schools, and hospitals throughout Indonesia, the organization has nevertheless faltered behind other modern Islamic reform-oriented institutions, like its sister organization, the Muhammadiyah (founded 1912). To date, al-Irsyad has only 450 schools (from kindergarten to high school), eight hospitals, and no university. Muhammadiyah, on the other hand, has a total of 5,754 schools, twenty-nine universities, and seventy-two hospitals. Equally important has been the decline in Arabic proficiency and general Islamic knowledge among young Irsyadis.

In their attempt to ameliorate the state of the organization, several al-Irsyad leaders began to develop relationships with, and send Irsyadi youth to, the

Saudi-sponsored Islamic sciences and Arabic language institute (LIPIA) in Jakarta. Founded in 1980, LIPIA was established as part of the Saudi response to the international impact of the Iranian Revolution. Offering both intensive and nonintensive preuniversity Arabic courses, LIPIA was able to recruit talented students from different reformist-oriented schools.[21] While admission standards are high, once matriculated, students enjoy free tuition and stipends. Directly associated with the Imam Muhammad Ibn Saʿud Islamic University in Riyadh and under the direct supervision of the Saudi embassy in Jakarta, the institute's objective was to expand Saudi Arabia's sphere of influence and reshape young minds to receive Salafi theological doctrines. Several young Irsyadis who were admitted to LIPIA received scholarships to study in Saudi Arabia, Pakistan, and North Yemen, including Jaʿfar ʿUmar Thalib, who later founded the Laskar Jihad (Jihad Front) in 1999. Upon return to Indonesia, these graduates actively preached Salafism through different means, including study circles, campus organizations, and publications.[22]

The expansion of Salafism within the Irsyadi community happened quite dramatically. Many local branches of the organization came under the influence of Salafi thought. They began to question and criticize the Irsyadi leadership, who in their view had softened up and were no longer involved in the original idea of purifying idolatrous and erroneous Islamic practices. These young Irsyadis took a hard stance toward Sufi-oriented scholars, accusing them of straying from Prophetic *sunna* and misguiding Indonesian Muslims with their heretical rituals and discourses. The growing Salafi camp within al-Irsyad rallied around the figures of Farouk Zein Badjabier and the wealthy, Surabaya-based businessman Khalid Bawazier. During the al-Irsyad congress in Pekalongan in 1996, the Salafi camp attempted to take over the organization's leadership from the then national chairman Geys Amar. An intra-Irsyadi rift ensued, with both camps claiming to be legitimate. Each side began to hold its own congress and form its own administration.[23] Bawazier funded the expansion of the Salafi movement in different areas, building mosques, schools, and dormitories as well as providing scholarships for students to attend Salafi educational centers abroad.

One of these newly built Salafi mosques is located in the neighborhood of Kwijan, Pekalongan, within walking distance of Habib Luthfi's congregational center. The mosque was formally opened in July 2011 by Mayor Basyir and ʿAlī Ḥasan al-Ḥalabī, a Syrian Salafi scholar who studied under the famed Albanian Salafi ideologue Muḥammad Nāṣir al-Dīn al-Albānī (d. 1999). Ever since its opening, the mosque has caused the displeasure of its traditionalist Muslim neighbors. Almost every day, following the dawn and afternoon prayers, the mosque holds classes by Salafi preachers, most of which revolve around criticizing the Islamic practices of the traditionalist Muslims—like *mawlid*, saintly commemoration, and grave visitation—deemed as *bid'a* that violate Prophetic *sunna* and may even constitute idolatry (*shirk*). While only ten to twenty people attend these daily classes, the Salafi teachings are amplified by powerful speakers perched on the mosque's minaret. As a result, adversarial Salafi discourses resonate through the urban soundscape, entering people's homes and private spaces, including Habib Luthfi's balcony, where he enjoys his afternoon coffee. This has caused growing resentment among the traditionalist Muslims in Pekalongan, particularly those living in the vicinity of the mosque.

Attempting to address the situation, local traditionalist Muslim activists began to look into the mosque's permit. They ascertained that the subdistrict head (*lurah*) had never issued a formal authorization for the construction of the mosque. Those building the mosque had never asked for an official permit, nor did they request consent from the neighbors. These activists subsequently discovered that the permit for the building of the mosque had come directly from the mayor, without going through the standard procedure involving neighbors and the subdistrict head. The activists and the traditionalist Muslims living in the mosque's vicinity have repeatedly filed complaints to the mayor, but to no avail. They have also brought their grievances to Habib Luthfi. His strained relationship with the mayor, however, curtailed the *habib*'s ability to address the complaints of his followers.

In contrast, the *manṣab*'s close relationship with the mayor has enabled him to exert his influence upon Basyir. The *manṣab* may be personally close to the mayor, but he strongly disagrees with Basyir's Salafi inclinations. Like Habib Luthfi, the *manṣab* has repeatedly criticized the Salafis, both in formal and informal settings, even if they agree and have even worked together on issues pertaining to the protection of public morality. Consequently, local Muslim scholars, including those who are close to Habib Luthfi, had to rely on the *manṣab*'s friendship with the mayor, as they were not on good terms with Basyir owing to their support for Mafakhir during the election. While Habib Bagir himself has not been able to persuade the mayor to reconsider the permit for the Salafi mosque, he nevertheless has been able to apply some degrees of pressure on the mayor in the following Salafi-related case.

The city council owns a big congregational mosque located in one of the city's major town squares. For years, a traditionalist scholar served as the mosque's prayer leader. When Basyir became the mayor, however, he unilaterally replaced the traditionalist scholar with a Salafi scholar, although the old prayer leader was still under working contract for another three years. The mayor's action alarmed traditionalist scholars, who feared a Salafi take-over of the mosque. While these scholars were close to Habib Luthfi, they nonetheless turned to the *manṣab* because of the latter's connection to the mayor. Habib

Bagir pleaded with the mayor on their behalf and, weeks later, the mayor removed the Salafi imam and restored the old prayer leader. Thus, in contrast to Habib Luthfi's inability to address the grievance of his followers over the expansion of the Salafi movement, the *manṣab*'s personal relationship with the mayor enabled him to pressure the mayor into revising his decision, notwithstanding Basyir's Salafi leanings.

* * *

A strained relationship with the mayor of Pekalongan does not mean that Habib Luthfi is left with no state allies. The fact that there is more than one state institution in a given location means that a Muslim community leader like Habib Luthfi can work with other state actors when there is one he cannot work with. Indeed, the *habib* can use his alliance with one state actor to work against other state actors or Muslim leaders. The tension among Habib Luthfi, the mayor, and the *manṣab* over the growth of nightclubs in Pekalongan highlights this intricate dynamic.

Upon becoming mayor in 2005, Basyir issued a mayoral decree banning the sale of alcohol in Pekalongan, a policy that disadvantaged nightclub owners. Habib Luthfi, on the other hand, chose to address the growth of nightclubs pragmatically. In his view, nightclubs should be allowed to operate freely in Pekalongan to generate employment and increase revenues to the city. Faced with an unfriendly mayor, the nightclub owners sought the protection of Habib Luthfi in the hope of benefiting from his intimate connection to the police and the military. While the police and the military no longer have the same degree of power and political influence that they enjoyed during the New Order, both institutions remain active in protecting various business ventures, including mining and the entertainment industry.[24] In many cases, influential middlemen like community leaders broker this cooperation. Such a description may sound disparaging, and indeed it does to many people. Nevertheless, Habib Luthfi himself has been open about his stance and does not see it negatively. As he has often made clear to his followers, his decision to protect such businesses is based on the fact that they have generated employment opportunities for Muslims. Clarifying his position in a meeting with local scholars at his congregational center, Habib Luthfi explained:

> I am not thinking about the bosses, I am thinking about Muslims whose livelihoods depend on those bosses. I maintain good relationships with the bosses because I am entrusting our children to them. If these entertainment sites are closed, are you willing to provide jobs for the workers, most if not all of whom are Muslims? One should think long and hard before making

any hasty decision. *Sharīʿa* should be a mercy rather than a disaster for the Muslims.

Here, Habib Luthfi deploys the notion of the common good, or *maṣlaḥa*, which has long been used by Muslim jurists to adjust "the boundaries of any existing consensus, via modes of public reasoning concretely applied to any given situation."[25] But despite his efforts to persuade his fellow scholars to accept his reasoning, objections from other Muslim leaders remain in place.

Through the triangular relationship among Habib Luthfi, the police and military, and the nightclub owners, the nightclubs have remained in operation and continued the sale of alcohol, notwithstanding the mayoral decree. One big nightclub complex owned by local Chinese textile giant and confidante of Habib Luthfi Tiong Hoe, hosts DJs and performers from Jakarta every week. In return for Habib Luthfi's support, Tiong Hoe financially supports the *habib*'s congregational center and its events. Strangely, there was no debate among Habib Luthfi's followers—at least, that I was aware of—over whether Tiong Hoe's money is lawful (*ḥalāl*) or otherwise, considering the nature of his business. Tiong Hoe also built a sizable edifice in his entertainment complex to accommodate Habib Luthfi's followers from out of town free of charge. When I first visited the place, there was a big sign stating: "Rest area for the guests of Habib Luthfi" (*tempat peristirahatan tamu Habib Luthfi*), which sparked a controversy in Pekalongan owing to its location within an entertainment complex. While the building remains in use, the sign has now been taken down.

In contrast to Habib Luthfi, the *manṣab* adopts a zero-tolerance attitude toward nightclubs and the sale of alcohol. Both the *manṣab* and the mayor are infuriated by the continuing existence of nightclubs in Pekalongan and their inability to intervene effectively. During a Friday prayer in Pekalongan's grand congregational mosque, the mosque's officials distributed a weekly bulletin to the congregants containing a report of the *manṣab*'s condemnation of the nightclubs, explicitly naming Tiong Hoe's entertainment complex. The report describes how the *manṣab* called on the public to keep pressuring all government institutions to take action. "Yes Pekalongan needs investments, but we do not want projects that can cripple public morality," states the *manṣab*.[26]

The *mansab*'s insistence on protecting public morality brought him closer to the Salafis and a controversial Jakarta-based vigilante organization, the Islamic Defenders Front (FPI), which had opened its branch in Pekalongan in 2011.[27] The *manṣab* was asked to sit on its advisory board and accepted the invitation. The presence of the FPI in Pekalongan was welcomed by the mayor and the Salafis, although it angered Habib Luthfi and many traditionalist Muslims. The organization's tendency to take the law into its own hands, together with its leader's persistent criticism of certain traditionalist scholars for their lukewarm commitment to "enjoin the good and forbid the wrong" have alienated the FPI from most traditionalist Muslims in Java.[28] Habib Luthfi himself publicly warned the FPI during one of his *mawlid* sermons not to wreak havoc in Pekalongan, threatening to deploy "our brothers in uniform" against it. In response to the traditionalist Muslims' antipathy toward the FPI, the *manṣab* withdrew himself from the organization less than two months after the opening of the Pekalongan branch.

Through his relationship with two state institutions—the military and the police—Habib Luthfi has been able to extend his protection over the nightclub owners and consequently receive their support, whether employment or financial donations, for his community. Such a relationship, in turn, limits the ability of the mayor to exercise power and enforce his regulation, despite his alliance with other Muslim leaders. If in this case we have a constellation whereby a Muslim leader works with two state institutions on behalf of the private sector against another state institution, the final case that I now turn to shows how Habib Luthfi works against other Muslim leaders on behalf of a state actor.

* * *

Around eighteen miles southeast of the city of Pekalongan, in the village of Wonobodro, Batang, stands an old shrine believed to contain the grave of a mysterious saintly figure known simply as Mawlānā Maghribī (Our Lord from the West, or the Maghreb).[29] A popular local and regional pilgrimage destination, the shrine holds a public commemoration every year attended by around five to six thousand people. Since its inception, the commemoration has been organized by the shrine's keeper, together with the family of the aforementioned Kyai Tolha and the *manṣab*. Due to the uneasy relationship between the *manṣab* and Habib Luthfi, the organizers of the commemoration had never invited the latter. Indeed, for a long time, Wonobodro was outside of Habib Luthfi's sphere of influence.

One evening, as I was sitting with the *habib* on the balcony of his house, the village head of Wonobodro made an unexpected appearance. The annual commemoration of Mawlānā Maghribī was only a few weeks away, and I assumed that the village head had come to extend an invitation to Habib Luthfi. I was wrong. He was there to inform Habib Luthfi that the sole bridge that connects the village to the outside world had collapsed. As a result, the village had to lease an emergency mobile bridge from the Army Regional Command (Kodam) in Semarang, which cost Rp. 90 million (more than $6,000). The village head, however, had failed to raise enough funds to cover the expense.

He thus requested Habib Luthfi's help to intercede on behalf of the village to the Kodam commander. Instead of agreeing to help, Habib Luthfi explained to the village head that since the end of the New Order, the military had been in dire financial straits, and as such, the Kodam had good reason to levy a rental charge for the emergency bridge. At the same time, Habib Luthfi explicitly expressed his disappointment that the rental cost was burdened on the village rather than on the district government of Batang. Habib Luthfi could have helped by bringing the case to the district head, but he was not on good terms with the incumbent owing to his support for another candidate in the previous election.

Habib Luthfi then told the village head to use the money accrued from pilgrimage donations to pay for the emergency bridge. The village head, however, informed the *habib* that the shrine keeper controlled the income of the shrine and that the money had been spent on the shrine's renovation. Habib Luthfi frowned. He began to criticize the village head for allowing the money to be used for a superfluous purpose, ignoring the more pressing need. "You are the representative of the state," Habib Luthfi told him. As the personification of the state in the village, he ought to have the final say over how the income from the shrine was spent. Habib Luthfi lit a cigarette. For at least fifteen minutes he did not utter a single word. His eyes were fixated on the flickering cigarette. When the *habib* exhibits such a pensive mood, nobody dares to interrupt.

Suddenly the *habib*'s eyes gleamed. He smiled and turned to the village head, who had been sitting quietly, while nervously holding his handkerchief. He asked one of his attendants to get a pen and paper and give them to the village head. "Write," Habib Luthfi instructed him, and began to dictate a donation request letter. Once the dictation concluded, Habib Luthfi told the village head to type it as a formal document with the letterhead of the village government, and circulate it to wealthy businesspeople, government officials, and Muslim leaders. He instructed the village head to start by sending the letter to the family of Kyai Tolha and the *manṣab*. "If they claim to be benefactors of the shrine, then they should pay attention to this problem and donate," Habib Luthfi exclaimed. He then left the balcony and went into his bedroom. Minutes later, he returned carrying a thickly filled envelope, presumably containing money, and gave it to the village head. "There, that is my share," he said.

Habib Luthfi then told the village head that he would sign the donation letter as a witness, to lend further credibility. "My signature as a witness will strengthen you to act on behalf of the village, and you should never be subservient to the shrine keeper," he said. Having Habib Luthfi's signature on the letter would allow prospective donors from outside the village to take the village head's request seriously, while strengthening his standing among the villagers, including the shrine keeper. After all, the keeper's authority over the shrine is partly built on his relationship with outside Islamic authorities, whether the family of Kyai Tolha or the *manṣab*. By signing the letter and instructing the village head to circulate it to other scholars and state actors, Habib Luthfi effectively directed the village head to question and test the dedication of the shrine keeper, the *manṣab*, the family of Kyai Tolha, and even the district head to the village of Wonobodro.

Wonobodro may be a small village. Nevertheless it is a social arena where contestations between Muslim leaders and different state actors have played out. These contestations mapped onto internal village politics like the uneasy relationship between the village head and the shrine keeper over the management of the pilgrimage economy. The collapse of the bridge afforded Habib Luthfi the opportunity to intercede on behalf of the village to the military or the district head, but he did not do so. Even if he had, the Kodam commander might still have been unwilling to waive the rental fee for the emergency bridge, in which case it would reflect badly on Habib Luthfi. What is fascinating is how Habib Luthfi used the crisis to proclaim himself a supporter and protector of the village head, who is the personification of the state in the village, not only in garnering donations but also in facing up to the shrine keeper and his backers. By adding his signature to the formal letter of a village head that was to be sent to the *manṣab* and the family of Kyai Tolha, Habib Luthfi was able to borrow the authority of the state as personified by the village head and instantiated in a formal letter with government bureaucratic form, like the letterhead. This enabled him to discursively and graphically present himself as a custodian of not just the shrine, but also the village. The donation letter thus endorsed Habib Luthfi as he endorsed the village head's fundraising attempt. The signature of the state, to use Veena Das's term, and that of the Muslim leader mutually reinforced each other.[30] The donation letter becomes a nodal point, constructed through articulatory labor between a Muslim leader and a state actor that occurred on a micro level, but which nevertheless allows the former to borrow the apparatus of the state to lay claim on a shrine and challenge other claimants to the position.

Conclusion

Alliances with state actors have enabled Habib Luthfi to organize events in and through which he can transmit the *sunna* in new territories, where he was not previously welcomed. Such maneuvers have facilitated wider recognition of Habib Luthfi's role as a religious authority—that is, as a connector to the Prophetic past. Such alliances have also allowed for the state to be reproduced and become immanent in diverse social settings, like Islamic rituals, thereby bolstering the ideological image of the state as an all-encompassing sociopolitical entity. At the heart of these alliances is articulatory labor—the creation of nodal points that facilitate the production of shared meanings and agendas, allowing the articulated elements, notwithstanding their contradictions, to act in concert, however momentarily.

Despite various internal regimenting operations, the state is instantiated in diverse actors and institutions that are often locked in contradictions and contestations. Different state actors form alliances with various Muslim leaders, fixating different meanings and pursuing diverse and often conflicting projects, some of which become efficacious in certain conjectural and relational contexts, while others fail to do so. The increasingly plural and conflictual terrain of social life in decentralized Indonesia means that state power is distributed among different state actors who have to form contingent relations with community leaders to enable effective exercise of power.[31] In the dense religious marketplace of contemporary Indonesia, such relationships have ensnared the state in the competitions between Muslim leaders. Despite the state's purported neutrality and palliative function toward social conflicts, different state institutions do take sides in the contestations between Muslim scholars. A state actor may work with a Muslim leader against other state actors and Muslim leaders. Consequently, relationships between the state and Islamic communities do not intersect only in mutually supportive ways. Often, they block, undermine, and interfere with one another. Moreover, these alliances fluctuate depending on the issue at hand. We see how the Sufi-oriented *manṣab* teamed up with the mayor and the Salafis over the problem of nightclubs and the sale of alcohol, notwithstanding their theological differences. This, in turn, suggests that analytic frameworks that delineate contestations between Islamic communities in terms of ideological or theological streams do not do fully capture these shifting constellations. As Alexander Knysh recently noted, "general observation of Sufi-Salafi conflicts does not carry far, for behind the apparent universality of the Salafi-Sufi conflict we find a myriad of indigenous factors that shape, often decisively, its concrete sociopolitical manifestations."[32]

Habib Luthfi's success in assembling and expanding his community with the help of state actors has led him to become increasingly recognized as one of the leading Islamic authorities in Indonesia. Equipped with this sociocultural capital, he has embarked on a project of composing the hagiography of his own little-known and unrecorded forefathers. This hagiographical composition allows Habib Luthfi to situate himself as the terminus of different authoritative genealogies of Islamic transmission that have connected contemporary Java to the Prophetic past. It is to this that we now turn.

7

Genealogies

ONCE UPON A TIME, an itinerant saintly *habib* passed by a small, sparsely inhabited village. Honored by the presence of a descendant of the Prophet, the villagers implored the *habib* to take up residence among them. The *habib* agreed and settled down in the village. Many years later, a delegation from a neighboring village visited the *habib* and invited him to move to their village. Seeing that the other village was in dire need of religious instruction, the aging *habib* accepted the invitation. The inhabitants of the first village, however, were deeply disappointed with the decision and begged the *habib* to stay. The *habib* tried to reason with them, saying that over the years they had received adequate guidance from him. Still, they refused to accept. That night, as the *habib* was deep in slumber, the villagers killed him. They buried his body in the village, built a mausoleum over it, and instituted an annual commemoration to honor his memory.

This story is one among the many satirical tales that are often told in jest among Indonesian Bā ʿAlawīs when they get together to engage in "empty talk." More often than not, those who laugh at such satires are themselves regular attendees of saintly commemorations. This is understandable, as to appreciate such stories requires familiarity with practices of saintly veneration and hagiographic literature, upon which the satires are modeled.[1] This particular story is interesting because it does not depict the villagers as passive victims of a power-hungry or money-grabbing *habib*, a trope most famously typified by Joseph Conrad in the villainous figure of Sherif Ali of Patusan.[2] Instead, they are portrayed as active actors driven by a combination of religious belief, emotional bond, and calculative reasoning. Killing the saintly *habib* ensures that his remains, and the *baraka* (blessing) associated with them, stays in the village. This, in turn, may transfigure the village into a pilgrimage destination, thereby gracing its inhabitants with *baraka* that is as much socioeconomic as it is spiritual and symbolic.

That saintly tombs enhance the prestige and welfare of a locality is a dynamic that has been repeatedly observed by historians of Christianity and

Islam.[3] It is also one that has come to be understood by the current mayor of Central Java's capital Semarang, Hendrar Prihadi. Since being elected mayor in 2013, Prihadi—who hails from the secular-nationalist Indonesian Democratic Party of Struggle (PDIP)—has been proactive in developing Semarang's potential as a destination for the increasingly lucrative religious tourism (*wisata religi*). The last two decades have indeed witnessed a remarkable growth of Islamic religious tourism in Indonesia.[4] The annual commemoration of the Bā ʿAlawī scholar-poet ʿAlī b. Muḥammad al-Ḥabashī in the Central Javanese city of Solo, to give one notable example, attracts more than two hundred thousand pilgrims from all over Indonesia, bringing the circulation of money to more than 200 billion rupiah (approximately $14 million) during the three-day event.[5] Unlike Solo, however, Semarang is not a fully established pilgrimage destination. In developing Semarang's potential, Prihadi has been working with Habib Luthfi to recover the city's saintly past. The city government assisted Habib Luthfi in constructing the mausoleum of one of Habib Luthfi's ancestors, Ḥasan b. Ṭāha Bin Yaḥyā, and funded the first commemoration in 2018.[6] On January 17, 2019, Indonesia's premier newspaper, *Kompas*, carried a report about a ground-breaking ceremony held to mark the construction of another mausoleum in Semarang.[7] Initiated by Habib Luthfi and Mayor Prihadi, the planned shrine will house an old grave that had recently been identified by the Sufi master as the tomb of Ḥasan's father, Ṭāhā b. Muḥammad al-Qāḍī Bin Yaḥyā. In a speech delivered during the ceremony, Prihadi expressed that "Habib Taha's tomb is a pride for the people of Semarang, as the city can now be a part of the history and genealogy of the Prophet's descendants in Indonesia."[8]

This final chapter follows Habib Luthfi's labor of recovering Indonesia's saintly past. For more than two decades, Habib Luthfi has been preoccupied with recovering saintly histories that have been reduced to obscurity or left unrecorded in historiography. In his view, Muslims have a responsibility to conserve their history and to preserve it for future generations. Muslims, he argues, must produce their own histories, particularly because both colonial and national historiographies have obscured, if not systematically erased, Indonesia's saintly past. He has accomplished this by identifying old unmarked graves as saintly tombs, providing them with recognizable histories and genealogies, and instituting commemorative rituals.[9] Such labors take place not only in his hometown of Pekalongan but also in different locations across Indonesia. In most cases, the Sufi master has been quite successful owing to his alliances with state actors, who, like Mayor Prihadi, have been interested in capitalizing on the growth of religious tourism in the country. For Habib Luthfi, saintly shrines facilitate the intimacy and connectivity that enable Muslims to viscerally imagine themselves as part of a transgenerational relationship that links them to the Prophetic past.[10] Materializing a topographically rooted Islam that hinges on embodied "participation" and engages with "the visceral register of being"—to use William Connolly's term—however, is not the only projected outcome of Habib Luthfi's historical recovery project.[11] Much of his labor has been devoted to the hagiographical composition of his own little-known and unrecorded forebears. In composing their hagiographies, the Sufi master employs old and new material to produce an interconnected ensemble of oral narratives, texts, and tombs that corroborate one another. This hagiographical composition projects Habib Luthfi not merely as someone who has been genealogically adopted into the Naqshbandī-Khālidī and Shādhilī *silsila*s, but also as a lineal successor of an old, but forgotten, Bā ʿAlawī saintly dynasty closely linked to the Ḥaddādian scholars on the one hand and the Javanese royal dynasty on the other.[12] Consequently, in the hands of Habib Luthfi, the hagiography works to articulate competing genealogies and itineraries of Islamic transmission like those that have been discussed in this book. The convergence of multiple genealogies of Islamic transmission in Habib Luthfi, in turn, allows him to situate himself as the living terminus of diverse historical itineraries that connect contemporary Java to the Prophetic past. Being an embodiment of several genealogies of authority affords Habib Luthfi the possibility to authoritatively nest himself in different Islamic communities in Java and articulate the *sunna* for them, albeit without necessarily determining its success.

In focusing on an ongoing hagiographical composition that involves saintly talk, texts, and tombs, this chapter contrasts with those studies that focus on finished or institutionalized hagiographies, or those that limit their analysis of hagiography to textual forms.[13] Following an unfinished hagiographical composition opens up a contextualized perspective into the politics and infrastructures of hagiography. The historian Shahzad Bashir, for example, observes how hagiography has served as the primary arena "in which various masters and their hagiographers constructed their own rights of spiritual inheritance and negated those of their rivals."[14] Bashir's observation highlights how hagiographies cannot be understood independently of their articulations in and of social life. Indeed, hagiographies have provided Muslims with vehicles for talking about theology, causation, justice, power, and ethics.[15] This, however, should not necessarily entail that their meanings are to be found in social phenomena. Rather, it should mean simply that the significance, truthfulness, and authoritative status of a hagiographical product emerge (or fail to emerge) in a field made up of different kinds of practice and discourse, and thus need to be explained as outcomes of historically specific politics and forces.[16] The case of Habib Luthfi's hagiographical composition is particularly useful for thinking about this process, considering that its authority and truthfulness are still very much in flux. This, in turn, enables us to explore the infrastructure of hagiography—that is, the various material forms, including, but not limited to, texts—that allows for its composition and enables it to become authoritative. The case of Habib Luthfi suggests how the authority of a hagiographical composition is built on the contingent involvement of different actors, material forms (old and new), and regimes of knowledge, all of which require careful orchestration to ensure that they are articulated in a coherent manner.

To speak of hagiography as an outcome of composition is to underline the heterogeneous materials that come to be articulated to create a hagiographic product that has recognizable themes, but also variations. I use the term "composition" because it resonates with an old Javanese notion of authorship that posits an author as a composer (*panganggit, pangiket*)—that is, someone who productively *interlaces* (*nganggit*) and *binds together* (*ngiket*) old and new texts, thereby blurring the distinction between the act of writing "as physical 'replication' of prior inscription," and "as 'original' composition."[17] Hagiographical composition, as will be shown in this chapter, generates factual ambiguity that cannot be easily resolved. This suggests that a useful way of approaching a hagiographical composition is not to ascertain its possible truth but to observe how people have come to accept or reject its truth and authority.[18]

Saintly Talk

"Does the donkey give birth to the lion? No. The lion is born of lions," said the Jordanian Dr. Ahmad to the anthropologist Andrew Shryock. Dr. Ahmad, Shryock explains, is a "self-made man," who has accomplished so much without genealogical capital. Nevertheless, Shryock adds, "unlike the self-made man of Western tradition, who boasts proudly of his humble origins and arduous climb to the top, Dr. Ahmad inhabits a world of *uṣūl*, of roots and foundations, in which the low status of one's ancestors is conveyed, quite literally, *in the blood*."[19] Shryock recounts how Dr. Ahmad has tried to make sense of, and further accelerate, his upward mobility by uncovering his noble origins. He uses the story of Dr. Ahmad to illustrate the ideology of *aṣl* (Ar. pl. *uṣūl*, roots), which posits nobility of birth as conferring moral qualities and distinctions, such as excellence, honor, sincerity and honesty, and generosity.[20] While Shryock discusses this ideology in relation to the Bedouin Arabs, the question of *aṣl* (Ind. *asal-usul*, Jav. *bibit*) has also been prevalent among non-Arabs.[21] For traditionalist Muslims of Indonesia, *nasab* (bloodline) remains an important evaluative category commonly deployed to explain the noble qualities or achievements of a religious leader, although it is less so among the urban-based, modern, educated Muslims who follow religious leaders owing to their teachings and marketing techniques.[22] *Nasab menentukan nasib* (bloodline shapes destiny), as my traditionalist interlocutors like to say. Those who are schooled in the *pesantren* often deploy an Arabic phrase believed to come from a Prophetic *ḥadīth*, to explain the importance of *aṣl*: *al-ʿirq dassās*. The phrase translates roughly as "blood will tell, what is bred in the bone will come out in the flesh."[23]

While, technically, sanctity does not depend on bloodline, in reality many traditionalist Muslims I conversed with tend to highlight the centrality of *nasab*. The notion of hereditary sanctity has a long history. As a textual and sociological phenomenon, hereditary sanctity proliferated across the Muslim world from the fourteenth century onward, as piety began to be increasingly identified with the Prophet and his family.[24] As early as the eleventh century, hagiographical sources were presenting *sayyid* families as the privileged sites for the transmission of sanctity. Scholarly and saintly *sayyid* families, like the ʿAydarūs of the Ḥaḍramawt and India, the Wafāʾ of Egypt, and the Jubāyrī of Bukhara were perceived as the institutional loci and training grounds in and through which sanctity is passed on from father or uncles to sons or nephews.[25] Teachings on how saints are born with congenital knowledge and inherit spiritual potentialities have been actively disseminated by scions of saintly dynasties in Java and have taken root among the Bā ʿAlawīs and traditionalist Javanese Muslims.[26] In expressing the notion of hereditary sanctity, Bā ʿAlawī preachers frequently quote the following verses, penned by the Bā ʿAlawī scholar-poet Alī b. Muḥammad al-Ḥabashī (d. 1915):

> Path [*ṭarīqa*] of guidance, filled with secrets
> obtained by the nobles [*amjād*]
> who succeeded the Noblest [the Prophet]
> A father received it from his father, and so on
> How honorable are those fathers and sons[27]

A Bā ʿAlawī preacher speaking during the commemoration of al-ʿAṭṭās in Pekalongan in 2013 even went as far as quoting the Qurʾān to justify hereditary sanctity. "Behold," he said, "God raised Adam, and Noah, and the House of Abraham, and the House of ʿImrān above all mankind in one line of descent" (Q. 3:33–34).

* * *

In contrast to most contemporary Bā ʿAlawī community leaders like the *manṣab*s who inherit their position through lineal succession, Habib Luthfi can be fairly described as a self-made leader. He did not inherit his leadership position from his father or grandfather. Rather, as discussed in the preceding chapters, he inherited a leadership position through genealogical adoption, and subsequently worked tirelessly to expand his following. Like the Jordanian Dr. Ahmad, however, Habib Luthfi "inhabits a world of *uṣūl*."[28] More often than not, his claim to religious authority has been dismissed on the basis of his relatively less-known ancestors, notwithstanding his Prophetic descent. Many Bā ʿAlawīs spurn Habib Luthfi's authority by saying, "ʿarafnā man abūh!" (we knew who his father was!), meaning that the father was not a scholar, a saint, or a *manṣab*. To be taken as legitimate in a world of *uṣūl*, an aspiring religious leader needs to articulate his leadership claim in kinship terms vis-à-vis the previous holder of the position.[29] Often, the contingency of succession unfolds in the terms of the cultural field of genealogy, from which actors drew their reasons and actions found their meanings.[30]

Habib Luthfi can, of course, claim that his ancestors were saints. Indeed, he has repeatedly done so in his sermons and during informal conversations. The following is an example of Habib Luthfi recounting the history of one of his ancestors during a sermon delivered at a *mawlid* celebration in Semarang in January 2013. The ancestor in question is Muḥammad al-Qāḍī, the father of the aforementioned Ṭāhā, whose mausoleum in Semarang is under construction at the time of this writing:

> Habib Muḥammad al-Qāḍī studied with his father, uncles, and other great Bā ʿAlawī imams, including Habib ʿUmar al-ʿAṭṭās. He was a close friend of Imam ʿAbdallāh al-Ḥaddād. He was among the great scholars of *ḥadīth*. He traveled around the Middle East, Africa, Fez, Tangier, Marrakech, and the Comoros. Wherever he went, he built mosques. He built more than five hundred mosques. He then traveled to India, to Naserabad, Ahmadabad, Jaipur, and studied under the Aydarūs scholars of Surat. He built mosques in the villages of India, where the majority of the population were Hindus. Many embraced Islam through him. . . . [*thirty seconds of silence*] . . . Then he entered Malaya and established an Islamic school in Penang. From Penang, he went to [the Sultanate of] Banten, where he was appointed as the *shaykh al-akbar* [the greatest shaykh] by the Sultan. The Dutch were eyeing him, but through his strategies, Habib Muḥammad was able to expand his influence without confronting them directly. He then went to Cirebon, and finally to Semarang, where he became known as *Ki Ageng Semarang* [the great master of Semarang]. His students rose to become eminent scholars. Among them was Prince Mangkubumi, who became HB I [Hamengku Buwono I, the first Sultan of Yogyakarta]. Habib Muḥammad was known as the *quṭb al-ʿulūm* [the axial saint of the sciences].

In this talk, Habib Luthfi presents a portrait of Muḥammad al-Qāḍī as a highly mobile Bā ʿAlawī saint. His biography resonates with the biographies of famous and "successful" Bā ʿAlawī personalities that can be found in hagiographies and biographical encyclopedias (*tarājim*). It is a success built on the combination of scholarship, sanctity, mobility, and worldly position.[31] Note how Habib Luthfi presents Muḥammad al-Qāḍī not only as an axial saint (*quṭb*) but also as a reputable *ḥadīth* scholar—that is, as a credible connector to the Prophetic past and articulator of Prophetic teachings. Notice also how al-Qāḍī is portrayed as closely connected to notable personalities, Bā ʿAlawī or otherwise, whose histories are amply recorded. These include the founder of the sanctuary of Ḥurayḍa, ʿUmar al-ʿAṭṭās (see chapter 1), the reformer ʿAbdallāh al-Ḥaddād (see chapter 2), the ʿAydarūs scholars of Surat, and the founder of the Yogyakarta Sultanate. It seems that saintly talk opens up the possibility for interweaving multiple histories through the articulation of different genealogies of authority that have been posited as unconnected or unrelated.

* * *

Saintly talk, however, is not durable and can be easily dismissed as mere talk. Among the textually erudite Bā ʿAlawīs, utterances do not invoke the same authority as texts.[32] They are believed to be polluted by lies, and more so when they are uttered by those deemed to have a personal interest. The marks of the storytellers, as Walter Benjamin once wrote, "cling to the story the way the handprints of the potter cling to the clay vessel."[33] To take on higher authority, saintly talk has to be corroborated, or travel across different material forms to set itself apart from the profanity of oral traditions. It needs to be linked to forms of truth posited to be higher than, and external to, the interested parties.

Take, for example, the *manṣab* of Pekalongan, whose leadership position is built on his descent from an ancestral saint whose hagiographies are widely known.[34] As discussed in chapter 3, the saint's hagiographies are instantiated in different material forms, including texts authored by numerous authors, a mausoleum, and a mosque, as well as rituals that continue to be observed down to the present day. The saint's biography is even recorded in the genealogical tome kept by the Bā ʿAlawī association, the Rabithah Alawiyyah (discussed in chapter 3), which contains a comprehensive scheme of descent of the Bā ʿAlawīs from the Prophet Muḥammad. For the Bā ʿAlawīs, the genealogical tome is considered as a transparent and higher form of truth as it consists simply of names and their lines of descent, with almost no narrative. After all, its purpose is simply to record names and serve as the final arbiter in solving the question of genealogical authenticity. The tome, however, includes short biographical addenda next to the names of outstanding Bā ʿAlawīs who have achieved saintly fame during their lives (see figure 7.1), including the saint

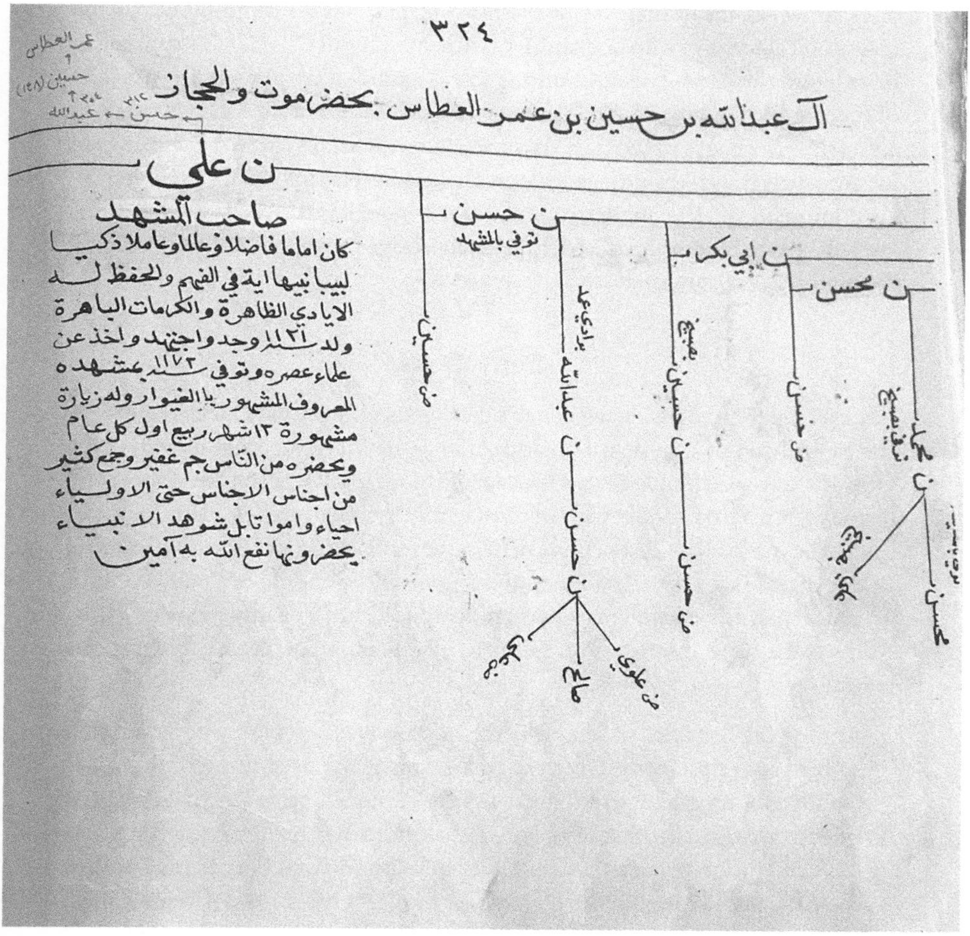

FIGURE 7.1 A page from the Bā ʿAlawī genealogical tome kept at the Rabithah Alawiyyah, showing a biographical addendum below the name of an outstanding individual. (Photo by the author)

of Pekalongan, Aḥmad al-ʿAṭṭās. The presence of al-ʿAṭṭās's biographical addendum in the genealogical tome lends further credence to the inherited authority of his descendants.

Contrastingly, no biographical addenda accompany the names of Habib Luthfi's immediate ancestors. Of course, this does not necessarily mean that Habib Luthfi's ancestors were individuals whose biographies are not worth mentioning. The absence of biographical addenda may be due to the genealogists' unawareness of their saintly fame or the lack of other textual records. It does, however, mean that, unlike the *manṣab*, Habib Luthfi cannot utilize the genealogical tome—whose authority is accepted by all Bā ʿAlawīs—to bolster his religious leadership claim. Among the *aṣl*-minded Bā ʿAlawīs, the absence of biographical addenda has been used to discredit Habib Luthfi's claim to authority. The pages of the Bā ʿAlawī genealogical tomes that list the names of his ancestors thus become a genealogical arena for Habib Luthfi's hagiographical composition. The challenge is to fill the blanks next to the names of his ancestors with biographical addenda. Such labors, however, take place outside the genealogical tome.

Saintly Texts

At times, canonical Bā ʿAlawī genealogical texts may provide an aperture that can be utilized to establish transitional links between saintly talk and texts. One illustrative example of this is a capsule biographical narrative of someone from the Bin Yaḥyā family who is known only by the moniker Ṭāhir in one of the authoritative Bā ʿAlawī genealogical compilations, the *Shams al-ẓahīra*. While Ṭāhir is a proper name commonly used by the Bā ʿAlawīs, the biographical narrative describes it ambiguously as either a proper name or a title. At the same time, the text does not provide the name of Ṭāhir's father or his genealogy:

> Among the notables of this [Bin Yaḥyā] family is a person who was called Ṭāhir [*yudʿā ṭāhiran*]. He went to Penang at the beginning of the nineteenth century and married the daughter of the Sultan of Yogyakarta. Then he accompanied the Sultan to Java and settled down in Semarang. Such was the description given by the Dutch orientalist Van den Berg in his book on the Arab population [of the Dutch East Indies]. He also said: two of Ṭāhir's children remained in their Arabness [*baqī ithnān min abnāʾ ṭāhir ʿalā ʿurūbatihimā*]. The third son, known as Aḥmad, became Javanized [*ṣār jāwiyan*] and was known by the title Sumodirjo. He actively took part in the war of Dipanagara. When the war ended in 1830, he settled in Pekalongan and married one of the daughters of the Bā ʿAbūd *sayyid* family. His son, Ṣāliḥ, became part of the city's government, known as Raden Sumoputra, and rose to become the attorney [*jaksa*] of Cilacap. He was then appointed as the chief of police in Pekalongan. When he retired, he went back to wearing Arab dress and married one of his daughters to an Arab from the Ḥaḍramawt.[35]

The *Shams al-ẓahīra* was initially written in 1890 by the Bā ʿAlawī master genealogist and *muftī* of Tarīm ʿAbd al-Raḥmān b. Muḥammad al-Mashhūr (d. 1902) as an abridgment of the seven-volume genealogical tome, kept in

Tarīm (and now also kept at the office of the Rabithah Alawiyyah in Jakarta). This abridgement was first printed in Hyderabad in 1911 and was subsequently republished in Jeddah in 1984 with copious biographical footnotes describing notable members of each Bā ʿAlawī family in Ḥaḍramawt and the diaspora prepared by an Indonesian Bā ʿAlawī journalist, Muhammad Dhiya Shahab (d. 1986). In compiling the extensive footnotes, Shahab relied on interviews as well as Bā ʿAlawī and non–Bā ʿAlawī texts such as hagiographies, histories, and newspaper articles, including the ethnographic work of the Dutch scholar L.W.C. van den Berg. The footnotes enrich the list of names in the original text with colorful biographical narratives. While, strictly speaking, the notes are later additions to the *Shams al-ẓahīra*, today they are not regarded by the Bā ʿAlawīs in Indonesia as a separate text. Rather, both are regarded as one unified text. After all, genealogical texts are a living, cumulative corpus.[36]

The biographical description of Ṭāhir and his descendants quoted above does not come from the original text of the *Shams al-ẓahīra*. It appears in a fourteen-page footnote on famous personalities from the Bin Yaḥyā family written by Shahab. Indeed, Shahab explicitly mentions that the information comes from L.W.C van den Berg's 1886 ethnographic work, *Le Hadhramout et les Colonies Arabes dans l'Archipel Indien*. While Shahab incorporates Van den Berg's narrative into the text, he does not provide any genealogical information for Ṭāhir, except for mentioning him as a member of the Bin Yaḥyā family. Presumably, Shahab himself was not aware of Ṭāhir's genealogy.

The presence of a name with a biographical addendum in one of the most authoritative Bā ʿAlawī genealogical texts, combined with the absence of a clear genealogy, opens up what I call a *genealogical aperture*. A genealogical aperture allows other actors—particularly those with knowledge of genealogy—to extend a proprietary claim on the name by superimposing it into a known genealogy. Such an opening, however, is limited by several other pieces of information given in the text, including: (1) Ṭāhir is a member of the Bin Yaḥyā family, who had (2) a son called Aḥmad (Sumodirjo), and (3) a grandson named Ṣāliḥ (Sumoputra). The prospect of reclaiming the mysterious Ṭāhir is quite appealing, owing to his affinal ties to the royal court of Yogyakarta and the involvement of his son in the Java War. More so as Prince Dipanagara has achieved legendary status as a national hero in postcolonial Indonesia. At the same time, Ṭāhir's biography is featured not only in a Bā ʿAlawī genealogical text, but also in a Dutch ethnographic work. The veracity of Ṭāhir's biography is, therefore, sustained by more than one regime of knowledge.

Habib Luthfi claims the mysterious Ṭāhir in the *Shams al-ẓahīra* as his ancestor. He maintains that Ṭāhir is not a proper name, but a title—*al-sayyid al-ṭāhir* (the pure *sayyid*)—borne by his ancestor Ṭāha b. Muḥammad al-Qāḍī, whose mausoleum in Semarang is currently under construction. Here is Habib Luthfi recounting Ṭāha during a sermon delivered in Semarang in January 2013:

> Habib Ṭāha was born in ʿInāt [Ḥaḍramawt]. His mother was from the family of the *manṣab* of ʿInāt. He studied under great scholars of Ḥaḍramawt like Habib ʿAlī b. Ḥasan al-ʿAṭṭās [founder of the sanctuary of Mashhad] and Imam ʿAbdallāh al-Haddād. Following his studies in Ḥaḍramawt, Habib Ṭāha traveled to Penang to see his father Muḥammad al-Qāḍī, who had established an Islamic school there. He taught at the school and fought against the British. He then went to Semarang, where his father had settled down, and then accompanied HB II [Hamengku Buwono II, the second sultan of Yogyakarta] to his exile in Penang. He married one of the daughters of HB II. He was known as *al-sayyid al-ṭāhir.* You can all check his biography in the *Shams al-ẓahīra*.

Note how Habib Luthfi has superimposed Ṭāha b. Muḥammad al-Qāḍī on the mysterious Ṭāhir. On the one hand, the saintly talk furnishes Ṭāhir with a clear genealogy—as Ṭāhir/Ṭāha b. Muḥammad al-Qāḍī—and background history, both of which are left unrecorded in the brief textual biography. On the other hand, by superimposing Ṭāha onto Ṭāhir, Habib Luthfi can finally point to a Bā ʿAlawī textual source deemed to be authoritative to corroborate his oral narratives. The presence of Ṭāhir's biography and the absence of his genealogy thus make him into a genealogical aperture that can facilitate alignment between saintly text and talk. The text corroborates the utterance, and the utterance enriches the text.

One cannot, however, simply dismiss Habib Luthfi as making things up, as indeed the Bā ʿAlawī genealogical tome does record Ṭāha b. Muḥammad al-Qāḍī as having several sons, one of whom was Aḥmad, who in turn begot Ṣāliḥ (see figure 7.2). Thus, there is a triangular alignment between the *Shams al-ẓahīra,* Habib Luthfi's saintly talk, and the Bā ʿAlawī genealogical tome. The question becomes whether Ṣāliḥ b. Aḥmad b. Ṭāha of the genealogical tome was indeed Ṣāliḥ Sumoputra b. Aḥmad Sumodirjo b. Ṭāhir of the *Shams al-ẓahīra*. The *Shams al-ẓahīra* mentions only one son of Ṭāhir. Habib Luthfi's ancestor, Ḥasan b. Ṭāha, is not mentioned. Nevertheless, the correspondence between the *Shams al-ẓahīra* (and Van den Berg's *Le Hadhramout*), Habib Luthfi's oral narratives, and his own genealogical record in the Bā ʿAlawī tomes already supports an important genealogical claim—namely, that through Ṭāha/Ṭāhir's marriage to the daughter of the second sultan of Yogyakarta, Habib Luthfi is theoretically connected to a Javanese royal dynasty. Habib Luthfi further enriches the biographical record in the *Shams al-ẓahīra* by claiming that his ancestor Ḥasan (the brother of Aḥmad Sumodirjo?) and the son of the Sultan's daughter—was known as Ḥasan Sumodinigrat. According to Habib

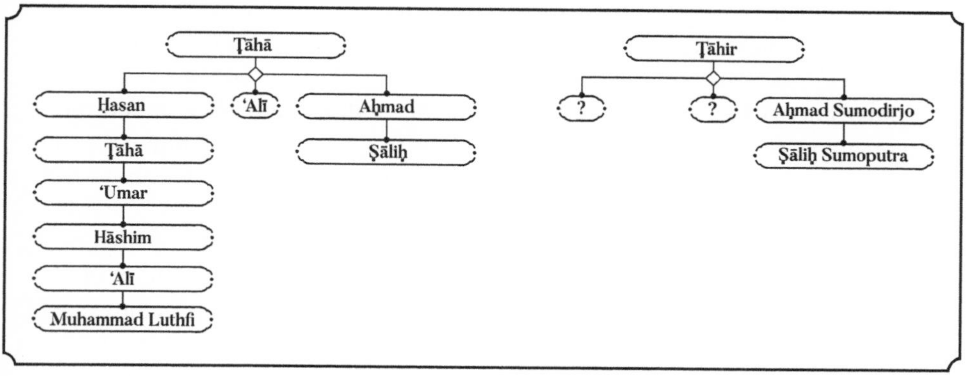

FIGURE 7.2 Schematic showing Habib Luthfi's genealogy from the Bā ʿAlawī genealogical tome (*left*) and the genealogy of Ṭāhir from the *Shams al-ẓahīra* (*right*).

Luthfi, Ḥasan also fought for Prince Dipanagara during the Java War, like his brother Aḥmad, and was known as the *senapati agung* (great commander).

Habib Luthfi's claim of connection to the Yogyakarta royal dynasty was reinforced through his personal relationship with the younger brother of the current Sultan, G.B.P.H. Joyokusumo, who for several years was his disciple. Habib Luthfi had developed a relationship with Prince (*Gusti*) Joyo, as he was usually called, through the former's Yogyakarta-based disciples, many of whom were connected to the royal court. Habib Luthfi's knowledge of Javanese history, together with his sensitivity to Javanese culture, attracted Prince Joyo. The prince, in turn, regarded the Sufi master with utmost respect. Several times a year, Prince Joyo would visit Pekalongan. He also invited Habib Luthfi to Yogyakarta to lead Islamic gatherings at the royal court. As the sultanate's Penghageng Kawedanan Hageng Panitra Putra—a post akin to a secretary of state—Prince Joyo was able to support Habib Luthfi's hagiographical composition. With his backing, Habib Luthfi obtained a *serat kekancingan*—that is, a genealogical certificate issued by the sultanate's genealogical office, the Tepas Darah Dalem, to those who can prove genealogical relation to the dynasty. Habib Luthfi's own *serat kekancingan*, authorized by the seal of the sultanate, thus becomes another piece of textual evidence that corroborates his oral narratives.

* * *

Oral narratives may enrich saintly and genealogical texts. Nevertheless, they are evanescent, malleable, and subjectively tied to the speaker. Such characteristics are what diminish the credibility of saintly talk among those who subscribe to the superiority of textual authority. Saintly talk, however, can be made durable and more authoritative, through the work of entextualization—that is, "the process of rendering discourse extractable, . . . [so that] it can be lifted out of its interactional setting."[37] Entextualization diminishes the control of interested speakers over the utterance, creating a perception of internal cohesion, autonomy, and consistency across contexts. This, in turn, allows a stretch of saintly talk to be reinserted in new interactional contexts, thereby prolonging its life and expanding its reach.[38] While linguistic anthropologists have directed our attention to the dialectical process of entextualization of a stretch of discourse and its contextualization in new interactional contexts, here I want to draw attention to how entextualization also allows for subsequent contextualization of discourse in new texts that are deemed to be more authoritative.

In 2014, a disciple of Habib Luthfi by the name of Ahmad Tsauri (b. 1985) published a book entitled *Sejarah Maulid Nabi: Sejak Khaizuran hingga Habib Luthfi Bin Yahya* (A history of the Prophetic Mawlid: From Khaizuran to Habib Luthfi Bin Yahya). The book traces the history of the *mawlid* celebration from the Abbasid era to the annual event held at Habib Luthfi's congregational center, the Kanzus Shalawat. Since its publication, more than seven thousand copies have been sold. The 285-page, heavily footnoted book has begun to be recognized by Habib Luthfi's disciples and followers as the official history of the annual *mawlid* at the Kanzus Shalawat. The book is not only sold online and at the congregational center during the monthly gathering, but is distributed to the bookshops of the traditionalist *pesantrens* in Java. It begins with a chapter on the meaning and social efficacy of ritual commemoration by drawing on modern anthropological and sociological theories. The following chapter charts the history of the *mawlid* celebration in the Abbasid, Fatimid, Ayyubid, and Mamluk eras, drawn from classical Arabic historiographical texts together with modern academic works. Another chapter recounts the history of the *mawlid* in Indonesia. The last two chapters specifically focus on Habib Luthfi's annual *mawlid.*

Significantly, Tsauri describes the annual *mawlid* at the Kanzus Shalawat not as Habib Luthfi's innovation, but as a yearly ritual that the Sufi master inherited from his ancestors. Based on Habib Luthfi's oral narratives, Tsauri depicts the annual *mawlid* as a continuation of a tradition instituted by Habib Luthfi's ancestor, the aforementioned Ṭāha/Ṭāhir:

> The Great *mawlid* [*mawlid akbar*] at Kanzus Shalawat has a long history. The annual event organized by Habib Luthfi is a continuation of a *mawlid* tradition that was instituted by Sayyid Ṭāha, also known as Sayyid Ṭāhir, whose full name is Habib Ṭāha b. Muḥammad al-Qāḍī Bin Yaḥyā (d. 1202 AH). It is said that when Sayyid Ṭāha began calling people to Allāh [*da ʿwa*

ilā Allāh] in Java, he used *mawlid* as his medium. He used drums and gamelan to accompany the singing of praises in honor of the Prophet.... During his life, Habib Ṭāha was known as a very knowledgeable scholar, particularly in the sciences of *ḥadīth* and *fiqḥ* [jurisprudence]. At first, Habib Ṭāha lived in Penang, Malaysia. He then traveled and proselytized in Banten, Cirebon, Surabaya, and finally Semarang. Habib Ṭāha died and was buried in Semarang. He had fourteen children, eleven sons and three daughters, all of whom were saints and scholars.

When Habib Ṭāha passed away, the *mawlid* was continued by his sons, particularly Habib Ḥasan, who lived and proselytized in Kramat Jati, Semarang. During his life, Habib Ḥasan fought valiantly against the Dutch colonizers and was feared by them. He fought along the northern coast of Java. His courage won him the appellation of *Singo Barong* [a lion-like mythological creature]. When Habib Ḥasan passed away, the *mawlid* was continued by his eldest son, Habib Ṭāha of Ciledug, West Java, and his younger siblings.

After the death of Habib Ṭāha b. Ḥasan, the *mawlid* was continued by his sons: Habib Hāshim, a reputable scholar who died in Medina, and Habib Muḥsin who lived and proselytized in Kutai, East Kalimantan, and was buried on the Senumpak Island off Kalimantan. The *mawlid* was also continued by his other son, Habib ʿUmar b. Ṭāha, who established a *pesantren* in Sindang Laut, Cirebon [West Java]. That *pesantren* produced eminent scholars who rose to prominence in Cirebon and West Java.

When Habib ʿUmar passed away, the *mawlid* was continued by one of his sons, Habib Hāshim. Habib Hāshim was the first Bā ʿAlawī scholar to establish a *pesantren* in Pekalongan. Before Habib Hāshim, there were several *pesantrens* in Pekalongan established by the local scholars, among others, Kyai Khomsa in Landungsari, Kyai Agus in Kenayagan, Kyai Murtado in Sampangan, Kyai Abdul Aziz in Banyu Urip, and others. Together with Habib Hāshim, those *kyai*s worked hand-in-hand to institute a *mawlid* tradition as a medium for proselytization. Through the *mawlid*, people became aware of the teachings of Islam, understood the Qurʾān and the *sunna*, as well as social ethics [*etika bermasyarakat*]. Through the *mawlid*, people became acquainted with our leader, the Prophet Muḥammad.... Habib Hāshim was very influential. Even scholars as great as Shaykh Hasyim Asy'ari [the founder of the Nahdlatul Ulama] recognized Habib Hāshim's authority.... When he passed away, the *mawlid* was continued by his children and sons-in-law, albeit not as big as it used to be, and finally, his grandson [Habib Luthfi]. The *mawlid* tradition has therefore been persistently carried out from generation to generation [*turun temurun*] until today.[39]

Several points can be deduced from Tsauri's entextualization of Habib Luthfi's oral narratives. First, the above description provides an old genealogy for a ritual established in the 1980s, while presenting Habib Luthfi as a lineal successor of an old Bā ʿAlawī line of spiritual leadership in Java. By positing Ṭāha/Ṭāhir as the one who instituted the annual *mawlid* tradition, the text avails itself to be aligned with other texts, including the *Shams al-ẓahīra*, where Ṭāhir's capsule biography can be found. Tsauri's description also reinforces Ṭāha/Ṭāhir's son, Ḥasan (Sumodinigrat), as someone who was involved in armed struggle against the Dutch, although it does not explicitly mention the Java War or Prince Dipanagara. It presents all of Habib Luthfi's ancestors as saints and scholars who left their mark on the history of Java.

Secondly, the *mawlid* is exclusively presented as a Bin Yaḥyā Bā ʿAlawī tradition. The description does not mention Habib Luthfi's teacher Abdul Malik, or the annual *mawlid* at Kedungparuk discussed in chapter 4. Thirdly, in discussing Habib Luthfi's direct grandfather, Hāshim (d. 1930), the description does not mention his leading Bā ʿAlawī contemporary, the principal Bā ʿAlawī saint of Pekalongan, Aḥmad al-ʿAṭṭās, who also established an annual *mawlid*, which continues to be observed at the al-Rawḍa mosque (see chapter 3). Instead, Hāshim's annual *mawlid* is described as the only big *mawlid* in Pekalongan. The absence of the principal saint of Pekalongan from the narrative seems to suggest that there exists in Pekalongan an older Bā ʿAlawī saintly dynasty with historical links to local Javanese scholars and even to the founder of the premier traditionalist Islamic organization, the Nahdlatul Ulama (NU).

In writing the book, Tsauri lodges Habib Luthfi's oral narratives in a more durable semiotic form and liberates them from "the finite horizon of [their] author."[40] Transformed into text, saintly talk has the potential to generate new publics beyond the confines of Habib Luthfi's disciples or followers. This potential is aided by the way the book presents itself as a universal history of the *mawlid*. After all, the discussion of Habib Luthfi's *mawlid* is only one part of a long history of the ritual celebration that begins with the Abbasid empress dowager al-Khayzurān (d. 789) and continues to present-day Pekalongan. While the discussion of the genealogy of Habib Luthfi's *mawlid* is based solely on oral narratives, the rest of the book is heavily referenced. Aside from pointing to classical Islamic historiographies, the book's footnotes also cite works that instantiate different regimes of knowledge, from Raffles's *History of Java* to contemporary Western social theories and contemporary academic works on Islam in Indonesia and on the practice of *mawlid* written by Nico Kaptein and by Marion Katz.[41] These references to a variety of texts of varying provenance may lend further credence to the veracity of the entextualized oral narratives that are nested in their midst, particularly for those who accept the legitimacy of such sources.

* * *

Another text that bolsters Habib Luthfi's saintly talk is the *Rātib al-kubra*. A *rātib*, as discussed in chapter 2, is a litany. It is an anthology made up of Qur'ānic verses, poetic prayers, and invocations, some of which are to be repeated several times during recitation. Al-Ḥaddād's litany, the *Rātib al-shahīr* (The renowned litany), for example, has struck deep roots across the Indian Ocean. Bā 'Alawīs and other traditionalist Muslims regularly recite the litany, whether singularly or collectively. In 1999, Habib Luthfi introduced his followers to a previously unknown litany entitled the *Rātib al-kubrā* (The great litany). While the cover of the text states the name of Habib Luthfi, the Sufi master claims that it was composed by his saintly ancestor Ṭāha, the son of the aforementioned Ḥasan (Sumodinigrat). He also claims that Ṭāhā studied with the disciples of 'Abdallāh b. 'Alawī al-Ḥaddād. Indeed the *Rātib al-kubrā* concludes with a prayer for Ṭāha b. Ḥasan Bin Yaḥyā, described as "our master, the compiler of the litany [*ṣāḥib al-rātib*], the sultan of the saints [*sulṭān al-awliyā'*]."[42] Reading through the contents of the *Rātib al-kubrā*, one can see that the litany is, to a large extent, similar to the Ḥaddādian litany. What differentiates the former from the latter is the ordering of the prayer formulas and several additional salutations to the Prophet (*ṣalawāt*), all of which can be found in *Al-Miftāḥ al-maqāṣid*—that is, the anthology of *ṣalawāt* compiled by Habib Luthfi's teacher Abdul Malik (see chapter 4). In other words, the *Rātib al-kubrā* reads more like a synthetic litany made up of the Ḥaddādian litany and several *ṣalawāt* formulas from Abdul Malik's *Al-Miftāḥ al-maqāṣid*. While this seems to suggest that the *Rātib al-kubrā* is a new litany composed by Habib Luthfi and retroactively attributed to his ancestor, the reality is more ambiguous, for two reasons. First, Habib Luthfi claims that Ṭāha was a disciple of al-Ḥaddād's disciples, which means that Ṭāha could have been the one who incorporated parts of the Ḥaddādian litany into his own new composition. Such a practice of combining litanies to form a new one is not unheard of. For example, an eighteenth-century Bā 'Alawī scholar, Saqqāf b. Muḥammad al-Saqqāf (d. 1781), studied with the son and disciples of al-Ḥaddād and composed a new litany that combines the litany of al-Ḥaddād with the litany of his other teacher, 'Alī b. 'Abdallāh al-Saqqāf (d. 1767).[43] Secondly, Abdul Malik's *Al-Miftāḥ al-maqāṣid* is a compilation of *ṣalawāt* formulas that he inherited from his teachers. Thus, theoretically, Abdul Malik could have inherited those formulas from Habib Luthfi's ancestors, including Ṭāha. Whatever the true provenance of the *Rātib al-kubrā,* for Habib Luthfi's followers the litany is considered to be the work of Ṭāha b. Ḥasan.

Unlike the aforementioned *Awrād al-ṭarīqa al-shādhiliya al-ʿalawiyya* (Litanies of the Shādhilī-ʿAlawī Sufi order) prescribed by Habib Luthfi to his initiated disciples (see chapter 5), the *Rātib al-kubrā,* like the Ḥaddādian *rātib,* is composed as an unrestricted litany that can be recited by anyone, without needing a permit or authorization. As a result, members of Habib Luthfi's community, whether initiated disciples or noninitiated followers have begun to recite the litany regularly. Furthermore, if the *Awrād al-ṭarīqa al-shādhiliya al-ʿalawiyya* evinces Habib Luthfi's Shādhilī *silsila* through Abdul Malik, the *Rātib al-kubrā* is presented as an exclusively Bā ʿAlawī litany. Abdul Malik's name is nowhere mentioned in the *Rātib al-kubrā.* In contrast, the name of the founder of the Ṭarīqa ʿAlawiyya, Muḥammad b. ʿAlī, is mentioned alongside those of the Prophet and Ṭāha b. Ḥasan in the intercessory prayer. These two characteristics make the *Rātib al-kubrā* similar to the Ḥaddādian litany. Indeed, the *Rātib al-kubrā* has become increasingly popular in Pekalongan alongside the Ḥaddādian *rātib.* The increasing popularity of a litany attributed to one of Habib Luthfi's ancestors serves to further corroborate the saintly talk that posits the Sufi master as a scion of a Bā ʿAlawī saintly dynasty.

This, however, does not mean that the Bā ʿAlawīs of Pekalongan or those living elsewhere accept the authority of the new litany. The prevailing view among the Bā ʿAlawīs of Pekalongan posits the *Rātib al-kubrā* as Habib Luthfi's invention rather than an inherited litany. The fact that most Bā ʿAlawīs had never heard of the litany before 1999 is taken to suggest its recent provenance. One Bā ʿAlawī scholar from Jakarta even ridiculed the name of the litany:

> The name is grammatically erroneous! *Rātib* is a masculine singular noun [*ism mufrad mudhakkar*]. The adjective [*ṣifat*] *kubrā* is feminine [*muʾannath*]. So how can the name be *Rātib al-kubrā*? It should use the masculine adjective *akbar* rather than *kubra.* So *Rātib al-akbar* and not *Rātib al-kubrā.* If you want to use the feminine adjective *kubrā,* then the noun should be made plural [*jamʿ taqsīr*]: *rawātib al-kubrā,* and not *Rātib al-kubrā.* If the name is already grammatically erroneous, what makes you think we ought to believe that the text was written by a great saint or scholar?

Despite rejection by most Indonesian Bā ʿAlawīs, the *Rātib al-kubrā* continues to circulate among Habib Luthfi's disciples and followers. It may be the case that with the persistent growth of Habib Luthfi's community, the *Rātib al-kubrā* will one day achieve the same fame as the Ḥaddādian litany in Java. Perhaps.

Saintly Tombs

Thus far, I have shown how Habib Luthfi's hagiographical composition consists of oral narratives and texts of various types that are regimented so that they can corroborate one another. I have also described how Habib Luthfi and other actors associated with him have utilized old and new materials in composing hagiographies. Such materials instantiate different regimes of knowledge and thus may be deemed authoritative by those who do not necessarily recognize Habib Luthfi's authority. To observe how people who are not, strictly speaking, Habib Luthfi's followers have come to accept the truth and authority of the Sufi master's hagiographical composition, I turn to another material form employed by Habib Luthfi—namely, mausoleums. Taking mausoleums as part of an ongoing hagiographic composition, in turn, allows us to expand analysis of Islamic hagiography beyond discursive or textual forms.

Habib Luthfi has spent the last three decades identifying old unmarked graves as saintly tombs, building new mausoleums, and instituting new pilgrimage practices. Many of these mausoleums belong to his ancestors. They are modeled on the mausoleums of well-known Bā ʿAlawī saints, like that of Aḥmad al-ʿAṭṭās in Pekalongan (see chapter 3). With the assistance of his disciples and followers, and owing to his alliances with different state actors, Habib Luthfi has been able to construct mausoleums over the graves of Ḥasan (Sumodiningrat) in Kramat Jati (Semarang, Central Java), his son Ṭāha (the putative composer of the *Rātib al-kubrā*) in Cileduk (West Java), and his grandson ʿUmar in Indramayu (West Java). He has also built a mausoleum over the graves of his father ʿAlī and grandfather Hāshim in Pekalongan. These mausoleums form an interconnected spatial network that serves as a material attestation of Habib Luthfi's saintly talk.

Mausoleums are statements. In a place like Java, where they tend to be associated with saints or kings, mausoleums work to proclaim spiritual or temporal authority. They declare that the person buried therein is worthy of pilgrimage. After all, a mausoleum is an infrastructure built to host living visitors. Mausoleums also serve as sites to physically inscribe claims of authority, particularly when that authority is not recognized elsewhere, say in hagiographical or genealogical texts. For example, the new marble tombstone of ʿUmar b. Ṭāha, enclosed by the recently built mausoleum in Indramayu, reads:

> This is the grave of our master, the noble Imam, the knower of Allāh, the great axial saint [*quṭb al-kabīr*], Habib ʿUmar b. Ṭāhā b. Ḥasan b. Ṭāhā b. Muḥammad al-Qāḍī b. Ṭāha Bin Yaḥyā Bā ʿAlawī, the Ḥusaynī.

Note how the tombstone proclaims ʿUmar as an axial saint. Yet the Bā ʿAlawī genealogical tome does not have anything to say about ʿUmar, save for his name. Read alongside the tome, the mausoleum and tombstone may work as arguments for historicity and discursive presence. They question the biographical exclusion of ʿUmar's biography from the genealogical tome.

As statements, mausoleums can trigger competition with one another, particularly when they are located in proximity to each other. In 2005, Habib Luthfi decided to build a mausoleum over the graves of his father ʿAlī and grandfather Hāshim, who were buried side by side in the public cemetery of Sapuro, around four hundred meters from the mausoleum of Pekalongan's principal saint, Aḥmad al-ʿAṭṭās. The building of the mausoleum irritated the *manṣab*, who stated on several occasions that building a private mausoleum in a public cemetery is unlawful as the land does not belong to that particular family. The *manṣab* repeatedly reminds people that his great-grandfather's mausoleum was not built within the public cemetery but on an endowed land adjacent to the cemetery. Unlike al-ʿAṭṭās's mausoleum with its constant flow of pilgrims, the mausoleum of Habib Luthfi's family tends to be empty most of the time. Most pilgrims who come to visit the former do not continue their visitation to the latter. On certain occasions, however, like the eve of Habib Luthfi's monthly gathering or the annual *mawlid*, the family mausoleum is filled with the Sufi master's disciples and followers. This suggests that while mausoleums are statements, their intensity varies. Mausoleums that succeeded in becoming popular pilgrimage destinations present a stronger argument compared with others. It follows that a mausoleum requires other mechanisms that would allow it to become a popular pilgrimage destination. The al-ʿAṭṭās mausoleum, for instance, has been a popular pilgrimage destination owing to the circulation of hagiographical texts, the annual commemoration, the continuous cultivation of a stable community by the three succeeding *manṣab*s, and the networks that connect these *manṣab*s with other Bā ʿAlawī scholars and their communities elsewhere. Habib Luthfi's family mausoleum, on the other hand, has become a pilgrimage destination only for the disciples and followers of Habib Luthfi, as neither Hāshim nor ʿAlī are known as scholars or saints except through the Sufi master's oral narratives. Consequently, the significance of the dead hinges exclusively on the authority of the living. At present, those who visit the mausoleum are those who recognize Habib Luthfi's authority.

* * *

Aside from building the mausoleums of his direct ancestors, Habib Luthfi has also been involved in building the mausoleums of other members of the Bin Yaḥyā family whose biographies have not been included in the Bā ʿAlawī genealogical tome. Unlike the tombs of his direct ancestors, however, some of these tombs had prior, albeit obscure, histories tied to their localities. In reclaiming these tombs and providing them with new Bin Yaḥyā genealogies, Habib Luthfi has had to persuade the locals to accept his claim. His authority as a Sufi master, his expanding communities of followers and disciples, and his social network—particularly his relationship with state actors—have all been crucial in enabling him to render his claim socially consequential.

Take the tomb of Abū Bakr b. Muḥammad Bin Yaḥyā (d. *c.*1755) in the hamlet of Geritan, Pekalongan. As discussed in the last chapter, Habib Luthfi was able to build this mausoleum thanks to his close relationship with the district head of Pekalongan, Siti Qomariyah. Before Habib Luthfi's appropriation, this unmarked tomb was believed to contain the remains of an obscure local Javanese saint known as Granpa (*mbah*) Angsono. The tomb had been a site of *local* pilgrimage. More than a decade ago, Habib Luthfi publicly identified the tomb as belonging to Abū Bakr b. Muḥammad Bin Yaḥyā, who, according to him, was a leading scholar at the court of the Mataram sultan Pakubuwana II (d. 1749), the last ruler of the united Mataram Sultanate before its partition into Yogyakarta and Surakarta. According to Habib Luthfi, Abū Bakr was the brother of his ancestor Ṭāha/Ṭāhir. With the backing of the district head, Habib Luthfi embarked on a project of rebuilding the tomb. Today, the tomb rests within the enclosure of an august mausoleum that was officially inaugurated in 2010.

Some disgruntled locals, however, protested Habib Luthfi's appropriation of the tomb without any conclusive historical evidence. At the same time, they could not provide any alternative identity, genealogy, or history of the tomb, as the only information they have inherited from their elders is the mere name of Granpa Angsono. Opposition also came from the scion of a local scholarly family whose forefathers were buried in the vicinity of Granpa Angsono's tomb. He, however, did not risk a confrontation with Habib Luthfi, opting instead to stop visiting the saint's tomb and discontinue the family tradition of interring their dead in the tomb's vicinity. In the prospect of conflict over the tomb's identity, the plaque commemorating the rebuilding of the mausoleum does not state either the name of Abū Bakr b. Muḥammad Bin Yaḥyā or Granpa Angsono. Instead, it uses a more equivocal and accommodating description: "*Makam Wali Agung Geritan*" (The tomb of the Great Saint of Geritan).

Since 2010, Habib Luthfi has taken over the guardianship of the tomb. He organizes annual commemoration for Abū Bakr at the site. Owing to Habib Luthfi's prominence, the tomb has begun to attract pilgrims from faraway places. Aside from his disciples and followers, those who have visited the tomb include notable Muslim scholars, high-ranking government officials, politicians, and generals from Jakarta, as well as members of the Javanese royal family, all of whom are connected to Habib Luthfi. Habib Luthfi himself sometimes receives his guests in Geritan, thereby acquainting them with the shrine. Over time, merchant stalls began to emerge outside the mausoleum complex, as the increasing volume of pilgrims to this revamped old site has created business opportunities for the locals. While opposition to Habib Luthfi's appropriation has remained among some locals, its strength has generally weakened.

A similar dynamic occurred in regard to an old unmarked grave in the village of Kedung Dowo, Batang (Central Java), believed by the locals to belong to a mysterious local saint, Granpa Surgi Jatikusumo. Habib Luthfi claimed that the tomb belongs to Muḥammad b. Ḥasan Bin Yaḥyā, and led a project of building a mausoleum. In this case, Habib Luthfi combined both names, arguing that Surgi Jatikusumo was not a proper name, but the title of Muḥammad b. Ḥasan Bin Yaḥyā, bestowed by the Sultan of Yogyakarta. The new tombstone reads:

> This is the grave of the Knower of Allāh [*al-ʿārif bi-llāh*], the most knowledgable [*al-ʿallāma*] the majestic *sayyid*, the noble, the distinguished, our master the Imam, Habib Muḥammad b. Ḥasan b. Ṭāhā Bin Yaḥyā Bā ʿAlawī, known famously as [*al-shahīr bi-*] Kyai Surgi Jatikusumo. He died in 1253 [1837] after the migration of the Prophet, upon him God's salutation and peace.

In contrast to the mausoleum of Geritan, Habib Luthfi did not attempt to erase the older name. Instead, he added another name and history that provided the tomb with a Prophetic genealogy and connection to the royal court of Yogyakarta. According to Habib Luthfi, Granpa Surgi/Muḥammad was the son of the aforementioned Ḥasan (Sumodinigrat) and grandson of Ṭāha/Ṭāhir. This makes him the brother of the compiler of the *Rātib al-kubrā*, Ṭāha b. Ḥasan. Like his brother, Granpa Surgi/Muḥammad was sent to the Ḥaḍramawt and studied with the disciples of ʿAbdallāh b. ʿAlawī al-Ḥaddād. He fought valiantly for Prince Dipanagara during the Java War and died in a skirmish with the Dutch seven years after the conclusion of the war.

Interestingly, the villagers of Kedung Dowo do not object to Habib Luthfi's renaming of the shrine, as they themselves are not aware of Granpa Surgi's history. For the villagers, Habib Luthfi's intervention has generated new pilgrimage traffic that did not previously exist. The assistant (*carik*) of the village head proudly informed me how "through Habib Luthfi we now know that Granpa Surgi was an offspring of the Prophet [*putro wayahe kanjeng nabi*] and a national hero [*pahlawan nasional*]." Every year Habib Luthfi organizes a commemoration for Granpa Surgi attended by the district head of Batang, local military and police officers, and around three thousand of his own followers. Through Habib Luthfi's interventions, local shrines such as that of Granpa Surgi have become known outside their localities. These mausoleums, in turn, further substantiate Habib Luthfi's saintly talk, although the Bā ʿAlawīs of Pekalongan remain skeptical about these tombs' new identities. One person told me how "Habib Luthfi likes to claim old graves of *kyai*s as belonging to the members of the Bin Yaḥyā family." Another described to me how Habib Luthfi had been engaged in the "Yaḥyānization of old tombs" (*Yaḥyānisasi kuburan kuno*).

Due to their obscure histories and identities, old unmarked tombs with local significance like those of Granpa Angsono and Granpa Surgi may work as spatial apertures susceptible to be enfolded into a hagiographical composition and genealogical articulation. Owing to Habib Luthfi's intervention, Geritan and Kedung Dowo have now become bourgeoning pilgrimage sites. Habib Luthfi's prominent position in diverse networks and his expansive following enabled him to draw people to the revamped tombs, thereby generating economic opportunities for the locals. Against the lack of clear documentary evidence to the contrary, the appearance of important personalities, money, and commodities from elsewhere is taken as evidence of Habib Luthfi's claim. The veracity of the tombs' new identities and genealogies is attested not by textual sources, but by the social consequences, which are as much socioeconomic as symbolic. Concurrently, these new histories were built on the exclusion of local histories that are more or less dormant for the time being, but may reemerge in the future.

Conclusion

Habib Luthfi's hagiographical composition consists of an interconnected ensemble of saintly talk, texts, and tombs, all of which reinforce one another. Familiarity with the hagiographical tradition and genealogies of Islamic transmission allows Habib Luthfi to utilize old and new materials to produce the hagiography of his family with recognizable themes and variations. Hagiographical narrative opens up the possibility for the interlacing of multiple histories and itineraries of Islamic transmission that have been previously posited as unconnected or unrelated through genealogical articulation. Similar to a musical composition that brings different sounds that come before, after, and simultaneously into a state of "constant interdependency," hagiographical composition opens up the past to various contingent processes and unstable relationships with the present.[44] This generates ambiguity in the relationship between the past and the present, such as with regard to whether the Bin Yaḥyā saintly dynasty truly existed historically or whether it is just a contemporary construction aimed for present and future expansion of Habib Luthfi's Islamic community. In the absence of conclusive evidence, the veracity of a hagiographical composition is often based on the authority of its composer, combined with the orchestrated involvement of other actors—particularly those with leverage over different regimes of knowledge—and its concrete social consequences. While hagiographical composition posits the past as real and not mere fiction, its reality cannot be divorced from the reality of its composition.[45] Like a symphony, a hagiographical composition is realized and becomes efficacious when it is performed as an ensemble involving multiple actors, each with his or her own role, who nevertheless make up "a larger system of community authorship."[46] The significance, truthfulness, and authority of a hagiographical composition are sustained by labor and social relations, which in turn subject it to the risk of disentanglement.

Through hagiographical composition, Habib Luthfi has been able to project himself as a lineal successor of a hitherto forgotten Bā ʿAlawī saintly dynasty with historical ties to the Ḥaddādian scholars and the Yogyakarta royal dynasty. Hagiographical composition thus affords him the ability to present himself not only as a master of the Naqshbandī-Khālidī and Shādhilī Sufi orders but also of the Ṭarīqa ʿAlawiyya that he inherited from his forefathers. It is partly in this bid for recognition from his fellow Bā ʿAlawīs that in 2006 Habib Luthfi replaced Abdul Malik's Naqshbandī-Khālidī-Shadhilī manual, the *Al-Tarqīb al-uṣūl li tashīl al-wuṣūl*, with his own prayer manual, the *Awrād al-ṭarīqa al-shādhiliyya al-ʿalawiyya* (Litanies of the Shādhilī-ʿAlawī Sufi order) as discussed in chapter 5. Through hagiographical composition, Habib Luthfi has tried to suture himself into a Bā ʿAlawī–Ḥaddādian *silsila*. So far, however, the result of this effort has been tepid at best. Most Bā ʿAlawīs remain skeptical of Habib Luthfi's hagiographical composition. Consequently, he has not been fully recognized by the Bā ʿAlawīs as an authoritative connector to the Prophetic past and articulator of Prophetic teachings. This, in turn, reaffirms an important point that has been made over the course of this book: that while Islamic religious authority is built on a connection to the Prophetic past, the particularities of that connection—whether its form, shape, or genealogy—truly matter. Some connections may be deemed authoritative by one community but rejected by others. Theoretically, the accrual of more recognizable forms of connection to the Prophetic past may lead to the strengthening of authority.

While Habib Luthfi has not been able to authoritatively nest himself in Bā ʿAlawī communities, he has been able to penetrate the *kraton* (royal court) of Yogyakarta. During the 2011 anniversary (*hadeging nagari*) of the *kraton*, Habib

Luthfi was invited by Prince Joyo to lead the annual pilgrimage of the royal family and court retainers (*abdi dalem*) to the tomb of the first sultan, Hamengku Buwono I, in the royal graveyard of Imogiri. On the evening following the royal pilgrimage, a ritual recitation (*semaan*) of the Qurʾān followed by a sermon by Habib Luthfi was held at the *kraton*. This public event was attended by Habib Luthfi's followers, the traditionalist Muslims of Yogyakarta, and members of the royal family and courtiers, although the sultan himself did not attend. During his welcome speech, Prince Joyo declared to the audience that the year's anniversary theme was "realizing a Javanese Caliphate" (*mewujudkan kekhalifahan jawi*). "There is no need to be afraid of the word 'caliphate,' as this is in the context of culture [*tidak perlu takut dengan khalifah, ini konteksnya budaya*]," he told the audience.[47] In his sermon, Habib Luthfi reinforced Prince Joyo's point that the time has come for the *kraton* to become recognized once again as the principal Islamic center of Java. He explained that the sultanate was actually a Javanese caliphate built through the relationship between the monarch and the saints. "But the colonizers divided us," Habib Luthfi continued,

> and now is the time for Muslim scholars to return to the *kraton*. Since the time of HB I, the *kraton* of Yogyakarta has been the center of Sufism. In those days, they followed the Shaṭṭāriyya order. Today there are many Sufi orders, and they are all good. They are all teaching the *sunna*. It's about time that Sufi orders return home so that the *kraton* may become the dispenser of the *sunna*.

The message was loud and clear. Both Habib Luthfi and Prince Joyo had been preparing to repair the old fractured connection between the sultan and the saints, now configured as a relationship between Yogyakarta's Mataram royal dynasty and the Bin Yaḥyā Bā ʿAlawī saintly dynasty.

This articulatory labor, however, was not supported by the reigning sultan. Hamengku Buwana X did not make an appearance in the events featuring Prince Joyo and Habib Luthfi. Without the sultan's support, Prince Joyo's maneuver was limited, notwithstanding his position as the sultanate's second-highest official. But Habib Luthfi and Prince Joyo were not thinking about the present. They were preparing for the future. The sultan, after all, does not have a male heir. According to the customary rules of the *kraton*, only a male can ascend the throne. Prince Joyo was the heir apparent to the throne of Yogyakarta. This vision for the future was brought home to me during a dialogue that occurred in April 2013. The conversation took place in Yogyakarta between Habib Luthfi and Prince Joyo's son, K.R.T. Jayaningrat. Habib Luthfi told Jayaningrat that, one day, he would become "the sun of Mataram" (*suryo mentaram*). Habib Luthfi assured him that he and his disciples would stand behind the young prince, just as saints stood behind his royal ancestors. The young prince listened assiduously to Habib Luthfi, humbling himself before the presence of the Sufi master. At the time, the scene looked anachronistic to me, as if it came out of a Javanese court chronicle or a Sufi hagiography. But perhaps such is the history of Islam in Java, an ongoing tale of cooperation and contestation between saints and sultans, scholars and rulers. A classic theme, indeed, but one with endless variations.

EPILOGUE

Authority and Universality

ON THE LAST DAY OF 2013, G.B.P.H. Joyokusumo breathed his last. The death of the fifty-eight-year-old heir apparent to the throne of Yogyakarta left the royal family and courtiers questioning who would succeed Hamengku Buwono X. Less than two years after his younger brother's death, the sultan issued a royal decree (*sabdaraja*). Read on April 30, 2015, the decree contains, among other things, the monarch's decision to erase the epithet "Caliph of God" (*khalifatullah*) from his regnal title. As mentioned in chapter 1, the rulers of Yogyakarta have borne the caliphal title since the inception of the sultanate in 1755. The regnal title of the sultan was: His majesty the Sultan Hamengku Buwono, commander in the battlefield, servant of the Most Gracious, the master regulator of religion (*sayyidin panatagama*), the Caliph of Allāh, the tenth in Yogyakarta. The sultan explained that he based his decision on an instruction that he had received from God and his ancestors. In his words: "I received an instruction from our Lord Allāh Most Great, the powerful creator, my father, and my forebears, the ancestors of Mataram [*nampa welinge dhawuh gusti Allah, gusti agung kuasa cipta lan rama ingsun eyang-eyang ingsun, para leluhur Mataram*]."[1] The sultan's sudden decision to eliminate the caliphal title shocked many people, who, at the time, could not understand its motivation. The reasoning behind the monarch's abandonment of his caliphal title became more apparent a few days later when he issued another decree, this time elevating the title of his eldest daughter to that of G.K.R. Mangkubumi, a rank usually reserved for a formal heir to the throne. It became obvious to many that abandoning the caliphal title was a measure taken by the sultan to mitigate objections to his decision to name his daughter as heir apparent. While there have been, historically, many sultanas, there has never been a female caliph. In fact, as the historian Hugh Kennedy makes clear, the idea of a female caliph was never even entertained in the historical debates over the question of who should be a caliph.[2]

The two royal decrees sparked protests from the sultan's brothers, who criticized the monarch for violating the customary rule of the sultanate. Regrets were also expressed outside the royal court. Indonesia's two largest Islamic *jam'iyyas* (associations), the traditionalist Nahdlatul Ulama and the modernist Muhammadiyyah, expressed their disappointment, viewing the decrees as a concerted attempt to efface the sultanate's Islamic identity.[3] Later, the two associations, together with several disgruntled princes, took the sultan to the Indonesian court in an effort to annul the decrees. Whatever results from this ongoing drama of royal succession, one thing is clear: the articulatory labor of realigning the royal and the saintly that had been pursued by Habib Luthfi and Prince Joyo over the past decade came to an abrupt end.[4] The 2015 *sabdaraja* of Hamengku Buwono X thus brings home one simple but crucial point that has been maintained in the foregoing pages—namely, that any form of articulatory labor can fail. Indeed, we have repeatedly observed such failures, from Prince Dipanagara's failure to defend his claim as a royal regulator of religion (chapter 1) and Ibn Yaḥyā's forced return to the Ḥaḍramawt (chapter 2), to the *manṣab*'s and the mayor's impotence in ridding Pekalongan of nightclubs despite their cooperation (chapter 6) and Habib Luthfi's inability to win the recognition of his fellow Bā ʿAlawīs (chapters 4, 6, and 7).

This book has shown how, as a sociological reality, Islam is an outcome of a historically and culturally situated articulatory practice that seeks to align a cultivated community to the normative teachings of the Prophet Muḥammad so that the former can serve as the site for the transmission and social realization of the latter. Temporal estrangement from the Prophetic past necessitates the labor of connecting to, along with reconstructing, selecting, and representing, that past as a model for action to others. Different actors use different means to recover, connect to, and represent that foundational past in the face of an incessantly changing problem-space, thereby opening up multiple and selective versions and interpretations of that past. This, in turn, generates a plethora of normative teachings and practices deemed to be authoritative owing to their recognizable connection to the Prophetic past.

Just as there has been a vast plurality in the ways Prophetic teachings are imagined, understood, and realized, there have also been multiple ideas regarding the form, shape, and scale a community ought to take, as well as ways of materializing it. Consequently, the notion of Islamic community—that is, a social formation that serves as the site for the transmission and social realization of Prophetic teachings—has taken on different shapes with varying scales throughout history. At times, these communities come into conflict with one another. At other times, they work together or merge to form an even bigger community. Some Islamic communities have mirrored, formed alliances with, or clashed with other sociopolitical formations, like the state. Others have even morphed into a state.

To posit Islam as a contingent outcome of articulatory labor is to take seriously the role of human actors who perform the labor of cultivating communities and connecting their contemporaries to the Prophetic past. These human actors, including the individuals discussed in this book, are multifaceted moral actors capable of acting upon history—including the small histories that make up their everyday lives—and compelled to respond to history, even when they themselves are constituted by that history.[5] Even when examining texts and their role in disseminating Prophetic teachings and forming Islamic communities, we need to be careful not to fall into the trap of textual fetishism. That is, we need to be cognizant of the extratextual dynamics that enable the production and circulation of texts and generate their authority. This includes the role of human actors associated with textual production, dissemination, and consumption, such as their authors, copyists, printers, binders, translators, vendors, and those who teach them. In performing articulatory labor, actors are informed by different moral and social visions and rely on various conceptual and material infrastructures that are available to them—including, but not limited to, texts—to form credible connections with the foundational past and maintain durable relationships to their contemporaries, thereby generating multiple articulatory modes, some of which have become paradigmatic and shape the labors of subsequent generations.

Insofar as Islam involves teachings and practices about being human and attempts to realize and extend forms of social relation, it is fundamentally political. Politics, as Bruno Latour suggests, is "what allows many heterogeneous resources to be woven together into a social link that becomes increasingly harder and harder to break."[6] Latour's conception of politics is useful to think with as it defines politics as *a type of situation* and a *periodic phase* constitutive of any social formation. Indeed, it allows us to comprehend politics as a graded dynamic, in that an assemblage can be more political at one point and become less so at another. For instance, a neighborhood mosque might become a fierce political arena when its imam passes away and several competing actors vie for the position, thereby dividing the community and demanding the reknitting of ties. When a social formation stabilizes, it may become less political. This entails that politics and the political should not be used to describe and differentiate particular variants of Islamic movement or social formation (like Islamist movements) from the supposedly nonpolitical variants, as implied in the still-common dichotomy between "political" and "cultural" Islams inherited from colonial scholarship.[7]

Successful articulatory labor results in the enactment of a durable hierarchical relationship premised on the recognition of the laboring actor as an Islamic authority—that is, as a connector to the Prophetic past who can augment and transform that past into realizable models without resorting to coercion. Understood this way, authority has less to do with blind obedience than with the often convoluted process of evaluation, recognition, and acknowledgment.

This understanding of authority contrasts with the Enlightenment dichotomy of authority and reason. Immanuel Kant, to give one prominent example, conflated submission to the authority of another with the reluctance to use one's rationality, which in his view constituted a state of immaturity.[8] In contrast, this book has shown how freedom and reason are central to the processes through which Muslims recognize, evaluate, and acknowledge religious authority. Acknowledging authority, as Hans-Georg Gadamer has noted, is "always connected with the idea that what the authority says is not irrational and arbitrary but can, in principle, be discovered to be true."[9] This entails that while someone who is recognized as an authority can legitimize discourse and practice, the source of that legitimacy is a form of truth external to the involved parties (both those who recognize and those who are being recognized) and is amenable to demonstration through a variety of ways, even when it is historically conditioned. Owing to the highly contingent nature of recognition, an aspiring religious authority has to persistently engage in articulatory labor in the hope of earning and maintaining that recognition. But actors may suddenly die, leaving their labor incomplete and the community they cultivate leaderless. Other actors who have historically performed such articulatory labors may suddenly decide to stop to allow for the realization of other agendas. Shifting conditions may also hinder actors from performing such labors, despite their willingness to do so. In short, articulatory labors may go wrong, and indeed they have often gone awry. The notion of articulatory labor is analytically helpful to accentuate the highly contingent and continuously shifting terrains of human social life in and through which religion and religious authority take shape.

In substantiating this theoretical argument, the book follows one itinerary of Islamic transmission spearheaded by the Bā ʿAlawī *sayyid*s to unravel the various historically and culturally situated labors of articulating Prophetic teachings and the community. Such labors have generated different articulations and social realization of the *sunna*, divergent forms of Islamic community, and diverse figurations of religious authority. The case of the Bā ʿAlawīs attests to how such manifold understandings of Prophetic teachings and their social realizations as *sunna* cannot be divorced from diverging ways of imagining and materializing a community. Indeed, the history of this particular lineage group already demonstrates the myriad ways in which different actors have defined and articulated the *sunna* and the community. It is this polyphonic reality that the book demonstrates by telling a story of how different and discordant Islamic communities came to be formed and interacted with one another in transgenerational and transregional settings.

In this sense, the history of Islam may be thought of not in terms of continuity or evolution, but in terms of unceasing reproduction. The central analytic problem of the history of Islam can thus be shifted to the question of articulatory variation. Positing Islam as a sociological achievement—that is, as the outcome of historically contingent and culturally embedded articulatory labor—allows us to develop an analytic approach that stays true to the religion's doctrinal and practical polyphony, while still retaining a notion of *monophyletic commonality*. In stressing the centrality of monophyletic commonality, this book calls for a reconsideration of Islam's universality. To say that universality is a site of contest, or that universal claims are indissoluble from particularities, has now become an academic truism.[10] More historically and ethnographically grounded empirical works, however, are needed to help us comprehend how universality works, the shapes and forms it has taken, and the labor and infrastructures needed to sustain it.[11] Here I want to conclude by proposing the need to understand Islam's universality as a *concrete universality* premised not in terms of ideational commonality, but in terms of an ancestral or monophyletic commonality.

In the literal sense, the term *universal* carries the meaning of "common to all." What is common between two entities, for example, has usually been understood as something that belongs to the composition of each entity. Such a commonality can be established (if it is possible at all) only through an abstraction that sets apart the available common feature of the two entities. What is common is imagined as a genus that hovers above its species and can be abstracted only from a given set, which in the final analysis requires that the set that constitutes the genus has been well defined in the first place. An idea of universality built on this conception of commonality is ultimately an *abstract universality*.[12]

Commonality or family likeness that can be accessed only through abstraction, however, is not the only way of making sense of universality. Commenting on Marx's reformulation of the Hegelian notion of *concrete universality* (as opposed to *abstract universality*), the Soviet philosopher Evald Ilyenkov notes how commonality can also be defined as something that exists apart from, say, two different entities, as its own entity, like the notion of a common ancestor. Here, what is common to both entities stands prior to them as its own entity and may not necessarily be present in its extensions, modifications, or descendants. Ilyenkov uses the figure of a triangle to clarify this notion of commonality. As a figure, the triangle can be found in the square and the pentagon, although it exists self-evidently and not simply in abstraction or thought. The figure of the triangle "is never retained as such in a square or pentagon, nor is it given in inherence or contemplation, although it can be identified analytically within their composition."[13] This makes the triangle a *concrete universal*—that is, a universal that exists self-evidently, not in abstraction or thought, but as objective reality as real as the particulars and existing along with its derivatives like the square or the pentagon. Ilyenkov further explains that, for Marx, the task of finding a *concrete universal* was to establish the original form of "human vital activity which is historically and essentially the universal foundation and condition of the emergence of all the rest."[14] An example of a concrete universal is labor—that is, "the direct remaking of nature (both external and one's own) as accomplished by social man with the tools of his own creation."[15] The most basic form of labor performed by human ancestors has historically developed into diverse variants and generated different relationalities from the simplest to the most complex modes of production, all of which share a common ancestor.

Islam's universality, I propose, can be more fruitfully thought of as a *concrete universality.* What is concretely universal about Islam is the labor of articulating the *sunna* and the community as an ongoing process. This articulatory labor is the concrete activity that reproduces various social realizations of Islam, each of which is particular and may differ from others (like dates and coconuts), but all are historically connected to, and developed from, one foundational moment of Prophetic labor. Posited as such, the universal exists as a concrete material reality as real as the particulars and existing alongside—instead of hovering abstractly over—its derivatives, albeit historically prior. Thus, what makes Islam a universal religion is not simply the presence of common ideas and practices that can be abstracted only from a given set. Instead, Islam's universality is something that *historically develops* out of a unity of genesis or descent from a common but vanished ancestral labor. What is deemed to be universal may outwardly express itself equally well through differences, and even opposites. We can thus identify Islam's universality as neither an essence nor a particular outlook integral to the religion, but as a historical becoming involving contingent processes of reproduction and extension across time and space. At the heart of this historical development is the labor of human actors recognized by their coreligionists as religious authorities, be they saints or sultans, scholars or teachers, all of whom reproduce Islam in their own way by performing different modes of articulatory labor, some of which have been more socially consequential than others. Posited as such, Islam's universality can become an object of historical and ethnographic inquiry. This book is one small and partial attempt in that direction.

NOTES

Introduction

1. Habib (Ar. *ḥabīb*, Ar. pl. *ḥabāʾib*), meaning "beloved," is an honorific used in the Ḥaḍramawt and Southeast Asia to address a Muslim scholar who is recognized as a *sayyid* or descendant of the Prophet Muḥammad.

2. Written by the Egyptian scholar Ibn Ḥajar al-ʿAsqalānī (d. 1449), the *Fatḥ al-bārī* is a commentary on the ninth-century anthology of *ḥadīth*s collected by al-Bukhārī (d. 879). See Blecher 2018.

3. Tsing 1993, 232. See also Ginzburg [1980] 2013.

4. I use "saint" to refer to *walī* or *walī Allāh*, meaning "intimate of God" or "friend of God." The term *walī* carries the connotations of "guardian," "protector," and "intercessor." As God's intimate, a *walī* is believed to have the capacity to protect and intercede for others. Despite its Christocentric connotations, the term saint is used in this book to ease comprehension and hopefully allow comparative readings. One should not, however, conclude that "saint" conveys the full meaning of the term *walī*. See Cornell 1998, xvii–xxi.

5. J. Brown 2009, 3. See also Bowen 2012, 18–19; J. Brown 2014, 8.

6. Brown 2009, 3.

7. Asad 1986. For a useful survey of recent approaches in the anthropology of Islam, see Bowen (2012).

8. Arendt [1968] 2006, 122.

9. Ahmed 2017; Anthony 2019; W. Graham 1977.

10. I. Alatas 2020, 80–83; Bashir 2014, 521.

11. Asad 2018, 95. See also Ernst 2005, 20.

12. Arendt [1968] 2006, 122. While Arendt's discussion of authority is based on her account of Roman political tradition, it is nevertheless relevant to the Middle East considering that the region was influenced by the Greco-Roman experience. See Asad 2015, 181.

13. Arendt [1968] 2006, 93.

14. Weber 1968, 48. On Weber's influence on the study of Islamic religious authority, see Knysh (2017, 26–28, 161–64). On the survival and flourishing of "charismatic" Islamic authorities in the modern world, see Bruinessen and Howell (2007), Rozehnal (2007), Sedgwick (2005), and Seesemann (2011).

15. Arendt [1958] 1998, 126.

16. Lambek 2010, 15.

17. MacIntyre 1981, 187–88.

18. Asad 1993, 2003.

19. Latour 2005, 39. See also Larkin 2013.

20. Scholarly works on the Bā ʿAlawīs in the Indian Ocean world have continued to grow over the last two decades. See, among others, I. Alatas (2010, 2011), Bang (2003, 2014), Freitag (2003), Ho (2006), and Knysh (1999b, 2011).

21. See, for example, Habib Luthfi's recent interview with Indonesia's leading web-based media *detikNews*: Erwin Dariyanto, "Bicara Islam Nusantara, Habib Luthfi Contohkan Dakwah Sunan Kudus," DetikNews, January 2, 2019, https://news.detik.com/berita/d-4368115/bicara-islam-nusantara-habib-luthfi-contohkan-dakwah-sunan-kudus. One observer describes Habib Luthfi as a proponent of "nationalistic Sufism" (Arifin 2012).

22. On *Pribumisasi Islam*, see Kersten (2015, ch. 3).

23. Wahid [1989] 2015.

24. Burhani 2018, 1. For other works on *Islam Nusantara* and the debates that the concept generates, see Arifianto (2016), Kato (2018), and Sahal and Aziz (2015).

25. For example, in his monumental *History of Sumatra*—first published in 1783 and expanded in 1811—William Marsden wrote that the Malays "did not appear to possess much of the bigotry so commonly found amongst the western Mahometans" (1811, 346).

26. Mamdani 2004.

27. On the tension between Arabization and indigenization in contemporary Indonesia, see Baso (2006), Bruinessen (2013, 2015), Hefner (2011), and Ricklefs (2012).

28. Wahid [1989] 2015.

29. Scholars have long defined Islam in ways that privileged the religion's legalistic framework. For discussions and critiques of the tendency to define "Islam as law," see Ahmed (2015, 113–75). On law as a cultural process, see Comaroff and Roberts (1981), Merry (2000), and Moore (1978), and Rosen (1989).

30. Roy 2004, 258–65.

31. W. Brown 2006, 153.

32. Formichi 2020, 43–75.

33. DeWeese 1994.

34. Ben-Dor Benite 2005; Petersen 2018.

35. Thum 2014.

36. T. Stewart 2001, 273.

37. Flood 2009.

38. C. Stewart 1999, 53.

39. An entity is said to be *instantiated* by *x* when that entity does not exist apart from its individuation. In contrast, an entity is exemplified or manifested by *x* if the entity still exists even without the particular individuation. Thus, in Platonic philosophy, for example, the entity "human" is merely exemplified and manifested by a concretely living individual, as the archetype "human" ontologically exists in the realm of Ideas (Meillassoux 2008, 25).

40. Asad 1993; Mahmood 2005.

41. See, for instance, the work of Harry Munt (2014) on the making of Medina as a sanctuary (*ḥaram*).

42. On the historical contestation over what constitutes Prophetic practice, see Ansari (1972), J. Brown (2007, 2014), El Shamsy (2013), Hallaq (2005), Juynboll (1996), Melchert (1997), and Motzki (2002).

43. Lohlker 2016.

44. Ibid., 92.

45. Ansari 1972, 280; Duderija 2012, 400–401.

46. Ansari 1972, 280; J. Brown 2014, 24–25; El Shamsy 2013, 41–48.

47. El Shamsy 2013, 70. On entextualization as a mode of objectification, see Bauman and Briggs (1990), Keane (1997), and M. Silverstein and Urban (1996).

48. Keane 1997, 63.

49. El Shamsy 2013.

50. Ahmed 2015. Nonprescriptive Islamic authority includes Qurʾānic healers (Perrino 2002), dream interpreters (Mittermaier 2011), poets (Taminian 2001), and antinomian saints (Ewing 1997). One can argue that all of these forms of authority are modeled on Prophetic precedents.

51. Cornell 1998; Mittermaier 2011; Rozehnal 2007; Wright 2015.

52. On the ideological contestation over the term "people of the *sunna* and the *jamāʿa*" in contemporary Indonesia, see Feener (2007, 139–53).

53. Dakake 2007; Pierce 2016.

54. Donner 2010, 217–26.

55. On cross-pollination between early Islamic communities and other religious communities of late antiquity, see Fowden (2007) and Sizgorich (2009).

56. Hodgson 1974, 1:251.

57. Ibid., 248.

58. Ibid., 250. See also Anjum 2012, 74–89.

59. Hodgson 1974, 1:252.

60. For a discussion of pre-Islamic *sunna*, see Von Grunebaum (1963, 15–16).

61. Ahmed 2015.

62. Scott 2004, 4.

63. Ibid.

64. The Safavid is probably the clearest example. See Babayan 1994, 153–54. Lara Deeb (2006), for instance, discusses the transformation of "charismatic circles" into modern associations in her ethnography of Lebanon.

65. Abun-Nasr 2007; Cornell 1998; Green 2012; Mayeur-Jaouen and Papas 2014.

66. Khan 2012; Mittermaier 2011; Sirriyeh 2015; Taneja 2018.

67. Tsing 2005.

68. See, for example, Bruinessen 2015; Gladney 2004; Hefner 2011; Lapidus 2014; Ricklefs 2012.

69. Latour 2005, 64–65.

70. Sewell 2005, 143.

71. While this book takes Green's notion of religious economy seriously, it does not reduce Islam or religious economy to the logic of the market. By identifying the *sunna* as the raw materials used to create a variety of "religious products," this book considers the labor process that diversifies Islam and makes up different Islamic communities, without falling into the false dichotomy of orthodox and unorthodox Islam.

72. Speaking of nineteenth-century Bombay, Green notes how "different Muslims protected their customary community boundaries" and that "Pan-Islamic visions of a single *umma* under

Allah were insubstantial indeed, and visions that, in circumstances of increasing religious production, comprised only one of many Islams on offer" (2011, 6).

73. Althusser 2015, 243.

74. Ibid., 246–47.

75. Ibid., 245.

76. Ibid.

77. Ibid., 247.

78. Balibar 2015, 365.

79. Hall 1980, 329.

80. Laclau and Mouffe [1985] 2001, 105.

81. Ibid., 113.

82. Roy 2004, 200.

83. On literary networks and their role in connecting Muslims across time, space, and cultures, see Ricci (2011, 260–68).

84. For example, Mahmood (2005) and Hirschkind (2006). Compare these works, for instance, with messier ethnographies of Muslims that posit Islam as one among the many problems faced by Muslims in their everyday lives (Abu-Lughod 1986; Ewing 1997; Kloos 2018; M. Marsden 2005; Messick 1993; Soares 2005).

85. Schielke 2010, 3. See also M. Marsden and Retsikas 2013.

86. The notion of articulation I develop in this book shares a certain resemblance with that developed by Magnus Marsden and Konstantinos Retsikas, in that both refer to "processes of assembly and disassembly." I agree with Marsden and Konstantinos that the notion "allows for an analysis of intersections and trajectories of different arenas of social life, and also of the inflections that develop between these varying strands" (M. Marsden and Retsikas 2013, 14). Where I differ from them is in the way that they use articulation to foreground Islam in the everyday, which gives the impression that there is already a prepackaged religion that undergoes articulatory processes. In contrast, I argue that Islam itself is the contingent outcome of articulating the *sunna* and the community, the latter of which already presupposes the complexity of the everyday, including the multiple arenas of social life. Posited as such, Islam is a sociological achievement that is embedded in, and inseparable from, the vicissitudes of social life. Equally important is my emphasis on the labor of actors as the active dynamic behind any articulatory attempts.

87. Bashir 2014, 526.

88. Ibid.

89. Ibid., 529.

90. Ibid.

91. Shaw 2012, 16.

92. Bashir 2014, 530.

93. Kundera 1988, 74.

94. Latour 2005, 187–90.

95. Aydin 2017; Roy 2004, 183.

96. Gilsenan 1982, 5.

97. Ibid., 19.

98. Kundera 1988, 75.

99. Bulliet 1972.

100. Bujra 1971.

101. Ahmed 2015, 368.

102. Chamberlain 1995.

103. Ayubi 2019, 6.

104. Ibid.

105. Birchok 2016; Homerin 2019; Mernissi 1991; Sayeed 2013.

106. Sayeed 2013, 91.

107. Ibid., 66.

108. Ibid., 143.

109. Hoesterey 2016; Husein and Slama 2018; Slama 2017.

110. Abu-Lughod 1988 ; Mackey 1992; Spivak 1992; Minh-Ha 1989.

111. Abu-Lughod 1991.

112. Keane 2003a, 243. See also Rabinow [1977] 2007.

Chapter 1

1. al-Ṭabarī 1987, 4–5.

2. Pigeaud and De Graaf 1976, 7.

3. Quoted in Florida 1995, 167.

4. My reading of Sunan Kalijaga differs from that offered by Clifford Geertz (1968), who uses this figure to highlight the strong Indic undercurrent that made up the superficial and syncretic character of Islam among the Javanese.

5. For a work that explores the intersection between sanctity, pilgrimage, and hospitality, see Taneja (2017).

6. On Sunan Ampel's role in the conversion of Java as presented in Javanese court chronicles, see Ricci (2011, 202–7).

7. Moertono 1963, 30.

8. al-Ghazālī 2003, vol. 2, bk. 26, 1120–23; al-Māwardī 1955, 192–93; 1966, 146–52.

9. Kamali 2003, 355. Note that *siyāsa shar ʿiyya*, or king's law, remains in place today in Saudi Arabia, where it complements and can even compete with the law drawn up and adjudicated by the jurists (Vogel 2000).

10. Such a privilege was also said to be accorded to religious communities in the pre-Islamic period. The Dutch maintained the status and privileges of the *perdikan*s up to 1874, when the colonial government deemed them to be states within the state and reverted their status to ordinary villages (Fauzia 2013, 120; Kumar 1985, 42).

11. Kumar 1985, 42

12. Pigeaud and De Graaf 1976, 10–15.

13. For similar dynamics in other parts of the Muslim world, see Alam (2009), Cornell (1998), and Foltz (1996).

14. Pigeaud and De Graaf 1976, 91.

15. Kumar 1985, 3.

16. Moertono 1963, 31–33.

17. Ricklefs 1974.

18. Florida 1995, 336.

19. Moin 2012.

20. Ricklefs 1998; Florida 2019.

21. Ricklefs 2006, 187, 224.

22. Ibid., 230.

23. Ahmed 2015.

24. T. Stewart 2001, 273.

25. Carey 2008,150.

26. Carey 2008; Laffan 2011; Ricklefs 2007.

27. Carey 2008, 72.

28. Dipanagara 2016, 224.

29. Carey 2008, 104–5.

30. Ibid., 111–12.

31. Quoted in Carey 2008, 110.

32. Ibid., 103.

33. The popularity of this esoteric work among the Muslims of the Malay-Indonesian Archipelago drove the Medinan scholar Ibrāhīm al-Kurānī (d. 1690) to write an explanatory treatise entitled the *Itḥāf al-dhakī* (The gifting of the clever), which was addressed to the "people of Jawa" (Fathurahman 2012).

34. El Moudden 1990, 69.

35. Halman 2013,120.

36. Dipanagara 2016, 224–25.

37. Javanese Muslims did not consider spirits like the Goddess of the Southern Ocean as divine. Rather, they were treated as spiritual beings with limited God-given power. Recognizing their power was, therefore, not regarded as *shirk*, or associating other beings with the divine. Modern Muslim reformists, however, tend to overlook this subtle but important qualifier.

38. Dipanagara 2016, 374.

39. It is important to stress that in Sufi metaphysics, the imaginal world is not a mere imaginary. The imaginal is understood to have ontological reality, one that dwells in an intermediate domain between the spiritual or rational and the physical or sensible realities. The imaginal shares in the attributes of the two sides that define it. An imaginal thing is therefore "both the same as and different from each of the two sides that define it," just like a mirror image that bridges the reflected object and the mirror (Chittick 1994, 25). The mirror image is both the same as and different from the mirror and the reflected object.

40. Dipanagara 2016, 245–73.

41. Carey 2008, 504.

42. While today the Shaṭṭāriyya is a minor Sufi tradition in Indonesia, it was the dominant Sufi tradition in the Malay world from the time of its introduction in the 1660s until the middle of the nineteenth century. Shaṭṭārī initiates held important religious, political, and literary posts in the Mataram court, and included the Surakartan king Pakubuwana IV (Florida 2019, 155–62).

43. Carey 2008, 632.

44. Ibid., 632.

45. It should be noted that Kyai Maja, a Shaṭṭārī scholar who served as Dipanagara's principal religious advisor, was known to have been very close to members of the Surakartan royal family.

While Kyai Maja stood at the center of a Shaṭṭārī network of Islamic teachers that provided the core backing for Dipanagara's force, he was also well connected to members of the Javanese royalty, some of whom were his disciples. The case of Kyai Maja alone should deter us from projecting too strong a division between the *kraton* and the *santris* (Florida 2019, 160).

46. Carey 2008, 636.

47. Ibid., 758.

48. Ibid., 682.

49. Ibid., 745.

50. Ibid.

51. ʿAlī b. Aḥmad al-ʿAṭṭās, n.d.

52. Thum 2014, 31.

53. Ibid.

54. The empire style, characterized by a return to classicism, was widespread in the Ottoman realm in the mid-eighteenth century. See Göçek 1996, 41.

55. For a history of this mausoleum, see I. Alatas (2016a).

56. ʿAbdallāh al-Saqqāf 1984, 5:3.

57. Ibid.

58. Shihāb and Nūḥ 1980, 47–50.

59. Ho 2006, 39.

60. This discussion is based on three early texts of the Ṭarīqa ʿAlawiyya written by Tarīmi Bā ʿAlawī scholars: *Al-Kibrit al-aḥmar wa al-iksīr al-akbar* of ʿAbdallāh b. Abū Bakr al-ʿAydarūs (d. 1461); *Maʿārij al-hidāya* of ʿAlī b. Abī Bakr al-Sakrān (d. 1490), and the *Al-Juzʾ al-laṭīf fī taḥkīm al-sharīf* of Abū Bakr b. ʿAbdallāh al-ʿAydarūs (d. 1513). See ʿAbdallāh al-ʿAydarūs [n.d.] 2002; al-Sakrān [n.d.] 1931; Abū Bakr al-ʿAydarūs [1489] 2011.

61. Knysh 2010, 338.

62. This discussion is based on several Bā ʿAlawī hagiographical texts, including *Al-Mashraʿ al-rawī fī manāqib al-sāda al-kirām āl abī ʿalawī* of Muḥammad b. Abī Bakr al-Shillī (d. 1682), "Al-Qirṭās fī manāqib al-ʿAṭṭās" and "Al-Maqṣad fī shawāhid al-mashhad" of ʿAlī b. Ḥasan al-ʿAṭṭās (d. 1759), "Nahr al-mawrūd fī manāqib shaykh abī bakr b. sālim fakhr al-wujūd" of Ḥasan b. Ismāʿīl al-Ḥāmid (d. 1948), and *Al-Barāhīn wa al-bayyināt fī manāqib mawlaʿināt* of Sālim b. Aḥmad bin Jindān (d. 1969). See also the encyclopedia of towns in Ḥaḍramawt entitled *Idām al-qūt fī dhikr buldān ḥadramawt* composed by ʿAbd al-Raḥmān b. ʿUbaydillāh al-Saqqāf (d. 1956). See ʿAlī b. Ḥasan al-ʿAṭṭās 1942, n.d.; H. al-Ḥāmid, n.d.; ʿAbd al-Raḥmān al-Saqqāf 2005; al-Shillī 1901; Bin Jindān 2017.

63. Arai 2004, 23.

64. Knysh 1993.

65. Abū Bakr al-Ḥabashī 1979, 9.

66. Arai 2004, 25.

67. Evans-Pritchard 1949, 88.

68. Shryock 1997, 240.

69. H. al-Ḥāmid, n.d., 191.

70. Bā Faḍl 1956, 2:281.

71. Bujra 1971, 116–18.

72. Serjeant 1957, 14. See also Serjeant 1962, 41–58.

73. Munt 2014.

74. Wolf 1951; Serjeant 1962; Donner 2010; Munt 2014. In West Africa such enclaves began as Qurʾān school farms, which gradually developed into extensive clerical compounds and became off-limits to temporal authorities and exempted from taxation (Ware 2014, 97–98).

75. Serjeant 1957, 14–15.

76. Ho 2006; Bujra 1971.

77. Arai 2004, 72.

78. al-Bakrī 1936, 2:118.

79. Ibid.

80. Denny 1988, 91.

81. Lambek 1993, 189–90.

82. Eickleman 1985, 28–34.

83. Hefner 2007.

84. For a fascinating ethnographic example of such a failure, see Gilsenan ([1976] 2016, 515–19).

Chapter 2

1. Quoted in Siegel [1969] 2000, 264.

2. Eickelman and Piscatori 1996.

3. Kurzman 2002.

4. Abdullah 1971; Eickelman and Piscatori 1996; Laffan 2003, 2011; Milner 1994; Noer 1973.

5. For entextualization as a mode of objectification, see Bauman and Briggs (1990), Keane (1997), and M. Silverstein and Urban (1996).

6. For Islam as a social blueprint, see Gellner (1981). For Islam as core symbols, see Geertz (1968).

7. el-Zein 1977.

8. Asad 1986. For another anthropological work that describes the production of Islamic traditions through particular cultural understandings, see Bowen (1993).

9. Ahmed 2015.

10. Ibid., 517.

11. Ahmed 2015, 515.

12. Latour 2005, 187–90; Tsing 2000, 330.

13. Ricci 2011, 240.

14. Ibid.

15. Arai 2004; Clarence-Smith 2009; Freitag 2002, 2003; Ho 2006.

16. For works that examine Ḥaḍramī religious actors and infrastructures in the diaspora, see Bang (2003, 2014), Jacob (2019), and Kaptein (2014).

17. al-Shāṭirī 1983, 2:387–98; al-ʿAlawī 2002, 141–45.

18. ʿAbdallāh b. ʿAlawī al-Ḥaddād [1757] 1999, 1:72.

19. ʿAbdallāh b. ʿAlawī al-Ḥaddād [1702] 1994, 30.

20. Ibid., 23.

21. ʿAbdallāh b. ʿAlawī al-Ḥaddād [1757] 1999, 1:74.

22. ʿAlī al-Saqqāf 2009, 1:132.

23. ʿAbdallāh b. ʿAlawī al-Ḥaddād [1702] 1994, 22.

24. ʿAbdallāh b. ʿAlawī al-Ḥaddād [1757] 1999, 1:33.

25. Freitag 2003, 96.

26. For recent works on al-Ghazālī, see Moosa (2005) and Griffel (2009).

27. ʿAbdallāh b. ʿAlawī al-Ḥaddād [1702] 1994, 36.

28. Ibid., 14.

29. ʿAbdallāh b. ʿAlawī al-Ḥaddād [1702] 1994, 71. *Itḥāf al-sāʾil bi-jawāb al-masāʾil* (Bestowing answers on the enquirer) and *Al-Naṣāʾiḥ al-dīniyya wa-l-waṣāya al-īmāniyya* (Religious advice and counsels of faith) are the titles of two of al-Ḥaddād's works. The first was written in 1662 and the second in 1678. The Ḥaddādian creed, entitled "ʿAqīda ahl al-sunna wa-l-jamāʿa" (The creed of the people of the *sunna* and the *jamāʿa*) can be found in the concluding section of the *Al-Naṣāʾiḥ al-dīniyya* (ʿAbdallāh b. ʿAlawī al-Ḥaddād [1678] 1992, 349–52). This succinct and straightforward creed, however, has also been repeatedly published as a singular text. For example, the creed has been published as a booklet under the title *ʿAqīda ahl al-islām* (The creed of the people of Islam), together with an introduction and short commentary by the late *muftī* of Egypt, Ḥasanayn Muḥammad Makhlūf (d. 1990) (ʿAbdallāh b. ʿAlawī al-Ḥaddād [1974] 1993). The booklet has been reprinted multiple times since its first publication in 1971.

30. ʿAbdallāh b. ʿAlawī al-Ḥaddād [1702] 1994, 71–72.

31. Keane 2007.

32. Ibid., 68.

33. Fadel 1996, 198. *Al-Mukhtaṣar al-laṭīf* (The delicate abridgment), recommended by al-Ḥaddād, for example, presents a codified and univocal Shāfiʿī law accessible to the general public.

34. Similarly to al-Ḥaddād, the fifteenth-century Moroccan saint Muḥammad b. Sulaymān al-Jazūlī also authored his own creed and instructed his disciples to disseminate it to reform religious practice among the commoners (Cornell 1992, 206).

35. Bang 2014, 148.

36. Ahmed 2015, 368, 377.

37. Bang 2014; Jeppie 2018.

38. ʿAbdallāh b. ʿAlawī al-Ḥaddād [1713] 1993, 74.

39. Ibid. The term *shaykh al-taʿlīm* was also used by the Andalusian Sufi scholar Ibn ʿAbbād al-Rundī (d. 1390) to describe a Sufi master who imparts knowledge about Sufi wisdom in lecture or conversation, without directly intervening in the students' behavior. Al-Rundī differentiates a *shaykh al-taʿlīm* from a *shaykh al-tarbiya,* which is synonymous with what al-Ḥaddād described as *shaykh al-riyāḍa* (Meier 1999, 191–96).

40. ʿAbdallāh Ibn Yaḥyā 2008, 25–48; ʿAqīl Ibn Yaḥyā, n.d.; al-Ḥabashī [1887] 2009, 1:548–59.

41. al-ʿAlawī 2002,132; Freitag 2003, 129; al-Shātirī 1983, 2:388–91.

42. Feener 2010, 39–68; Freitag 2003; Gelvin and Green 2014, 1–24.

43. Clarence-Smith 2009, 140.

44. Ho 2006, 82–83; al-Junayd 1994, 167–68, 178–80.

45. See ʿAbd al-Raḥmān al-Saqqāf 2005, 601–2; Berg [1886] 1989, 106; Laffan 2011, 48; Bruinessen 1995, 122.

46. ʿAqīl Ibn Yaḥyā, n.d., 164.

47. Ibid., 325.

48. Ibid., 374–75.

49. For the complete text of this creed, see ʿAqīl Ibn Yaḥyā (n.d., 227). The other abridgments were on the proper performance of pilgrimage to Mecca, the etiquette of visiting the Prophet's tomb, and the righteous division of alms.

50. Kaptein 2014, 66, 137–38.

51. ʿUmar 1858, 16–30.

52. Ibid., 29.

53. Ibid., 22–23.

54. Ibid., 26.

55. Van Niel 1972.

56. Tagliacozzo 2013, 63–82.

57. Ricklefs 2009, 114.

58. Laffan 2011, 33. See also Bruinessen 1995, 71–87; Feener 2015. On al-Shaʿrānī's role in the reconfiguration of Sufi thought, see McGregor (2005, 380–94).

59. Kartodirdjo 1966, 162.

60. Florida 1995, 24–25. Such a project was cultivated in the new academic field of Javanology, which "worked in the interests of the authorities to frame 'traditional Java' through a delineation of that tradition's genuine high culture," while positing Javanese culture "as standing in opposition to Islam" (Florida 1997, 193).

61. This, however, does not mean that Muslim scholars were not active in the countryside prior to the Java War. Evidence suggests that they were already spread across the countryside and establishing educational institutions, like the famous *perdikan* of Tegalsari. Sources like the 1815 *Serat Centhini* suggest that the *kraton*, the countryside, and Muslim scholars were in dialogue (Florida 1997).

62. Ricklefs 2007, 52–53.

63. For the Great Post Road, see Nas and Pratiwo (2002) and Toer (2006). Later on when train travel became available in Java, Muslim scholars constituted "one segment of the Indies native population that used trains and trams radically more than the rest" (Mrázek 2002, 11).

64. Berg 1887, 518–55.

65. For a comprehensive list and discussion of these texts, see Bruinessen (1995, 112–71).

66. Indeed, Nancy Florida's examination of manuscripts stored in the three royal libraries of Surakarta suggests that the composition of Shaṭṭārī-oriented texts by the court's literati came to a near standstill with the end of the Java War, which suggest this development as a consequence of that war. Prince Dipanagara, his spiritual advisor Kyai Maja, and many, if not most, of the Islamic teachers who supported the prince were disciples of the Shaṭṭāriyya order. As such, affiliation with the Shaṭṭāriyya might had been seen by many as a liability (Florida 2019).

67. To ease comprehension, I will retain the term *traditionalist Muslims* in the rest of this book, while recognizing its limitations and its origin in early twentieth-century polemics.

68. Kumar 1985, 14; Kraus 2018, 5–8.

69. ʿAqīl Ibn Yaḥyā, n.d., 196–97.

70. A similar case involved a mid-nineteenth-century Javanese spiritual teacher, Hasan Mawlani, also known as Kyai Lengkong. Mawlani gradually attracted a large following, including the

sons of the Javanese elites, which, according to Michael Laffan, "raised the hackles of the rival gurus as much as it disturbed uncomprehending Dutch officials." Laffan adds that it is also likely that the rival gurus "saw to it that accounts of these teachers' activities were cast as an incipient danger to the state" (Laffan 2011, 52). In 1842, Mawlani was sent into lifetime exile in Tondano, North Sulawesi. It is highly possible that Ibn Yaḥyā experienced a similar conflict to that faced later on by Mawlani.

71. This is by no means unique to the Ḥaddādian paradigm. Since at least the sixteenth century, different Sufi orders have placed a great emphasis on the law-abiding moral rectitude of the Sufi as a social role model for Muslims in general. Sufism as it developed in different parts of the Muslim world had grown into "a powerful idiom of collective organization and communal solidarity," which went hand in hand with the systematic attempts of several Islamic polities to demote "the nomadic, charismatic, and 'anarchistic' Sufism associated with rural tribal groups" (Green 2012, 175). See also Kafadar 1995; Babayan 1994; Alam 2009.

Chapter 3

1. On the commemorative ritual, see I. Alatas (2014).
2. Denny 1988, 91.
3. On the impossibility of total purification, see Latour (1993).
4. Keane 2007, 80.
5. Ibid.
6. Abdullah 1971; Eickelman and Piscatori 1996; Laffan 2003, 2011; Milner 1994; Noer 1973.
7. Eickleman 1976; Geertz 1968; Gellner 1981.
8. Ahmed 2015; Berkey 1992; Cornell 1998; J. Katz 1996; Mahdi 1975; Munson 1993.
9. Messick 1993, 28. See also W. Graham 1987.
10. Quoted in Aḥmad al-ʿAṭṭās 2006, 89.
11. This biographical account of al-ʿAṭṭās is based on four hagiographical texts: Aḥmad al-ʿAṭṭās (2006), ʿAlī b. Ḥusayn al-ʿAṭṭās (1979), M. al-ʿAṭṭās (1949), and ʿAbdallāh b. Ṭāhir al-Ḥaddād (2009).
12. Laffan 2011, 133–36.
13. Bang 2014, 27–8.
14. Alī b. Ḥusayn al-ʿAṭṭās 1979, 2:311.
15. The livelihood of a *shaykh al-ta ʿlīm* like al-ʿAṭṭās depended on the support of the wealthy members of the Ḥaḍramī diaspora. One surviving letter, written by al-ʿAṭṭās to a scion of the wealthy āl-Junayd family of Singapore, ʿAbd al-Raḥmān al-Junayd (d. 1950), illustrates this relationship. In the letter, al-ʿAṭṭās requested financial assistance from al-Junayd to pay a government house tax (*fersel*) to the sum of three hundred rupiah (al-Junayd 1994, 342–43).
16. Alī b. Ḥusayn al-ʿAṭṭās 1979, 2:312; Shahabuddin [1944] 2000, 62.
17. Aḥmad al-ʿAṭṭās 2006, 76.
18. Shahabuddin [1944] 2000, 62–63.
19. ʿAbdallāh b. Ṭāhir al-Ḥaddād 2009, 1:728.
20. Mandal 2018, 66. See also Berg [1886] 1989, 69–70.
21. Jonge 1997, 94.

22. Reid 2003, 11.

23. Jonge 1997, 96.

24. Ibid., 97–101.

25. L.W.C. van den Berg reported that by the late nineteenth century, Javanese elites had stopped their former practice of marrying their daughters to the Ḥaḍramīs (Berg [1886] 1989, 138). See also Mandal 2018, 70.

26. Vuldy 1985, 95–119.

27. It is important, however, to note the disjuncture between colonial policies and their outcomes. Sumit Mandal recently suggested that the "exclusionary outcome was incremental rather than radical in character." He further noted how the Arab quarters of Java "retained a significant degree of ethnic diversity and cultural hybridity" (Mandal 2018, 205).

28. See, for example, Freitag 2003; Ho 2006; Mandal 2018; Mobini-Kesheh 1999.

29. Aḥmad al-ʿAṭṭās 2006, 83.

30. al-ʿAṭṭās's extant letters have been compiled by his grandson Aḥmad b. ʿUmar al-ʿAṭṭās and are appended to his hagiography (Aḥmad al-ʿAṭṭās 2006).

31. For example, another notable Ḥaḍramī *shaykh al-taʿlīm* active during this period was ʿAbdallāh b. Muḥsin al-ʿAṭṭās (d. 1933), posthumously known as the principal saint of Bogor, West Java. A survey of the condolence letters (*taʿazzī*) addressed to ʿAbdallāh's children on the occasion of his death provides us with a rough indication of the scope of his extended networks. Letters were sent from all over Indonesia, Singapore, Malaysia, the Ḥaḍramawt, and Egypt. Out of the eighty-nine extant letters, only three were written by non-Ḥaḍramīs (Saʿidī, n.d.). There are, of course, exceptions to this general trend as exemplified by the Batavia-born Ḥaḍramī *shaykh al-taʿlīm* ʿUthmān b. ʿAbdallāh Bin Yaḥyā (d. 1914), who was influential not only among the Ḥaḍramīs (Kaptein 2014).

32. I. Alatas 2016a.

33. This resemblance is captured by at least two travelers from the Ḥaḍramawt who left behind travelogues (*riḥla*) of their visit to Java. The first is the scholar ʿUmar b. Aḥmad Bā Faqīh (d. 1939), whose 1899 visit to Java was recorded in his *Ṣilat al-akhyār bi-l-rijāl al-aʾimmat al-kibār*. The second is the poet Ṣāliḥ b. ʿAlī al-Ḥāmid (d. 1995), who visited Pekalongan in 1928 and described his experience in his *Riḥla jāwā al-jamīla* (Bā Faqīh 1990, 81–85; S. al-Ḥāmid 2002, 206–7).

34. ʿAbd al-Raḥmān al-Saqqāf 2005, 577; ʿAbdallāh al-Saqqāf 1984, 5:3–6.

35. On al-Miḥḍār, see Freitag (2003, 163–64); "Index of Arabs in the Netherlands East Indies" (1919); al-Mashhūr ([1911] 1984, 1:283); ʿAbdallāh al-Saqqāf (1984, 5:84).

36. Shahabuddin [1944] 2000, 65.

37. For vivid descriptions of customs associated with the manṣabates of Ḥaḍramawt, see Stark (1936, 1940).

38. The earliest hagiography was written by al-ʿAṭṭās's disciple, Muḥsin b. Muḥammad al-ʿAṭṭās. This short work is the one that is recited annually during the commemoration. Al-ʿAṭṭās's hagiography is also included in a three-volume hagiography of his contemporary, Muḥammad b. Ṭāhir al-Ḥaddād (d. 1899), entitled *Qurrat al-nāẓir* and composed by ʿAbdallāh b. Ṭāhir al-Ḥaddād (d. 1947). Another disciple of al-ʿAṭṭās, ʿAlī b. Ḥusayn al-ʿAṭṭās (d. 1976), also wrote a hagiography as part of a two-volume hagiographical dictionary of Bā ʿAlawī saints and scholars who lived from the eighteenth to the twentieth century, entitled *Tāj al-aʿrās*.

39. For works on Prophetic and saintly relics and objects in Islam, see Margoliouth (1937) and Meri (2010).

40. This *mawlid* text is one that was composed by the Yemeni ʿAbd al-Raḥmān al-Dībaʿī (d. 1537). For the history of *mawlid* texts, see M. Katz (2007, 50–62).

41. For the *madkhal* as a long-established practice in the sanctuaries of Ḥaḍramawt, see ʿAlī b. Ḥusayn al-ʿAṭṭās (1979, 2:732–40).

42. I. Alatas 2014.

43. I have discussed this dynamic in greater detail elsewhere. See ibid.

44. Feener 2010; Laffan 2003.

45. Bowen 2012, 33.

46. Warner 2002, 105.

47. Abaza 1993; Abushouk 2007; Azra 1999; Bluhm 1983.

48. Mandal 2002, 163–84; Mobini-Kesheh 1996, 236–56.

49. For the role of the *jamʿiyya* in "negotiating the tension between face-to-face relationship and an anonymous public," see Deeb (2006, 177).

50. Freitag 2003, 233–45.

51. Mobini-Kesheh 1999, 36–37.

52. Ibid., 37.

53. Ibid.; Mandal 2018, 171–73.

54. Bujra 1967.

55. For the emergence and early development of al-Irsyad, see Mobini-Kesheh (1997, 1999).

56. Mobini-Kesheh 1999.

57. Knysh 1997; Mobini-Kesheh 1999.

58. al-Bakrī 1936, 2:324.

59. Ibid., 325.

60. Sirriyeh 1999; Loimeier 2016.

61. For the Muhammadiyah, see Nakamura (2012) and Federspiel (1970).

62. Abdullah 1971; Noer 1973.

63. Tsing 2005, 8.

64. Ibid.

65. Anderson 1991; Freitag 2003; Milner 1994; Mobini-Kesheh 1999.

66. Soares 2016, 280. On the moral narrative of modernity, see Keane (2007).

Chapter 4

1. Taneja 2018, 94.

2. Ernst 1992; Farhādī [1993] 1999; T. Graham [1993] 1999.

3. Keshani 2008, 450.

4. Green 2012, 60.

5. Birchok 2015; Buehler 1998; Ho 2006; Shaery-Eisenlohr 2009.

6. I. Alatas 2015; Cornell 1998; Ho 2006.

7. Cornell 1998; Mayeur-Jaouen and Papas 2014; McGregor 2004; Peskes 2015.

8. El Moudden 1990; Euben 2006; Gellens 1990; Netton 1996.

9. Gellens 1990, 53.

10. Ricci 2011, 196.

11. Ibid., 61. This is not unique to Islamic knowledge practice. In her study of the Meratus Dayaks, Tsing has shown how the ability to travel allows ambitious Meratus men to tap into different power and knowledge structures, and enables them to gather an audience, thereby making them more authoritative than those who do not travel (1993, 150–51).

12. Sayeed 2013.

13. Abaza 1993; Azra 2004; Laffan 2003, 2011; Tagliacozzo 2013.

14. M. Marsden 2010.

15. Ibid., 56.

16. Ibid., 56, 67.

17. For the latter, see Hirschkind (2006) and Mahmood (2005).

18. M. Marsden 2010, 68.

19. Ho 2006, 153–54.

20. Hoesterey 2016, 77, 87.

21. Ibid., 87.

22. Stearns 2011, 78.

23. Soemarsaid Moertono (1976), quoted in Carey 2008, 127.

24. El Moudden 1990, 96.

25. Muhaimin 2006, 250–51.

26. For al-Habsyi, see Zulkifli (2013, 52–62).

27. Rosen 1989; Messick 1993.

28. Indeed, one can compare *lelono/riḥla* with the Christian adoption of the Greek *paideia* in late antiquity. See P. Brown 1981.

29. Hammoudi 1997, 91.

30. One can compare Habib Luthfi's position with Michael Lambek's discussion of the role of practical wisdom/judgement (*phronesis*) in everyday ethics (Lambek 2010, 25–29).

31. Dhofier 2011.

32. Weismann 2001, 305–6.

33. Abu-Manneh 1982; Weismann 2001.

34. Bruinessen 1992, 164.

35. Abdul Malik, n.d.b.

36. Abun-Nasr 2007, 61–62; Hammoudi 1997, 96–97; Ohlander 2008, 200.

37. Green 2012, 87.

38. Abun-Nasr 2007, 82.

39. Bashir 2011, 153; Denny 1988, 80.

40. Trimingham 1971, 14–16.

41. ʿAlī al-Ḥabashī, n.d.a., 2:386–87.

42. Abdul Malik, n.d.a., 73–74.

43. Ibid., 74.

44. Felek and Knysh 2012; J. Katz 1996; Sirriyeh 2015.

45. Ricklefs 2012, 156.

46. Ibid.

47. Bruinessen 1992, 109–10; Kaptein 2014, 201–3; Laffan 2011, 58–60.

48. S. Alatas 1999; Assegaf 2015; Formichi 2014, 2015; Zulkifli 2013.

49. Formichi 2015.

50. Ibid., 272.

51. For the history of this association, see Bruinessen (1992, 171–73).

52. Azra 1997, 258. For a more accurate explanation regarding ʿUthmān's view of Sufi orders, see Kaptein (2014, 106–20).

Chapter 5

1. One prominent example is Machiavelli, who criticized the French king Louis XII's policy of helping Pope Alexander VI to occupy Romagna as a move that alienated him from his allies and strengthened the church *"by adding to it so much temporal power, in addition to the spiritual power from which it derives so much authority"* (Machiavelli 2005, 14; emphasis added). Another example is John Stuart Mill, who described tyrannical forms of government as deriving *"their authority from inheritance or conquest, who at all events, did not hold it at the pleasure of the governed"* (Mill 1999, 43; emphasis added). Another notable example is Michel Foucault, whose capacious conceptualization of power situates all forms of asymmetrical relations—including those that can be described as authoritative or authoritarian—within its fold, thereby emptying the notion of authority of any analytic purchase. See, for example, his discussion of the pastorate as a particular technique of power (Foucault 1982, 782–84).

2. Arendt [1968] 2006, 92.

3. Ibid. 122.

4. Ibid., 93.

5. Thus, historically, Sufi orders were one of the primary means of integration in the Muslim world in the face of the political fragmentation that followed from the downfall of the Abbasid period. See Hodgson 1974; Voll 1994.

6. Fadil and Fernando 2015.

7. For classic treatments of *ṭarīqa* as Sufi order, see Jong (1978) and Trimingham (1971).

8. Sedgwick 2005.

9. Bashir 2011, 11.

10. Hervieu-Léger 2000, 151–52.

11. For an example of a fruitful comparative approach between Islamic and Buddhist religious orders, see Blackburn and Feener (2019).

12. See Green 2012; Meier 1999; Ohlander 2008; Sviri [1993] 1999.

13. Similarly, Aryo Danusiri's work on Islamic youth movements in Jakarta underlines the generative force of mobile spatial practice as a means employed by Muslim preachers to create relations and networks that *may* lead to the formation of durable urban Islamic communities. While Danusiri focuses on urban contexts, the case of Habib Luthfi attests to how similar mobile practices are also at work in rural settings. Such similarity should serve as a reminder not to attribute dynamism solely to urban-based communities. See Danusiri 2014, 339–51.

14. Warner 2002, 67–74. This, however, does not mean that a member of a preacher's public cannot develop attachment to the preacher that perdures beyond the temporality of the speech event. Research conducted by Fatimah Husein and Martin Slama among Indonesian Muslim women who frequent Islamic study groups indicates how their interlocutors have developed

the practice of directly contacting a preacher using messaging apps like WhatsApp whenever they need guidance (Husein and Slama 2018; see also Slama 2017).

15. Chih 2007; Halman 2013; Hammoudi 1997.

16. Cornell 1998, 197–98.

17. Millie 2009.

18. Baker 1993, 108.

19. The *Jāmiʿ al-uṣūl fi-l-awliyāʾ* is a Khālidī text that was first brought to Java toward the end of the nineteenth century by Javanese pilgrims, who had been exposed to it during their stay in Mecca. Subsequently, it became popular in Naqshbandī-Khālidī circles of Java (Bruinessen 1992, 74).

20. B. Silverstein 2008, 141.

21. Bin Yahya 2006, 3–5.

22. Meri 2010; Renard 2008.

23. Eisenlohr 2009.

24. I. Alatas 2017.

25. Agrama 2012, 182.

26. See, for example, Bruinessen and Howell (2007), Seesemann (2011), and Weismann (2001).

27. Knysh 2017, 163.

28. Ibid., 163. For cases of failures, see J. Katz (1996) and Hoesterey (2016).

29. Beekers and Kloos 2018, 11.

30. Ibid.

31. This is by no means unique to Habib Luthfi. Scholars working on contemporary Sufism in Indonesia have noted how Sufi discipleship has significantly increased since 1977, owing to, among other things, the loosening of the entry requirements and the easing of spiritual practice (Howell 2001; Bruinessen and Howell 2007).

32. DeWeese 1999; Weismann 2001.

33. Cornell 1998; Mittermaier 2011; Renard 2008; Rozehnal 2007; Wright 2015.

34. Hirschkind 2006; Kloos 2018; Mahmood 2005.

35. Foucault 1990, 23–28; 1997, 225.

36. Asad 1993; Keane 2016; Laidlaw 2014; Lambek 2010.

37. Schielke 2009; Debevec 2012; M. Marsden 2010; Osella and Soares 2010. On the everyday as site of "moral pluralism," see Mattingly (2014).

38. Fadil and Fernando 2015.

39. Ahmed 2015.

40. Knysh 1999a, 271.

41. Ibid, 272.

42. al-Attas 1966; Laffan 2011, 11; Ricklefs 2006, 197.

43. Feener 2013, 120.

44. Keane 2003b.

45. On the so-called "newly pious" of Indonesia, see Hefner (2005).

46. S. H. Nasr et al. 2015, 1258.

47. Williams 2011, 140–41.

48. Ibid., 129.

49. The anthropologist Abdellah Hammoudi, to give one prominent example, describes how such a relationship is characterized by the disciples' submission and the negation of their virility (Hammoudi 1997).

50. Arendt [1968] 2006, 93.

51. Humphrey 1997, 38.

52. Ibid., 34.

53. Žižek 1999, 102.

Chapter 6

1. The chronicle has been translated in its entirety by Nancy Florida (1995, 183–84).

2. See, for example, Alam (2009), Jong (1983), Karamustafa (1993), Moin (2012), and S.V.R. Nasr (2001).

3. Bayat 2007; Hoesterey 2016; Kingsley 2018; Zaman 2007.

4. Ewing 1983, 1997; Pinto 2006; Rozehnal 2007.

5. Laclau and Mouffe [1985] 2001, 113.

6. Ibid., 142.

7. Foucault 1991. For a notable example of the traditional treatment of power, see Anderson ([1990] 2006, 17–77).

8. Das 2007; Ferguson and Gupta 2002; Hull 2012; Mitchell 1991, 2006; Salomon 2016; Trouillot 2001.

9. Abrams 1988.

10. Aretxaga 2003, 395.

11. Navaro-Yashin 2002.

12. Latour 2010, 260.

13. Mitchell 1991, 2006; Van der Veer 2001.

14. "PKB supporters attack PPP backers," *Jakarta Post*, May 28, 1999; "'Hired ulemas' behind Pekalongan PKB-PPP clash: Gus Dur," *Jakarta Post*, May 31, 1999.

15. Crouch [1978] 2007.

16. Rinakit 2005.

17. Aretxaga 2003, 401.

18. Taussig 1997.

19. *Pernyataan Keberatan* 2011, 3.

20. "Rahasia sang Pemenang," *Majalah Tempo* 38, no. 6 (April 2009).

21. The flow of Saudi theological influence to Indonesia, including the establishment of LIPIA, was facilitated by the Indonesian Council for Islamic Propagation (DDII) founded in 1967 by the former Indonesian prime minister Muhammad Natsir (d. 1993) (Hasan 2006, 39–40).

22. Hasan 2006.

23. Slama 2014b, 122.

24. See Kirsch 2010; Tsing 2005.

25. Salvatore 2007, 156.

26. "Habib Baqir minta Pemkot hentikan kemaksiatan," *Buletin Masjid Al-Jami' Kota Pekalongan*, April 28, 2012, 1–2.

27. For the history of the FPI, see Bamualim (2011) and Jahroni (2008).

28. Ricklefs 2012, 420–22.

29. The grave of Mawlānā Maghribī is claimed by a half-dozen villages in Java. John Pemberton notes how within a thirty-mile radius alone, there are at least four places claimed to be the tomb of Mawlānā Maghribī, each site bearing a particular history tied to its locality (1994, 286–87).

30. Das 2007, 177.

31. See Feener 2013; Kingsley 2018; Nordholt and Klinken 2007; Pribadi 2018.

32. Knysh 2017, 191.

Chapter 7

1. While such stories are of obscure provenance, it may be the case that they initially circulated among modern reformist critics of saintly veneration, who were known to use satires (Knysh 1997,152–53).

2. Conrad 2000, 233.

3. See, for example, Harris (1999), Kugle (2007), Taylor (1999), Wolper (2003), and Yasin (2009).

4. On the growth of religious tourism in Indonesia, see I. Alatas (2016b), Quinn (2019), and Slama (2014a).

5. "Wisata Religi Solo: Perputaran Uang Capai Rp.225 Miliar, Tamu Haul Habib Ali Belanjakan Rp1,5 Juta," *SoloPos*, February 10, 2015.

6. "Pemkot Semarang Gelar Haul Habib Hasan," *Tribunnews*, March 1, 2018.

7. "Pembangunan Makam Habib Diyakini Dongkrak Potensi Wisata Semarang," *Kompas*, January 17, 2019.

8. Ibid.

9. I. Alatas 2020.

10. Habib Luthfi's view on the importance of saintly discourse and practice is similar to the views expressed or embodied by traditionalist Muslims in other parts of the world. For comparison, see Bashir (2011), Ho (2006), Mittermaier (2011), Taneja (2018), Taylor (1999), and Thum (2014).

11. Connolly 1999, 29. For "participation" as a mode of relating to and constructing a shared reality, see Tambiah (1990, 107–8). Tambiah contrasts participation with what he calls causality. The latter is a mode of relating to reality that involves distancing, affective neutrality, and abstraction.

12. For example, in introducing the two aforementioned new saints of Semarang, Habib Luthfi claims that both Ṭāhā and his son Ḥasan were the sons-in-law of the first and second sultans of Yogyakarta. See "Pembangunan Makam Habib Diyakini Dongkrak Potensi Wisata Semarang," *Kompas*, January 17, 2019.

13. Gilsenan 1973; Green 2012; Kugle 2007; Millie 2009; Renard 2008. A notable exception to this is Daniel Birchock's study of female saints in Aceh (Birchok 2016).

14. Bashir 2011, 88.

15. Cornell 1998; Ernst 1992; Ewing 1997; Gilsenan 1973; Millie 2009; Renard 2008.

16. Asad 1993, 53–54.

17. Florida 1993, 24.

18. There is a resonance between what I am suggesting here and what the Egyptologist Jan Assmann has described as the objective of mnemohistory. Assmann defines mnemohistory as a subbranch of history concerned "not with the past as such but only with the past as it is remembered" (1997, 9).

19. Shryock 1997, 240.

20. See also Abu-Lughod 1986; Samin 2015.

21. For example, Louise Marlow (2003) has written about the importance of *aṣl* among the Persians.

22. Hoesterey 2016; Millie 2017; Rudnyckyj 2010; Slama 2017.

23. Wehr 1979, 710.

24. Mayeur-Jaouen and Papas 2014.

25. Foltz 1996; McGregor 2004; Papas 2007; Peskes 2015.

26. I. Alatas 2015, 146–47.

27. ʿAlī al-Ḥabashī, n.d.b., 147–48.

28. Shryock 1997, 240.

29. Similarly, the opponents of the notable twentieth-century West African scholar and Sufi master Ibrahim Niasse (d. 1975) "sought to undermine his spiritual authority by advancing the notion that he was the descendant of a blacksmith, and thus not qualified for a religious leadership position" (Seesemann 2011, 145).

30. Goody 1970; Sahlins 2004, 291; 2013, 62; Valeri 1990, 190.

31. Bang 2003; Freitag 2003; Ho 2006; Peskes 2015.

32. A similar observation has been made by Rian Thum in his study of Altishahri (Uyghur) praxis of history (2014, 24–25).

33. Benjamin 1968, 92.

34. For example, Aḥmad al-ʿAṭṭās 2006; ʿAlī b. Ḥusayn al-ʿAṭṭās 1979; M. al-ʿAṭṭās 1949; ʿAbdallāh b. Ṭāhir al-Ḥaddād 2009.

35. al-Mashhūr [1911] 1984, 324.

36. Ho 2006, xxiii, 115.

37. Bauman and Briggs 1990, 73. See also M. Silverstein and Urban 1996.

38. Boyarin 1993; Janowitz 1993; M. Silverstein 1996.

39. Tsauri 2014, 184–89.

40. Ricoeur 1973, 95.

41. Kaptein 1993; M. Katz 2007.

42. Bin Yaḥyā 1999, 20.

43. Ḥ. al-Saqqāf [1781] 2001, 290–93.

44. Barenboim and Said 2002, 112.

45. This makes hagiographical composition similar to Javanese poetic historiography. See Florida 1995, 398.

46. Thum 2014, 89.

47. Longing for the caliphate is an established trope in Muslim political, scholarly, and literary works. Such a desire has taken different forms throughout history and comes with a variety of imaginations of what a caliphate is (Hassan 2016).

Epilogue

1. "Berikut Isi Utuh Sabda Raja Yogya," *Koran Tempo*, May 9, 2015.

2. Kennedy 2016, xviii.

3. "NU dan Muhammadiyah Protes Sabda Raja Yogya," *Koran Tempo*, May 7, 2015.

4. After the failure of the articulatory project in Yogyakarta, Habib Luthfi is now attempting to approach the other Javanese royal court, that of Surakarta (Solo). The move came following several meetings between Habib Luthfi and the deputy ruler of the *kraton* Surakarta, K.G.P.H. Puger. In June 2015, Prince Puger announced to the press that Habib Luthfi "has agreed to work with me to re-enhance Islamic civilization in *kraton* Surakarta." He added that "in the past, *kraton* Surakarta was very attentive to the development of Islam both in civilizational and socio-cultural term due to its predicate as an Islamic kingdom. This is what I want to revive" ("KGPH Puger: Pererat Ukhuwah Islamiyah antara Kraton Surakarta dan Ulama," *Kedaulatan Rakyat*, June 9, 2015).

5. Mattingly 2014, 203.

6. For Latour's conception of politics and the political, see Harman (2014, 23).

7. One prominent example was the scholarship of the Dutch orientalist Christiaan Snouck Hurgronje (d. 1936). See Laffan 2011.

8. Kant [1784] 2009.

9. Gadamer 2004, 281.

10. Buck-Morss 2009; Butler, Laclau, and Žižek 1999; Duara 1995; Laclau and Mouffe [1985] 2001.

11. Excellent examples of this kind of empirical work include de la Cruz (2015), Li (2020), and Tsing (2005).

12. One can trace this conception of universality all the way back to St. Paul (Badiou 2003).

13. Ilyenkov 1975, 38–39.

14. Ibid., 43.

15. Ibid., 44.

BIBLIOGRAPHY

NB: Names beginning with the particle *al-* have been alphabetized under the element following the particle; so, *al-Junayd* will be found under *J*.

Abaza, Mona. 1993. *Changing Images of Three Generations of Azharites in Indonesia*. Singapore: ISEAS.

Abdullah, Taufik. 1971. *Schools and Politics: The Kaum Muda Movement in West Sumatra (1927–1933)*. Ithaca, NY: Cornell Modern Indonesia Project.

Abdul Malik b. Muhammad Ilyas. n.d.a. *Al-Miftāḥ al-maqāṣid li ahl al-tawḥīd*. Privately printed.

———. n.d.b. *Al-Tarqīb al-uṣūl li tashīl al-wuṣūl*. Privately printed.

Abrams, Philip. 1988. "Notes on the Difficulty of Studying the State." *Journal of Historical Sociology* 1 (1): 58–89.

Abu-Lughod, Lila. 1986. *Veiled Sentiments: Honor and Poetry in a Bedouin society*. Berkeley: University of California Press.

———. 1988. "Fieldwork of a Dutiful Daughter." In *Arab Women in the Field: Studying Your Own Society*, edited by Soraya Altorki and Camilia Fawzi el-Solh, 139–61. Syracuse, NY: Syracuse University Press.

———. 1991. "Writing against Culture." In *Recapturing Anthropology: Working in the Present*, edited by Richard Fox, 137–62. Santa Fe: School of American Research Press.

Abu-Manneh, Butrus. 1982. "The Naqshbandiyya-Mujaddidiyya in the Ottoman lands in the Early 19th Century." *Die Welt des Islams* 22 (1–4): 1–36.

Abun-Nasr, Jamil M. 2007. *Muslim Communities of Grace: The Sufi Brotherhoods in Islamic Religious Life*. New York: Columbia University Press.

Abushouk, Ahmed Ibrahim. 2007. "Al-Manār and the Ḥadhramī Elite in the Malay-Indonesian World: Challenge and Response." *Journal of the Royal Asiatic Society* 17 (3): 301–22.

Agrama, Hussein Ali. 2012. *Questioning Secularism: Islam, Sovereignty, and the Rule of Law in Modern Egypt*. Chicago: Chicago University Press.

Ahmed, Shahab. 2015. *What Is Islam? The Importance of being Islamic*. Princeton, NJ: Princeton University Press.

———. 2017. *Before Orthodoxy: The Satanic Verses in Early Islam*. Cambridge, MA: Harvard University Press.

Alam, Muzaffar. 2009. "The Mughals, the Sufi Shaikhs and the Formation of the Akbari Dispensation." *Modern Asian Studies* 43 (1): 135–74.

Alatas, Ismail Fajrie. 2010. "[Al-] ʿAlawiyya (in Hadramawt)." In *The Encyclopaedia of Islam Three*, edited by Gudrun Krämer, Denis Matringe, John Nawas and Everett Rowson. Leiden: Brill.

———. 2011. "Becoming Indonesians: The Bā ʿAlawī in the Interstices of the Nation." *Die Welt des Islams* 51 (1): 45–108.

———. 2014. "Pilgrimage and Network Formation in Two Contemporary Bā ʿAlawī *Ḥawl* in Central Java." *Journal of Islamic Studies* 25 (3): 298–324.

———. 2015. "'They Are the Heirs of the Prophet': Discourses on the *Ahl al-Bayt* and Religious Authority among the Bā ʿAlawī in Modern Indonesia." In *Shiʿism in Southeast Asia: ʿAlid Piety and Sectarian Constructions*, edited by Chiara Formichi and R. Michael Feener, 139–64. Oxford: Oxford University Press.

———. 2016a. "The *Pangeran* and the Saints: The Historical Inflection of a Mid 19th-Century Ḥaḍramī Mausoleum in East Java, Indonesia." *Indonesia and the Malay World* 44 (130): 285–306.

———. 2016b. "The Poetics of Pilgrimage: Assembling Contemporary Indonesian Pilgrimage to Ḥaḍramawt, Yemen." *Comparative Studies in Society and History* 58 (3): 607–35.

———. 2017. "Sufi Sociality in Social Media." In *Piety, Celebrity, Sociality: A Forum on Islam and Social Media in Southeast Asia*, edited by Martin Slama and Carla Jones. American Ethnologist website, November 8, 2017. http://americanethnologist.org/features/collections/piety-celebrity-sociality/sufi-sociality-in-social-media.

———. 2020 "Dreaming Saints: Exploratory Authority and Islamic Praxes of History in Central Java." *Journal of the Royal Anthropological Institute* 26 (1): 67–85.

Alatas, Syed Farid. 1999. "The Ṭarīqat al-ʿAlawiyyah and the Emergence of the Shiʿi School in Indonesia and Malaysia." *Oriente moderno* 18 (2): 323–39.

al-ʿAlawī, Muḥammad b. Hāshim. 2002. *Tārīkh al-dawla al-kathīriyya*. Tarim, Yemen: Tarīm li-dirāsāt wa al-nashr.

Althusser, Louis. 2015. "The Object of Capital." In *Reading Capital: The Complete Edition*, translated by Ben Brewster and David Fernbach, 215–355. London: Verso.

Anderson, Benedict R. O'G. (1990) 2006. *Language and Power: Exploring Political Culture in Indonesia*. Jakarta: Equinox.

———. 1991. *Imagined Communities: Reflections on the Origin and Spread of Nationalism*. 2nd ed. London: Verso.

Anjum, Ovamir. 2012. *Politics, Law, and Community in Islamic Thought: The Taymiyyan Moment*. Cambridge: Cambridge University Press.

Ansari, Zafar I. 1972. "Islamic Juristic Terminology before Šāfiʿī: A Semantic Analysis with Special Reference to Kūfa." *Arabica* 19:255–300.

Anthony, Sean W. 2019. "Two 'Lost' Sūras of the Qurʾān: Sūrat al-Khalʿ and Sūrat al-Ḥafd between Textual and Ritual Canon (1st–3rd/7th–9th Centuries)." *Jerusalem Studies in Arabic and Islam* 46:67–112.

Arai, Kazuhiro. 2004. "Arabs Who Traversed the Indian Ocean: The History of the al-ʿAttas Family in Hadramawt and Southeast Asia, c. 1600–c. 1960." PhD dissertation, University of Michigan.

Arendt, Hannah. (1968) 2006. *Between Past and Future: Eight Exercises in Political Thought*. New York: Penguin.

———. (1958) 1998. *The Human Condition*. 2nd ed. Chicago: University of Chicago Press.

Aretxaga, Begoña. 2003. "Maddening States." *Annual Review of Anthropology* 32:393–410.

Arifianto, Alexander R. 2016. "Islam Nusantara: NU's Bid to Promote 'Moderate Indonesian Islam.'" *RSIS Commentaries* 114. Singapore: Nanyang Technological University.

Arifin, Achmad Zainal. 2012. "Re-energising Recognised Sufi Orders in Indonesia." *RIMA: Review of Indonesian and Malaysian Affairs* 46 (2): 77–104.

Asad, Talal. 1986. "The Idea of an Anthropology of Islam." Occasional Papers Series. Washington, DC: Center for Contemporary Arab Studies, Georgetown University.

———. 1993. *Genealogies of Religion: Discipline and Reasons of Power in Christianity and Islam.* Baltimore, MD: Johns Hopkins University Press.

———. 2003. *Formations of the Secular: Christianity, Islam, Modernity.* Stanford, CA: Stanford University Press.

———. 2015. "Thinking about Tradition, Religion, and Politics in Egypt today." *Critical Inquiry* 42 (1): 166–214.

———. 2018. *Secular Translations: Nation-State, Modern Self, and Calculative Reason.* New York: Columbia University Press.

Assegaf, Umar Faruk. 2015. "Aspects of Shiʿism in Contemporary Indonesia: A Quest for Social Recognition in the Post-Suharto Era (1998–2008)." In *Shiʿism in Southeast Asia: ʿAlid Piety and Sectarian Constructions,* edited by Chiara Formichi and Michael Feener, 249–68. Oxford: Oxford University Press.

Assman, Jan. 1997. *Moses the Egyptian: The Memory of Egypt in Western Monotheism.* Cambridge, MA: Harvard University Press.

al-ʿAṭṭās, Aḥmad b. ʿUmar. 2006. *Mawrid al-ṭālib fī manāqib al-ḥabīb aḥmad bin ʿabdallāh bin ṭālib.* Privately printed.

al-ʿAṭṭās, ʿAlī b. Aḥmad. n.d. "Bughyat al-ṭālib fī safīnat al-ḥabīb ʿalī bin aḥmad bin ʿabdallāh al-ʿaṭṭās al-maʿrūf bi ibn ṭālib." MS 02328. Kanzul Hikmah Library, Jakarta.

al-ʿAṭṭās, ʿAlī b. Ḥasan. 1942. "Al-Maqṣad fī shawāhid al-mashhad." MS 00626. Kanzul Hikmah Library, Jakarta.

———. n.d. "Al-Qirṭās fī manāqib al-ʿaṭṭās." 2 vols. MS 2149. Al-Ahqaff Library, Tarim, Yemen.

al-ʿAṭṭās, ʿAlī b. Ḥusayn. 1979. *Tāj al-aʿrās ʿalā manāqib al-ḥabīb al-quṭb ṣāliḥ bin ʿabdallāh al-ʿaṭṭās.* 2 vols. Kudus, Central Java: Menara Kudus.

al-ʿAṭṭās, Muḥsin b. Muḥammad. 1949. "Manāqib al-imām al-ʿārif bi-llāh wa al-dāl ʿalayh al-walī al-kabīr wa al-quṭb al-shahīr qudwat al-akyās al-ḥabīb aḥmad b. ʿabdallāh b. ṭālib al-ʿattās." MS. Markaz al-Noor, Tarim, Yemen.

al-Attas, Syed Muhammad Naguib. 1966. *Rānīrī and the Wujūdiyah of 17th Century Aceh.* Kuala Lumpur: Malaysian Branch Royal Asiatic Society.

al-ʿAydarūs, ʿAbdallāh b. Abū Bakr. (n.d.) 2002. *Al-Kibrīt al-aḥmar wa-l-iksīr al-akbar fī maʿrifa asrār al-sulūk ilā malik al-mulūk.* Cairo: Dār jawāmiʿ al-kalim.

al-ʿAydarūs, Abū Bakr b. ʿAbdallāh al-ʿAydarūs. (1489) 2011. *Al-Juzʾ al-laṭīf fī al-taḥkīm al-sharīf.* Beirut: Dār al-ḥāwī.

Aydin, Cemil. 2017. *The Idea of the Muslim World: A Global Intellectual History.* Cambridge, MA: Harvard University Press.

Ayubi, Zahra. 2019. *Gendered Morality: Classical Islamic Ethics of the Self, Family, and Society.* New York: Columbia University Press.

Azra, Azyumardi. 1997. "A Hadhrami Religious Scholar in Indonesia: Sayyid ʿUthman." In *Hadhrami Traders, Scholars and Statesmen in the Indian Ocean, 1750s–1960s,* edited by Ulrike Freitag and William G. Clarence-Smith, 249–62. Leiden: Brill.

———. 1999. "The Transmission of *al-Manar's* Reformism to the Malay-Indonesian World: The Cases of al-Imam and al-Munir." *Studia Islamika* 6 (3): 75–100.

———. 2004. *The Origins of Islamic Reformism in Southeast Asia: Networks of Malay-Indonesian and Middle Eastern 'Ulama' in the Seventeenth and Eighteenth Centuries*. Crows Nest, NSW: Allen and Unwin.

Babayan, Kathryn. 1994. "The Safavid Synthesis: From Qizilbash Islam to Imamite Shi'ism." *Iranian Studies* 27 (1–4): 135–61.

Badiou, Alain. 2003. *Saint Paul: The Foundation of Universalism*. Stanford, CA: Stanford University Press.

Bā Faḍl, Muḥammad ʿAwaḍ. 1956. "Tanwīr al-aghlās bi dhikr anfās al-shihāb al-nibrās aḥmad b. ḥasan al-ʿaṭṭās." 2 vols. MS. Private collection of Manṣab Abdullah Bagir, Pekalongan, Indonesia.

Bā Faqīh, ʿUmar b. Aḥmad. 1990. *Ṣilat al-akhyār bi-l-rijāl al-aʾimmat al-kibār*. Singapore: Pustaka Nasional.

Baker, James N. 1993. "The Presence of the Name: Reading Scripture in an Indonesian Village." In *The Ethnography of Reading*, edited by Jonathan Boyarin, 98–138. Berkeley: University of California Press.

al-Bakrī, Ṣalāḥ. 1936. *Tārīkh ḥaḍramawt al-siyāsī*. 2 vols. Cairo: Muṣṭafā al-bābī al-ḥalabī.

Balibar, Étienne. 2015. "On the Basic Concepts of Historical Materialism." In *Reading Capital: The Complete Edition*, translated by Ben Brewster and David Fernbach, 357–480. London: Verso.

Bamualim, Chaider S. 2011. "Islamic Militancy and Resentment against Hadhramis in Post-Suharto Indonesia: A Case Study of Habib Rizieq Syihab and His Islamic Defenders Front." *Comparative Studies of South Asia, Africa and the Middle East* 31 (2): 267–81.

Bang, Anne K. 2003. *Sufis and Scholars of the Sea: Family Networks in East Africa, 1860–1925*. London: RoutledgeCurzon.

———. 2014. *Islamic Sufi Networks in the Western Indian Ocean (c. 1880–1940): Ripples of Reform*. Leiden: Brill.

Barenboim, Daniel, and Edward W. Said. 2002. *Parallels and Paradoxes: Explorations in Music and Society*. Edited by Ara Guzelimian. New York: Pantheon Books.

Bashir, Shahzad. 2011. *Sufi Bodies: Religion and Society in Medieval Islam*. New York: Columbia University Press.

———. 2014. "On Islamic Time: Rethinking Chronology in the Historiography of Muslim Societies." *History and Theory* 53 (4): 519–44.

Baso, Ahmad. 2006. *NU Studies: Pergolakan Pemikiran antara Fundametalisme Islam & Fundamentalisme Neo-Liberal*. Surabaya, East Java: Erlangga.

Bauman, Richard, and Charles L. Briggs. 1990. "Poetics and Performances as Critical Perspectives on Language and Social Life." *Annual Review of Anthropology* 19:59–88.

Bayat, Asef. 2007. *Making Islam Democratic: Social Movements and the Post-Islamist Turn*. Stanford, CA: Stanford University Press.

Beekers, Daan, and David Kloos. 2018. "Introduction: The Productive Potential of Moral Failure in Lived Islam and Christianity." In *Straying from the Straight Path: How Senses of Failure Invigorate Lived Religion*, edited by Beekers and Kloos, 1–20. New York: Berghahn.

Ben-Dor Benite, Zvi. 2005. *The Dao of Muhammad: A Cultural History of Muslims in Late Imperial China*. Harvard East Asian Monographs 248. Cambridge, MA: Harvard University Press.

Benjamin, Walter. 1968. *Illuminations: Essays and Reflections*. Edited by Hannah Arendt. Translated by Harry Zohn. New York: Shocken Books.

Berg, L.W.C. van den. (1886) 1989. *Hadramaut dan Koloni Arab di Nusantara*. Translated by Rahayu Hidayat. Jakarta: INIS.

———. 1887. "Het Mohammedaansche Godsdienstonderwijs op Java en Madoera: En de Daarbij Gebruikte Arabische Boeken." *Tijdschrift voor Indische Taal-, Land- en Volkenkunde* 31:1–38.

Berkey, Jonathan P. 1992. *The Transmission of Knowledge in Medieval Cairo: A Social History of Islamic Education*. Princeton, NJ: Princeton University Press.

Bin Jindān, Sālim b. Aḥmad. 2017. *Al-Barāhīn wa al-bayyināt fī manāqib mawla ʿināt*. Jakarta: Dār al-fakhriyya.

Bin Yahya, Muhammad Luthfi bin Ali. 1999. *Rātib al-kubrā*. Privately printed.

———. 2006. *Awrād al-ṭarīqa al-shādhiliyya al-ʿalawiyya*. Privately printed.

Birchok, Daniel A. 2015. "Putting Habib Abdurrahim in His Place: Genealogy, Scale, and Islamization in Seunagan, Indonesia." *Comparative Studies in Society and History* 57 (2): 497–527.

———. 2016. "Women, Genealogical Inheritance and Sufi Authority: The Female Saints of Seunagan, Indonesia." *Asian Studies Review* 40 (4): 583–99.

Blackburn, Anne M., and R. Michael Feener. 2019. "Sufis and *Saṅgha* in Motion: Toward a Comparative Study of Religious Orders and Networks in Southern Asia." In *Buddhist and Islamic Orders in Southern Asia: Comparative Perspectives*, edited by Feener and Blackburn, 1–19. Honolulu: University of Hawai'i Press.

Blecher, Joel. 2018. *Said the Prophet of God: Hadith Commentary across a Millennium*. Berkeley: University of California Press.

Bluhm, Jutta E. 1983. "A Preliminary Statement on the Dialogue Established between the Reform Magazine *al-Manar* and the Malayo-Indonesian World." *Indonesia Circle* 11 (32): 35–42.

Bowen, John R. 1993. *Muslims through Discourse: Religion and Ritual in Gayo Society*. Princeton, NJ: Princeton University Press.

———. 2012. *A New Anthropology of Islam*. Cambridge: Cambridge University Press.

Boyarin, Jonathan. 1993. "Voices around the Text: The Ethnography of Reading at Mesivta Tifereth Jerusalem." In *The Ethnography of Reading*, edited by Boyarin, 212–37. Berkeley: University of California Press.

Brown, Jonathan A. C. 2007. *The Canonization of al-Bukhārī and Muslim: The Formation and Function of the Sunnī Ḥadīth Canon*. Leiden: Brill.

———. 2009. *Hadith: Muhammad's Legacy in the Medieval and Modern World*. Oxford: Oneworld.

———. 2014. *Misquoting Muhammad: The Challenge and Choices of Interpreting the Prophet's Legacy*. Oxford: Oneworld.

Brown, Peter. 1981. *The Cult of the Saints: Its Rise and Function in Latin Christianity*. Chicago: University of Chicago Press.

Brown, Wendy. 2006. *Regulating Aversion: Tolerance in the Age of Identity and Empire*. Princeton, NJ: Princeton University Press.

Bruinessen, Martin van. 1992. *Tarekat Naqsyabandiyah di Indonesia: Survei Historis, Geografis, dan Sosiologis*. Bandung, West Java: Mizan.

———. 1995. *Kitab Kuning, Pesantren dan Tarekat: Tradisi-tradisi Islam di Indonesia.* Bandung, West Java: Mizan.

———. 2013. "Introduction: Contemporary Developments in Indonesian Islam and the 'Conservative Turn' of the Early Twenty-First Century." In *Contemporary Developments in Indonesian Islam: Explaining the "Conservative Turn,"* edited by Bruinessen, 1–20. Singapore: ISEAS.

———. 2015. "*Ghazwul Fikri* or Arabization? Indonesian Muslim Responses to Globalization." In *Southeast Asian Muslims in the Era of Globalization,* edited by Ken Miichi and Omar Farouk, 61–85. New York: Palgrave Macmillan.

Bruinessen, Martin van, and Julia Day Howell, eds. 2007. *Sufism and the "Modern" in Islam.* London: I. B. Tauris.

Buck-Morss, Susan. 2009. *Hegel, Haiti, and Universal History.* Pittsburgh, PA: University of Pittsburgh Press.

Buehler, Arthur F. 1998. *Sufi Heirs of the Prophet: The Indian Naqshbandiyya and the Rise of the Mediating Sufi Shaykh.* Columbia: University of South Carolina Press.

Bujra, Abdalla S. 1967. "Political Conflict and Stratification in Hadramaut—I." *Middle Eastern Studies* 3 (4): 355–75.

———. 1971. *The Politics of Stratification: A Study of Political Change in a South Arabian Town.* Oxford: Clarendon.

Bulliet, Richard W. 1972. *The Patricians of Nishapur: A Study in Medieval Islamic Social History.* Cambridge, MA: Harvard University Press.

Burhani, Ahmad Najib. 2018. "Islam Nusantara as a Promising Response to Religious Intolerance and Radicalism." *Trends in Southeast Asia* 21:1–29.

Butler, Judith, Ernesto Laclau, and Slavoj Žižek. 2000. *Contingency, Hegemony, Universality: Contemporary Dialogues on the Left.* London: Verso.

Carey, Peter. 2008. *The Power of Prophecy: Prince Dipanagara and the End of an Old Order in Java, 1785–1855.* Leiden: KITLV.

Chamberlain, Michael. 1995. *Knowledge and Social Practice in Medieval Damascus, 1190–1350.* Cambridge: Cambridge University Press.

Chih, Rachida. 2007. "What Is a Sufi Order? Revisiting the Concept through a Case Study of the Khalwatiyya in Contemporary Egypt." In *Sufism and the "Modern" in Islam,* edited by Martin van Bruinessen and Julia Day Howell, 21–38. London: I. B. Tauris.

Chittick, William. C. 1994. *Imaginal Worlds: Ibn al-'Arabī and the Problem of Religious Diversity.* Albany: State University of New York Press.

Clarence-Smith, William Gervase. 2009. "Entrepreneurial Strategies of Hadhrami Arabs in Southeast Asia, c. 1750s–1950s." In *The Hadhrami Diaspora in Southeast Asia: Identity Maintenance or Assimilation?* edited by Ahmed Ibrahim Abushouk and Hassan Ahmed Ibrahim, 135–58. Leiden: Brill.

Comaroff, John L., and Simon Roberts. 1981. *Rulers and Processes: The Cultural Logic of Dispute in an African Context.* Chicago: University of Chicago Press.

Connolly, William E. 1999. *Why I Am Not a Secularist.* Minneapolis: University of Minnesota Press.

Conrad, Joseph. 2000. *Lord Jim.* London: Penguin.

Cornell, Vincent J. 1992. "Mystical Doctrine and Political Action in Moroccan Sufism: The Role of the Exemplar in the *Ṭārīqa al-Jazūlīyya.*" *Al-Qanṭara* 13 (1): 201–31.

———. 1998. *Realm of the Saint: Power and Authority in Moroccan Sufism*. Austin: University of Texas Press.

Crouch, Harold. (1978) 2007. *The Army and Politics in Indonesia*. Jakarta: Equinox.

Dakake, Maria Massi. 2007. *The Charismatic Community: Shi'ite Identity in Early Islam*. Albany: State University of New York Press.

Danusiri, Aryo. 2014. "Performing Crowds: The Circulative Urban Forms of the Tariqa Alawiya Youth Movement in Contemporary Indonesia." In *Global Prayers: Contemporary Manifestations of the Religious in the City*, edited by Jochen Becker, Katrin Klingan, Stephan Lanz, and Kathrin Wildner, 338–51. Zürich: Lars Müller.

Das, Veena. 2007. *Life and Words: Violence and the Descent into the Ordinary*. Berkeley: University of California Press.

Debevec, Liza. 2012. "Postponing Piety in Urban Burkina Faso: Discussing Ideas on When to Start Acting as a Pious Muslim." In *Ordinary Lives and Grand Schemes: An Anthropology of Everyday Religion*, edited by Samuli Schielke and Liza Debevec, 33–47. New York: Berghahn.

Deeb, Lara. 2006. *An Enchanted Modern: Gender and Public Piety in Shi'i Lebanon*. Princeton, NJ: Princeton University Press.

de la Cruz, Deirdre. 2015. *Mother Figured: Marian Apparitions and the Making of a Filipino Universal*. Chicago: University of Chicago Press.

Denny, Frederick M. 1988. "God's Friends: The Sanctity of Persons in Islam." In *Sainthood: Its Manifestations in World Religions*, edited by Richard Kieckhefer and George D. Bond, 69–97. Berkeley: University of California Press.

DeWeese, Devin. 1994. *Islamization and Native Religion in the Golden Horde: Baba Tükles and Conversion to Islam in Historical and Epic Tradition*. University Park: Pennsylvania State University Press.

———. 1999. "Khojagani Origins and the Critique of Sufism: The Rhetoric of Communal Uniqueness in the Manaqib of Khoja ʿAli ʿAzizan Ramitani." In *Islamic Mysticism Contested: Thirteen Centuries of Controversies and Polemics*, edited by Frederick de Jong and Berndt Radtke, 492–519. Leiden: Brill.

Dhofier, Zamakhsyari. 2011. *Tradisi Pesantren: Studi pandangan hidup kyai dan visinya mengenai masa depan Indonesia*. Rev. ed. Jakarta: LP3ES.

Dipanagara. 2016. *Babad Dipanagara*. Translated by Gunawan et al. Yogyakarta: Narasi.

Donner, Fred M. 2010. *Muhammad and the Believers: At the Origins of Islam*. Cambridge, MA: Belknap Press of Harvard University Press.

Duara, Prasenjit. 1995. *Rescuing History from the Nation: Questioning Narratives of Modern China*. Chicago: University of Chicago Press.

Duderija, Adis. 2012. "Evolution in the Concept of Sunnah during the First Four Generations of Muslims in Relation to the Development of the Concept of an Authentic Ḥadīth as Based on Recent Western Scholarship." *Arab Law Quarterly* 26:393–437.

Eickelman, Dale F. 1976. *Moroccan Islam: Tradition and Society in a Pilgrimage Center*. Austin: University of Texas Press.

———. 1985. *Knowledge and Power in Morocco*. Princeton, NJ: Princeton University Press.

Eickelman, Dale F., and James Piscatori. 1996. *Muslim Politics*. Princeton, NJ: Princeton University Press.

Eisenlohr, Patrick. 2009. "Technologies of the Spirit: Devotional Islam, Sound Reproduction and the Dialectics of Mediation and Immediacy in Mauritius." *Anthropological Theory* 9 (3): 273–96.

El Moudden, Abderrahmane. 1990. "The Ambivalence of *Rihla*: Community Integration and Self-Definition in Moroccan Travel Accounts, 1300–1800." In *Muslim Travellers: Pilgrimage, Migration, and the Religious Imagination*, edited by Dale F. Eickelman and James Piscatori, 69–82. Berkeley: University of California Press.

El Shamsy, Ahmed. 2013. *The Canonization of Islamic Law: A Social and Intellectual History.* Cambridge: Cambridge University Press.

El-Zein, Abdul Hamid. 1977. "Beyond Ideology and Theology: The Search for the Anthropology of Islam." *Annual Review of Anthropology* 6:227–54.

Ernst, Carl W. 1992. *Eternal Garden: Mysticism, History, and Politics at a South Asian Sufi Center.* Albany: State University of New York Press.

———. 2005. "Situating Sufism and Yoga." *Journal of the Royal Asiatic Society* 15 (1): 15–43.

Euben, Roxanne L. 2006. *Journeys to the Other Shore: Muslim and Western Travelers in Search of Knowledge.* Princeton, NJ: Princeton University Press.

Evans-Pritchard, E. E. 1949. *The Sanusi of Cyrenaica.* Oxford: Clarendon.

Ewing, Katherine P. 1983. "The Politics of Sufism: Redefining the Saints of Pakistan." *Journal of Asian Studies* 42 (2): 251–68.

———. 1997. *Arguing Sainthood: Modernity, Psychoanalysis, and Islam.* Durham, NC: Duke University Press.

Fadel, Mohammad. 1996. "The Social Logic of Taqlīd and the Rise of the Mukhataṣar." *Islamic Law and Society* 3 (2): 193–233.

Fadil, Nadia, and Mayanthi Fernando. 2015. "Rediscovering the 'Everyday' Muslim: Notes on an Anthropological Divide." *HAU: Journal of Ethnographic Theory* 5 (2): 59–88.

Farhādī, A. G. Ravān. (1993) 1999. "The *Hundred Grounds* of ʿAbdullāh Ansārī of Herāt (d. 448/1056): The Earliest Mnemonic Sufi Manual in Persian." In *The Heritage of Sufism*, vol. 1, *Classical Persian Sufism: From Its Origins to Rumi (700–1300)*, edited by Leonard Lewisohn, 381–400. Oxford: Oneworld.

Fathurahman, Oman. 2012. *Itḥāf al-Dhakī: Tafsir Wahdatul Wujud bagi Muslim Nusantara.* Jakarta: Mizan.

Fauzia, Amelia. 2013. *Faith and the State: A History of Islamic Philanthropy in Indonesia.* Leiden: Brill.

Federspiel, Howard M. 1970. "The Muhammadiyah: A Study of an Orthodox Islamic Movement in Indonesia." *Indonesia* 10:57–79.

Feener, R. Michael. 2007. "Constructions of Religious Authority in Indonesian Islamism: 'The Way and the Community' Re-imagined." In *Islamic Legitimacy in a Plural Asia*, edited by Anthony Reid and Michael Gilsenan, 139–53. London: Routledge.

———. 2010. "New Networks and New Knowledge: Migrations, Communications and the Refiguration of the Muslim Community in the Nineteenth and Early Twentieth Centuries." In *The New Cambridge History of Islam*, vol. 6, edited by Robert Hefner, 39–68. Cambridge: Cambridge University Press.

———. 2013. *Shariʿa and Social Engineering: The Implementation of Islamic Law in Contemporary Aceh, Indonesia.* Oxford: Oxford University Press.

———. 2015. "ʿAbd al-Samad in Arabia: The Yemeni Years of a Shaykh from Sumatra." *Southeast Asian Studies* 4 (2): 259–77.

Felek, Özgen, and Alexander D. Knysh, eds. 2012. *Dreams and Visions in Islamic Societies*. Albany: State University of New York Press.

Ferguson, James, and Akhil Gupta. 2002. "Spatializing States: Toward an Ethnography of Neoliberal Governmentality." *American Ethnologist* 29 (4): 981–1002.

Flood, Finbarr B. 2009. *Objects of Translation: Material Culture and Medieval "Hindu-Muslim" Encounter*. Princeton, NJ: Princeton University Press.

Florida, Nancy K. 1993. *Javanese Literature in Surakarta Manuscripts*, vol. 1, *Introduction and Manuscripts of the Karaton Surakarta Manuscripts*. Ithaca, NY: Southeast Asia Program, Cornell University.

———. 1995. *Writing the Past, Inscribing the Future: History as Prophecy in Colonial Java*. Durham, NC: Duke University Press.

———. 1997. "Writing Traditions in Colonial Java: The Question of Islam." In *Cultures of Scholarship*, edited by S. C. Humphreys, 187–217. Ann Arbor: University of Michigan Press.

———. 2019. "Shaṭṭāriyya Sufi Scents: The Literary World of the Surakarta Palace in Nineteenth-Century Java." In *Buddhist and Islamic Orders in Southern Asia: Comparative Perspectives*, edited by R. Michael Feener and Anne M. Blackburn, 153–84. Honolulu: University of Hawaiʾi Press.

Foltz, Richard. 1996. "The Central Asian Naqshbandi Connections of the Mughal Emperors." *Journal of Islamic Studies* 7 (2): 229–39.

Formichi, Chiara. 2014. "Shaping Shiʿa Identities in Contemporary Indonesia between Local Tradition and Foreign Orthodoxy." *Die Welt des Islams* 54 (2): 212–36.

———. 2015. "One Big Family? Dynamics of Interaction among the 'Lovers of the *Ahl al Bayt*' in Modern Java." In *Shiʿism in Southeast Asia: ʿAlid Piety and Sectarian Constructions*, edited by Formichi and Michael Feener, 269–91. Oxford: Oxford University Press.

———. 2020. *Islam and Asia: A History*. Cambridge: Cambridge University Press.

Foucault, Michel. 1982. "The Subject and Power." *Critical Inquiry* 8 (4): 777–95.

———. 1990. *The History of Sexuality*, vol. 2: *The Use of Pleasure*. Translated by Robert Hurley. New York: Vintage Books.

———. 1991. "Governmentality." In *The Foucault Effect: Studies in Governmentality*, edited by Graham Burchell, Collin Gordon, and Peter Miller, 87–104. Chicago: University of Chicago Press.

———. 1997. *Ethics, Subjectivity and Truth*. Translated by Robert Hurley. Edited by Paul Rabinow. New York: New Press.

Fowden, Elizabeth Key. 2007. "The Lamp and the Wine Flask: Early Muslim Interest in Christian Monasticism." In *Islamic Crosspollinations: Interactions in the Medieval Middle East*, edited by Anna Akasoy, James E. Montgomery, and Peter E. Pormann, 1–28. Exeter, UK: Gibb Memorial Trust.

Freitag, Ulrike. 2002. "Arab Merchants in Singapore: Attempt at a Collective Biography." In *Transcending Borders: Arabs, Politics, Trade, and Islam in Southeast Asia*, edited by Huub de Jonge and Nico Kaptein, 107–42. Leiden: KITLV.

———. 2003. *Indian Ocean Migrants and State Formation in Hadhramaut: Reforming the Homeland*. Leiden: Brill.

Gadamer, Hans-Georg. 2004. *Truth and Method*. 2nd rev. ed. Translated by Joel Weinsheimer and Donald G. Marshall. London: Continuum.

Geertz, Clifford. 1968. *Islam Observed: Religious Development in Morocco and Indonesia*. New Haven, CT: Yale University Press.

Gellens, Sam I. 1990. "The Search for Knowledge in Medieval Muslim Societies: A Comparative Approach." In *Muslim Travellers: Pilgrimage, Migration, and the Religious Imagination*, edited by Dale F. Eickleman and James Piscatori, 50–65. Berkeley: University of California Press.

Gellner, Ernest. 1981. *Muslim Society*. Cambridge: Cambridge University Press.

Gelvin, James L., and Nile Green. 2014. Introduction to *Global Muslims in the Age of Steam and Print*, edited by Gelvin and Green, 1–22. Berkeley: University of California Press.

al-Ghazālī, Abū Ḥāmid. 2003. *Iḥyāʾ ʿulūm al-dīn*. 4 vols. Cairo: Dār al-salām.

Gilsenan, Michael. 1973. *Saint and Sufi in Modern Egypt: An Essay in the Sociology of Religion*. Oxford: Clarendon.

———. (1976) 2016. "Lying, Honor, and Contradiction." *Hau: Journal of Ethnographic Theory* 6 (2): 497–525.

———. 1982. *Recognizing Islam: Religion and Society in the Modern Arab World*. New York: Pantheon Books.

Ginzburg, Carlo. (1980) 2013. *The Cheese and the Worms: The Cosmos of a Sixteenth-Century Miller*. Translated by John and Anne C. Tadeschi. Baltimore, MD: Johns Hopkins University Press.

Gladney, Dru C. 2004. *Dislocating China: Muslims, Minorities and Other Subaltern Subjects*. London: Hurst.

Göçek, Fatma Müge. 1996. *Rise of the Bourgeoisie, Demise of Empire: Ottoman Westernization and Social Change*. Oxford: Oxford University Press.

Goody, Jack. 1970. "Sideways or Downwards? Lateral and Vertical Succession, Inheritance and Descent in Africa and Eurasia." *Man* 5 (4): 627–38.

Graham, Terry. (1993) 1999. "Abū Saʿīd ibn Abi'l-Khayr and the School of Khurasan." In *The Heritage of Sufism*, vol. 1, *Classical Persian Sufism: From Its Origins to Rumi (700–1300)*, edited by Leonard Lewisohn, 83–136. Oxford: Oneworld.

Graham, William A. 1977. *Divine Word and Prophetic Word in Early Islam: A Reconsideration of the Sources, with Special Reference to the Divine Saying or Hadîth Qudsî*. The Hague: Mouton.

———. 1987. *Beyond the Written Word: Oral Aspects of Scripture in the History of Religion*. Cambridge: Cambridge University Press.

Green, Nile. 2011. *Bombay Islam: The Religious Economy of the West Indian Ocean, 1840–1915*. Cambridge: Cambridge University Press.

———. 2012. *Sufism: A Global History*. Chichester, UK: Wiley-Blackwell.

Griffel, Frank. 2009. *Al-Ghazālī's Philosophical Theology*. Oxford: Oxford University Press.

al-Ḥabashī, Abū Bakr Aṭṭās. 1979. *Tadhkīr al-nās bimā wajada min al-masāʾil al-fiqhiyya wa mā taʿallaq bihā fī majmūʿ kalām al-imām aḥmad bin ḥasan al-ʿaṭṭās*. Cairo: Dār al-iḥyāʾ al-kutub al-ʿarabiyya.

al-Ḥabashī, ʿAlī b. Muḥammad. n.d.a. *Al-Jawhar al-maknūn wa al-sirr al-maṣūn: dīwān al-ḥumaynī*. 4 vols. Privately printed.

———. n.d.b. *Al-Jawhar al-maknūn wa al-sirr al-maṣūn: dīwān al-ḥakamī*. Seiyun, Yemen: Dār ʿimārat al-minhaj.

al-Ḥabashī, ʿAydarūs b. ʿUmar. (1887) 2009. *ʿIqd al-yawāqīt al-jawhariyya wa simṭ al-ʿayn al-dhahabiyya bi-dhikr ṭarīq al-sādat al-ʿalawiyya*. 2 vols. Tarim, Yemen: Dār al-ʿilm wa al-daʿwa.

al-Ḥaddād, ʿAbdallāh b. ʿAlawī. (1678) 1992. *Al-Naṣāʾiḥ al-dīniyya wa-l-waṣāyā al-īmāniyya*. Tarim, Yemen: Dār al-ḥāwī

———. (1702) 1994. *Al-Daʿwa al-tāmma wa-l-tadhkira al-ʿāmma*. Tarim, Yemen: Dār al-ḥāwī.

———. (1713) 1993. *Al-Nafāʾis al-ʿuluwiyya fī al-masāʾil al-ṣūfiyya*. Tarim, Yemen: Dār al-ḥāwī.

———. (1757) 1999. *Tathbīt al-fuʾād bi dhikr kalām majālis al-quṭb al-imām ʿabdallāh bin ʿalawī bin muḥammad al-ḥaddād*. Compiled by Aḥmad b. ʿAbd al-Karīm al-Shajjār. 2 vols. Tarim, Yemen: al-Maqām al-imām al-ḥaddād.

———. (1974) 1993. *ʿAqīda ahl al-islām*. With a short commentary by Ḥasanayn Muḥammad Makhlūf. Beirut: Maktaba al-hidāya.

al-Ḥaddād, ʿAbdallāh b. Ṭāhir. 2009. *Qurrat al-nāẓir bi manāqib al-ḥabīb al-quṭb muḥammad b. ṭāhir b. ʿumar al-ḥaddād*. 3 vols. Tarim, Yemen: Dār al-turāth.

Hall, Stuart. 1980. "Race, Articulation and Societies Structured in Dominance." In *Sociological Theories: Race and Colonialism*, by UNESCO, 305–45. Paris: UNESCO.

Hallaq, Wael B. 2005. *The Origins and Evolution of Islamic Law*. Cambridge: Cambridge University Press.

Halman, Hugh T. 2013. *Where the Two Seas Meet: The Qur'ānic Story of Al-Khiḍr and Moses in Sufi Commentaries as a Model of Spiritual Guidance*. Louisville, KY: Fons Vitae.

al-Ḥāmid, Ḥasan b. Ismāʿīl. n.d. "Nahr al-mawrūd fī manāqib shaykh abī bakr b. sālim fakhr al-wujūd." MS 02135. Kanzul Hikmah Library, Jakarta.

al-Ḥāmid, Ṣāliḥ b. ʿAlī. 2002. *Riḥla jāwā al-jamīla*. Tarim, Yemen: Tarīm li-l-dirāsāt wa al-nashr.

Hammoudi, Abdellah. 1997. *Master and Disciple: The Cultural Foundations of Moroccan Authoritarianism*. Chicago: University of Chicago Press.

Harman, Graham. 2014. *Bruno Latour: Reassembling the Political*. London: Pluto.

Harris, Ruth. 1999. *Lourdes: Body and Spirit in the Secular Age*. London: Penguin.

Hasan, Noorhaidi. 2006. *Laskar Jihad: Islam, Militancy, and the Quest for Identity in Post-New Order Indonesia*. Ithaca, NY: Southeast Asia Program, Cornell University.

Hassan, Mona. 2016. *Longing for the Lost Caliphate: A Transregional History*. Princeton, NJ: Princeton University Press.

Hefner, Robert W. 2005. "Introduction: Modernity and the Remaking of Muslim Politics." In *Remaking Muslim Politics: Pluralism, Contestation, Democratization*, edited by Hefner, 1–36. Princeton, NJ: Princeton University Press.

———. 2007. "Introduction: The Culture, Politics, and Future of Muslim Education." In *Schooling Islam: The Culture and Politics of Modern Muslim Education*, edited by Hefner and Muhammad Qasim Zaman, 1–39. Princeton, NJ: Princeton University Press.

———. 2011. "Where have All the Abangan Gone? Religionization and the Decline of Non-standard Islam in Contemporary Indonesia." In *The Politics of Religion in Indonesia: Syncretism, Orthodoxy, and Religious Contention in Java and Bali*, edited by Michel Picard and Rémy Madinier, 71–91. London: Routledge.

Hervieu-Léger, Danièle. 2000. *Religion as a Chain of Memory*. Translated by Simon Lee. New Brunswick, NJ: Rutgers University Press.

Hirschkind, Charles. 2006. *The Ethical Soundscape: Cassette Sermons and Islamic Counterpublics.* New York: Columbia University Press.

Ho, Engseng. 2006 *The Graves of Tarim: Genealogy and Mobility across the Indian Ocean.* Berkeley: University of California Press.

Hodgson, Marshall G. S. 1974. *The Venture of Islam: Conscience and History in a World Civilization.* 3 vols. Chicago: University of Chicago Press.

Hoesterey, James Bourk. 2016. *Rebranding Islam: Piety, Prosperity, and a Self-Help Guru.* Stanford, CA: Stanford University Press.

Homerin, Th. Emil. 2019. *Aisha al-Ba ʿuniyya: A Life in Praise of Love.* London: Oneworld.

Howell, Julia Day. 2001. "Sufism and the Indonesian Islamic Revival." *Journal of Asian Studies* 60 (3): 701–29.

Hull, Matthew S. 2012. *Government of Paper: The Materiality of Bureaucracy in Urban Pakistan.* Berkeley: University of California Press.

Humphrey, Caroline. 1997. "Exemplars and Rules: Aspects of the Discourse of Moralities in Mongolia." In *The Ethnography of Moralities,* edited by Signe Howell, 25–47. London: Routledge.

Husein, Fatima, and Martin Slama. 2018. "Online Piety and Its Discontent: Revisiting Islamic Anxieties on Indonesian Social Media." *Indonesia and the Malay World* 46 (134): 80–93.

Ibn Yaḥyā, ʿAbdallāh b. ʿUmar. 2008. *Al-Suyūf al-bawātir liman yuqaddim ṣalāt al-ṣubḥ ʿalā al-fajr al-ākhir.* Edited by Ṣāliḥ Bilfaqīh. Tarim, Yemen: Markaz al-nūr.

Ibn Yaḥyā, ʿAqīl b. ʿAbdallāh. n.d. "Tadhkirat al-aḥyāʾ bi-dhikr nubdha yasīra min baʿḍ manāqib sayyidinā wa imāminā al-sayyid al-sharīf al-wālid ʿabdallāh b. ʿumar bin yaḥyā bā ʿalawī." Transcript of the original MS together with his letters, poems, epistles, and sermons. In *Al-Imām ʿabdallāh b. ʿumar bin yaḥyā: Manāqibuhu, āthāruhu, shiʿruhu,* compiled and edited by Zayd b. ʿAbd al-Raḥmān Bin Yaḥyā, 21–115. Privately printed.

Ilyenkov, Evald E. 1975. "The Universal." In *Philosophical Investigations in the U.S.S.R,* edited by Frederick J. Adelmann, 26–51. Chestnut Hill, MA: Boston College.

"Index of Arabs in the Netherlands East Indies, Anti-British and Friendly." Enclosure in W. N. Dunn to A. J. Balfour, September 27, 1919. India Office (IO) Record R/20/A/1409. India and Oriental Office, British Library, London.

Jacob, Wilson Chacko. 2019. *For God or Empire: Sayyid Fadl and the Indian Ocean World.* Stanford, CA: Stanford University Press.

Jahroni, Jajang. 2008. *Defending the Majesty of Islam: Indonesia's Front Pembela Islam, 1998–2003.* Bangkok: Silkworm Books.

Janowitz, Naomi. 1993. "Recreating Genesis: The Metapragmatics of Divine Speech." In *Reflexive Language: Reported Speech and Metapragmatics,* edited by John A. Lucy, 393–405. Cambridge: Cambridge University Press.

Jeppie, Shamil. 2018. "The Little and the Large: A Little Book and Connected History between Asia and Africa." In *Migration and Agency in a Globalizing World: Afro-Asian Encounters,* edited by Scarlett Cornelissen and Yoichi Mine, 27–46. London: Palgrave Macmillan.

Jong, Frederick de. 1978. *Turuq and Turuq-Linked Institutions in Nineteenth-Century Egypt.* Leiden: Brill.

———. 1983. "Aspects of the Political Involvement of *Sufi* Orders in Twentieth Century Egypt (1907–1970): An Exploratory Stock-Taking." In *Islam, Nationalism, and Radicalism in Egypt and the Sudan*, edited by Gabriel R. Warburg and Uri M. Kupferschmidt, 183–212. New York: Praeger.

Jonge, Huub de. 1997. "Dutch Colonial Policy Pertaining to Hadhrami Immigrants." In *Hadhrami Traders, Scholars and Statesmen in the Indian Ocean, 1750s–1960s*, edited by Ulrike Freitag and William G. Clarence-Smith, 94–111. Leiden: Brill.

al-Junayd, ʿAbd al-Qādir b. ʿAbd al-Raḥmān. 1994. *Al-ʿUqūd al-ʿasjadiyya fī nashr manāqib baʿdh afrād al-usra al-junaydiyya*. Singapore: al-Mahdudah.

Juynboll, Gautier H. A. 1996. *Studies on the Origins and Uses of Islamic Ḥadīth*. Aldershot, UK: Variorum.

Kafadar, Cemal. 1995. *Between Two Worlds: The Construction of the Ottoman State*. Berkeley: University of California Press.

Kamali, Mohammad Hashim. 2003. *Principles of Islamic Jurisprudence*. 3rd ed. Cambridge, UK: Islamic Texts Society.

Kant, Immanuel. (1784) 2009. *An Answer to the Question: "What is Enlightenment?"* Translated by H. B. Nisbet. London: Penguin.

Kaptein, Nico J. G. 1993. *Muḥammad's Birthday Festival: Early History in the Central Muslim Lands and Development in the Muslim West until the 10th/16th Century*. Leiden: Brill.

———. 2014. *Islam, Colonialism and the Modern Age in the Netherlands East Indies: A Biography of Sayyid ʿUthman (1822–1914)*. Leiden: Brill.

Karamustafa, Ahmet T. 1993. "*Ḳalenders, Abdâls, Ḥayderîs*: The Formation of the *Bektâşîye* in the Sixteenth Century." In *Šuleymân the Second and His Time*, edited by Halil İnalcik and Cemal Kafadar, 121–29. Istanbul: Isis.

Kartodirdjo, Sartono. 1966. *The Peasants' Revolt of Banten in 1888: Its Conditions, Course and Sequel*. The Hague: Martinus Nijhoff.

Kato, Hisanori. 2018. "Religion and Locality: The Case of the Islam Nusantara Movement in Indonesia." *Fieldwork in Religion* 13 (2):151–68.

Katz, Jonathan G. 1996. *Dreams, Sufism, and Sainthood: The Visionary Career of Muḥammad al-Zawāwī*. Leiden: Brill.

Katz, Marion H. 2007. *The Birth of the Prophet Muḥammad: Devotional Piety in Sunni Islam*. London: Routledge.

Keane, Webb. 1997. "Religious Language." *Annual Review of Anthropology* 26:47–71.

———. 2003a. "Self-Interpretation, Agency, and the Objects of Anthropology: Reflections on a Genealogy." *Comparative Studies in Society and History* 45 (2): 222–48.

———. 2003b. "Semiotics and the Social Analysis of Material Things." *Language & Communication* 23 (3–4): 409–25.

———. 2007. *Christian Moderns: Freedom & Fetish in the Mission Encounter*. Berkeley: University of California Press.

———. 2016. *Ethical Life: Its Natural and Social History*. Princeton, NJ: Princeton University Press.

Kennedy, Hugh. 2016. *Caliphate: The History of an Idea*. New York: Basic Books.

Kersten, Carool. 2015. *Islam in Indonesia: The Contest for Society, Ideas, and Values*. Oxford: Oxford University Press.

Keshani, Hussein. 2008. "Architecture." In *The Islamic World*, edited by Andrew Rippin, 444–72. Abingdon, UK: Routledge.

Khan, Naveeda. 2012. *Muslim Becoming: Aspiration and Skepticism in Pakistan*. Durham, NC: Duke University Press.

Kingsley, Jeremy J. 2018. *Religious Authority and Local Governance in Eastern Indonesia*. Melbourne: Melbourne University Press.

Kirsch, Stuart. 2010. "Ethnographic Representation and the Politics of Violence in West Papua." *Critique of Anthropology* 30 (1): 3–22.

Kloos, David. 2018. *Becoming Better Muslims: Religious Authority and Ethical Improvement in Aceh, Indonesia*. Princeton, NJ: Princeton University Press.

Knysh, Alexander D. 1993. "The Cult of Saints in Hadramawt: An Overview." *New Arabian Studies* 1:137–53.

———. 1997. "The Cult of Saints and Religious Reformism in Hadhramaut." In *Hadhrami Traders, Scholars and Statesmen in the Indian Ocean, 1750s–1960s*, edited by Ulrike Freitag and William G. Clarence-Smith, 199–216. Leiden: Brill.

———. 1999a. *Ibn 'Arabi in the Later Islamic Tradition: The Making of a Polemical Image in Medieval Islam*. Albany: State University of New York Press.

———. 1999b. "The *Sada* in History: A Critical Essay on Hadrami Historiography." *Journal of the Royal Asiatic Society* 9 (2): 215–22.

———. 2010. "A Tale of two Poets: Sufism in Yemen during the Ottoman Epoch." In *Le Soufisme à l'époque Ottomane, XVIe–XVIIIe siècle*, edited by Rachida Chih and Catherine Mayeur-Jaouen, 337–67. Cairo: Institut Francaise de Archéologie Orientale.

———. 2011. "The '*Tariqa*' on a Landcruiser: The Resurgence of Sufism in Yemen." *Middle East Journal* 55 (3): 399–414.

———. 2017. *Sufism: A New History of Islamic Mysticism*. Princeton, NJ: Princeton University Press.

Kraus, Werner. 2018. *Raden Saleh: Kehidupan dan Karyanya*. Jakarta: Kepustakaan Populer Gramedia.

Kugle, Scott A. 2007. *Sufis and Saints' Bodies: Mysticism, Corporeality, and Sacred Power in Islam*. Chapel Hill: University of North Carolina Press.

Kumar, Ann. 1985. *The Diary of a Javanese Muslim: Religion, Politics, and the Pesantren, 1883–1886*. Canberra: Faculty of Asian Studies, Australian National University.

Kundera, Milan. 1988. *The Art of the Novel*. Translated by Linda Asher. New York: HarperPerennial.

Kurzman, Charles, ed. 2002. *Modernist Islam, 1840–1940: A Sourcebook*. New York: Oxford University Press.

Laclau, Ernesto, and Chantal Mouffe. (1985) 2001. *Hegemony and Socialist Strategy: Towards a Radical Democratic Politics*. London: Verso.

Laffan, Michael Francis. 2003. *Islamic Nationhood and Colonial Indonesia: The Umma below the Winds*. London: Routledge.

———. 2011 *The Makings of Indonesian Islam: Orientalism and the Narration of a Sufi Past*. Princeton, NJ: Princeton University Press.

Laidlaw, James. 2014. *The Subject of Virtue: An Anthropology of Ethics and Freedom*. Cambridge: Cambridge University Press.

Lambek, Michael. 1993. *Knowledge and Practice in Mayotte: Local Discourses of Islam, Sorcery and Spirit Possession*. Toronto: University of Toronto Press.

———. 2010. Introduction to *Ordinary Ethics: Anthropology, Language, and Action*, 1–36. New York: Fordham University Press.

Lapidus, Ira M. 2014. *A History of Islamic Societies*. 3rd ed. Cambridge: Cambridge University Press.

Larkin, Brian. 2013. "The Politics and Poetics of Infrastructure." *Annual Review of Anthropology* 42:327–43.

Latour, Bruno. 1993. *We Have Never Been Modern*. Translated by Catherine Porter. Cambridge, MA: Harvard University Press.

———. 2005. *Reassembling the Social: An Introduction to Actor-Network Theory*. Oxford: Oxford University Press.

———. 2010. *The Making of Law: An Ethnography of the Conseil d'Etat*. Translated by Marina Brilman and Alain Pottage. Cambridge: Polity.

Li, Darryl. 2020. *The Universal Enemy: Jihad, Empire, and the challenge of Solidary*. Stanford, CA: Stanford University Press.

Lohlker, Rüdiger. 2016. "*Jamā ʿa* vs. *Mulk*: Community-Centred and Ruler-Centred Visions of the Islamic Community." In *Meanings of Community across Medieval Eurasia: Comparative Approaches*, edited by Eirik Hovden, Christina Lutter, and Walter Pohl, 78–96. Leiden: Brill.

Loimeier, Roman. 2016. *Islamic Reform in Twentieth-Century Africa*. Edinburgh: Edinburgh University Press.

Machiavelli, Nicollò. 2005. *The Prince*. Translated and edited by Peter Bondanella. Oxford: Oxford University Press.

MacIntyre, Alasdair. 1981. *After Virtue: A Study in Moral Theory*. London: Duckworth.

Mackey, Nathaniel. 1992. "Other: From Noun to Verb." *Representations* 39 (Summer): 57–70.

Mahdi, Muhsin. 1975. "The Book and the Master as Poles of Cultural Change in Islam." In *Islam and Cultural Change in the Middle Ages*, edited by Speros Vryonis, 3–15. Wiesbaden, Germany: Otto Harrassowitz.

Mahmood, Saba. 2005. *Politics of Piety: The Islamic Revival and the Feminist Subject*. Princeton, NJ: Princeton University Press.

Mamdani, Mahmood. 2004. *Good Muslim, Bad Muslim: America, the Cold War, and the Roots of Terror*. New York: Three Leaves.

Mandal, Sumit K. 2002. "Forging a Modern Arab Identity in Java in the Early Twentieth Century." In *Transcending Borders: Arabs, Politics, Trade and Islam in Southeast Asia*, edited by Huub de Jonge and Nico Kaptein, 163–84. Leiden: KITLV.

———. 2018. *Becoming Arab: Creole Histories and Modern Identity in the Malay World*. Cambridge: Cambridge University Press.

Margoliouth, David S. 1937. "The Relics of the Prophet Mohammed." *Muslim World* 27 (1): 20–27.

Marlow, Louise. 2003. "Ḥasab O Nasab." In *Encyclopaedia Iranica*, 12 (1): 23–24. http://www.iranicaonline.org/articles/hasab-o-nasab.

Marsden, Magnus. 2005. *Living Islam: Muslim Religious Experience in Pakistan's North-West Frontier*. Cambridge: Cambridge University Press.

———. 2010. "A Tour Not So Grand: Mobile Muslims in Northern Pakistan." In *Islam, Politics, Anthropology*, edited by Filippo Osella and Benjamin Soares, 54–71. Chichester, UK: Wiley-Blackwell.

Marsden, Magnus, and Konstantinos Retsikas. 2013. Introduction to *Articulating Islam: Anthropological Approaches to Muslim Worlds*, edited by Marsden and Retsikas, 1–31. Dordrecht: Springer.

Marsden, William. 1811. *The History of Sumatra, Containing an Account of the Government, Laws, Customs, and Manners of the Native Inhabitants, with a Description of the Natural Productions, and a Relation of the Ancient Political State of That Island.* 3rd ed. London: Longman, Hurst, Rees, Orme, and Brown.

al-Mashhūr, ʿAbd al-Raḥmān b. Muḥammad. (1911) 1984. *Shams al-ẓahīra fī nasab ahl al-bayt min banī ʿalawī furūʾ fāṭima al-zahrāʾ wa amīr al-muʾminīn ʿalī*. 2 vols. Jeddah: ʿĀlam al-maʾrifa.

Mattingly, Cheryl. 2014. *Moral Laboratories: Family Peril and the Struggle for a Good Life*. Berkeley: University of California Press.

al-Māwardī, ʿAlī b. Muḥammad. 1955. *Adab al-dunyā wa al-dīn*. Cairo: Muṣṭafā al-bābī al-ḥalabī.

———. 1966. *Al-Aḥkām al-sulṭāniyya wa al-wilāyāt al-dīniyya*. Cairo: Muṣṭafā al-bābī al-ḥalabī.

Mayeur-Jaouen, Catherine, and Alexandre Papas. 2014. Introduction to *Family Portraits with Saints: Hagiography, Sanctity, and Family in the Muslim World*, edited by Mayeur-Jaouen and Papas, 7–25. Berlin: Klaus Schwarz.

McGregor, Richard J. A. 2004. *Sanctity and Mysticism in Medieval Egypt: The Wafa Sufi Order and the Legacy of Ibn ʿArabī*. Albany: State University of New York Press.

———. 2005. "Notes on the Transmission of Mystical Philosophy: Ibn ʿArabī according to ʿAbd al-Wahhāb al-Shaʿrānī." In *Reason and Inspiration in Islam: Essays in Honour of Hermann Landolt*, edited by Todd Lawson, 380–94. London: I. B. Tauris.

Meier, Fritz. 1999. *Essays on Islamic Piety and Mysticism*. Translated by John O'Kane. Leiden: Brill.

Meillassoux, Quentin. 2008. *After Finitude: An Essay on the Necessity of Contingency*. Translated by Ray Brassier. London: Continuum.

Melchert, Christopher. 1997. *The Formation of the Sunni Schools of Law: 9th–10th Centuries C.E.* Leiden: Brill.

Meri, Josef W. 2010. "Relics of Piety and Power in Medieval Islam." *Past and Present* 206 (suppl. 5): 97–120.

Mernissi, Fatima. 1991. *The Veil and the Male Elite: A Feminist Interpretation of Women's Rights in Islam*. Translated by Mary Jo Lakeland. New York: Perseus.

Merry, Sally E. 2000. *Colonizing Hawai'i: The Cultural Power of Law*. Princeton, NJ: Princeton University Press.

Messick, Brinkley. 1993. *The Calligraphic State: Textual Domination and History in a Muslim Society*. Berkeley: University of California Press.

Mill, John Stuart.1999. *On Liberty*. Edited by Edward Alexander. Peterborough, ON: Broadview.

Millie, Julian. 2009. *Splashed by the Saint: Ritual Reading and Islamic Sanctity in West Java*. Leiden: KITLV.

———. 2017. *Hearing Allah's Call: Preaching and Performance in Indonesian Islam*. Ithaca, NY: Cornell University Press.

Milner, Anthony C. 1994. *The Invention of Politics in Colonial Malaya: Contesting Nationalism and the Expansion of the Public Sphere.* Cambridge: Cambridge University Press.

Minh-Ha, Trinh T. 1989. *Woman, Native, Other: Writing Postcoloniality and Feminism.* Bloomington: Indiana University Press.

Mitchell, Timothy. 1991. "The Limits of the State: Beyond Statist Approaches and Their Critics." *American Political Science Review* 85 (1): 77–96.

———. 2006. "Society, Economy, and the State Effect." In *The Anthropology of the State: A Reader*, edited by Aradhana Sharma and Anil Gupta, 169–86. Malden, MA: Blackwell.

Mittermaier, Amira. 2011. *Dreams that Matter: Egyptian Landscapes of the Imagination.* Berkeley: University of California Press.

Mobini-Kesheh, Natalie. 1996. "The Arab Periodicals of the Netherlands East Indies, 1914–1942." *Bijdragen tot de Taal-, Land-en volkenkunde* 152 (2): 236–56.

———. 1997. "Islamic Modernism in Colonial Java: The al-Irshād Movement." In *Hadhrami Traders, Scholars and Statesmen in the Indian Ocean, 1750s–1960s*, edited by Ulrike Freitag and William G. Clarence-Smith, 231–48. Leiden: Brill.

———. 1999. *The Hadrami Awakening: Community and Identity in the Netherlands East Indies, 1900–1942.* Ithaca, NY: Southeast Asia Program, Cornell University.

Moertono, Soemarsaid. 1963. *State and Statecraft in Old Java: A Study of the Later Mataram Period, 16th to 19th Century.* Ithaca, NY: Southeast Asia Program, Cornell University.

Moin, A. Azfar. 2012. *The Millennial Sovereign: Sacred Kingship and Sainthood in Islam.* New York: Columbia University Press.

Moore, Sally Falk. 1978. *Law as Process: An Anthropological Approach.* London: Routledge.

Moosa, Ebrahim. 2005. *Ghazālī and the Poetics of Imagination.* Chapel Hill: University of North Carolina Press.

Motzki, Harald. 2002. *The Origins of Islamic Jurisprudence: Meccan Fiqh before the Classical Schools.* Translated by Marion H. Katz. Leiden: Brill.

Mrázek, Rudolf. 2002. *Engineers of Happy Land: Technology and Nationalism in a Colony.* Princeton, NJ: Princeton University Press.

Muhaimin, Abdul Ghoffur. 2006. *The Islamic Traditions of Cirebon: Ibadat and Adat among Javanese Muslims.* Canberra: Australian National University Press.

Munson, Henry. 1993. "The Political Role of Islam in Morocco (1970–90)." In *North Africa: Nation, State and Region*, edited by George Joffé, 187–202. New York: Routledge.

Munt, Harry. 2014. *The Holy City of Medina: Sacred Space in Early Islamic Arabia.* New York: Cambridge University Press.

Nakamura, Mitsuo. 2012. *The Crescent Arises over the Banyan Tree: A Study of the Muhammadiyah Movement in a Central Javanese Town, c. 1910–2010.* 2nd ed. Singapore: ISEAS.

Nas, Peter J. M., and Pratiwo. 2002. "Java and de Groote Postweg, la Grande Route, the Great Mail Road, Jalan Raya Pos." *Bijdragen tot de Taal-, Land-en Volkenkunde* 158 (4): 707–25.

Nasr, Seyyed Hossein, Canel K. Dagli, Maria Massi Dakake, Joseph E. B. Lumbard, and Mohammed Rustom, eds. 2015. *The Study Quran: A New Translation and Commentary.* New York: HarperCollins.

Nasr, Seyyed Vali Reza. 2001. *Islamic Leviathan: Islam and the Making of State Power.* Oxford: Oxford University Press.

Navaro-Yashin, Yael. 2002. *Faces of the State: Secularism and Public Life in Turkey*. Princeton, NJ: Princeton University Press.

Netton, Ian Richard. 1996. *Seek Knowledge: Thought and Travel in the House of Islam*. Abingdon, UK: RoutledgeCurzon.

Noer, Deliar. 1973. *The Modernist Muslim Movement in Indonesia, 1900–1942*. Singapore: Oxford University Press.

Nordholt, Henk Schulte, and Gerry van Klinken, eds. 2007. *Renegotiating Boundaries: Local Politics in Post-Suharto Indonesia*. Leiden: KITLV.

Ohlander, Erik S. 2008. *Sufism in an Age of Transition: ʿUmar al-Suhrawardī and the Rise of the Islamic Mystical Brotherhoods*. Leiden: Brill.

Osella, Filippo, and Benjamin Soares, eds. 2010. *Islam, Politics, Anthropology*. Chichester, UK: Wiley-Blackwell.

Papas, Alexandre. 2007. "Shaykh Succession in the Classical Naqshbandiyya: Spiritual, Heredity and the Question of Body." *Asian and African Area Studies* 7 (1): 36–49.

Pemberton, John. 1994. *On the Subject of "Java."* Ithaca, NY: Cornell University Press.

Pernyataan Keberatan atas pentas Barongsai dalam Peringatan Maulid Nabi SAW Desa Kebasen-Talang- Tegal. 2011. Privately printed.

Perrino, Sabina M. 2002. "Intimate Hierarchies and Qur'anic Saliva (*Tefli*): Textuality in a Senegalese Ethnomedical Encounter." *Journal of Linguistic Anthropology* 12 (2): 225–59.

Peskes, Esther. 2015. "Sainthood as Patrimony: ʿAbd Allāh al-ʿAydarūs (d. 1461) and His Descendants." In *Family Portraits with Saints: Hagiography, Sanctity, and Family in the Muslim World*, edited by Catherine Mayeur-Jaouen and Alexandre Papas, 125–57. Berlin: Klaus Schwarz.

Petersen, Kristian. 2018. *Interpreting Islam in China: Pilgrimage, Scripture, and Language in the Han Kitab*. New York: Oxford University Press.

Pierce, Matthew. 2016. *Twelve Infallible Men: The Imams and the Making of Shiʿism*. Cambridge, MA: Harvard University Press.

Pigeaud, Theodore G. Th., and H. J. de Graaf. 1976. *Islamic States in Java 1500–1700: A Summary, Bibliography and Index*. The Hague: Martinus Nijhoff.

Pinto, Paulo G. 2006. "Sufism, Moral Performance and the Public Sphere in Syria." *Revue du mondes musulmans et de la Méditerranée* 115/116:155–171.

Pribadi, Yanwar. 2018. *Islam, State and Society in Indonesia: Local Politics in Madura*. Abingdon, UK: Routledge.

Quinn, George. 2019. *Bandit Saints of Java: How Java's Eccentric Saints Are Challenging Fundamentalist Islam in Modern Indonesia*. Burrough on the Hill, UK: Monsoon Books.

Rabinow, Paul. (1977) 2007. *Reflections on Fieldwork in Morocco*. Berkeley: University of California Press.

Reid, Anthony. 2003. *Kekacauan dan Kerusuhan: Tiga Tulisan tentang Pan-Islamisme di Hindia-Belanda Timur pada akhir abad kesembilan belas dan awal abad kedua puluh*. Jakarta: INIS.

Renard, John. 2008. *Friends of God: Islamic Images of Piety, Commitment, and Servanthood*. Berkeley: University of California Press.

Ricci, Ronit. 2011. *Islam Translated: Literature, Conversion, and the Arabic Cosmopolis of South and Southeast Asia*. Chicago: University of Chicago Press.

Ricklefs, Merle C. 1974. *Jogjakarta under Sultan Mangkubumi, 1749–1792: A History of the Division of Java*. Oxford: Oxford University Press.

———. 1998. *The Seen and Unseen Worlds in Java, 1726–1749: History, Literature and Islam in the Court of Pakubuwana II.* Honolulu: University of Hawai'i Press.

———. 2006. *Mystic Synthesis in Java: A History of Islamization from the Fourteenth to the Early Nineteenth Centuries.* Norwalk, CT: Eastbridge.

———. 2007. *Polarizing Javanese Society: Islamic and Other Visions, c. 1830–1930.* Singapore: National University of Singapore Press.

———. 2009. "The Middle East Connection and Reform and Revival Movements among the *Putihan* in 19th Century Java." In *Southeast Asia and the Middle East: Islam, Movement, and the Longue Durée*, edited by Eric Tagliacozzo, 111–34. Stanford, CA: Stanford University Press.

———. 2012. *Islamisation and Its Opponents in Java: A Political, Social, Cultural and Religious History, c. 1930 to the Present.* Singapore: National University of Singapore Press.

Ricoeur, Paul. 1973. "The Model of the Text: Meaningful Action Considered as a Text." *New Literary History* 5 (1): 91–117.

Rinakit, Sukardi. 2005. *The Indonesian Military after the New Order.* Copenhagen: NIAS.

Rosen, Lawrence. 1989. *The Anthropology of Justice: Law as Culture in Islamic Society.* Cambridge: Cambridge University Press.

Roy, Olivier. 2004. *Globalized Islam: The Search for a New Ummah.* New York: Columbia University Press.

Rozehnal, Robert. 2007. *Islamic Sufism Unbound: Politics and Piety in Twenty-First Century Pakistan.* New York: Palgrave Macmillan.

Rudnyckyj, Daromir. 2010. *Spiritual Economies: Islam, Globalization, and the Afterlife of Development.* Ithaca, NY: Cornell University Press.

Sahal, Akhmad, and Munawir Azis, eds. 2015. *Islam Nusantara Dari Ushul Fiqh hingga Paham Kebangsaan.* Bandung, West Java: Mizan-Teraju.

Sahlins, Marshall. 2004. *Apologies to Thucydides: Understanding History as Culture and Vice Versa.* Chicago: University of Chicago Press.

———. 2013. *What Kinship Is—and Is Not.* Chicago: University of Chicago Press.

Sa'idī, Haji n.d. "Al-Kutub al-wārida fī ta'ziya sayyidinā al-ḥabīb al-quṭb 'abdallāh b. muḥsin bin muḥammad al-'aṭṭās mawla būqūr." MS. Private collection of Muhammad b. Husein Alatas, Jakarta, Indonesia.

al-Sakrān, 'Alī b. Abī Bakr. (n.d.) 1931. *Ma'ārij al-hidāya ilā dhawq shahid janā thamarāt al-mu'āmalāt fī al-nihāya.* Cairo: al-Maṭba'a al-miṣriyya bi-l-azhar.

Salomon, Noah. 2016. *For the Love of the Prophet: An Ethnography of Sudan's Islamic State.* Princeton, NJ: Princeton University Press.

Salvatore, Armando. 2007. *The Public Sphere: Liberal Modernity, Catholicism, Islam.* New York: Palgrave Macmillan.

Samin, Nadav. 2015. *Of Sand or Soil: Genealogy and Tribal Belonging in Saudi Arabia.* Princeton, NJ: Princeton University Press.

al-Saqqāf, 'Abdallāh b. Muḥammad. 1984. *Tārīkh al-shu'arā' al-ḥaḍramiyyīn.* 5 vols. Ta'if, Saudi Arabia: Maktabat al-ma'ārif.

al-Saqqāf, 'Abd al-Raḥmān b. 'Ubaydillāh. 2005. *Idām al-qūt fī dhikr buldān ḥaḍramawt.* Sana'a, Yemen: Dār al-minhaj.

al-Saqqāf, 'Alī b. Muḥsin. 2009. *Al-Istizāda min akhbār al-sāda.* 2 vols. Amman, Jordan: Dār al-fatḥ li-dirāsāt wa al-nashr.

al-Saqqāf, Ḥasan b. Saqqāf. (1781) 2001. *Nashr maḥāsin al-awṣāf fī dhikr manāqib al-ʿārif bi-llāh quṭb zamānihi sayyidinā al-imām saqqāf bin muḥammad bin ʿumar al-saqqāf.* Beirut: Dār al-ḥāwī.

Sayeed, Asma. 2013. *Women and the Transmission of Religious Knowledge in Islam.* Cambridge: Cambridge University Press.

Schielke, Samuli. 2009. "Being Good in Ramadan: Ambivalence, Fragmentation, and the Moral Self in the Lives of Young Egyptians." *Journal of the Royal Anthropological Institute* 15:S24–S40.

———. 2010. "Second Thoughts about the Anthropology of Islam, or How to Make Sense of Grand Schemes in Everyday Life." *Zentrum Moderner Orient Working Papers,* no. 2: 1–16.

Scott, David. 2004. *Conscripts of Modernity: The Tragedy of Colonial Enlightenment.* Durham, NC: Duke University Press.

Sedgwick, Mark J. 2005. *Saints and Sons: The Making and Remaking of the Rashidi Ahmadi Sufi Order, 1799–2000.* Leiden: Brill.

Seesemann, Rüdiger. 2011. *The Divine Flood: Ibrāhīm Niasse and the Roots of a Twentieth-Century Sufi Revival.* New York: Oxford University Press.

Serjeant, Robert B. 1957. *The Saiyids of Ḥaḍramawt, An Inaugural Lecture Delivered on 5 June 1956.* London: School of Oriental and African Studies.

———. 1962. "Haram and Hawta: The Sacred Enclave in Arabia." In *Mélanges Taha Husayn,* edited by ʿAbd al-Raḥmān Badawī, 41–58. Cairo: Dār al-maʿārif.

Sewell, William H. 2005. *Logics of History: Social Theory and Social Transformation.* Chicago: University of Chicago Press.

Shaery-Eisenlohr, Roschanack. 2009. "Territorializing Piety: Genealogy, Transnationalism, and Shi 'ite Politics in Modern Lebanon." *Comparative Studies in Society and History* 51 (3): 533–62.

Shahabuddin, Abubakar. (1944) 2000. *Rihlatul Asfar: Otobiografi Sayyid Abubakar bin Ali bin Abubakar Shahabuddin.* Jakarta: privately printed.

al-Shāṭirī, Muḥammad b. Aḥmad. 1983. *Adwār al-tārīkh al-ḥaḍramī.* 2 vols. 2nd ed. Jeddah: ʿĀlam al-maʿrifa.

Shaw, Wendy M. K. 2012. "The Islam in Islamic Art History: Secularism and Public Discourse." *Journal of Art Historiography* 6:1–34.

Shihāb, Muḥammad Ḍiyāʾ, and ʿAbdallāh b. Nūḥ. 1980. *Imām al-muhājir: aḥmad bin ʿīsā bin muḥammad bin ʿalī al-ʿurayḍī b. jaʿfar al-ṣādiq, mā lahu wa-li-naslihi wa al-aʾimma min aslāfihi min al-faḍāʾil wa al-maʾāthir.* Jeddah: Dār al-shurūq.

al-Shillī, Muḥammad b. Abī Bakr. 1901. *Al-Mashraʿ al-rawī fī manāqib al-sāda al-kirām āl abī ʿalawī.* 2 vols. Cairo: al-ʿĀmira al-sharafiya.

Shryock, Andrew. 1997. *Nationalism and the Genealogical Imagination: Oral History and Textual Authority in Tribal Jordan.* Berkeley: University of California Press.

Siegel, James T. (1969) 2000. *The Rope of God.* 2nd ed. Ann Arbor: University of Michigan Press.

Silverstein, Brian E. 2008. "Disciplines of Presence in Modern Turkey: Discourse, Companionship, and the Mass Mediation of Islamic Practice." *Cultural Anthropology* 23 (1): 118–53.

Silverstein, Michael. 1996. "The Secret Life of Texts." In *Natural Histories of Discourse,* edited by Silverstein and Greg Urban, 81–105. Chicago: University of Chicago Press.

Silverstein, Michael, and Greg Urban, eds. 1996. *Natural Histories of Discourse.* Chicago: University of Chicago Press.

Sirriyeh, Elizabeth. 1999. *Sufis and Anti-Sufis: The Defense, Rethinking and Rejection of Sufism in the Modern World.* Richmond, VA: Curzon.

———. 2015. *Dreams & Visions in the World of Islam: A History of Muslim Dreaming and Foreknowing.* London: I. B. Tauris.

Sizgorich, Thomas. 2009. *Violence and Belief in Late Antiquity: Militant Devotion in Christianity and Islam.* Philadelphia: University of Pennsylvania Press.

Slama, Martin. 2014a. "From Wali Songo to Wali Pitu: The Travelling of Islamic Saint Veneration to Bali." In *Between Harmony and Discrimination: Negotiating Religious Identities within Majority-Minority Relationships in Bali and Lombok,* edited by Brigitta Hauser-Schäublin and David D. Harnish, 112–43. Leiden: Brill.

———. 2014b. "Hadhrami Moderns: Recurrent Dynamics as Historical Rhymes of Indonesia's Reformist Islamic Organization Al-Irsyad." In *Dynamics of Religion in Southeast Asia: Magic and Modernity,* edited by Volker Gottowik, 113–32. Amsterdam: Amsterdam University Press.

———. 2017. "A Subtle Economy of Time: Social Media and the Transformation of Indonesia's Islamic Preacher Economy." *Economic Anthropology* 4 (1): 94–106.

Soares, Benjamin F. 2005. *Islam and the Prayer Economy: History and Authority in a Malian Town.* Ann Arbor: University of Michigan Press.

———. 2016. "New Muslim Public Figures in West Africa." In *Islamic Education in Africa: Writing Boards and Blackboards,* edited by Robert Launay, 268–84. Bloomington: Indiana University Press.

Spivak, Gayatri Chakravorty. 1992. "Acting Bits/Identity Talk." *Critical Inquiry* 18 (4): 770–803.

Stark, Freya. 1936. *The Southern Gates of Arabia: A Journey in the Hadhramaut.* London: Murray.

———. 1940. *A Winter in Arabia.* London: Murray.

Stearns, Justin K. 2011. *Infectious Ideas: Contagion in Premodern Islamic and Christian Thought in the Western Mediterranean.* Baltimore, MD: Johns Hopkins University Press.

Stewart, Charles. 1999. "Syncretism and Its Synonyms: Reflections on Cultural Mixture." *Diacritics* 29 (3): 40–62.

Stewart, Tony K. 2001. "In Search of Equivalence: Conceiving Muslim-Hindu Encounter through Translation Theory." *History of Religions* 40 (3): 260–87.

Sviri, Sara. (1993) 1999. "Hakīm Tirmidhī and the Malāmatī Movement in Early Sufism." In *The Heritage of Sufism,* vol. 1, *Classical Persian Sufism: From Its Origins to Rumi (700–1300),* edited by Leonard Lewisohn, 583–613. Oxford: Oneworld.

al-Ṭabarī, Abū Jaʿfar. 1987. *The History of al-Ṭabarī.* Vol. 7, *The Foundation of the Community.* Translated and annotated by W. Montgommery Watt and M. V. McDonald. Albany: State University of New York Press.

Tagliacozzo, Eric. 2013. *The Longest Journey: Southeast Asians and the Pilgrimage to Mecca.* New York: Oxford University Press.

Tambiah, Stanley J. 1990. *Magic, Science, Religion, and the Scope of Rationality.* Cambridge: Cambridge University Press.

Taminian, Lucine D. 2001. "Playing with Words: The Ethnography of Poetic Genres in Yemen." PhD dissertation, University of Michigan.

Taneja, Anand V. 2018. *Jinnealogy: Time, Islam, and Ecological Thought in the Medieval Ruins of Delhi.* Stanford, CA: Stanford University Press.

Taussig, Michael. 1997. *The Magic of the State*. New York: Routledge.

Taylor, Christopher. 1999. *In the Vicinity of the Righteous: Ziyāra and the Veneration of Muslim Saints in Late Medieval Egypt*. Leiden: Brill.

Thum, Rian. 2014. *The Sacred Routes of Uyghur History*. Cambridge, MA: Harvard University Press.

Toer, Pramoedya Ananta. 2006. *Jalan Raya Pos, Jalan Daendels*. Jakarta: Lentera Dipantara.

Trimingham, J. Spencer. 1971. *The Sufi Orders in Islam*. Oxford: Clarendon.

Trouillot, Michel-Rolph. 2001. "The Anthropology of the State in the Age of Globalization: Close Encounters of the Deceptive Kind." *Current Anthropology* 42 (1): 125–38.

Tsauri, Ahmad. 2014. *Sejarah Maulid Nabi: Sejak Khaizuran (173 H.) hingga Habib Luthfi Bin Yahya (1947 M.-Sekarang)*. Pekalongan, Central Java: Menara.

Tsing, Anna Lowenhaupt. 1993. *In the Realm of the Diamond Queen: Marginality in an Out-of-the-Way Place*. Princeton, NJ: Princeton University Press.

———. 2000. "The Global Situation." *Cultural Anthropology* 15 (3): 327–60.

———. 2005. *Friction: An Ethnography of Global Connection*. Princeton, NJ: Princeton University Press.

ʿUmar, ʿAbdallāh b. 1858. "Tadhkira ʿAbdallāh bin ʿUmar." MS A594. National Library of Indonesia, Jakarta.

Valeri, Valerio. 1990. "Constitutive History: Genealogy and Narrative in the Legitimation of Hawaiian Kingship." In *Culture through Time: Anthropological Approaches*, edited by Emiko Ohnuki-Tierney, 154–92. Stanford, CA: Stanford University Press.

Van der Veer, Peter. 2001. *Imperial Encounters: Religion and Modernity in India and Britain*. Princeton, NJ: Princeton University Press.

Van Niel, Robert. 1972. "Measurement of Change under the Cultivations System in Java, 1837–1851." *Indonesia* 14:89–109.

Vogel, Frank. E. 2000. *Islamic Law and Legal System: Studies of Saudi Arabia*. Leiden: Brill.

Voll, John O. 1994. "Islam as a Special World-System." *Journal of World History* 5 (2): 213–26.

Von Grunebaum, Gustave E. 1963. "The Nature of Arab Unity before Islam." *Arabica* 10 (1): 5–23.

Vuldy, Chantal. 1985. "La communauté arabe de Pekalongan." *Archipel* 30 (1): 95–119.

Wahid, Abdurrahman. (1989) 2015. "Pribumisasi Islam." *NUOnline*, July, 19, 2015. https://www.nu.or.id/post/read/60985/pribumisasi-islam.

Ware, Rudolph T. 2014. *The Walking Qur'an: Islamic Education, Embodied Knowledge, and History in West Africa*. Chapel Hill: University of North Carolina Press.

Warner, Michael. 2002. *Publics and Counterpublics*. New York: Zone Books.

Weber, Max. 1968. "The Nature of Charismatic Authority and Its Routinization." In *On Charisma and Institution Building: Selected Papers*, edited by S. N. Eisenstadt, 48–65. Chicago: University of Chicago Press.

Wehr, Hans. 1979. *A Dictionary of Modern Written Arabic*. 4th ed. Edited by J. Milton Cowan. Wiesbaden, Germany: Otto Harrassowitz.

Weismann, Itzchak. 2001. *Taste of Modernity: Sufism, Salafiyya, and Arabism in Late Ottoman Damascus*. Leiden: Brill.

Williams, Bernard. 2011. *Ethics and the Limits of Philosophy*. New York: Taylor and Francis.

Wolf, Eric R.1951. "The Social Organization of Mecca and the Origins of Islam." *Southwestern Journal of Anthropology* 7 (4): 329–56.

Wolper, Ethel Sara. 2003. *Cities and Saints: Sufism and the Transformation of Urban Space in Medieval Anatolia.* University Park: Pennsylvania State University Press.

Wright, Zachary. 2015. "Salafi Theology and Islamic Orthodoxy in West Africa." *Comparative Studies of South Asia, Africa and the Middle East* 35 (3): 647–56.

Yasin, Ann Marie. 2009. *Saints and Church Spaces in the Late Antique Mediterranean: Architecture, Cult, and Community.* Cambridge: Cambridge University Press.

Zaman, Muhammad Qasim. 2007. *The Ulama in Contemporary Islam: Custodians of Change.* Princeton, NJ: Princeton University Press.

Žižek, Slavoj. 1999. *The Ticklish Subject: The Absent Centre of Political Ontology.* London: Verso.

Zulkifli. 2013. *The Struggle of the Shiʿis in Indonesia.* Canberra: Australian National University Press.

INDEX

A NOTE ON THE TYPE

This book has been composed in Arno, an Old-style serif typeface in the classic Venetian tradition, designed by Robert Slimbach at Adobe.

CPSIA information can be obtained
at www.ICGtesting.com
Printed in the USA
LVHW091145010222
709936LV00012B/1612

9 780691 204314